JAY BOCHNER is a member of the Department of English at the Université de Montréal

In *Blaise Cendrars: Discovery and Re-creation,* Jay Bochner presents a revealing account of Cendrars' life and establishes the importance of his work in the mainstream of modern literature. Prolific and versatile, Cendrars wrote poetry, radio plays, novels, essays, autobiography, and books on the cinema. An early contributor to the Dada movement, he was at the forefront of the Paris avant-garde before and after the first world war, and his powerful poetic style influenced such writers as Apollinaire, Henry Miller, and John Dos Passos. Although he was well known to the French reading public, lavishly praised by his peers, and well received by the important critics of his day, Cendrars' critical reputation has not endured.

The first part of the book is biographical, and in this section Professor Bochner suggests that the reasons for Cendrars' obscurity have more to do with his life than his works. Cendrars himself cared little about his reputation. Although he knew most of the important writers and artists working in Paris, he spent relatively little time actively engaged in the literary life there, frequently disappearing to work on films in southern France and Italy, to travel with gypsies, or to live in isolation. In fact the attention he attracted as an adventurer has perhaps overwhelmed and obscured his stature as a writer.

The critical analysis of Cendrars' writing is divided into seven chapters, each corresponding to a period in which a particular genre dominated his publications. Professor Bochner's premise is that the serious reading of Cendrars shows that for him *bourlinguer,* knocking about the world, was discovery, not only of the world at large but of the self. He believed writing to be a re-creation of the self as well as the creation of a mythical world for an alternately disbelieving and enchanted reader. The title of his collected poetry, *Du monde entier au cœur du monde,* expresses the essential fusion of this writer's life and art.

Professor Bochner's study is both a major contribution to the critical history of modern literature and an absorbing account of a fascinating personality.

Blaise Cendrars:
Discovery
and Re-creation

JAY BOCHNER

University of Toronto Press

TORONTO / BUFFALO / LONDON

Library of Congress Cataloging in Publication Data

Bochner, Jay, 1940–
    Blaise Cendrars: discovery and re-creation.

    Bibliography: p .
    Includes index.
    1. Cendrars, Blaise, 1887–1961. 2. Authors,
    Swiss – 20th century – Biography.
    PQ2605. E55Z563   841'.9'12 [B]   77-2580
    ISBN 0-8020-5352-1

This volume has been published with the help of
a grant from the Humanities Research Council of Canada,
using funds provided by the Canada Council, and
with the help of grants from the University of Toronto and
the Publications Fund of the University of Toronto Press.
The author would particularly like to thank
Howard Riddle of the HRCC for his interest in
a study of Blaise Cendrars.

Cover: Cendrars by Modigliani,
from a special printing of the original edition of
Dix-neuf poèmes élastiques (1919)
ADAGP   Photo Bibliothèque Jacques Doucet

Au dernier dada, Jacques-Henry Lévesque, 1899–1971

Grateful acknowledgment is made to the following for permission to use material in copyright:

Mme Miriam Gilou-Cendrars: Blaise Cendrars, *Inédits secrets,* published by Le Club français du livre (© 1969)

Mme Raymone Cendrars: unpublished letters of Blaise Cendrars to John Dos Passos

Éditions Denoël: Blaise Cendrars, *Oeuvres Complètes* (© 1960, 1961, 1962, 1963, 1964)

Mrs Elizabeth Dos Passos for permission to quote from an unpublished letter from John Dos Passos

Bernard Grasset: Blaise Cendrars *Aujourd'hui* (© 1931), *Hollywood* (© 1936), *La Vie dangereuse* (© 1938), *Rhum* (© 1930), and *Moravagine* (© 1926)

La Guilde du Livre and M. Albert Mermoud: Blaise Cendrars, *Vol à voile (© 1960)* and *Une Nuit dans la forêt* (© 1929)

Harcourt Brace Jovanovich and Routledge & Kegan Paul Ltd: C.G. Jung, *Modern Man in Search of a Soul* (© 1968)

New Directions Publishing Corporation: Henry Miller, *The Books in My Life* (copyright © 1960 by New Directions Publishing Corporation. All rights reserved); and Henry Miller, *The Henry Miller Reader* (© by Henry Miller, reprinted by permission of New Directions Publishing Corporation)

Oxford University Press: Frank Budgen, *Myselves When Young* (© Oxford University Press 1970. By permission of the Oxford University Press)

Georges Simenon: Georges Simenon, *Quand j'étais vieux,* published by Les Presses de la Cité (© 1970 by Georges Simenon)

Contents

TOP Cendrars in Abel Gance's *J'accuse* (1919) (*front centre*),
the bandage unravelling from his stump as he leans for support on the
shoulder of the film's star, Séverin Mars
Cinématique française

BOTTOM Cendrars at Le Tremblay in the twenties

La Prose du transsibérien by Cendrars and Sonia Delaunay (1913), 2 metres by 0.36 metres, shown here in two sections

ADAGP   Photo Musées nationaux

Cendrars by Modigliani, from a special printing of the
original edition of *Dix-neuf Poèmes élastiques* (1919)
ADAGP   Photo Bibliothèque Jacques Doucet

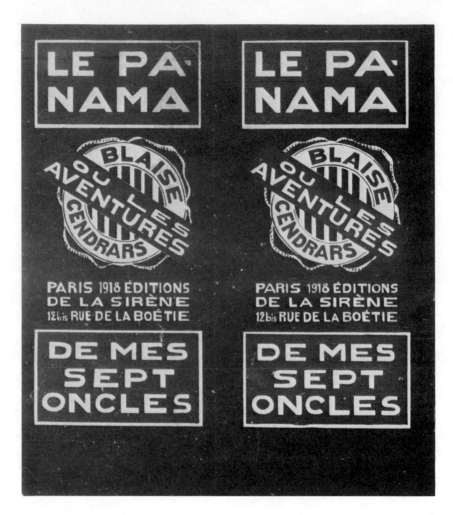

ABOVE AND OPPOSITE The front and back cover of *Le Panama* (1918) and
its inspiration, a Union Pacific train schedule, which contains the maps of
train-routes and bits of information Cendrars used in his poem
Photo above Bibliothèque nationale

ABOVE *Left to right:* Cendrars, Vera and Igor Stravinsky, and Raymone
at a fair some time in the twenties

OPPOSITE TOP Cover by Fernand Léger of
La Fin du monde filmée par L'Ange Notre-Dame (1919)
SPADEM   Photo Bibliothèque nationale

OPPOSITE BOTTOM Cover of the 1926 Russian edition of *L'Or,*
hitherto unknown even to Cendrars,
who thought it might have been published in 1929.
The bottom lines read: Editions of the State 1926.
Photo Staatsbibliothek Preussischer Kulturbesitz

Cendrars hiking in the Alps in the twenties
Collection Roger Viollet

Cendrars (*left*) and Francis Picabia at Le Tremblay (1923)
Bibliothèque Jacques Doucet

Cendrars in the fifties

Blaise Cendrars:
Discovery and Re-creation

Introduction

The praise I give Blaise Cendrars in this study will no doubt make the reader wonder why he has been relatively neglected up to now. Why have some students of French literature never heard of him, and why have others who have heard of him not felt the interest to say more? The problem of neglect is irksome when every corner of the arts is being searched for any trace of talent that might furnish an academic topic. All too many authors are being recommended to us as 'unjustly neglected,' and each time that phrase is used again we are in effect being asked to be less discriminating, though the pretence is the reverse. I should like to examine here a few reasons for Cendrars' neglect in order to show that it comes mainly from the way he lived and very little from the quality of his writing itself.

Firstly, we are confronted with a rather erratic combination of recognition and non-recognition. A growing number of critics now consider that his influence upon Apollinaire was decisive. Marcel Raymond, in his important study *De Baudelaire au Surréalisme,* says that it was Cendrars, more than Apollinaire, who prepared the way for French poetry after the first world war.[1] Nevertheless, few critics have bothered to examine this further, and fewer yet have examined his poetry for itself. Cendrars' novels are reasonably well known to the reading public in France, since five are in the Livre de poche series, Denoël has published his complete works in eight volumes, and the Club français du livre has published another in sixteen plus one volume of early notebooks, letters, and manuscripts. *L'Or* has seen over twenty editions in French and been translated into ten languages. Still, the relative popularity of these novels has not aroused much interest on the part of critics or scholars. Yet many of the works were extremely well received by perceptive and well-known critics of the day, and the problem, it seems, is that there has been no continuity, no accumulation of the acclaim, with the accompanying growth of a 'reputation.'

As Cendrars wrote almost no poetry after 1924, devoting himself thenceforth to prose, he is subcategorized by genre-minded literary histories, which are obliged to split his work in two. Thus he further suffers from rarely being considered for all of his very varied work as a piece. The intriguing corollary of this, however, is the number of different places you may run across his name, from material on cubist poetry, Dada, Surrealism, and Modernism in Brazil, to work about Henry Miller and John Dos Passos. And as his activites, or at least the little we know of them, were not in the least restricted to poetry and fiction, we also find material in unsuspected places such as Ilya Ehrenburg's memoirs, Marie Seton's biography of Eisenstein, or Jean-Paul Clébert's book on gypsies. An amusing and revealing bibliographical item is that in the October 1967 issue of the *Magazine Littéraire* Cendrars appears in three unrelated articles, on Malraux, on 'Montparnasse, patrie des "louftingues," ' and on Henry Miller. [2] All the separate pieces of Cendrars' life and work have yet to be reassembled.

A further hindrance in the recognition of Cendrars the writer is Cendrars the legend. Far less than in the case of Hemingway can the two be separated, especially as it seems that Hemingway's reputation as a writer may well be improved in the end by the deflation of the legend. Cendrars is famous as an adventurer, and much of his work reflects his experiences, real and imaginary. So fantastic is this life as it has come down to us in his work and the reminiscences of others that the author has often been called a great liar. The exoticism of Cendrars attracted popular attention, and most of the critics bothered to search no further; they have made him out to be the sort of fellow Claude Lévi-Strauss lashes out against so violently in the first two chapters of *Tristes Tropiques* – a traveller who voyages not for discovery but rather the slides he will show at home or at lectures. But I think the serious reading of Cendrars will show that for him *bourlinguer,* knocking around the world, was discovery, not only of the world at large but of oneself. The title of his collected poetry beautifully describes this double voyage, *Du Monde entier au cœur du monde.* Cendrars is an 'aventurier humaniste,' as Raymond Warnier has called him, [3] and we must see past the obstruction of an escape-seeking readership. The outer world serves as the required terms of the inner; that is how I shall deal with the legend. Cendrars' reach is on the cosmic scale, though his mysticism is not ethereal. It thrives not on transcendence but on the variety of the discovered and yet-to-be-discovered world. This grounded mysticism sets him in the only tradition I would find for him, the Whitman tradition. That remains ill-defined, for as William Carlos Williams wrote: 'The only way to be like Whitman is to write *unlike* Whitman. Do I expect to be a companion to Whitman by mimicking his manners? I might even so please some old dotard, some "good grey poet" by kow-towing to him; but not Whitman.'[4] Whitman stands for a marginal tradition in France, and that is one important reason why Cendrars has been so difficult to swallow, why he is so often compared, in France, to American writers, and why his two most famous and energetic admirers, Henry Miller and John Dos Passos, are American, as well as admirers of Whitman. I have not gone into the Whitman tradition at any great length or in any systematic fashion here, but his name will reappear often.[5] Further, I have made much of parallels with certain Americans and with aspects of American poetry and fiction in general which shed light on this Whitmanesque quality in Cendrars. One premise behind this study is that from 1908 or so onward America provided a virgin – and barbaric – source for the avant-garde, which was attempting to discover what was indeed modern and therefore in its view *real*. In Europe the sources seemed too contaminated with the past, and no one could see to the bottom of the stream. Cendrars, Picabia, and Duchamp, foremost among the most revolutionary elements of the avant-garde in Paris, struck upon new material and forms in New York, the last two in collaboration with Alfred Stieglitz and his circle. This 'Americanness' of Cendrars provides a context in which to present him to the English-speaking reader. On the other hand it helps to explain why he appears too brutal, too lacking in taste for French critics, and has not been granted a tidy niche in the literary pantheon. The understanding of Cendrars should benefit from a less national view.

We cannot say that Cendrars has lacked praise from eminent fellow-writers, but the praise has not found fertile soil. A short history of acclaim by his peers might run as follows: from Apollinaire: 'Blaise Cendrars, poète suisse, à mon avis constitue avec moi et Fleuret, la seule trinité de poètes qui aient aujourd'hui un talent véritable et du lyrisme'; from Max Jacob: 'Les deux dernières pages de 'La Guerre au Luxembourg' sont parmi les plus belles choses que j'ai jamais lues'; from Malraux, who praised *Les Pâques à New York* in his very first article, on 'cubist' poetry; from the film-maker Abel Gance, who, like Apollinaire, set his own trinity of poets, Novalis, Rimbaud, and Cendrars (upon reading Cendrars' *Moravagine,* a novel); from Philippe Soupault: 'Ce qu'il faut d'abord rappeler, c'est que Blaise Cendrars fut un grand précurseur. Avec Apollinaire et Pierre Reverdy, il est un des principaux responsables de la révolution qui a bouleversé la poésie française et lui a redonné toute sa vitalité et tout son souffle'; from John Dos Passos, who called Cendrars the 'Homer of the Transsiberian'; from Henry Miller, who termed him the 'Chinese rock-bottom man' of his imagination, which students of Miller will recog-

nize as his highest possible praise; and, finally, from Georges Simenon in
an open letter to Cendrars:

> N'en avez-vous pas du boucanier le besoin de découvertes toujours nou-
> velles en même temps qu'un calme mépris pour tout ce qui ne compte pas
> réellement, pour ce qui n'est pas essentiel? ...
> Je vous tire mon chapeau, Cendrars ...[6]

Yet despite such admiration on the part of peers, despite the sales and the
legend, Cendrars has only a minor reputation among critics generally and
is highly regarded by only a very small number of enthusiasts.

The principal reason is that Cendrars did not care enough about his
reputation, and did virtually nothing to promote it. Although he knew,
at one time or another, most of the painters, poets, musicians, and their
Maecenases in Paris between, say, 1912 and 1924, only for short, intermit-
tent periods did he engage actively in the literary life there; for during
those twelve years he also worked on films in Southern France and Italy,
travelled with gypsies, and lived in isolation for long periods. When he
was invited to Brazil in 1924, he merely dropped what he was doing and
left. The talk about Cendrars in the artistic circles of Paris is always of
arrivals and departures and of meetings in hotels and cafés between trips,
even if they were only trips to the obscure world of Paris suburbs and the
'Zone.' There is occasional bitterness on Cendrars' part for the lack of
recognition, but that does not change the fact that he preferred the freedom of his separation from the artistic world, and that he would never
have made the trade if it had been offered. Thus Soupault has written that
Cendrars felt neglected when Dada monopolized the literary avant-garde
scene (although Dada needed Cendrars, publishing his poetry in the first
issue of *Littérature* and in the one number of *Le Cabaret Voltaire,* this last
without authorization); but he also says in the same passage that Cendrars
had already 'choisi d'être un solitaire, avec dignité et avec insolence.'[7]
René Hilsum, editor of the Au Sans Pareil avant-garde publishing house,
remembers Adrienne Monnier's bookstore where, about 1918, Cendrars
'figurait déjà parmi les notabilités,' but 'dans cette librairie où les grands
hommes étaient fort cossus, Gide, Claudel, Larbaud, etc., Blaise formait
avec eux un contraste marqué ... '[8]

Except for the period of revolution in French poetry and painting that
took place before the first world war, with Le Douanier Rousseau, Apollinaire, Max Jacob, Cravan, Duchamp, Delaunay and the early cubist
painters, Cendrars purposely lived outside the artistic community. The
reason for his *congé,* as he called it, will be examined in the biographical
section, but it is important to speak of it here because it defines his entire

attitude and also explains the great difficulty of establishing any biography at all.

In Cendrars' radio interviews we find the following exchange with Michel Manoll:

> ... vous n'êtes pas l'homme qui subit des influences mais l'homme qui fait subir des influences aux autres, et beaucoup d'écrivains contemporains sont influencés par vous...
>
> – J'ai horreur de ça!
>
> – Vous n'y pouvez rien. *Les Pâques à New York*, le *Transsibérien*, le *Panama*, les...
>
> – On en parle depuis quand, dites?
>
> –... les *19 Poèmes élastiques* ...On en parle et on les cite précisément parce que ces poèmes sont à la base de la poésie moderne, sont à la source du lyrisme moderne...
>
> – Vous êtes bien gentil, Manoll, de me dire des choses aussi aimables...
>
> – Mais enfin, vous êtes célèbre, Cendrars!
>
> – Alors, comme un cocu, je suis le dernier à y croire! Non, non, pas du tout, je ne suis à la base de rien du tout. C'est le monde moderne qui est à la base, 'énorme et délicat' comme le moyen âge.[9]

Cendrars' low opinion of his influence points to the importance he attached to the re-creation of life as opposed to the making of art. I hope to make clear, in this study that re-creation is somewhat different from mimesis. There is great vibrancy in his work, and the main source of that vibrancy is his permanent connection to life rather than to art. It is just such an *élan* which manifestly permeates all of Cendrars' work, for it is never the work of a *littérateur*. That is why Hilsum, along with practically every eyewitness who is not openly hostile, describes him as a man different from most artists, truly on the open road. Cendrars' influence is two-fold: the revelation of a new, modern world as a subject for poetry, to replace the ageing objective correlatives of Symbolism; and the reevaluation of art and culture, which led inevitably to Dada.

'La poésie est dans la rue,' he wrote in a number of places, and, in fact, Rilke is quoted as calling *Le Transsibérien* 'die höhere Bänkelsängerei,' which Frank Budgen translates roughly as 'superior street corner balladry.'[10] But although the words may tame the idea, it is a long, long way from the street to poetry. Essentially, for both artists and critics Cendrars was a foreigner, an outsider. The insolence Soupault speaks of is his full knowledge that the artistic community takes itself too seriously and, jealously, is ever protecting its opinion of itself. Yet art is not so much separate from and above life as one part of it which is about it. Cendrars is an emissary from a non-literary world, and the hardest task in discussing him is to interpret with necessarily literary criteria. In 1930 Cendrars dedicated *Rhum*

> aux jeunes gens d'aujourd'hui
> fatigués de la littérature
> pour leur prouver
> qu'un roman
> peut aussi être un acte.

Later Sartre quoted this statement in *What is Literature*[11] in support of a literature *d'engagement,* but Sartre here misunderstood the full import. Cendrars was not a political, or even a 'social-consciousness' writer. His meaning of 'act' went deeper. The problem will be examined later, but briefly one might say that Cendrars was only barely writing. Marcel Raymond wrote: 'Avec Cendrars, on croit étreindre, en une espèce de corps-à-corps, la réalité rugueuse que Rimbaud découvrit à l'âge d'homme (mais Rimbaud, l'ayant découvert, se tut).'[12] Cendrars is the man who could still write. The terrible world is more than art, and Cendrars' writing lies somewhere between the *Logos* and its mistranslation, the Word. He knew that to be a literary man, with all that entailed, need have little to do with being a poet. Quite the contrary, since it entailed so much. To be a free poet one had precisely to forgo the promotion of Poetry and of oneself, that is, forgo fame, or immortality: 'Je ne trempe pas ma plume dans un encrier, mais dans la vie. Écrire, ce n'est pas vivre. C'est peut-être se survivre. Mais rien n'est moins garanti.'[13]

Whether immortality is forthcoming or not, the search for it, the consolidation of an image, is an all-consuming pursuit. Cendrars hardly had a literary career, and this freedom is always apparent in his work. As Jeanine Moulin wrote of Cendrars and Apollinaire as they were in 1912 when they first met: 'A cette époque Cendrars a déjà "bourlingué," et a rapporté de ses randonnées des œuvres qui sonnent comme un défi à tout conformisme. Il est, à proprement parler, l'aventurier tel que Guillaume rêve d'être et tel qu'il ne sera jamais.'[14] And Ribemont-Dessaignes has written: 'Blaise Cendrars est le seul parmi les auteurs contemporains qui sache que la vie vaut mieux que la littérature. La vie est une aventure, l'homme un aventurier. Cendrars est leur poète.'[15] In both his life and his work, Cendrars is as elusive and suspect as, say, Casanova.

The bearing of all this on Cendrars' biography is that he did not often sit still in his study or appear regularly in well-known literary haunts. It is very important constantly to remind oneself that, for the most part, he was away. There is a whole life outside his involvement with art, which itself is outside the main current. Furthermore, he liked his privacy. In 1929 Nino Frank wrote: 'Quant à savoir quelles sont les affaires qu'il traite, on n'y parviendra jamais: "Ma vie ne vous regarde pas," est-il toujours prêt à vous répondre. Publicité, vente d'une île dans la baie de Rio de Janeiro, trust des cacahuètes, institut de beauté, films de propagande ...'[16] Thus the biographical section of this book is filled with lacunae. Over thirty years after Frank's article, in the introduction to the special number of the *Mercure de France* devoted to Cendrars after he died, such friends and admirers as Paul Gilson, Robert Kanters, Jacques-Henry Lévesque, Georges Piroué, Soupault, and Frank agreed that it was impossible to draw up a precise and detailed biography, as they had originally hoped to do.[17] For the most part I am in a poorer position than they, the main exceptions being t'Serstevens' memoirs published in 1972 and some of Cendrars' early letters and notebooks which have come to light. So the biographical project as I have seen it may appear eccentric – extremely detailed when details are available and at other times covering whole years in a sentence or two. However, I felt it was worth supplying what is known, not only for the interest of the scholar but because from these details a fleeting picture is drawn which may suggest the spirit of what is missing and of what may well be lost for good.

The other peculiarity of my short biography is that I have chosen to include material which may not be factual. It is in its legendary aspects that the life may be most important for the work – and the work remains my primary concern. I attempt to distinguish the real from the imagined where possible, but I prefer to believe much of what has been put in doubt, since, when we indeed can check, we find that what Cendrars wrote or said was more often fact than fiction. This only goes further to show how different he must have been from most of us; as Maurice Nadeau, the historian of Surrealism, has written: 'Tout ce qui lui arrive est extraordinaire simplement parce qu'il est un homme extraordinaire.'[18] Attempts to make him appear less extraordinary may be merely the result of jealousy, and such scepticism may be more detrimental to a truthful picture than going a certain way with Cendrars or with his game. If, however, someone were to show that Cendrars in fact led an armchair existence, that would only serve to make the fiction and poetry more extraordinary, for they themselves maintain their strength. Whether a given occurrence was extraordinary fact or merely legend its main relevance to Cendrars' work remains the same – it provides the material for a modern mythopoeia.

Part two of this volume, the critical analysis of Cendrars' writing, is divided into seven chapters, each corresponding to a period during which a particular genre dominated his published production. However, publication itself does not tell us what Cendrars was doing at a given moment. Almost every work was in progress for years; and, as he said himself, he could not write about an event for some ten years after it happened. *L'Or* is dated 1910-24, and *Moravagine,* begun in 1912, was finished the night of 1 November 1925.[19] In the original edition of *Moravagine* (1926) Cendrars announced as 'en préparation' *D'Outremer à indigo,* which was published in 1940 (in fact this title is listed in a series of projects he drew up in 1918), and as 'sous presse' *Des Hommes sont venus,* published only in 1952 as *Le Brésil.* These works represent respectively the biographical novel, the novel, the short story, and the reportage genres. Despite some violations of strict chronology, the works may be grouped by genre, and these divisions represent an attempt to combine chronological, generic, and thematic approaches. The effect is meant to be cumulative. Each chapter of this volume is a study of Cendrars' retooling of a genre to suit his needs, and one step in our own discovery of a general thematic pattern. Thus I become most theoretical near the end, especially in chapter eleven. In that chapter some specialists may miss a specific study of the middle two of the four autobiographical novels, *La Main coupée* and *Bourlinguer.* The four novels together represent, in my view, an extraordinary and variegated whole which deserves a separate study. I have, however, concentrated on *L'Homme foudroyé* and *Le Lotissement du ciel* in order to draw more forcefully the main lines of my pattern. It has been my foremost intention to offer good reason for reading Cendrars as seriously as any other writer this century.

PART ONE
In place of biography

1 Beginnings, 1887-1912

Blaise Cendrars was born Frédéric Louis Sauser in the small Swiss city of La Chaux-de-Fonds (canton of Neuchâtel) on 1 September 1887. The address was Paix 27. We know these elementary facts from Jean Buhler's research for his book *Blaise Cendrars*.[1] But for a long time the date and particularly the place were not known. In 1948 Louis Parrot still did not know the place when he wrote his book on Cendrars, and he gives none. In a group of poems called 'Au Cœur du monde' written in 1917, Cendrars says he was born at 216 rue Saint-Jacques, at the Hôtel des Étrangers,[2] and it is probably from this source that, in 1948, André Bourin felt he could write: 'C'est la poésie qui lui souffle son âge, comme elle lui souffle aussi parfois des lieux de naissances imaginaires. La vérité, c'est qu'il naquit à Paris ...'[3] And in 1962 Nino Frank wrote:

> ... me sachant né en Italie, dans les Pouilles, il m'avait confié qu'il y était né lui-même, mais en chemin de fer, dans la malle des Indes qui ramenait sa mère d'Égypte: or c'était pure gentillesse, car, à quelques jours de là, il me déclarait qu'il avait vu le jour à Paris, rue Saint-Jacques, et, plus tard, que sa naissance s'était produite en Égypte même ... Ce n'était pas lui qui plaisantait, mais nous, avec notre manie d'emprisonner sa poésie dans les limites étroites d'une vérité.[4]

The word *gentillesse* is as relevant as the last sentence. Most of the doubtful anecdotes which seem too coincidental partake of this sympathy of Cendrars, of which all his friends speak – in this case the offering of a kind of kinship.

Actually we have little reason to suspect that Cendrars went out of his way to hide his origins (although on matters which were important to him he was most secretive). In Conrad Moricand's *Portraits astrologiques* the

information necessary for Cendrars' chart and analysis are correct enough,
if we accept Neuchâtel, which is the right area.[5] Moricand even has the
hour, only fifteen minutes off the official birth certificate, which gives
19:45 (Moricand gives 19:30). And once we have the correct information
we discover Cendrars playing games, such as the following in his long
poem *Le Panama ou les aventures de mes sept oncles:*

> La dernière lettre de mon troisième oncle:
> Papeete, le 1er septembre 1887.
> Ma sœur, ma très chère sœur
> Je suis bouddhiste membre d'une secte politique ... [6]

La Chaux-de-Fonds was until recently the most important centre of the
watch industry in Switzerland, and had been since the beginning of the
eighteenth century. It is a modern city, set out with streets at right angles,
and the citizenry is bourgeois in the best Swiss sense of the word. Jean
Buhler tells us that in 1900 one out of every ten Swiss lived abroad,[7] and
we may imagine that many of these must have fled complacent towns just
as Rimbaud fled his Charleville. Thus La Chaux-de-Fonds' most famous
sons left: Blaise Cendrars, Le Corbusier, born a month later only a hundred yards away, and Louis Chevrolet, born in 1879 and in America by
1900. Cendrars did not, however, leave under his own steam, as the entire
family moved to Egypt soon after his birth, where his father attempted to
go into the hotel business.

Cendrars' father was Georges Frédéric Sauser, originally from Sigriswil
(Bern), and his mother was Marie Louise Dorner, from Zürich. Sauser
gave his own first name to his first son (1884-1966), who later became a
famous jurist and drafted the Turkish civil code. Then a girl was born,
Marie, and then Freddy, as he was called, the youngest. The sister is barely
mentioned in all of Cendrars' writing, but there are warm letters to
Georges in the *Inédits* volume of the Club français du livre complete
works, and Cendrars shows, I think, a particular fondness for Georges'
wife, Agnès, to whom his first important work, *Les Pâques à New York,*
is dedicated. Otherwise, we find all too little about Cendrars' family in his
own writing, autobiographical as it was, and what we do find carries a
strong note of the kind of fondness or nostalgia for people with whom one
has broken off relations. 'La famille, si on ne rompt pas avec elle, c'est un
malentendu qui ne va que s'envenimant ... ' Cendrars wrote;[8] yet there
is often great warmth in some of the passages quoted below, as well as in
many others besides.

G.F. Sauser was a professor of mathematics, and no doubt came to La
Chaux-de-Fonds to teach in one of the schools that trained boys for the

watch industry. But well before the birth of Freddy he had forgone teaching for financial speculation:

> Dès le lendemain de son mariage, mon père avait quitté le professorat des mathématiques où il s'était distingué de bonne heure pour se lancer la tête la première dans la mêlée des affaires, et non seulement il s'était fait gruger, voler, rouler sur toute la ligne, mais encore, ayant perdu du premier coup toute sa fortune personnelle, il avait engagé par la suite dans des affaires de plus en plus extravagantes ... la dot de sa femme et avait dû avoir recours, un peu trop regulièrement à leur gré, à l'argent de ses beaux-parents pour éviter, souvent de justesse, la faillite.[9]

Sauser alienated thus not only his wife and parents-in-law, but also Freddy's brother and sister, who sided with their mother, whereas Freddy, as he later told it in *Vol à voile* (the only autobiography Cendrars described as such), grew up after the family's initial shock of failure and chronic insecurity and was often seduced by his father's adventurous dealings. Yet the weakness of his father was also apparent to the boy, and when the time came for him to break the strongest link to his family the groundwork for his act of independence was already laid.

The paterfamilias was also an inventor; he originated

> ... les lettres de cristal des devantures de magasins, les premières enseignes lumineuses, le char romain qui courait sur la façade de la maison qui fait le coin de la rue Taitbout et de la rue Lafitte sur le boulevard, des appareils à sous. Il touchait à tout, il bouillonnait d'idées. C'était un fantaisiste et un impatient ... C'était un précurseur mais c'était aussi un réalisateur. Il a inventé la première machine à tisser automatiquement les tapis de Smyrne, y compris le stop, cette touffe de cheveux que les ouvrières nouent au bout de leur enfilée de laine en fin de journée pour marquer la reprise de leur travail du lendemain. Il aurait dû faire fortune avec cette unique invention. Mais dès qu'il avait fait une invention, papa n'avait qu'une seule hâte, c'était d'en faire une autre, si bien qu'il n'exploitait pas la première, se dépêchant de vendre ses patentes et de liquider ses droits pour se procurer de l'argent frais et mettre au point la nouvelle invention qui lui trottait par la tête. Et c'est pourquoi il a connu tant de hauts et de bas, dont nous subissions les contrecoups à la maison sans jamais savoir au juste d'où cela venait. Alors, je gagnais peu à peu la rue, au grand désespoir de maman.[10]

Once Freddy found himself at a certain remove from the insecurity the rest of his family felt so acutely, his father's activities as a speculator and an inventor must have shown him glimpses of a world full of excitement, from the extravagant hotel Mr Sauser built in Heliopolis around 1890 in anticipation of a tourist boom in Egypt which failed to materialize, to land speculation on the slopes of the Vomero in Naples near the mythical burial place of Virgil, and the introduction of Munich beer in the Mediterranean countries. *Le Panama* indicates that the financial scandal around de Lesseps' canal project about 1889 must also have affected his father's investments, so that Cendrars wrote in that poem: 'C'est le crach du Panama qui fit de moi un poète!' Clearly his father's failures, and probably his failure overall, provided the object-lesson that success may not be the point, but rather the activity and creativity involved, and most particularly the quality of one's involvement. So in 1930 Cendrars could write (with special reference to the inevitable break):

> Mais qu'il me soit permis de déclarer ici, justement parce qu'en définitive rien ne lui a réussi dans la vie, que sa vieillesse a été tragique et sa fin lamentable, qu'il me soit permis d'affirmer, malgré toutes les apparences contraires que mon père était un homme de cœur et que depuis qu'il n'est plus, et justement parce que j'ai été si longtemps brouillé avec lui à cause de son entêtement dans cette malencontreuse question de l'École de Commerce, je pense que c'était tout de même un type, un grand et un chic type.[11]

We can see that what attention Cendrars gave to telling of his family revolved mainly about his father. We know that his mother was much taken with botany and loved the piano. Freddy played a great deal, and from all indications quite well. During his one year in school in Neuchâtel, about 1902 or 1903, he played the organ at the Temple-Vieux a few times each month for his teacher, M. Hess-Ruetschi, who suffered from arthritis. *Vol à voile* ends with a discussion of invention in musical composition which is extremely important in understanding the way Cendrars approached his craft, and *Le Transsibérien* is dedicated 'aux musiciens.'

When Freddy was one year old he was baptised in La Chaux-de-Fonds, at the Hôtel de la Balance owned by his maternal grandfather. Six months later the family was in Egypt, but for perhaps no more than two years:

> Je me souviens d'un grand bruit d'usine autour de mon berceau et de beaucoup, beaucoup d'activité à la maison, des visites, des réceptions, puis de beaucoup de luxe en Egypte, avec palais, yacht, domestiques, victoria, chevaux, puis d'une vie un peu plus retirée en Angleterre dans un château appartenant à mon grand-père, puis d'une grande maison en Italie, puis d'une enfilade de pièces désertes à Paris, puis d'une toute petite villa au

> bord du lac à Montreux, enfin, coup sur coup, de plusieurs déménage-
> ments en Suisse, déménagements précipités, déménagements dans des
> appartements de plus en plus pauvres, avec, puis sans jardin, mais où alors
> je gagnais la rue ... [12]

To this list we may add Alexandria alternating with Heliopolis (unless the
family never actually resided at Heliopolis). The stay in England appears
the most questionable one, but it is possible that the maternal grandfather,
wherever he was, and always against his son-in-law, at some time took
Freddy, and perhaps the other children and their mother, under his wing;
for it seems Freddy's parents led separate lives for a number of periods,
such as when Cendrars says he visited his mother ('vacances chez Maman')
about 1900 in Paris, at 29 avenue Victor Hugo, bringing along from
Naples his schoolmate, Paul de Muralt. [13]

The early school years were spent in Naples, from 1891 or 1892 to
1897. The dates are examined at length by Cendrars in a long footnote
to 'Gênes' in *Bourlinguer*, [14] and, for obvious reasons, we can unravel the
discrepancies no better than he. For example, on this evidence, the 1900
trip to Paris was not made from Naples. From where? Montreux, or one
of the other homes in Switzerland? I suppose the most likely explanation
would be that his home in 1900 was in Paris, and he was at boarding
school. At any rate, in the nineties he spent his first school years at Dr
Pluss' Scuola Internazionale, which catered to foreigners and rich
Neapolitans, and notably to a sizable Swiss colony. A school photograph
taken in 1896 shows Freddy as a short boy in a sailor suit among conserva-
tively dressed schoolmates. [15]

There must have been a number of schools between this one and the
École de Commerce in Neuchâtel, which Cendrars says he attended in
1901-2 but may actually have attended a year or two later since he was
not in Russia until about 1904. At some point he spent three years in
school in Basel, where he met August Suter, the grandson of the 'Emperor
of California,' the hero of Cendrars' novel *L'Or*. He also attended boarding schools in Germany. It does not seem that his academic education
showed any greater continuity than his home life and, again in *Le Panama*,
the poet wrote:

> Comment voulez-vous que je prépare des examens?
> Vous m'avez envoyé dans tous les pensionnats d'Europe
> Lycées
> Gymnases
> Université

Perhaps, even quite likely, examinations were failed. Mr Sauser then decided to put his younger son in a trade school in Neuchâtel, where the family moved about 1901 and was to stay for some ten years:

> Les parents se font parfois de bien drôles d'idées quand ils pensent à l'avenir de leurs enfants. Ainsi mon père s'était mis en tête que puisqu'il destinait mon frère à une carrière libérale, il devait me mettre, moi, dans le commerce. Ceci ne correspondait à rien de réel, sinon ce besoin obscur de symétrie qui pousse les bourgeois à décorer leur cheminée du grand salon avec des objets la plupart du temps hétéroclites mais qui se font pendant, ce qui leur cause une satisfaction intime et les fait se complaire dans leur mauvais goût.[16]

But it was far too late to stabilize Freddy, who made love to three young English girls, went boating, rode an unpaid-for American motorcycle, ran up large debts at wine-shops, florists, and newspaperstands ('chez la marchande de journaux qui tenait le kiosque de la gare ... je m'étais abonné à la *Vie au Grand Air,* à la *Culotte rouge,* au *Nu académique* de Vignola, à la *Kleines Witzblatt,* à des publications obscènes qu'elle recevait de Londres, au *Guguss'* de Genève ... '[17]) and accumulated, by the end of his year at the École de Commerce, 375 unexcused absences (counted in class hours). *Vol à voile* tells in detail the story at this juncture: confessions to his father, a relationship with another, older woman, the boy being locked in his room, and, finally, his escape out of the window, with stops in his father's and sister's rooms for cigarettes and money. Freddy Sauser jumped on the first express through Neuchâtel, which as it happened was headed for Basel. The first station out of Neuchâtel, one at which express trains do not stop, is Saint-Blaise.

After wandering in German train stations for a few weeks Freddy ran short of funds. In Munich he played the piano in a piano shop. Then, in Pforzheim, he was befriended by a Jew from Warsaw named Rogovine who traded in jewelry and took the boy into his wandering business. However, this is Cendrars' story. The other, less romantic version is that Freddy's father, exasperated by his son's academic performance, entrusted him to this or another traveller headed for Russia. Whether in fact Freddy ran away from home, as he said, is a major subject of discussion among Cendrars scholars. Almost all come out against his having done so, but I am not yet convinced. It is not so unusual to run away from home, after all. Furthermore Cendrars devoted his only work of avowed autobiography to the event. Whatever the truth of the matter, we do know that his destination was the Swiss colony in Saint Petersburg which mainly dealt with clocks and watches, and it is likely he arrived with some form of recommendation. Perhaps the most secure position to take is that Cendrars was rewriting the break with his father to disguise a strictly private matter, such as his father's violently exiling him. We find, for example, in a letter to Suter sent from Russia during a second stay there in 1911: 'Je ne possède point les talents qui permettent aux autres de gagner leur vie. Pour se moquer de moi, on m'a surnommé Hans-sans-soucis et l'on m'a chassé de chez moi.'[18] Cendrars' public version gives him more independence; but it also protects his privacy. A photograph of Freddy with members of the transplanted Swiss group in Saint Petersburg shows him pensive, and not especially youthful-looking, but the only clean-shaven man. There are seven other men and seven women, no doubt their wives.[19] Perhaps a few of the frequently doubted uncles in *Le Panama ou les aventures de mes sept oncles* are here. One of them is surely H.A. Leuba, watchmaker, of 34 'rue aux Pois,' or Gorokhovaïa Street, where Freddy worked for almost three years.[20]

Freddy made a number of trips with Rogovine, beginning with an epic one on the newly finished Transsiberian railroad, starting in Moscow and going as far as Kharbin (Harbin) and thence to Peking, as the Russians were being routed by the Japanese at Port Arthur; as Cendrars' poem *Le Transsibérien* describes it:

> Et à Khilok nous avons croisé un long convoi de soldats fous
> J'ai vu dans les lazarets des plaies béantes des blessures qui saignaient à
> pleines orgues
> Et les membres amputés dansaient autour ou s'envolaient dans l'air rauque

It took Freddy three weeks to get to Peking, where he arrived in September of 1904 and spent the winter. It was an extremely cold one, and he practically died of hunger before finding a job as a stoker in the newly opened Hôtel des Wagons-Lits. He spent the winter reading, then burning for fuel, copies of the *Mercure de France* pillaged in the Western consulates during the Boxer Rebellion; perhaps this provided him with his first introduction to the most important of his immediate literary predecessors, Remy de Gourmont. But the life he intermittently led with Rogovine from 1904 to 1906, whether Rogovine was a real traveller or merely a fantasy made up from reading in the Saint Petersburg library, was the great influence of this period:

> ... je devais faire durant quelques années tant de voyages avec lui, dont
> trois à la foire de Nijni, deux en Chine, un en Arménie, un peu de

contrebande de perles via l'hinterland du Farsistan, les hauts plateaux
d'Ispahan, les déserts de l'intérieur, les passes de Merv, Boukhara, une
expédition à l'embouchure de la Léna, expédition qui avait pour but
d'atteindre des gisements d'ivoire fossile et qui faillit nous coûter la vie
et à Rogovine tout son avoir si, en nous rabattant de plusieurs centaines
de kilomètres dans l'est du delta, nous n'avions découvert dans la toundra
sibérienne des peuplades totalement inconnues où nous échangeâmes le
chargement de nos trente-sept traîneaux remplis de disques de sel gemme
contre autant de disques d'argent pur et quelques sacs de *xhisli* qui est du
saumon pourri, un court séjour à Bombay, où Rogovine avait été con-
voqué pour estimer un diamant ... [21]

It is about this point, in 1906, that we may pick up the very valuable
letters, agendas, and notebooks published by the Club français du livre in
1969. These *Inédits* represent mainly the years 1907 to 1914, and they
provide details and corroborate certain facts hitherto unverified. However, like each new discovery, they also widen, in a sort of geometrical
progression, the realms of the unknown. Thus they shed no light at all on
Cendrars' activities in China, if he went there, or in Russia during the
three years 1904–7, except to verify by the letter cited in footnote 20
above that he was in fact in Russia. We continue to have little verification
of his travels in this period. A. t'Serstevens, in his recent book of memoirs
L'Homme que fut Blaise Cendrars, doubts that Cendrars ever left Saint Petersburg in all the time he was in Russia, though he seems to base this
opinion on the *Inédits,* which, as I say, hardly bear on the matter. [22] Even
that all-important letter contains at least one error, as the young Sauser,
perhaps for reasons of simplification, gives his birthplace as Neuchâtel.
Furthermore, the *Inédits* contain not a word about the period October
1907 to March 1909, about a year and a half out of a total of eight covered.
Scholars will have to await the release of the actual documents used as the
source of this volume, as the material has been rearranged and many items
translated, excerpted, or omitted. I am told that Miriam Cendrars, the
author's daughter, has a roomful of manuscripts and papers in unopened
boxes.

The two most important revelations of the *Inédits* relative to this period
are a love-affair with a young Russian girl, Hélène (the only name we have
for her), and his earliest writing, *Alea,* dated Saint Petersburg 1907 – New
York, 15 February to 15 April 1912, and signed Freddy Sausey, a first
pseudonym. *Alea,* much revised even to the spelling of the title, was
eventually published in *Les Feuilles Libres* in 1921 under the enigmatic title
Moganni Nameh; Cendrars never seemed to give it much importance, as

he never had it published as a volume, nor is it listed in his own bibliographies.[23]

Letters to Hélène span the period from January 1907 in Saint Petersburg to June 1907, when Freddy had returned to Neuchâtel. They reveal an intense, *Sturm und Drang* sort of love on the part of the boy (we have no letters from Hélène in the *Inédits*), who seemed to have been suddenly liberated: 'Vous avez su réchauffer mon cœur, faire vibrer mon âme que j'avais volontairement endurcie, des plus doux sentiments que j'avais étouffés depuis longtemps.'[24] His intimacy with Hélène released him from a stoicism founded upon alienation from his family and even from any kind of home or country, a self-protective mortification (one is reminded of Joyce's *Portrait of an Artist as a Young Man*). This was now succeeded by what it was hiding, a powerful, suffering romanticism which mixed, or alternated between, French, German, and even Russian qualities. This romanticism pervades his letters to Hélène, those to his brother, some of the literary projects through 1912, and even letters to Féla, his wife to be, written after *Les Pâques*. During these few years his style and taste evolved from an early romanticism through neo-symbolism and then, almost simultaneously with the demise of the latter, to the powerful, unadorned modernism he is now known for; Freddy Sauser went from Lamartine to Blaise Cendrars in roughly five years.

Freddy left Saint Petersburg in April of 1907 for Neuchâtel and passed through Basel, where he saw his brother and probably Suter, and where he was shocked to discover himself a foreigner in his own country. In Neuchâtel his father refused to recognize him. In May he wrote Hélène that he was reading, preparing exams, and studying Chopin's *Trauermarsch* and that he was more and more alone within his family: 'Comme vous le voyez, je suis seul, isolé, expatrié au milieu de ma famille et dans ma patrie! Comme Ibsen je me dis: "l'homme fort est celui qui vit seul." '[25] It was a prophetic statement, and an idea I shall return to in connection with Cendrars as a 'modern' man in C.G. Jung's sense. Practising the funeral march at this point was strangely foreboding, as in June 1907 Hélène was seriously burned in a fire and died in hospital soon afterwards. The 1907 notebook, a black one, ends in September with the following inscription, the furthest note from stoicism; if the words are not entirely exceptional, yet their violence and, in this case, their precise relevance, make them much more than a post-romantic imitation:

Je crache sur la beauté qui amène le malheur,
Je crache sur la raison qui veut être trop belle,
Je crache sur le destin qui ne veut rien admettre,

Je crache sur les mots qui trompent l'animal,
Je crache sur la vie qui n'écoute pas la vie![26]

Cendrars would always distrust reason, language, any ordering of reality which might pretend to make life itself more trustworthy, less dangerous.

From this point to April 1909 we have almost no information from the *Inédits*. It is likely Freddy was in Paris during 1908 as he makes reference to his stay in a letter to Georges. If so, it is probably at this time that he raised bees in a Paris suburb, Tribardou, near Meaux; later he compared his experiences with bees to the moralistic attitude of Maeterlinck's then well-known book *The Life of the Bee* (1901).[27] He may also have met the writer of potboilers Gustave Lerouge, from whom he later lifted entire passages with the explanation that he was proving Lerouge to be a great 'poet of reality,' an 'anti-poet.' The verification of Cendrars' plagiarisms for his volume *Kodak (Documentaire)* of 1924 has actually helped to fire a revival of Lerouge's work. If these accounts of bee-raising and meetings, this early, with Lerouge are not factual, at least they show Cendrars projecting his later sense of poetic realism back into a very romantic youth.

Also in April of 1909 he was studying medicine in Bern. His mother had just died, but we have little indication of his state of mind. Certainly what little home he had had at one time could no longer claim a hold on him. The same month a short-lived but passionate love for Bella Bender, a Polish student, was reciprocated, but by May or June he and Féla Poznanska, another Polish girl studying in Bern, were lovers. Bella and Féla remained best friends, and so the threesome were often together. Féla became Freddy's wife in 1914, and the mother of his children. Yet we have had to await the publication of parts of her journal in the *Inédits* even to learn of her existence, as Cendrars never mentioned her, or even the fact of ever being married, despite the autobiographical nature, or at least the autobiographical appearance, of most of his work. His great secrecy concerning certain matters obliges us to be openminded, on the one hand about what he has hidden, and on the other about what he has chosen to tell, which may not be so fanciful after all. For example, what are we to make of these two lines near the end of *Le Transsibérien?*

Bella, Agnès, Catherine et la mère de mon fils en Italie
Et celle, la mère de mon amour en Amérique

Féla was in New York, and we know Bella and Agnès. If we have found three of the five women, certainly we must continue to believe in the possibility of the two others, and another child who to this day remains unknown.

Féla's journal provides an early reflection upon the writer from the outside; for it is clear that the tortured, sometimes self-indulgent tone of his own meditations represented only one facet of his personality. Her first notes are the most revealing. Her introduction to him by a classmate is: 'Il est suisse, mais par pur hasard. Il aurait pu naître dans n'importe quel autre pays, et il s'y trouverait parfaitement chez lui.' This was often said of Cendrars when he was famous; here we see that he was already more than just a tourist. Féla then goes on in her own voice: 'Il ressemble peu aux gens de son pays. Il porte la chevelure d'un Gorki, la vareuse de velours et la large cravate d'un Baudelaire et, dans les gestes, la grâce d'un Italien. Il pourrait aussi être polonais.'[28] Freddy first courted her by sending huge bouquets of flowers during all the month of May, incognito and on credit, for he had no money at all, he soon admitted to her. Already Féla sensed that Freddy was not one to stand still, to build a home, and she resisted her attraction. This no doubt explains their travels and long separations, until they parted permanently during the war years. (They were not divorced, however. Féla died in 1942 in England.) In April of 1910 Freddy visited Bella in Brussels (179 rue Brogniez, Anderledt, Brussels). Féla's journal had read:

> Il est assis sur un banc. Il me dit: 'Je regarde les couleurs du couchant qui me donnent le mal du départ.'
>
> Et moi, j'ai gardé dans l'armoire les 30 francs nécessaires à son départ pour Bruxelles ... [29]

In May 1910 he was back at school; then he and Féla both spent the summer near Brussels with Bella at the sea-side resort of La Panne:

> Je te vois à Bruxelles, le soir. Tu études dans le gros dictionnaire Hatzfeld et Darmesteter. Tu dis: 'Dix ans d'études. Il me faut dix ans. Je trouverais ma langue. Mon style. Une fois que j'aurai commencé. Mais je ne sais rien. Je ne sais pas mon français ... ' J'étais dans mon lit. Dans le lit. Toi, à la table. J'étais heureuse. Je regardais ton front, ta main.
>
> J'étais souffrante. Tu vendais des livres de la planche pour m'acheter des oranges. Tu étais beau. J'étais belle ... [30]

So Freddy went on writing, waiting for his style: at La Panne, an essay on Remy de Gourmont; in Paris in October, a sixty-seven-page fable, never published by the author; and in October and November, contributions to *L'Étudiant de Paris* and *La Forge,* so far not recovered. In Brussels Freddy worked as an extra in *Carmen* at the Théâtre de la Monnaie and made some money. In Paris from October 1910 to April 1911 he lived with Féla at the Hôtel des Étrangers, 216 rue Saint-Jacques. 'C'est la maison où fut écrit "Le Roman de la rose" ' he wrote in the poem 'Au Cœur du monde,' and his claim in that poem to have been born there may refer to the lovers' life together, or to his birth as a writer, or again to both as facets of a new life. At times he worked as a multilingual long-distance telephone operator; Féla translated letters, at one franc apiece. The *Inédits* hint at ambitious projects, with irony: 'Et me voici maintenant, rempli d'une ardeur nouvelle, à Paris, avec dans ma serviette un manuscrit de quatre cent pages, visitant un éditeur après l'autre pour caser convenablement ma "nostalgie romantique"!'[31] Cendrars voyaged much of his life with an overflowing briefcase, and later a trunk, full of manuscripts, projects which often took decades to finish and publish. Many never saw the light. That fall of 1910 he translated the Polish writer Stanislaw Prybyzewski's *La Messe des morts* from German into French; the Pole's introduction is a first source for Raymond, the narrator of Cendrars' *Moravagine,* published fifteen years later.

In Paris Freddy renewed his friendship with August Suter, who made a sculpture of his head, now lost to us except for a photograph. He met through Suter the Swiss poet Sigfried Lang, the English artist Frank Budgen, and perhaps also the Swiss painter Lejeune. But in March 1911 Féla left for New York to stay with relatives there, and soon thereafter Freddy returned to Saint Petersburg. *Alea* in its final version deals mainly with this second stay. Much of his time was spent in Strelna, where he read, wrote, and mainly loafed: 'Je vis sans vergogne comme un parasite,' he wrote to Suter in June, and of his book, now *Alia,*

> ... en allemand, *Noitzen,* ou mieux, comme Spitteler, *Allotria.* J'y jette tout, ma vie antérieure, tout ce que je sais, tout ce que j'ignore, mes idées, mes croyances, mes vulgarités, mes démences, mes stupidités: la vie et la mort, Nietzsche et saint Jean de la Croix, Rivarol et Kant, la Bible et mon cœur. C'est un 'omnibus': la poésie populaire et le Professeur Haeckel.[32]

He was giving lessons and hoping to give lectures (on what, we do not know), but was generally impatient to return to Paris. Besides his experiences in the wider world, which had in fact only just begun, he already knew the habits of a local, seamier side of life, as witness the following in a letter to Suter:

> Pour répondre à Monsieur B: à partir de onze heures du soir, Place Blanche, vis-à-vis du Moulin-Rouge, on trouve de temps en temps, au *Grelot,* des garçons maquillés, des démaquillés toujours. Monsieur B. pourrait y aller une fois. Et s'il n'y en avait pas ce soir-là, il n'aurait qu'à

s'adresser sans crainte à une des hétaïres qui y paradent. Au prix d'une bouteille de champagne, elle le conduirait dans un des nombreux endroits où l'on trouve de tels garçons. Mieux encore, qu'il se rende à l'adresse suivante: Louise Darmont, 3 bis, rue Capron. C'est une brave fille, une Montmartroise, enfant de la Butte Sacrée! (Attention: je crois qu'elle est malade!) Lui donner rendez-vous au *Grelot* et alors passer une nuit avec elle à Montmartre. Elle s'y connaît! Avec elle, aux *Gaies filles du Portugal,* j'ai pris part à une orgie. On y a présenté à table, au dessert, une fille nue, âgée de seize ans, dans une corbeille de violettes bleu-pâle.[33]

Still at Strelna in July, Freddy translated Richard Dehmel's poem *Verwandlungen der Venus,* a Nietzschean work that was considered very shocking in its day (1893). In September he was teaching French in a mysteriously foggy Saint Petersburg and spending much of his time in the library: 'On cherche refuge tantôt dans une église, tantôt dans une bibliothèque. On vit dans ce pays presque comme dans une hallucination de fumeur d'opium. Cela me plaît.'[34] He read, and wrote at some length, about paintings, visiting all the museums and sending critiques to Suter. He was no doubt keeping abreast of Paris news, for in a letter dated 10/23 September 1911 he asked: 'Qu'est-il advenu de la "Joconde"? L'a-t-on vraiment volée?'[35] Apollinaire had been arrested for the theft of the *Mona Lisa* on September 7 (a year later, on 17 September 1912, Cendrars would be in jail in Paris for the theft of Apollinaire's *L'Hérésiarque et cie.* from the publisher Stock's bookstall). Freddy also read about this time Apollinaire's pornographic novel *Les Onze mille verges* 'par G... A...' and published that year. We cannot say if Freddy knew who the author was, though Raymond Warnier, who has made a case for Cendrars already being one of Apollinaire's 'nègres' in Paris in 1910, feels that certain chapters of the book show signs of their collaboration.[36]

In November prospects for work seemed poor, or at least without advantageous issue. Suddenly Féla sent him a boat ticket for New York, and he jumped at the opportunity. He was impoverished, sometimes starving, violently unhappy, and vindictive in his letters and journal as he awaited the moment of departure, in the train to Libau (Latvia), and even on the boat, the *Birma,*[37] despite the fact that he was looking forward to this voyage and would remember it a few months later with nostalgia. In Saint Petersburg he wrote:

J'entreprends ce voyage pour être loin de l'hideuse face humaine ...

Les agglomérations humaines ont la sombre attirance de la mort. Elles sont les purulentes plaies de l'immonde corps qu'est la terre. Elles sont fétides, spongieuses; en pus continuel, la foule humaine en découle. Le monde pourrit. La terre est ulcérée. L'idéalisme, sur les dômes aurés des temples, allume de squameuses dartres. [Piqûre] des vers, monnaies d'or, morsures. Cybèle s'exténue.

Ave, Virgo siphilitica! Je vais en Amérique.[38]

In Warsaw he stopped over to see Bella; we have yet to discover the exact nature of their love or friendship.[39] 'Je rôde insatisfait de F... à B..., la tête troublée, incapable d'une pensée juste, d'un sentiment vrai, d'une sensation aiguë.' He was tense, torn between damning the world and praising it:

> Je passe par des hauts et des bas, des abattements et des [ancrages] d'éner-
> gie ... 'Lasciva est nobis pagina, vita proba.' Ausone. Ainsi, je veux, moi
> aussi, une littérature exultatrice de la Vie, quand en réalité je la méprise
> supérieurement, la vie, impuissant, voluptueux, frileux et délicat.[40]

At the heart of this tension was the fact that he viewed his trip as a concession to Féla, a failure on his part to do without her:

> Tu as peur de l'avouer, mais avoue donc que tu as peur ... ELLE, la
> femme au cœur de tendresse, t'attend; – mais il est peut-être déjà trop tard;
> mais ce n'est pas elle que tu cherches. Une chambre, des livres, le silence
> et la paix: travailler. Pourquoi vas-tu vers elle? Pourquoi rampes-tu quand
> même vers elle? Lâche. Frousseux de la vie... Tu as peur de ne pouvoir
> assez l'aimer.[41]

Too late for what?

Freddy boarded the *Birma* on 21 November 1911, to disembark in New York on 12 December. Raymond Dumay calls Freddy's exhilarating experience during a great storm at sea his 'mise à feu,' a night of transformation during which the poet is born.[42] Dumay goes on to connect this experience with a central quality of Cendrars' later attitude: 'La paix qui doit loger le bonheur est au cœur du risque.'[43] Dumay's first idea seems too simple; it depends on a more traumatic view of man's nature and development than I can subscribe to, especially as the travails of Freddy Sauser continue to plague the emerging Blaise Cendrars for months to come, as witness the letters to Féla during the following summer. I tend to agree, however, that the tempest, as we view it through Freddy's account, affords a fine instance of the poet's discovery of his own authentic nature. It is an epiphany of sorts, a moment of insight which must have occurred before and had to occur again any number of times before its lesson would take hold, the intimation of a dangerous mortality: 'Le bateau semble bondir sur les flots, léger, heureux, fleuri d'écume, une nef aventureuse. Les flancs palpitent. Cela me rappelle mon temps d'école buissonnière, mes après-midi passés en voilier sur le lac de Neuchâtel.'[44] Perhaps the major relevance of the storm to the poet's art, a storm which the captain declares to be one of the three worst he has experienced in twenty-six years at sea and which forces the *Birma* to St John's in New-foundland for repairs, is Freddy's discovery that such danger still exists in our modern world, which is supposed to have spoiled us:

> J'ai partagé tous les sorts du marin. Beau temps des premiers jours, enchantements, vagues, vents, tempêtes, ouragan, dépontement, avaries, dérive, refuge dans un port de fortune. Je n'attendais pas ces choses au xxᵉ...
> J'ai eu de la chance.[45]

As I shall attempt to show in part two, however, danger will come to mean more than adventure in the common sense, though it includes adventure as well. It will point not so much to a particular kind of strenuous life as to the attitude that everything we participate in is dangerous, if not for our bodies then for our souls.

I would add another important discovery of this voyage – Goethe, in particular *Dichtung und Wahrheit*. I have purposely avoided, for the most part, reference to young Sauser's reading precisely because we have an unusual amount of information, from different sources including Cendrars himself, notably the library callslips found in the trunk which followed him for many years, callslips which serve to verify some of Cendrars' much-questioned memories. So at this crucial moment, a few months before *Les Pâques à New York* are composed, I should like to make a digression which demonstrates quite a different side to Freddy's wandering life so far. For if a real storm in November and December of 1911 could decisively enlist Sauser in the conflagration of life, a more reflective influence played a large part about the same time, giving him, among other things, his name in the embers and ashes of desire and of action. The editors of the *Inédits* recount discovering the following on a small piece of paper from this period:

> En cendres se transmue
> Ce que j'aime et possède
> Tout ce que j'aime et que j'étreins
> Se transmue aussitôt en
> Cendres.
> Blaise Cendrars[46]

He later attributed the original to Nietzsche, quoting: 'Und alles wird mir nur zur Asche / Was ich liebe, was ich fasse' and adding 'Et Blaise vient de braise.'[47]

In 'Paris, Port-de-Mer,' the last section of *Bourlinguer,* Cendrars discusses both books and their readers, and readers of different sorts; he writes of Apollinaire, Chadenat the bookseller, Remy de Gourmont, his friend t'Serstevens and himself: '... et depuis ma plus tendre enfance, depuis que maman m'a appris à lire, j'avais besoin de ma drogue, de ma dose dans les 24 heures, n'importe quoi, pourvu que cela soit de l'imprimé! C'est ce que j'appelle être un inguérissable lecteur de livres ... '[48] Many friends and acquaintances confirm this on both scores, quantitatively and qualitatively; that is to say that he read enormously, enough that some suggest that the vast riches of his writing come not from experience but rather from reading; and also that he read virtually anything, or perhaps I should say everything; from *Fantômas,* the *Répertoire général du tarif des douanes,* the books of Captain Lacroix, such as *Les Derniers Voyages de forçats et de voiliers en Guyane et les derniers voiliers antillais,* and the dime novels of his friend Gustave Lerouge, to Migne's 221-volume *Patrologia Latina* and *The Encyclopaedia Britannica,* which he was memorizing at one point during his youth, tearing out a page a day. Writes t'Serstevens of the years 1912–13:

> Sa grande source d'inspiration, et la plus féconde, a toujours été la lecture, non celle des livres purement littéraires, qui ne pouvaient rien lui apporter, mais tout ce que l'imprimé peut nous offrir de neuf et de substantiel. Il a été le plus ardent liseur que j'aie connu, depuis les livres les plus élevés de la philosophie et de la mystique, jusqu'à des prospectus et des dépliants de compagnies maritimes et aériennes ... N'ayant au surplus aucun respect pour la chose imprimée, il n'hésitait pas à découper dans les volumes les passages qui l'intéressaient; et il est bien vrai qu'il avait déjà, lorsque je l'ai connu, cette serviette remplie de pages arrachées, dont il a parlé dans un de ses bouquins. Doué d'une mémoire extraordinaire, il aurait pu se passer de cette brocante qu'il n'a pas dû consulter souvent, et qu'il a d'ailleurs égarée au cours d'un de ses vagabondages.[49]

Whether it be fact or projection, Cendrars reconstructs his earliest reading as Balzac and Nerval, at about the age of ten. These two, representing life as monstrous and profuse variety and life confused with dream, are perfect masters for Cendrars, in whom they interpenetrate. In his introduction to Balzac's *Ferragus* for the Club français du livre *Comédie humaine*, Cendrars tells of his father's buying a complete Balzac and giving him Nerval's *Les Filles du feu* to keep him away from the fine leather-bound volumes. Naturally the boy read both. Cendrars writes: 'Balzac n'est pas un précurseur. Il est le créateur du monde moderne. C'est pourquoi tout jeune auteur d'aujourd'hui doit passer par lui. Plus j'avance dans mes écritures, plus je me rends compte combien j'ai subi son empreinte.' And to Raymond Radiguet's sceptical 'Vous trouvez qu'il écrit bien?' he replies: 'Peu importe. Il ne s'agit pas tant d'écriture dans un roman, que de création, de vie. Vous n'apprendrez jamais rien dans *La Princesse de Clèves,* où l'on ne parle jamais d'argent, ce puissant ressort psychologique et bien moderne mis en place par le seul Balzac.'[50] In 'Paris, Port-de-Mer' Cendrars calls Balzac his third master (speaking of prose only). The second is the precursor of the third: '... quant au duc, le grand Saint-Simon, l'homme de cour, je le considère comme le précurseur de Balzac, ses *Mémoires* étant plus formidables et beaucoup plus romanesques que *La Comédie humaine.* C'est mon second maître, après Remy de Gourmont, pour l'usage des mots et le maniement de la langue, sans rien dire de ses histoires vraies ... '[51] De Gourmont I shall leave for later discussion.

Nerval is also extremely important. Four lines from 'El Desdichado' are given in the notes to the extremely complex 120-page story 'Gênes' in *Bourlinguer* as one of the keys to the meaning of the narrative. As his preferred poets for the famous 'questionnaire de Marcel Proust' Cendrars gave 'Nerval et les chinois'[52] and in the radio interviews of 1950 he said: 'Je dois à Gérard de Nerval mon amour des chansons et de la poésie populaires et dans tous les pays du monde je me suis efforcé d'entendre et de noter et de lire presque exclusivement de la musique, de la poésie, de la littérature populaires, notamment en Russie, en Chine, au Brésil.'[53] It may seem surprising to find Nerval considered so close to the common man, but Cendrars' is not the sociologist's interest; quite the contrary, what he is always searching out, and what constitutes the touchstone of his work, is the popular *imagination:*

> Depuis toujours, le cœur de la poésie française tient entre la Tour Saint-Jacques, Saint-Merri, la Cité, et le centre en était la lanterne où Gérard de Nerval s'est pendu. La pierre de touche est là. Il est, au portail de l'église Saint-Martin, une pierre où se cache la formule de l'or. L'a-t-on déchiffrée? La formule de la pierre philosophale est la formule de la poésie.[54]

Thus Balzac and Nerval blend somewhere at the source of all Cendrars' work. Asked twenty years before the above interview to define his writing in four or five lines he answered: 'En un mot: l'irréalisme.'[55]

However, our first sure introduction to Cendrars' reading, in the *Inédits* in 1906, indicates a different story, one which interrupts an attractively

simple development from Balzac and Nerval straight to Cendrars. This
other progression is a Rimbaud-like accelerated history of poetry, in which
Freddy Sauser's interest runs from Lamartine through Maeterlinck to
Remy de Gourmont, who in turn introduces Blaise Cendrars, all in about
five years.

The first authors mentioned in the *Inédits* are Lamartine and Châteaubriand, whose works Freddy copied into his notebooks. Then there are
notes on Benjamin Constant, quotations from Coleridge, and reading lists
extending to September of 1907 which include the following poets, in this
order: Nerval (but not poetry – *Les Filles du feu*), Verlaine, Poe, Baudelaire. There are many more novelists, including, in order: Fogazzaro
(*Malombre*), Tolstoy, l'Abbé Prévost, Goethe, a great deal of Maupassant,
Turgenev, George Sand, J. H. Rosny (*Résurrection*), Dostoyevsky, Octave
Mirbeau (*Sebastien Roch*), Paul Adam, Machiavelli (*Belfagor*), and Heine.
He was also reading the theatre of Molière (taking many notes) and that
of Maeterlinck, whose sombre symbolism runs through much of Freddy's
writing. In *Le Transsibérien* he will write of the sounds of different trains.
'Et il y en a qui dans le bruit monotone des roues me rappellent la prose
lourde de Maeterlinck.'

But two other kinds of reading are of special interest. One may be called
social philosophy, and includes Darwin, F. Huet's *Le Christianisme social,*
John Stuart Mill, and, grouped in March 1907, Taine, Michelet, E. de
Laveleye's *De la Propriété,* and Tarde and Durkheim, two sociologists
usually considered to have greatly influenced Jules Romains' *Unanimisme.*
Within a year (and perhaps while Sauser was in Paris during 1908), *La Vie
unanime* would appear. But if Romains' Whitmanesque poetry has been
accused of being too intellectually calculating, Sauser's reading in soci-
ology must have led more likely to the rejection of theories. Frank Budgen
paraphrases Cendrars, who would be speaking about 1913: 'Revolution
was a different matter. It smacked of the pedantries of pretentious sociologists, with their ideological straitjackets ... '[56] It is extremely important to
the understanding of all of Cendrars to distinguish between an intellectual
position, which he disdained, and a position as an act and as a fact. He
wrote in 1920:

> Il y a l'époque: Tango, Ballets Russes, cubisme, Mallarmé, bolchevisme
> intellectuel, insanité.
> Puis la guerre: un vide.
> Puis l'époque: construction, simultanisme, affirmation. Calicot: Rim-
> baud: changement de propriétaire. Affiches. La façade des maisons man-
> gées par les lettres. La rue enjambée par le mot. La machine moderne dont
> l'homme sait se passer. Bolchevisme en action. Monde.[57]

The second kind of reading, and certainly the most important as it developed over the next few years, is religious, mystical, visionary, and sometimes pathological, as witness the following: Dante's *Commedia;* Sacher-Masoch, who taught us masochism; Max Nordau's *Les Mensonges conventionnels* (perhaps at some other time Nordau's famous *Degeneration* also supplied material for *Moravagine*); Malebranche's *Recherche de la vérité;* A. Karr's *Dieu et le diable;* Poe; A. Forel's *Question sexuelle;* Swedenborg; Robert Fludd; Campanella; Ludwig Holberg; and J.L. Tieck.

Unfortunately, at this point the eighteen-month break in the *Inédits* prevents us from establishing any continuity in Freddy's reading. Furthermore, the editors chose to arrange alphabetically all the references they found to reading in the libraries of Bern (1909–10), Saint Petersburg (1910), and New York (1911–12). We have dates only for the text on de Gourmont and the books bought in Paris at the end of 1910.

In August of 1910, in Brussels, Freddy made detailed studies, chapter by chapter, of de Gourmont's anthology *Le Latin mystique* and his *Physique de l'amour,* and wrote an article on him which appeared in 1912 in *Les Hommes Nouveaux,* Cendrars' own journal. Without any hesitation we may say that Remy de Gourmont is the most crucial writer for Cendrars, who said that the critic revealed to him all the authors who ever mattered to him, from the church fathers to Rimbaud and Lautréamont. He also said that he believed he had mentioned de Gourmont's name in almost everything he wrote. Quotations from de Gourmont serve as epigraphs to *Les Pâques à New York* and *Moravagine.* Cendrars' second son was named Rémy (de Gourmont did not use the accent), and there is the extraordinary 'coincidence' of Cendrars losing his arm the day de Gourmont died. The then-famous symbolist critic for the *Mercure de France,* which was the most important periodical in Paris before the ascendancy of *La Nouvelle Revue Française,* has suffered an eclipse, but the praise of Ezra Pound and T.S. Eliot demonstrates his importance for modern poetry.[58] In this month of August 1910 Freddy wrote (I excerpt a few ideas):

> Mécislas Golberg a démontré que chaque grand homme crée [sa légende]. Ainsi, Pythagore, Jésus, Napoléon. Des amis ont rédigé celle de Socrate, et Baudelaire, comme tout ce qu'il entreprenait, a construit la sienne avec beaucoup d'application. C'est peut-être un des traits les plus caractéristiques du génie que ce besoin de se créer une légende. Comme les enfants, le génie, ce suprême enfant, veut rêver à des histoires dont il est le héros. C'est ce que Nietzsche appelait la volonté de puissance.
>
> Je ne touche jamais aux légendes. C'est la forme sous laquelle les génies (et les dieux) communient avec l'humanité.

Remy de Gourmont n'a pas d'idées: c'est un sensuel. Quand tout un peuple d'hommes de lettres s'abrutit sur des idées prostituées, comme dans les brasseries avec les filles, lui n'a que des images.

Remy de Gourmont est un cerveau en train de dissocier l'idée de l'amour.[59]

The first two quotations could serve to support the argument that Cendrars invented his legend rather than lived it. If so, he does not appear to have been the victim of it, as is often the case. I continue to take the view that he lived most of his story. Still, we can see here his search for mythopoesis, in order to 'communicate with humanity.' I also note the use of Nietzsche's 'will to power,' which is often associated with Malraux and his heroes' quest for domination, over others or over circumstances. For Cendrars it seems to mean more the will to create, or re-create oneself; the phrase bears a more direct relation to mythopoesis. The last two quotations are both interesting in the light of developments in England about the same time; a poetry of images, not ideas or rhetoric, and a variation on Eliot's use of de Gourmont's dissociation of sensibility.

Along with a complete bibliography of Remy de Gourmont we find mentioned in the *Inédits* his *Le Latin mystique,* and, from Cendrars' later comments throughout his life, we may guess that this volume is the fountainhead for most of the single largest category of his reading, the church fathers. Most of this reading must have been done in Migne's 221-volume *Patrologia Latina,* but many separate works are cited, usually in very old editions.[60] Late in his life Cendrars said he bought a volume of Migne each year, not as a follower of the faith or even as a scholar, but strictly for the language.[61]

Thus we may see the great influence of de Gourmont, which is threefold. The first influence is as the foremost proponent of Symbolism – an influence which dominates Freddy Sauser's work, almost despite him, in 1910, 1911, and into 1912. *Séquences* shows the influence strongly; it is the only work Cendrars published as a separate volume which does so, and he called it a 'péché de jeunesse.'[62] The *Inédits* indicate that he sent a manuscript of *Séquences* to Remy de Gourmont just before leaving New York, around April 1912. The second influence of de Gourmont is the revelation of the Latin fathers and religious medieval poets as writers. Such prose and poetry was undermining Freddy's overwrought symbolist rhetoric, which, of course, he also owed in some degree to de Gourmont. The effect is found most directly in *Les Pâques,* though it can also be discovered already in *Séquences,* as a poetic language of entirely unaffected and quite unadorned faith, of naïveté in the oldest sense of the word. And thirdly, we see the beginning of Cendrars' project to metamorphose himself and his world into a myth sufficient for a modern world without centre or gods.

In Paris at the end of 1910 Freddy bought eight volumes of de Gourmont, along with books by Judith Gautier, Saint-Evremond, Cyrano de Bergerac, Nerval, Rivarol, Heine, Rétif de la Bretonne, Théophile de Viau, and Saint-Amant. The consistency of such a list resides in its focus on marginal, rebellious writers, some of them more interesting for themselves as men and women than for their works; or, conversely, we might say the focus presupposes a certain knowledge of the mainstream and, generally, a desire to find something else. Thus, in the case of Baudelaire Cendrars would later distinguish the major poetry from his lesser-known art criticism, and show a marked preference for the latter:

> Quant à Baudelaire, certes j'en ai subi l'influence. C'est un très grand poète, mais c'est surtout un profond esprit catholique dans sa critique de la modernité. Comme critique c'était même un type étonnant, bien en avance sur son époque et je crois que durant longtemps encore, mettons jusqu'au bout du XXᵉ siècle, il influencera les jeunes gens par sa critique et son dandyisme. Ses plus beaux vers datent déjà. Je me place sous le signe de François Villon.[63]

For someone as concerned as Cendrars already seemed to be with marginal characters, peculiar habits and customs, and the accursed poets as witnesses to their times, we are not surprised finally to come upon Rimbaud in these notebooks, where he serves to condemn the whole mainstream of literature: 'Littératuricide d'un rhétoricien émancipé: Racine... peuh! Victor Hugo... pouah! Homer... oh! la! la! l'École Parnassienne... pfuit!'

We see Cendrars' great curiosity in his scholarly and scientific pursuits. There are many books on music, including a Rachmaninov score; works on entomology and biology in general, including Maeterlinck's book on bees, Fabre, and A.R. Wallace on evolution; a dossier of works with his notes on hypnotism and its applications to physical disorders, including Charcot, and Bernheim and Liébaut of the school of Nancy;[64] books on precious stones, on perfumes, and on cosmetology; works on painting (the Flemish schools, French religious art of the thirteenth century, Vasari's *Lives,* Rodin's *L'Art*); works on the Orient and the Middle East (and Théophile Gautier's *Voyage en Russie*); books on Celtic poetry and Franciscan poets, and a dossier labelled 'rhythm' with quotations from Saint Augustine, Aristides, Quintilian, and Aristotle's *Poetics*; philosophical works mainly by two men – Bergson, whose *Essai sur les données immédiates*

de la conscience is cited, and Schopenhauer, for whom no titles are given.
Schopenhauer is mentioned often in Cendrars' writing, and the poet saw
dangerous action as a natural outcome of a philosophical pessimism. (A
third philosopher is often mentioned in other places in the *Inédits,* but
infrequently in Cendrars' published work – Friedrich Nietzsche.)

There is more contemporary reading, in this list and among the books
he read on the boat for New York: Gustave Kahn, Huysmans, and the
Swiss epic poet Spitteler (twenty-two works listed). On the boat Freddy
read Baudelaire's volume *Mon Cœur mis à nu,* which he referred to
throughout his life and published in 1919 when he was running La Sirène
editions. But I think the discovery, or rediscovery, of the trip is Goethe.
My justification for this long literary digression at this point in the author's
life is that it is the conjunction of Goethe and the sea-voyage which
probably gives him a grand, powerful insight into what will become
Cendrars' unique entwining of art and reality. On 26 November 1911,
three days before the storm, he writes in his journal:

> *Dichtung und Wahrheit* de Goethe m'ouvre toutes les portes du rêve,
> toutes les avenues qui mênent au loin, hors du brumeux de la conscience.
> Je suis un voluptueux.[65]

December 2 (when, after twenty-four hours of calm, the storm returns):

> Oh! que je comprends bien le 'Déjà' de Baudelaire. Oui, le voyage en
> mer a un grand charme pour le poète qui n'est jamais pressé d'arriver.
> L'insouciance matérielle, la retraite et la solitude relatives, à bord; l'ordre
> et l'appropriété du navire; la cabine, étui du dandy; la grandeur élémen-
> taire du spectacle, vents, vagues, soleils, immensités et infinis, tout cela
> porte l'esprit contemplatif au rêve, au rêve et à la création poétique.
> *Dichtung und Wahrheit. Voyages en Italie. Autobiographie de Goethe.* C'est
> le livre, par excellence, du voyage.[66]

Then, in his notebooks for December 4, he writes a comparison of the
powers of artists and nature, followed by what amounts to a literary
manifesto:

> Michel-Ange et Léonard et, parmi les littérateurs, seul, je crois Spitteler,
> peuvent subir l'épreuve d'être vus et lus dans ce milieu. Mais surtout,
> certains hymnes, certaines proses, certaines [tropes] en bas latin ...
> Que peu de poètes, en somme, ont la synthèse de la grandeur. Les
> anciens sont loin de l'âme humaine; les modernes ont des notations, des

à-coups; semblent préparer et rassembler les éléments d'une œuvre à
venir.

Il faut purger Spitteler du jeu enfantin des mythologies, Huysmans de
l'encombrant bric-à-brac, Remy de Gourmont de son érudition, tous les
poètes et tous les livres de la mise en scène, des coulisses, de l'anecdote,
éplucher tous les poèmes des rimes, jusqu'au vers rythmiquement élémen-
taire qui en est le noyau, réduire tous les livres à quelques pages essen-
tielles et nues, etc., pour découvrir ce que j'appelle 'le lyrisme cosmique.'
   Peu d'œuvres sont pures; il n'y a eu jusqu'ici que des essais.
   Plus de commentaires, mais des inventaires; plus d'encyclopédies, mais
des incentripédies; plus de gloses, mais des clefs, des florilèges, des essen-
tiaires; l'analytique synthèse, le scelle mortuaire, la Pyramide.[67]

Sauser strips his poets of their artifices, descriptions, reflections, which is
to say their cover, because they withhold the facts from the touch. The
very counting of the real will suffice, as in Whitman's inventories. But, as
with Whitman, the purpose of such accounting is not to be encyclopedic,
which would be a strictly rational enterprise; Sauser wants to evoke
through the facts their connection, the active centre around which they all
dance, their real, unrhetorical lyricism. Thus, on 11 December 1911,
Freddy Sauser disembarks in New York as if he had been reborn, not so
much to a different life as to the same one over again, with renewed
innocence: 'J'attends le point du jour, l'aube de ma vie ... C'est une
nouvelle naissance!' At the same time he recognizes that he has not, in fact,
changed: 'La nature est partout la même, je suis partout le même: ingué-
rissablement musical.'[68] If there had been any escapism before now,
henceforth it becomes less and less likely; the changes and the permanence
reside within, and the very discoveries of the voyage, while new and real,
time after time reiterate that principle.

In New York Freddy stayed for a time with Féla, at 845 Jennings Street
in the Bronx, and he let her support him while he wrote. There were many
projects, works begun or finished: *Alea,* or *Moganni Nameh*; portraits of
people he met under the title *Hic Haec Hoc* (he later used this title for a
poem in *Feuilles de route* [1924, 1928] to refer to the names of three
marmoset monkeys; I read this as a little private irony about his post-
symbolist beginnings); a *Séjour à New York*; *New York in Flashlight,* which
contains the fast, metaphorical language of Cendrars' poems after *Les
Pâques* and of the prose *Profond aujourd'hui*: 'Triste pays, maigre recette.
Les ménagères repartent. Les monstres redéfilent, sautent les mêmes

méridiens à rebours, rentrent dans les écuries de la Malchance. Ils ne reviendront jamais plus, les forains, et ils m'auront une fois de plus oublié.'[69] He wrote two or perhaps three dramas, of which *Danse macabre de l'amour* seems to revolve about Hélène's death; *Séquences,* poems not mentioned in the *Inédits* except for the following in a letter to Féla dated 14 April 1912, a few weeks before he left America: 'Comme je veux rire, j'envoie, aujourd'hui même, les *Séquences* à Remy'[70] and finally the long poem *Les Pâques à New York,* dated 6-8 April 1912 (Easter Sunday was the 7th) and written at the same time as *Danse macabre* (5–8 April). Cendrars had made his first contribution to the valuable literature of the modern age, and we may begin to treat him as one who has found a way more than as one who is still searching.

Freddy had to leave Féla, who could not continue to support him, whether because she disliked the idea or lacked the money, or for both reasons. In March at the latest he lived at 70 West 96th Street, in Manhattan 'dans la dernière maison en bois ... chez un gangster hongrois qui avait une chouette petite femme et où j'avais comme voisin de chambre un gentleman anglais, un aveugle, absolument abracadabrant et chichiteux.'[71] Parts of *Les Pâques* no doubt refer to his small room and his neighbours in this wooden house:

> Dans la chambre à côté, un être triste et muet
> Attend derrière la porte, attend que je l'appelle!   [ll. 18-19]

> Ma chambre est nue comme un tombeau ...   [l. 196]

The poem, in fact, may tell us more about Freddy in New York than the *Inédits.* We have no idea whom he met there. He later said he stayed with Caruso for a few weeks. The unpublished *Hic Haec Hoc* describes people he met, some of whom seem to have come to him, but they are referred to only by initials: W, a professor; L ... sky, a painter to whom Freddy talks of modern painting, including cubism; H, a dramatist who perhaps prompted the three plays Freddy was writing (he never had any published in his lifetime). He tried to spend all the time he had wandering about idly or reading at the New York Public Library at 42nd Street and Fifth Avenue. One wonders if, in his many rambles further downtown, he did not stop more than once at 291 Fifth Avenue, Stieglitz' Photo-Secession gallery. Here, earlier in 1911, Picasso had had his first one-man show anywhere, from his early work down through analytical cubism, two years before the cubist scandal of the Armory Show. The *Inédits* have Freddy talking to L ... sky about 'Pigazzaro, le cubiste.' Could this be Picasso?

But essentially Freddy was alone, and he prized his solitude despite the

drawbacks: 'Isolement absolu de Gérard de Nerval; de par sa vie décou-
sue, ses voyages, son foyer désert, ses fréquentations louches et ses nuits
malsaines. Et malgré l'horreur du drame final, je ne trouve pas qu'il ait
payé trop cher son indépendance.'[72] Freddy explored New York, very
much alone. The Bronx, upper Manhattan, and Harlem (then a white
neighbourhood) looked to him like Basel's Gurdeldinger or Paris'
'Levois-Perret' districts (I presume Levallois-Perret; as with Pigazzaro
above, we cannot say if the error is Cendrars' or that of the *Inédits*). These
places struck him as unusually ugly, but essentially not different from their
European counterparts; over the years, and starting with *Les Pâques,* he
would reverse his distaste radically and find the century's new men in this
pitiful environment:

> Nous revenions de plus en plus souvent au quartier des Ternes ... Un
> peuple net et propre s'y engouffrait, des hommes d'une jeune élégance,
> des femmes en chandail. On était loin de l'Angleterre, de l'Amérique ou
> de la Chine et, pourtant, on y était en étroite communion avec le monde
> entier ...
>
> Peuple magnifique de Levallois-Perret et de Courbevoie, peuple en
> cotte bleue ... [73]

These areas of New York are not named in *Les Pâques,* though they are
present. The poem becomes more specific downtown, where the poverty
is more shocking; the Lower East Side, which was the Jewish ghetto,
Chinatown, or the area of armed robbers and bandits between the two,
around Mulberry and Rivington Streets, Nerval's 'fréquentations
louches':

> Seigneur, je suis dans le quartier des bons voleurs,
> Des vagabonds, des va-nu-pieds, des recéleurs
>
> [ll. 98-9]

Freddy let his beard and hair grow long. He attempted to get a publisher for some of his work, but without success. He contemplated suicide,
perhaps not seriously, and even proposed a suicide pact to Féla. He was
constantly hungry from the ever-persistent rebellion against work:

> Je crevais la faim parce que je ne voulais pas travailler ... De temps en
> temps, j'acceptais un job, contraint et forcé, mais je n'y restais pas huit
> jours et, si je pouvais me faire balancer avant et toucher ma semaine, je
> le faisais, impatient d'aller reprendre mes séances de lecture à la Central-
> Library. C'est ainsi que j'ai été vingt-quatre heures tailleur pour dames, me

recommandant de Mme Paquin, la créatrice de la robe entravée, une amie de ma marraine; durant deux, trois séances pianiste dans un cinéma du Bowery et que j'ai travaillé toute une semaine aux abattoirs sans arriver à me faire vider, malheur![74]

He was perhaps more alone in New York than at any time previously, and his refusal, or inability, to work weighed more heavily than ever as there was only Féla to help him, and she had very little. Yet he embraced this poverty as a part of his independence, which was cheap enough at that price. Certainly it would not prevent him from writing, which was what he wanted to do more than anything else: 'J'ai des choses à faire que j'accomplirai. Ce n'est pas d'être pauvre ou crève-la-faim qui m'empêchera d'écrire.'[75] In such conditions Les Pâques was written, the eve of Easter Sunday after he left a church where they were playing Hayden's Creation because a minister insisted on a donation he did not have.[76] The detail is worth reporting as it seems to provide an impetus for the poem. The spirit in an age – here, a city – of money-making is a recurring theme in Cendrars, from L'Or and Rhum to the violent tirades against both the USA and the USSR in Le Lotissement du ciel.

Although New York gave him his first great poem, Paris was the place to be a poet. In Saint Petersburg he had wanted to return to Paris, and in New York, once a job with the Swiss legation in Washington failed to materialize, he felt he had no alternative. Leaving Féla behind, as their relationship was too much of a burden for her, at least in his mind,[77] he returned to Paris via Geneva, where he arrived at the end of June. The boat crossing cost him five dollars: 'Il est vrai que c'était un bateau de bœufs.'[78] This was possibly the Uranium Steam Ship Company's Volturno, mentioned in Le Panama; like the Birma, the Volturno carried immigrants to America, and I suppose the same accommodations were good enough for cattle on the return voyage. A few years earlier Isadora Duncan had fled a philistine America in the same manner.

2 Paris and the avant-garde before the war, 1912-14

Freddy Sauser, Sausey, Blaise Cendrart, already signing Blaise Cendrars, reached Paris in July of 1912, and lived in the studio of Richard Hall (the brother of Agnès, his sister-in-law), at 40 rue Lauriston. Hall had already lent him money, and now he lent him more; he was away for a month or so and Freddy resumed a life of industrious writing, this time in luxurious poverty: 'J'ai le superflu, mais non le nécessaire.'[1] Periods of elation about working alternate with the most severe depressions the *Inédits* tell us of. It would seem that Raymond Dumay's view of a transformation, at one spectacular point, from boy to artist is too simplistic. There was a continuing transformation, interrupted by numerous re-evaluations and sombre doubts, during which man and artist both became more and more virulent so that the artist became less and less artistic; witness this letter of 7 August 1912, which might properly take its place in the history of the sources of Dada from Lautréamont to Jarry to Cendrars' own 'La critique d'art est aussi imbécile que l'espéranto'[2]:

> Je ne lis presque plus, moi. Je ne lis presque plus rien. L'art m'ennuie. Je pourrais mettre le feu à tous les musées de Paris. Il y a des heures où l'art m'embête comme la morale. Je n'en veux plus. Je n'en peux plus. On en parle trop. C'est d'un 'omatich' comme la théologie. Il n'y a plus que le style qui me retienne. Des bas noirs, l'érotisme, le jeûne du cœur. Et toutes les saletés de la sexualité que je m'entête à vouloir embellir.
>
> J'ai ce soir une telle heure de nervosité que j'ai envie de descendre dans la rue pour chercher une femme-garçon. Peut-être que l'équivoque de la pédérastie me chatouillera. Suis-je assez neurasthénique? J'ai envie de pleurer ou de rire![3]

Hall returned, and with a straining of their relationship, which remains

obscure in the *Inédits,* Freddy was obliged to move out. Certainly now he
had to search harder than ever for a job ('Je fais cent mille démarches à
tous les diables'[4]) but we do not know what he did until we find him at
the end of August with an old friend from Leipzig, Émile Szittya, in a little
hotel at 4 rue Saint-Étienne-du-Mont. A few weeks later they were at 4
rue de Savoie, an address in the Latin Quarter near the Seine which
remained a sort of clearing house and depository for Cendrars for some
six years to come. Within a few weeks he, Szittya, and Marius Hanot
transformed Szittya's dormant journal *Neue Menschen* (first series in Paris
1910, second series in Vienna and Munich 1911) into *Les Hommes Nouveaux,* 'revue libre (franco-allemande), rédaction et administration, 4 rue
de Savoie.' Publisher-editor F. Sauser's pseudonyms, Blaise Cendrars, Jack
Lee, and Diogène, signed articles (including one on André Suarès) and
poetry in the first issue, about the end of October. The same address was
also the centre for a 'Bureau international de traduction.' A list of journals
given in the *Inédits* may indicate contributions Cendrars made, none of
which has been retrieved (the editors of the *Inédits*[5] consider these to be
published contributions), or perhaps only prospective outlets for social
criticism, or business translation: *Das Buch* (Berlin), *Les Feuillets* (Genèva),
*Revue Internationale de l'Industrie, du Commerce et de l'Agriculture, La Revue
Moderne, Le Monde Industriel, La Revue des Industries de l'Alimentation, La
Terre, Les Échos de Silence,* and *Der Pionier* (Berlin). At the end of September
'camarade' Sauser addressed the 'Freiheitlicher Diskutiert Klub' at their
weekly Friday meeting ('au restaurant "Jules," boulevard Magenta 6,
vis-à-vis de la bourse du travail') on the subject of 'Beauté et Anarch-
isme.'[6] For Sauser-become-Cendrars the relationship of the title is not as
forced as it may seem: 'La Beauté n'est pas la norme, elle s'érige hors de
la norme ... Les lois de la nature sont les béquilles de l'esprit.' In this text
of 1912 we can already hear Raymond the doctor speaking at the beginning of *Moravagine;* normalcy is entropy. For Cendrars anarchy is all of life
without sense or order, and 'l'anarchiste est l'homme de la Vie ... Il est
le grand romantique.'[7] Beauty here is the vision Rimbaud was willing to
derange the senses for; it is reality unexpected, unknown, seen or sensed
without the crutch of reason, and only the most daring and determined
find it, or at least find themselves in it. Cendrars later called saints 'ces
enfants terribles de l'église'; for what a saint does is, paradoxically, ana-
thema to the church; she, properly, must remain normative.

   This lecture and Cendrars' involvement with *Les Hommes Nouveaux*
point to some relationship with anarchists in Paris, possibly dating back
to 1910. Bonnot is mentioned here, and in the poems, but Cendrars does
not say he knew him (Bonnot was shot in April of 1912).[8] On the other
hand Cendrars speaks of knowing Raymond-la-Science, Kibaltchich (Vic-

tor Serge), and Armand and Rirette Maîtrejean. Raymond is the putative narrator of *Moravagine,* and Victor Serge translated *L'Or* into Russian. Roch Carrier makes a case for Cendrars' knowing Victor Méric around 1910.[9] But Szittya himself says Cendrars was no anarchist, or at best only on an ideal and personal level, out of the work of Stirner and Nietzsche.[10] And yet many details do add up, not to armed political anarchism but to one just as potent given the right circumstances, a revolutionary cultural anarchism. Szittya's disdain may in fact be aimed not strictly at Cendrars but rather at a group whose ideas Cendrars seemed to be emulating, and whom I suspect Szittya knew well enough from having published *Neue Menschen* in Vienna and Munich – the Viennese secession group, and particularly the Munich Schwabing bohemia so well described in Martin Green's *The Von Richthofen Sisters.*[11] The centre, or even vortex, of this group preaching anarchy in art and life was the psychoanalyst Otto Gross, discussed below in my section on *Moravagine.* Green's book is the first to treat Gross as a serious and seminal thinker who exerted a good deal of influence on D.H. Lawrence and Max Weber through his relationships with the Von Richthofen sisters, who both had children by him. Later, when Gross was in Prague during the war, Kafka, Max Brod, and Franz Werfel fell under his influence. Gross' erotic revolution, quickly suppressed by the opposition of both political authorities and orthodox psychoanalysis, survived only through literary variation and interpretation – Cendrars' *Moravagine* and D.H. Lawrence's *Lady Chatterley's Lover,* for example – but we can trace most of the essential ideas of Marcuse and Norman O. Brown back to Gross, who in 1913 was writing about psychoanalysis freeing man from an authoritarian state (his own father, a world-renowned criminologist, had him committed). In 1912 Cendrars wrote to Gross asking for contributions to *Les Hommes Nouveaux,* and offered him a free hand, even the editorship of the German section if he wanted to come to Paris.[12] A year later Cendrars was one of those who, in an issue of *Revolution* entirely devoted to the psychoanalyst, protested Gross' incarceration. He called him 'un esprit des plus appréciés en France de l'Allemagne contemporaine,'[13] but we must think of the appreciation coming more from Cendrars personally than from France as a whole, where even the name of Freud was hardly known.

Cendrars clearly had something quite precise in mind at this time, his own conception of the *libertin,* a subject on which he had been accumulating a dossier since his second stay in Saint Petersburg – research, notes, bibliographies on the libertines at Geneva, Gassendi, Epicurus, Margaret of Valois, Calvin (*Contre le secte phantastique et furieuse des Libertins qui se nomment spirituels,* Geneva, 1545) – and in Paris at the Bibliothèque nationale in September and October of 1912 – Nietzsche, Socrates, Des-

cartes, Spinoza, Plato, Pythagoras, Thales, Cellini, Bruno, Dante, Rabe-
lais, Erasmus, Théophile de Viau, Saint-Amant, de Bergerac, Barbey
d'Aurevilly, Schopenhauer, Epicurus, Rimbaud, and others yet. The study
never materialized, though at a much later date (1952) there was a 'dossier
volumineux' on adventurers for a projected volume in the 'Dans l'Histoire' collection for Buchet and Chastel.[14] The main drive must have
been, over two or three years, to uncover his own position, or anti-
position, and we may see a few fruits of the enterprise in the following
definitions:

> 'Libertaire,' en ces temps de politique, a une nuance politique, donc
> sentimentale. Je choisis *libertin:* celui qui vit dans la liberté de penser et
> surtout de *sentir,* et j'accepte le sens méprisant qui est, au moins, franche-
> ment sexuel.
>
> Le libertin: le représentant de ces esprits qui méprisent le bonheur et
> qui seuls l'ont peut-être goûté car, grâce à l'ironie, ils ont vécu une vie
> grave et ample, intellectuelle et sensuelle, et ont connu toutes les ivresses
> d'*être*.[15]

It is the last paragraph in particular which is the key to many passages in
the letters. It describes that moral position, no doubt still a little vague,
which dictated the self-inflicted suffering, the refusals to work, to belong,
even to love too much: 'Quand on aime il faut partir.'[16] He had still to
make freedom destructive in order to be sure he had any.

So in September or October of 1912 Cendrars found himself in Paris,
on the threshold if not of Dada at least of what Apollinaire was to call
l'esprit nouveau. Sometime near the end of October *Les Pâques à New York*
was printed as a special number of *Les Hommes Nouveaux:*

> J'ai trouvé un imprimeur, un anarchiste, qui possédait une petite presse
> clandestine installé dans une caisse de piano, aux Buttes-Chaumont, rue
> Botzaris. Je travaillais avec lui pour gagner quatre sous sur
> les frais d'édition. J'ai profité de l'occasion pour faire mon apprentissage
> de typographe. C'est moi qui ai composé plus de la moitié du texte. La
> plaquette a été publiée avec un méchant dessin de moi. Cela m'a coûté
> quelque chose comme cent francs.[17]

With the publication of *Les Pâques* Cendrars entered the Parisian literary
community. He met Apollinaire and some of his friends, especially those
who were trying to do something new. Paris was beginning to fulfil his
expectations.

I shall not try here to settle the problem which has been raised in connection with Apollinaire's 'Zone' and Cendrars' *Les Pâques à New York*. I will say quite openly that I think Cendrars' poem was written first and Apollinaire had the opportunity to use it, perhaps subconsciously, when he wrote his own. I refer the reader to the notes to this section if he wishes to follow the debate which has taken place; he will find that few arguments have been accepted by both sides. I would like to attempt here, instead of more polemic, an account of the relationship of the two poets as I see it, with emphasis on Cendrars of course, adding where possible information which other scholars have omitted or slighted. Perhaps the most important aspect of my version – as it must be viewed – is how closely Cendrars was working and thinking at one point with the most famous poet and theoretician of the avant-garde in Paris before the Great War.

Apollinaire was, of course, well established in Paris among the painters and poets by 1912. He was a close friend of Picasso, for one, and is a prominent figure in the various accounts of the famous Rousseau banquet which took place in 1908 at the Bateau Lavoir; the Douanier painted his portrait in 1909 (*Le Poète et sa muse*). Nevertheless, in 1912 Apollinaire was far from famous. The Cubist revolution already had its masters, but the poetic revolution still had no direction. Apollinaire was not yet the 'impressario of the avant-garde,' as Roger Shattuck has called him,[18] nor was he, for the public, a poet of any note; he was, in fact, approaching a turning point, as was Cendrars. In 1913 his poems would be collected and, with the addition of 'Zone,' published as *Alcools;* and his evaluation of Cubism and the Cubist painters would appear as *Les Peintres cubistes, méditations esthétiques.* Thenceforth Apollinaire would indeed become the hub of artistic activity in Paris, and the best pre-war writing would be read in his *Soirées de Paris.*

Cendrars seems to have gone to some pains to make contact with Apollinaire in 1912, and this would indicate he knew who else in Paris was trying to give up Symbolism. He seems to have sent Apollinaire a manuscript copy of *Les Pâques* as soon as he arrived in Paris, let us say no later than early August, but he failed to get a response. Perhaps merely in order to get one he had himself arrested on 17 September for stealing a copy of Apollinaire's *L'Hérésiarque et Cie* from the publisher's stall. The theft may have had no deeper motive than the desire for the book; but a letter drafted in jail, perhaps never sent, makes us wonder. At any rate, the letter mentions the sending of *Les Pâques,* and it is the first of two documents which seem to prove irrefutably the precedence of Cendrars' poem. Also, the poets had not yet met: 'Je suis l'auteur de *Pâques à New York,* Blaise Cendrars, le poème que je vous ai fait parvenir dernièrement.'[19] Almost precisely a year earlier Apollinaire had been arrested for the theft to the *Mona Lisa;* quite a flattering comparison Cendrars was making, if that was his intention!

In October a witness mentions Cendrars in the company of Apollinaire, André Salmon, Reverdy, Max Jacob, and André Billy at the famous 'Section d'Or' salon at the Boëtie galleries.[20] Gabrielle Buffet remembers that in October Apollinaire read a poem like 'Zone,' which was then called 'Cri,' at her mother's home in the Jura. Her husband, Francis Picabia, had brought Apollinaire and Marcel Duchamp to visit, and the poem is supposed to have acquired its final title from the area, which was in a *zone franche* ('duty-free,' implying ruleless).[21] Another source for the title could have been 'la Zone' outside Paris where many poor people, gypsies, thieves, and generally unwanted or undesirable people tried to live; years later Cendrars wrote a great deal about these people. Apollinaire was already making revisions on 'Zone' in October, and when *Les Pâques* appeared about the second week in November he was correcting proof for its appearance in the December issue of the *Soirées.* Thus the actual publications of the two poems are almost simultaneous, a matter of a few weeks apart. As for the manuscripts, Cendrars' would seem to have been available to the older poet, and Michel Décaudin's analysis of the various drafts of 'Zone' confirm, in my view, that Cendrars was his source. Décaudin writes: 'Tout se passe comme si, dans ses corrections, Apollinaire avait voulu différencier son poème des *Pâques.*' The second half of 'Zone,' Marc Poupon finds, goes even further: 'L'inspiration le cède à une imitation plus flagrante encore que ne l'a dit Robert Goffin ...'[22]

On 15 November 1912 Cendrars could already write to his friend Suter that *Les Pâques* was published and that he had met Apollinaire, who had introduced him to Remy de Gourmont and the *Mercure de France* staff. Apollinaire 'm'a dit que *Pâques* était meilleur que tous les poèmes publiés depuis dix ans dans le *Mercure*';[23] magnanimous praise indeed since, as J.-P. Goldenstein has pointed out, Apollinaire's own poem 'La Chanson du mal-aimé' appeared in the *Mercure* in 1909.[24] At this time Apollinaire was living with different friends before moving to Boulevard Saint-Germain at the beginning of 1913. Much of his time was spent at the studio of Robert and Sonia Delaunay, and Cendrars was soon very close to these two painters and worked with Sonia on 'simultaneous' paintings and poems. Within a few months Cendrars was doing all sorts of work for Apollinaire, mainly 'travail de nègre' – ghostwriting which Apollinaire could farm out and which Cendrars spoke of in later life. The *Inédits* have come to verify his account, which has often been taken to be fabrication. He wrote, under his own name, a monograph entitled *Rimsky-Korsakov et les maîtres de la musique russe* in December of 1912 for a series at Figuière which Apollinaire was to direct (Apollinaire may have made his contact through Wilhelm Uhde, an early collector of modern art and Sonia Delaunay's first husband; Uhde had written on the Douanier Rousseau for Figuière). Proof was corrected and returned to the editor by February of 1913, but the volume never appeared. Cendrars translated anonymously the pornographic *Mémoires d'une chanteuse* by one Mme Schroder-Devrient, published with an introduction by Apollinaire in 1913. He also transcribed the twelfth-century novel *Perceval le gallois* which Apollinaire was supposed to be doing for Pierre-Paul Plan's 'Nouvelle Bibliothèque Bleue'; this volume finally saw the light in 1918, but had been ready in 1914.[25] Cendrars also transcribed, at the Bibliothèque nationale, *Lancelot du lac* and *Mélusine,* but these books were never published. One wonders if Cendrars ever received any payment for these abortive projects as, of course, the main point was always the few francs which should filter down from *nègre* to *nègre.*

Early in 1913 Cendrars was writing Apollinaire's art reviews for *L'Intransigeant.*[26] No doubt Apollinaire was busy enough with the publication of *Les Peintres cubistes* on 17 March, *Alcools* in April, and reviews of the same Salon des Indépendants for Canudo's *Montjoie!,* a little magazine where he had more freedom to speak his mind. On 1 April Apollinaire wrote a very peculiar account of Walt Whitman's funeral for his column 'La Vie anecdotique' in the *Mercure,* and this article was to cause a great deal of trouble, of which more below. Perhaps this, or a follow-up which was never printed, was another one of the articles written by Cendrars. If so, Cendrars was hoaxing the public through his friend, and their relationship may already have begun to suffer as Apollinaire attempted to consolidate a few beginnings of respectability. The *Inédits* further confirm a statement by Raymond Warnier that Cendrars was translating Apollinaire's *Les Peintres cubistes* for Herwarth Walden's *Der Sturm.*[27] The text may be found in the *Inédits* (pp. 297-311), translated back into French by the editors, who failed to recognize Apollinaire's book and assumed they were dealing with an original essay by Cendrars writing in German.

At the same time that Cendrars was performing this purely remunerative work for Apollinaire the two were trading poetic homage in their poems. If we may consider that 'Zone' contains conscious reference to *Les Pâques,* we also find in *Le Transsibérien* of 1913 references to Apollinaire's work:

'Pardonnez-moi mon ignorance
'Pardonnez-moi de ne plus connaître l'ancien jeu des vers'
Comme dit Guillaume Apollinaire.

The two lines are from Apollinaire's 'Les Fiançailles,' originally published

in *Pan* in November-December 1908, but they may not have found their
way into *Le Transsibérien* until after the poem appeared in *Alcools,* in April
of 1913. Cendrars' poem was being written as early as December of 1912,
and Apollinaire must have seen it in manuscript in order to write in
'Arbre,' published in *Le Gay Sçavoir* on 10 March 1913:

> Nous avions loué deux coupés dans le Transsibérien
> Tour à tour nous dormions le voyageur en bijouterie et moi
> Mais celui qui veillait ne cachait point son révolver aimé.

(For the *Calligrammes* version, 1918, the last phrase was altered to 'un
révolver armé.') Cendrars wrote in *Le Transsibérien:*

> Et je partis moi aussi pour accompagner le voyageur en bijouterie qui se
>   rendait à Kharbine
> Nous avions deux coupés dans l'Express et 34 coffres de joaillerie de
>   Pforzheim
> De la camelote allemande 'Made in Germany'
> Il m'avait habillé de neuf et en montant dans le train j'avais perdu un
>   bouton
> – Je m'en souviens, je m'en souviens, j'y ai souvent pensé depuis –
> Je couchais sur les coffres et j'étais tout heureux de pouvoir jouer avec le
>   Browning nickelé
> Qu'il m'avait aussi donné

Another item the poets seem to have juggled between them was a clock
in Prague, 'l'horloge du quartier juif de Prague qui tourne éperduement
à rebours,' as it appears in *Le Transsibérien,* and in 'Zone':

> Tu ressembles au Lazare affolé par le jour
> Les aiguilles de l'horloge du quartier juif vont à rebours
> Et tu recules aussi dans ta vie lentement.

But the detail appeared before either of those two places in *L'Hérésiarque
et Cie,* in a story called 'Le Passant de Prague.' So, in a way, Cendrars stole
the book twice. These were, I cannot but believe, friendly gestures, not
plagiarisms, which would have been recognized by almost anyone in the
avant-garde. Besides, Cendrars was on the threshold of the 'found poem'
and Apollinaire of what he called the 'poème-conversation.' Yet such
intimacy was bound to sour at times, particularly because of the divergent
directions the poets were taking and the public bluntness of Cendrars; the
same clock image supplied him with an ironical comment on Apollinaire

as a real leader of the avant-garde in a poem called originally 'Apollinaire'
and later 'Hamac.'[28] The reference to Prague is only oblique, via reference to the lines in 'Zone,' and Cendrars picks up Apollinaire's own
comment upon himself as a hesitant Lazarus:

> Cadran compliqué de la Gare Saint-Lazare
> Apollinaire
> Avance, retarde, s'arrête parfois.

The poem ends with double-edged homage:

> Apollinaire
> 1900-1911
> Durant 12 ans seul poète de France.

Presumably there were at least two poets in France now. *Le Transsibérien*
was written between December 1912 and June 1913; in the critical section
of this study I will discuss this extraordinary production, 'premier livre
simultané,' seven feet long, with a painting by Sonia Delaunay. Even
before this collaboration, Sonia had painted an abstract binding for her
copy of *Les Pâques*. This represented the sort of break with the past which
Apollinaire was sometimes hesitant to endorse. It is worth quoting an
appraisal of the binding by Michel Hoog, curator of the Museum of
Modern Art in Paris, as I shall not have occasion to return to it later:

> On ne saurait donner trop d'importance à cette précieuse reliure ex-
> écutée le 1er janvier 1913, en présence de Blaise Cendrars, et qui consti-
> tue, autant et plus que le numéro précédent, l'inauguration d'un langage
> nouveau. Libérées de toute intention figurative, les taches de couleurs sont
> constituées par des morceaux de papier découpés et collés avec grand soin,
> déterminant des à-plats de forme régulière, sans aucune modification.
> L'utilisation du papier a permis à l'artiste un progrès décisif vers ce qu'il
> faut bien appeler l'abstraction géométrique, que R. et S. Delaunay n'ont
> approché dans leurs peintures à l'huile que plus tard. Cette reliure, expo-
> sée à Berlin en 1913, citée et reproduite plusieurs fois au lendemain de
> la guerre, montrée à ses visiteurs par R. Delaunay, qui y attachait beau-
> coup d'importance, n'a pu qu'influencer Klee, Freundlich, les peintres du
> *Stijl* et de l'abstraction géométrique.[29]

About this time Cendrars wrote two articles of his own on painters he
greatly admired, one on Odilon Redon which was not published, and one

on the Douanier Rousseau which appeared in *Der Sturm* in September of
1913. This article is the first work Cendrars had published by someone
other than himself. We do not know if it was Apollinaire or Delaunay, or
someone else, perhaps in Szittya's circle, who introduced him to Herwarth
Walden; but in the same month *Le Transsibérien* was exhibited at *Der
Sturm*'s important Erster Deutscher Herbstsalon. Also on exhibit was
Sonia's copy of *Les Pâques* described above, as well as the proofs for
Cendrars' *Séquences.*

The article on Rousseau afforded Cendrars a chance to declare himself
against intellectualized art:

> En ouvrant la première académie à Milan, Léonard de Vinci a commis
> une funeste erreur. Il a introduit le canon dans l'art. Et c'est peut-être à
> cause de lui que nous souffrons comme dans un hôpital.
>   'La philosophie de la composition' de Poe, cette amère ironie, en est un
> mémorable exemple.[30]

The reference to Poe has its importance. Two American poets, Poe and
Whitman, were very much at the source of French literary activity at this
time. F.O. Matthiessen formulated their opposing influences in the most
simple terms, poet as 'inspired genius' or poet as 'craftsman'; it was Poe's
'strict if brittle insistence on the principles of art that helped free Baudelaire and the French symbolists from the effluvia of romanticism, and so
cleared the way for the emergence of Pound and Eliot.'[31] But by 1912
the counter-influence of Whitman had taken a strong hold in France. As
early as 1886 Jules Laforgue had translated Whitman for Gustave
Kahn's *La Vogue* (28 June, 5 July, 2 August), and soon thereafter Laforgue, Kahn, Moréas, and Paul Adam were writing their first 'vers libre.'
The influence of Whitman is unequivocal in Maeterlinck's *Les Serres chaudes*
(1889), Verhaeren, Claudel, Gide's first *Nourritures terrestres* (1897), Valery Larbaud's *A.O. Barnabooth* (1908), and Jules Romains' *La Vie unanime*
(1908). The same year of 1908 Léon Bazalgette's long study *Walt Whitman, l'homme et l'œuvre* appeared, followed in 1909 by a full translation of
Leaves of Grass. By 1912 a short-lived *Whitmanisme* had emerged (a few
times brilliantly misspelled as *Withmanisme*), described by Henri Ghéon
for *La Nouvelle Revue Française.*[32] 'Maintenant il faut des barbares,' wrote
Ghéon, quoting an often reiterated statement of Charles-Louis Philippe.
All this activity around the figure of Whitman was in the name of artistic
freedom, but suddenly he risked becoming institutionalized in his own
turn. Apollinaire's article on Whitman's burial, presumably reported to
him by an eye-witness, appeared in the *Mercure* for 1 April 1913 (All

Fools' Day of course), and reported an orgy with 3,500 participants: 'Les pédérastes étaient venus en foule ...'[33] This 'accusation' of homosexuality brought down a veritable storm of letters, which raged in the pages of the *Mercure* for almost a year,[34] and in December Apollinaire printed an excuse cum retraction: 'J'ai rapporté le détail des funérailles tel qu'il m'a été raconté en présence d'un jeune poète de talent, M. Blaise Cendrars.'[35] This is the main evidence upon which Poupon bases his suggestion that Cendrars was, in fact, the source.[36] I do not mind thinking so myself, as it is an amusing hoax which shows Cendrars in the best Dada light. At the same time it would be surprising if Apollinaire had not been in on the joke, as he could hardly have thought Cendrars had been an eye-witness in 1892 at the age of five! But Apollinaire, who had begun to write for the very important *Mercure* only in 1911, had a new-found prestige to protect, and if indeed he did swallow whole this amusing 'poisson d'avril' the unexpected polemic may have caused serious uneasiness between him and Cendrars. On 4 April 1913, only a few days later, Cendrars wrote to his friend Suter that Apollinaire and he were founding a new art journal, *Zones* (I am reminded of a slightly earlier association between similarly divergent minds, de Gourmont's and Jarry's *L'Ymagier*), but we hear no more of this project. And in September in Saint-Cloud, where Cendrars was living with Féla, who had returned to Paris in May, he scribbled across a recent number of *Die Aktion* a letter to Apollinaire which is well worth citing in its entirety:

> On me dit que je parle trop de vous.
> Ce n'est pas ma faute, car je pense beaucoup à vous. Je ne tiens pas à dire ici pourquoi. Vous, vous le savez bien. Car nous sommes bons amis.
> Je vous ai une fois envoyé Pâques.
> Vous, vous auriez dû me dédier Zone.
> Nous avions fait de beaux projets et nous voulions travailler ensemble.
> Puis quand je me suis cassé la jambe, les *Alcools* ont paru. Je les aime beaucoup et je les ai beaucoup lus. Si je n'ai pas fait un article, ce n'est pas de ma faute. Aucun journal ne voulait alors de ma prose. Et si j'en parle aujourd'hui, c'est grâce à H. Walden qui veut bien reproduire mon avis. Nous ferons encore de grands voyages ensemble.[37]

A good deal of bitterness is reflected in this letter, apparently on the part of both poets. Possibly Cendrars had yet to praise *Alcools* in print because he had been given no acknowledgment there; if he had not deserved Eliot's 'il miglior fabbro' dedication to Pound, he felt he at least deserved something like Pound's to Whitman: 'It was you that broke the new wood.' We could add, on the authority of Tristan Tzara, that *Alcools* also owed its title to Cendrars, as Apollinaire had originally planned to call the volume *Eau de vie.*[38] Then, on the back of this number of *Die Aktion*, we find the first draft of 'Crépitements,' including the words italicized in the following excerpt, which were omitted in the final version:

> L'Intransigeant ce soir
> Publie les vers pour carte postale
> *de G. A.*
> *Moi je suis triste de voir tant de génie*
> *s'en aller à vau l'eau ...*[39]

There is in these lines, perhaps written only a few hours earlier or later than the letter, instead of bitterness a great sadness, possibly resignation, at the inevitable distance growing between them.

'Crépitements' is the third of the eighteen short poems Cendrars wrote between August 1913 and July 1914 while he and Féla lived in Saint-Cloud for a short time (at the Hôtel du Palais) and later in many different suburbs, Sèvres, Saint-Martin-en-Bière, Forges-par-Barbizon – a list of no less than fifteen is given at the end of *Le Panama*, which is dated June 1913-June 1914. *Le Panama ou les aventures de mes sept oncles* was not published until after the war, but the short poems fared a bit better, if not well enough to please Cendrars who, when these eighteen plus one written in 1919 were published as *Dix-neuf Poèmes élastiques* in 1919, complained that established French periodicals would not publish his work.

The complaint has seemed a distortion to some critics, and it is worth examining. Strictly speaking, and as evidenced by the bibliography which Cendrars openly printed along with his complaint (termed 'notule d'histoire littéraire, 1912–1914'), what he said is not true, to the following extent; he wrote 'à l'exception de deux ou trois' whereas the correct number is five (out of eighteen in all), these in three issues of *Les Soirées de Paris,* run by Apollinaire and his friends. But Cendrars was not really talking about numbers. The other journals he named, the *Mercure de France,* Paul Fort's *Vers et Prose,* and Henri-Martin Barzun's *Poème et Drame,* did turn down his poetry. Further, of the eighteen poems the first three were published in Berlin, in *Der Sturm,* and the next three in *Montjoie!,* a small magazine founded in Paris by an Italian, Ricciotto Canudo; seven did not appear at all before the war, yet two of these seven were important enough for one to be stolen by the first Dada publication, *Le Cabaret Voltaire,* in 1916 and the other to be quoted in *De Stijl* in 1918; finally, although Apollinaire and Cendrars were friends by the time the first poem, 'Journal,' was written in August 1913, and although Apollinaire owned the *Soirées* by November 1913, he printed nothing of Cendrars' until April 1914. It was a qualified friendship. But in April Apollinaire finally took 'Journal'; he accepted another for the 15 June issue and three for the July-August issue (two of these three were in fact written in July). For a few months Cendrars was indeed being published by a good French magazine, but then war broke out in August. Otherwise the *notule* might have proved unnecessary. Yet the facts remain; Cendrars had a great deal of trouble publishing his poetry at first, though it did not go unnoticed whenever it appeared. *Les Pâques, Le Transsibérien,* and the *Séquences* were all published by Cendrars himself at *Les Hommes Nouveaux.* Even in 1919 *Le Panama* was published by him, at La Sirène, though this was no longer his own money nor, by this time, were publishers scarce for him. In 1919, by way of consecration, the NRF reprinted the three long poems as one volume, *Du Monde entier* (that journal had suspended publication during the war and had just resumed in June, 1919, under the direction of Jacques Rivière; see footnote 32 of this chapter). The *notule* was supposed to serve as a reminder, as Roger Allard did not fail to notice in his review of *Dix-neuf Poèmes élastiques:*

> Dans une 'notule d'histoire littéraire' l'auteur de *Poèmes élastiques* rappelle avec une discrète amertume que 'les aînés, les écrivains classés et le soi-disant avant-garde refusaient ma collaboration.' J'admire surtout qu'elle soit acceptée sans nulle gêne aujourd'hui par ses imitateurs directs. Il est vrai que le voisinage si dangereux d'un vrai poète n'est guère redouté des mauvais, car ceux-ci sont les derniers à s'aviser de leur infirmité.[40]

Cendrars' first public fame came as a small *succès de scandale* with the September 1913 publication of *Le Transsibérien,* or as it was originally called *Prose du transsibérien et de la petite Jehanne de France.* It was widely attacked in the press, Cendrars responded with letters of explanation, and a polemic around the seven-foot sheet with parallel text and abstract painting (with an announced printing of 150 copies which would all together reach the top of the Eiffel Tower) developed in the pages of *Paris-Midi, Gil Blas* (columns by André Salmon), *Paris-Journal,* and particularly with Henri-Martin Barzun in his *Poème et Drame.* Cendrars and the Delaunays and soon Apollinaire found themselves aligned in a dispute with Barzun and some of the Italian futurists over the paternity and usage of the term *Simultanéisme,* or *Simultanisme,* or again *le Simultané.* Pär Bergman has examined the debate in detail in his more general view of this movement and its ideas and techniques, which were at the source of many aspects of Dada, Cubist poetry (or verbal montage), and the kind of simultaneous narration later used by John Dos Passos in *USA.*[41] *Le Trans-*

sibérien is billed as the 'premier livre simultané,' and I shall explain the meaning of this in the second part of this study.

During these pre-war years Cendrars, Robert Delaunay, and Arthur Cravan were often seen together, at the Bal Bullier notably, which was one of the earliest places of popular entertainment to enter the burgeoning modernist mythology. Their antics or mere appearance prefigured the public outrages of Dada. They would wear 'simultané' clothes designed by Sonia – colourful geometric patterns which made them look like walking abstract paintings. Sonia and Blaise went into advertising and composed a series of publicity projects for Zenith watches: 'Record! Midi bat sur son enclume solaire les rayons de la lumière – ZENITH.'[42] Cendrars knew the more famous painters whom Apollinaire promoted in his *Méditations esthétiques:* Picasso, Braque, Gris, Léger, Picabia, and Duchamp. Braque is reputed to have redesigned an Alfa-Romeo for him in the twenties (a Gran Sport 6, a famous racer). Picabia drew his portrait for *Kodak (Documentaire)* in 1924, and in the twenties he and Cendrars were neighbours in Le Tremblay-sur-Maudre, not far from Paris (the two of them must have made the area vastly more dangerous than it had been before, the one in his Alfa and the other in his Bugatti). Picabia, Duchamp, and Cendrars were the three luminaries of Jacques-Henry Lévesque's Dada journal *Orbes* (1928-32), which attempted to continue the spirit of Dada, though not the movement.[43]

But Cendrars was closer, before the war, to other artists, notably those who were the subjects of the *Dix-neuf Poèmes élastiques:* Chagall, Roger de la Fresnaye, Archipenko, Delaunay, and Léger. In fact, if Apollinaire was the poet of the Bateau Lavoir in Montmartre, Cendrars was the poet of La Ruche, at 2 passage Dantzig, and drank at le père Lampion's La Rotonde café in Montparnasse with Soutine, Lipschitz, Csaky, Kisling, and Modigliani. Cendrars and Chagall were close in their beginnings, Cendrars providing titles for the artist's early paintings in Paris and encouraging him to paint in his own manner and resist the cubists. In his 1911-12 painting *Hommage à Apollinaire* Chagall placed the names of Apollinaire, Cendrars (spelled Cendras), Canudo, and Walden in a circle around a heart with an arrow through it. Jean-Paul Crespelle, in *Chagall, l'amour, le rêve et la vie,* tells of the dispersal of Chagall's work left at La Ruche during the war, their subsequent authentication by Cendrars, and how Cendrars managed Chagall's return to Paris for the art dealer Vollard. But it seems that the sale of his paintings so angered Chagall that a break ensued; however, as Cendrars had nothing to do with the actual sales, there may have been other reasons for their troubles. Crespelle reports that Chagall visited Cendrars when the poet was ill and dying, and that they were reconciled. There are no paintings or drawings of Cendrars by

Chagall, nor any to illustrate the poet's books. A number of drawings which Cendrars possessed he gave away to Philippe Soupault for his volume of poetry *La Rose des vents,* published in 1920.[44]

Almost all of Cendrars' early books were illustrated. Kisling made drawings for *La Guerre au Luxembourg* (1916), and Csaky did the cover for *Anthologie nègre* (1921). Cendrars and Modigliani were a legendary pair, drunk throughout Montparnasse, promenading in colourful dress in Nice; *Dix-neuf Poèmes élastiques* appeared with a portrait of Cendrars by Modigliani, and there are two different portraits in the first fifty copies. A third was inscribed by Cendrars:

> Le monde intérieur
> Le cœur humain avec
>> ses 17 mouvements
>> dans l'esprit
> Et le vaetvient de la
>> passion

There is also a full size oil-painting of Cendrars by Modigliani.

Léger collaborated with Cendrars on many of his works, and they remained close throughout their lives. They first found themselves together in the pages of *Les Soirées de Paris* for 15 June 1914 which contained 'Fantômas,' the three prose 'Amours,' and the painter's 'Les Réalisations pictorales actuelles.' The last 'elastic' poem is about Léger and was written while the latter drew the poet's portrait. Léger illustrated *J'ai tué* (1918) and supplied artwork and presumably layout for *La Fin du monde filmée par l'Ange Notre-Dame,* in which text and picture interpenetrate. One did the sets and the other the scenario for Milhaud's *La Création du monde.* Émile Szittya wrote: 'Il m'est arrivé une seule fois de voir Cendrars abattu: c'était à l'enterrement de Fernand Léger.'[45] Much of the later writing of Léger resembles that of Cendrars in both style and ideas, especially their views of streets, circuses, dance-halls, the cinema, and modern life in general.[46]

We could summarize by saying Cendrars preferred the work of painters who were less cerebral, or less classical, which is how he termed Picasso's painting. Léger, Chagall, and Modigliani well indicate his taste – no academics, only the 'vaetvient de la passion,' with, in Léger's case, 'ses 17 mouvements.' Cendrars was always more interested in lyricism as the first element of any art, and his own writing resembles at times the violent yet tender visions of Chagall and at other times the muscular, even mechanized grace of Léger. In 1919 Cendrars wrote a number of articles on painters and painting for *La Rose Rouge* (he was assistant editor at the time).[47] There are short pieces on Picasso, Braque, Léger, and Delaunay, and the well-known 'Pourquoi le "cube" s'effrite' on the failure and demise of Cubism. This article, partially written in 1913, shows his distaste for the analytical styles of Cubism and the importance he gave to colour, thus to Delaunay and Léger as opposed to Picasso and Braque. Other artists Cendrars knew well before and after the war include Zadkine, André Lhote, Lejeune, Gabriel Fournier, Rouault, and the dealers Vollard and Zborowski.

In May of 1913 Féla had returned to Paris and to Blaise, and she lived with him throughout this period of great activity – the publication of *Le Transsibérien*, the composition of *Dix-neuf Poèmes élastiques* and *Le Panama*, and the constant travelling between the Paris garret and the many suburbs. Cendrars was in the thick of the battle at the opening of Stravinsky's *Sacre du printemps* on 28 May 1913 at the Théâtre des Champs-Élysées and celebrated the remainder of the night with an orchestra seat around his neck.[48] Although Cendrars and Stravinsky lived in Saint Petersburg during the same period there is no evidence that they knew each other at that time, but they must have met often in Paris, especially after the war. Stravinsky's scores were published at Cendrars' La Sirène press, and I reproduce on page xiv a photograph of them together, peering out the windows of a fairground cardboard train. In *Blaise Cendrars vous parle...* Cendrars praised the composer's great knowledge of Catholic symbolism, and Henry Miller wrote that when he met Stravinsky in 1942 in Los Angeles all the latter could talk about was Cendrars and Cingria, the Swiss essayist.[49] The late Frank Budgen has left a portrait of Cendrars as he appeared in 1913:

> A bird man – chough or raven? Cendrars seemed to have been everywhere: Russia. America. New York. St. Petersburg. Forests of the Amazon. He knew them all. And any suspicions of longbrow practice had soon to be set aside in face of the simplicity of his narrative. Bird is not quite right. Birds' flights, song, and nestings are as predictable as tax demands. The comings and goings of Cendrars had no such fixed pattern.
>
> As he was, so his writing, so his preferences. He held that the lurid stories of Fantomas then running in a Parisian daily newspaper were the modern equivalent of the *Iliad* and the *Odyssey*.
>
> Cendrars and his wife Féla, a Polish girl, were living in the neighbourhood of the Porte de Versailles when their son was born. August and I bore witness in the Mairie of the *quatorzième arrondissement* to the birth of Odilon.
>
> In one of his periods of domesticity Cendrars lived in or near Sèvres,

a rural retreat but agreeably near the great city. It was there that he thought of setting up a sort of translation factory. I heard of projects for turning Russian and Czech into French. I was to join forces with Féla in translating into English the letters of the Douanier Rousseau. I sent a specimen of our work back to London, to Taylor, who at the time was connected with some art publication or other, but he returned it. Interest in the Douanier was not sufficient to justify, etc. The project fell through.

At St. Sèvres [*sic*] on Sundays Cendrars' friends were welcome. Frequent visitors were the painters Delaunay and Chagall. I was a visitor one Sunday when Chagall arrived all furious about some scurrilous references to Madame Delaunay in an article on the *Exposition des Indépendants* written by Arthur Cravan. Cendrars thought highly of Cravan's poetry and also of Robert Delaunay's painting.

Sometimes Cendrars' funds rose to the level of fairly good living: at other times they were hardly sufficient for any living at all.[50]

When Odilon was born, on 7 April 1914, Féla and Blaise were not married, and it seems likely that only the war and Cendrars' departure to the front were responsible for the ceremony, on 16 September 1914 at the Town Hall of the sixth *arrondissement;* even after this Féla had to endure the suspicions of a small suburban village for any sort of foreigner, particularly one from the east. But at least she was the wife of a *poilu.*

3 War, and the return of the poet-legionnaire, 1914-24

A few days before the declaration of war Cendrars and Canudo had already drafted an *appel* which appeared in all the papers on 29 July 1914 – an appeal to all foreigners to join the side of the French in the inevitable conflict. Roch Carrier feels the *appel* is entirely the writing of Cendrars, though the rhetoric seems to me conventional enough for its purpose. The first signatures are Blaise Gendrars [*sic*], Csaki, and Canudo.[1]

In August Cendrars started to train as a flyer, but he could not be a pilot because the foreign volunteers were attached to the Légion étrangère, which was part of the army. In September, as a corporal in the 'ier Régiment étranger de Paris,' about to leave by foot for the front (the trains went empty), he worried about Féla and their friends the Jaenni-chens as aliens in France, and also for friends in Germany and Russia; still, in the same letter, he could write: 'Cette guerre est une douloureuse délivrance pour accoucher de la liberté. Cela me va comme un gant. Réaction ou Révolution – l'homme doit devenir plus humain. Je revien-drai. Cela ne fait point de doute.'[2] Cendrars' rush to war encompassed not only this expectation of forthcoming social change but also a release from the cavilling, ingrown life of the artistic community: 'La guerre m'a sauvé la vie. Ça a l'air d'un paradoxe, mais cent fois je me suis dit depuis que si j'avais continué à vivre avec tous ces gens-là, j'en aurais claqué.'[3] In the war Cendrars would discover and rediscover with renewed intimacy the common people, outside artistic cliques and ivory towers classical or mod-ernist. It was a re-education. He turned down promotions and years later wrote scathingly of the officers' aristocratic disdain for the ordinary sol-dier. And he would not be a writer while he was in the trenches, voicing afterwards his bewilderment at those poets capable of doing so, for he could never conceive of war as primarily 'useful experience' for a writer: 'Quand on écrit, on ne combat pas à coups de fusil et quand on tire des

coups de fusil, on n'écrit pas, on écrit après. On aurait bien mieux fait
d'écrire avant et d'empêcher tout ça ... '[4] And so in the next war he was
to serve as a 52-year-old war-correspondent and, after the fall of France,
retire to the South and not write a word for over three years.

Soon after his marriage to Féla, Cendrars was marched to the front, first
to Frise, then to Herbécourt for the winter. In May of 1915 he survived
Foch's attacks in Artois, where 100,000 men were lost in a month. Cendrars fought at the Carency cemetery and the Bois de la Vache, and
actually found himself with a few men on the Crête de Vimy, so far in
advance of their own lines that they were being fired upon by French
artillery (the Crête was not to be retaken until 1917, by the Canadians in
their most illustrious battle). He was at Souchez, Notre-Dame-de-Lorette,
and Givenchy, all remembered as horrendous disasters. The generals
generously sacrificed thousands of lives for ten feet of no man's land and
a few inches in the Parisian dailies. The losses of the four foreign regi-
ments were so great that the survivors were transferred to a single one,
'La Marocaine,' which was the real Légion étrangère. At Souchez, about
May 13, the Moroccan division, always famous for its daring, counted
7,000 men lost, out of a total of 15,000 for the whole Tenth Army.[5] In
June, and after the battle of Sainte-Marie-les-Mines, there was some respite
as the division was relieved and sent behind the lines to Roye. In July
Cendrars went on leave to Paris, and his 1946 novel *La Main coupée* ends
with his arrival 'à Paname.' He saw Féla and Odilon in Forges-par-Barbizon (at other times during the war the two stayed in the studio of the
Delaunays, who had fled to Portugal), and went to see his first Chaplin
film. His is now a classic account of France's heartening war-time discovery of 'Charlot':

> Charlot est né au front. Jamais je n'oublierai la première fois que j'ai
> entendu parler de lui. C'était au Bois de la Vache par une soirée d'automne
> pluvieuse et détrempée. Nous pataugions dans la boue dans un entonnoir
> de mine qui se remplissait d'eau quand Garnier vint nous rejoindre, retour
> de permission... Il radinait tout droit de Paris. Toute la nuit il ne nous parla
> que de Charlot. Qui ça, Charlot? Garnier était plein comme une bour-
> rique. Je crus que Charlot était une espèce de frangin à lui et il nous fit
> bien rigoler avec ses histoires. A partir de ce soir-là et de huit en quinze
> jours, chaque fournée de permissionnaires nous remenait de nouvelles
> histoires de Charlot... Tout le front ne parlait que de Charlot... J'aurais
> bien voulu connaître ce nouveau poilu qui faisait se gondoler le front.
> Charlot, Charlot, Charlot, Charlot dans toutes les cagnas et, la nuit, on
> entendait rire jusqu'au fond des sapes. A gauche et à droite, et toute la
> ligne des poilus derrière nous, on se trémoussait. Charlot, Charlot, Char-
> lot. Un jour, ce fut enfin mon tour de partir en perme. J'arrivai à Paris.

Quelle émotion en sortant de la gare du Nord, en sentant le bon pavé de
bois sous mes godillots et en voyant pour la première fois depuis le début
de la guerre des maisons pas trop chahutées. Après avoir salué la Tour
Eiffel, je me précipitai dans un petit ciné de la Place Pigalle. Je vis Charlot
... Charlot! Quelle bosse je me suis payée!
       – Hé, soldat! On ne rit pas comme ça. C'est la guerre! me dit un digne
monsieur de l'arrière.
       – Merde! Je viens voir Charlot.
       Il ne pouvait pas comprendre. Je riais aux larmes.[6]

Then, back to the front. In September 1915 the Moroccan division was
in Champagne and participated in a vast and fruitless campaign there
under Castelnau, which began on the 25th, in pouring rain. One may read
about the Legion's early successes and its failure to break the Germans'
second line of defence in Alan Seeger's letters, as the American poet
fought in the same division (he was erroneously reported killed in this
battle, but in fact survived until the following July). Cendrars' luck had
run its course, and on the 28th he lost his right arm at 'La Ferme Navarin.'
His military citation reads: 'Bien que grièvement blessé au début de
l'attaque du 28.9.15 et épuisé par la perte du sang a continué à entraîner
son escouade à l'assaut et est resté avec elle jusqu'à la fin de l'action.'[7] He
was evacuated to Sainte-Croix hospital at Châlons-sur-Marne, and thence
to the Lycée Lakanal, now serving as a hospital, in Bourg-la-Reine
(Sceaux). In *Bourlinguer* he wrote of his missing arm:

> L'esprit s'égare à vouloir suivre, situer, identifier, localiser la survie d'une
> main coupée qui se fait douloureusement sentir, non pas au bout du moi-
> gnon ni dans l'axe radial ni dans le centre de la conscience, mais en aura,
> quelque part en dehors du corps, une main, des mains qui se multiplient
> et qui se développent et s'ouvrent en éventail, le rachis des doigts plus ou
> moins écrasé, les nerfs ultra-sensibles qui finissent par imprimer à l'esprit
> l'image de Çiva dansant qui roulerait sous une scie circulaire pour être
> amputé successivement de tous ses bras, que l'on est Çiva, lui-même,
> l'homme divinisé. C'est effarant. D'où le sourire.[8]

Both Sonia Delaunay and Féla reported that they saw the man wounded
in dreams.[9]
       Cendrars was soon writing with his left hand, but it is such an altered
script that all of his papers can be easily dated as pre- or post-war by the
penmanship. One of his first concerns was the extraordinary coincidence
of his own loss with the death of Remy de Gourmont: 'Mort Remy de

Gourmont. Pouvez-vous m'envoyer journaux la relatant? J'ai le bras droit amputé. Cela me rajeunit jusqu'au barbouillage.'[10] He also wrote to Apollinaire on November 2:

> Mon cher Apollinaire
> J'ai été blessé le 28 septembre en Champagne devant la ferme de Navarin, à l'attaque de la tranchée de la Kultur. On a dû m'amputer du bras droit. Cela va aussi bien que possible. L'humeur est bonne. J'aurais eu grand plaisir à vous rencontrer là-bas. J'ai demandé aprés vous. Je vous embrasse; Blaise Cendrars.[11]

Within a short time Cendrars resumed the artistic life in Paris, but of course life was no longer the same. Many of his friends and acquaintances in the arts were still at the front or in self-imposed exile. Apollinaire, to whom the above card had been addressed in Champagne, did not return to Paris for another six months, after being wounded in March of 1916. Léger was at the front, the Delaunays in Portugal, and Cravan in Spain, where he fought Jack Johnson in April 1916, and then in New York with Picabia and Duchamp. But the absence of the avant-garde was also a liberation for Cendrars. At the same time that he wrote and published the very moving *La Guerre au Luxembourg,* in which small children play at war in the bucolic Luxembourg Gardens, he may have lived several months with gypsies. There is much which may be invented in his narratives of life with gypsies in *L'Homme foudroyé* (1945), some sheer verve, some lifted from or inspired by George Borrow's work, which he said he had been translating before the war; but it is true that the main character of that volume, Sawo, was a gypsy and a good friend from the Legion, and much of Sawo's story must be based on fact.

In April of 1916 his second son, Rémy, was born. But Cendrars and Féla were less and less frequently together. T'Serstevens recounts that Cendrars lived with him at quai Bourbon, when he left the hospital; they would prowl the city, often go to movies where 't'Ser' would lend him one hand to applaud ('What is the sound of one hand clapping,' asks the Zen koan!). A few months later Cendrars moved into the Hôtel Notre-Dame with a girl named Gabrielle, a model for Modigliani.[12]

The Swiss painter Lejeune had been holding concerts at his studio at 6 rue Huyghens, a block from the Dôme café, since 1914 in order to finance a canteen. Cendrars persuaded him to make it a centre for art and poetry as well,[13] and the first presentation took place from 19 November to 5 December 1916; in his book on Jean Cocteau Frederick Brown has written that this was 'a pivotal event in the history of the avant-garde, for it brought on stage figures whose stars would rise meteorically between the two wars and collected an audience heralding Montparnasse of the 1920s.'[14]

The Salle Huyghens affairs well deserve a full study. For those in the know some of the artists shown and read there were already 'stars,' while others, such as Cocteau, who brought swarms of stylish people from the Right Bank, were really latching on. Eventually Cocteau the showman would take over and make Montparnasse fashionable. But the originators of the new spirit, Apollinaire, back from the war with a serious head-wound, Max Jacob, Reverdy, and Cendrars, read their poetry at many Huyghens recitals, and such performances would multiply and spread, to the Vieux-Colombier for example, where Jeanne Bathori was in charge. In June of 1917 Cendrars organized a concert at Huyghens with several new composers whom Satie, also a friend of Cendrars and much admired by him, thereupon proposed to call 'les Nouveaux Jeunes.' This group was 'les Six' (Milhaud, Honegger, Auric, Poulenc, Durey, and Tailleferre), who were first presented all together by Bathori but whom Cocteau would quickly claim as his own discovery.

On 31 December 1916, Gris, Picasso, Dermée, Jacob, Reverdy, and Cendrars organized a banquet at the Palais d'Orléans, boulevard du Maine, in honour of Apollinaire, whose spirits after his wound and trepan-ning were often low. Ninety guests, including the most important literary figures of the day – Fort, Gide, Romains, Copeau, Salmon, de Régnier, Alfred Valette – attended this launching of the ominously entitled volume *Le Poète assassiné.* The luncheon degenerated quickly enough into a shout-ing, enthusiastic brawl which pleased Apollinaire greatly: 'L'air était empli de moignons menaçants,' he wrote in an exuberant letter, unmistakenly identifying Cendrars, who a year after his amputation was not afraid to clobber a journalist.[15]

But despite his literary activities Cendrars was not living in Paris in 1917. After taking leave of his gypsy friends he rented a barn in the village of La Pierre (Loiret). Here he returned to the land, as it were, while his imagination flew very high above it in *La Fin du monde filmée par l'Ange Notre-Dame* and in *L'Eubage,* which he was writing for the *couturier* and collector Jacques Doucet:

> M. Doucet m'envoyait 100 francs par mois pour reçevoir chapitre par chapitre mon manuscrit (mon premier manuscrit écrit de la main gauche, ce qui en faisait toute l'originalité dans cette célèbre collection d'auto-graphes, léguée aujourd'hui à la Bibliothèque Sainte-Geneviève); à la moisson, je travaillai comme charretier dans les riches fermes de la Beauce (ces fermes étaient menées par les femmes, tous les hommes étant au front); à l'automne, je me mis à chasser au filet perdreaux et faisans qui

pullulaient dans la plaine au crépuscule et que je remettais au passage du
train du soir, en gare à Méréville (Loiret), à un serre-frein de la Compa-
gnie qui me les payait à vil prix, lui-même les vendant très cher à Paris (à
des gens dont je lui avais donné l'adresse); et, l'hiver, je tirai du cresson
un sel pour l'estomac, le *Camosel* dont je vendis la formule à un pharmacien
de la rue Jacob qui venait en villégiature dans la région (un brave juif) qui
y mit sa firme, le lança comme spécialité et fit fortune.[16]

The dates of composition for *L'Eubage* ascribe limits to this arcadian year
– 3 May to 28 December 1917. But the places of composition are given
as Paris, Courcelles, Nice, and La Pierre. The dedication is further revealing, as well as purposely amusing: to Doucet dated Paris, and to Conrad
Moricand dated Cannes, both on the same day, Thursday, 3 May 1917 –
a double dedication made before the book was written and from two cities
six hundred miles apart. The Doucet-Paris half is given first, but Cendrars
had been in Cannes in January and in Nice in February where, on the 14th,
at the terrace of the café Monnot he drew up a list of projects which he
expected to finish soon and which shows the busy program he had outlined
for himself (I omit three which cannot be traced from the titles): *Le
Panama* (finished July 1918); *Aux Antipodes de l'unité* (*L'Eubage*) (May
1919); *L'ABC du cinéma* (1919); *J'ai tué* (September 1918); *Les Atlandes*
(a film script for Abel Gance, 1918; not produced); *La Fin du monde*
(1919); *D'Outremer à indigo* (it is difficult to say what this was originally
meant to be, but it is the title of a volume of stories published in 1940);
Poèmes élastiques (July 1919). To this already considerable list we should
add the extremely important *Profond aujourd'hui* (see part two of this
study), written one day before this program was drafted. Indeed, as
Picasso is reported to have quipped: 'Blaise Cendrars revient de la guerre
avec un bras en plus.'[17]

A decisive break with the world of literature took place about this time,
in the autumn of 1917. Cendrars referred to it often, so there is little doubt
about its importance, though he appeared in Paris at different literary
activities almost as often as in the previous two years. The difference, then,
is one of emphasis, of attitude, and can only be seen in subtle ways. We
do not find Cendrars involved in the politics of art, the debates, the
haggling among jealous movements; notable we will not find him in the
famous battles of Dada, though *Dix-neuf Poèmes élastiques* was published by
René Hilsum at Au Sans Pareil editions, one of the first and foremost
organs for Dada, and *Littérature* would publish his work in the first and
later issues. The *Inédits* end during this period, and with it we lose our only

close record of his activities, t'Serstevens' *L'Homme que fut Blaise Cendrars*
notwithstanding. We have left only sporadic appearances here or there,
reported as if a legend had suddenly risen from the past only to disappear
as quickly. Cendrars' leave-taking was not a sudden or categorical one, but
rather the symbolic gesture of a renewed and confident independence. It
seems to have been precipitated at least in part by his meeting with
Raymone; forty years later the actress and leave-taking were explicitly
connected in an interview for *Le Figaro:* '1917. Ayant rencontré Raymone,
j'ai pris congé de la poésie.'[18] It was Canudo who introduced Cendrars
and Raymone, and their love-affair lasted the rest of their lives. They were
finally married in 1949, Fela having died in England during the second
world war. Raymone survives Blaise; at first she continued to live in the
apartment in Paris where they moved in 1956, and currently she lives in
Lausanne. She figures discreetly, sometimes unnamed, in many of his
works, and a number of them are dedicated to her. For example, *Le
Lotissement du ciel* (1949) is dedicated to 'La Folle de Saint-Sulpice.' Raymone played this role in the original production of Giraudoux's *La Folle
de Chaillot* (Raymone was a regular member of Louis Jouvet's company).
And yet one wonders how much they actually saw of each other between
the two wars, with Raymone's career and Cendrars' congenital wanderings. Her mother is reputed to have remarked that there was only one
poet-bum in Paris, and Raymone had got him. Although we cannot underestimate the part Raymone played in Cendrars' leave-taking we have his
testimony that the life of poetry in Paris played just as great a part:

> Le comput de ma vie d'homme commence en octobre 1917 le jour où,
> pour de nombreuses raisons dont je vous fais grâce mais dont la principale
> était que la poésie qui prenait vogue à Paris me semblait devenir la base
> d'un malentendu spirituel et d'une confusion mentale ... et que je quittai
> mes amis les poètes sans qu'aucun d'eux ne se doutât que je m'éloignais
> pour m'épanouir et me fortifier dans l'Amour, sur un plan où tout: actes,
> pensées, sentiments, paroles, est une communion universelle, après quoi,
> chose que j'ignorais moi-même alors, comme on entre en religion et
> franchit le cloître dont la grille se referme silencieusement sur vous, sans
> avoir prononcé de vœux, on est dans la solitude intégrale. En cage. Mais
> avec Dieu. C'est une grande force. Et l'on se tait par désir du verbe ... [19]

It is not easy to read much religious solitude at the heart of the life I am
attempting to describe, and it is perhaps only in the works that we can see
it looming so large.

For the next few years Cendrars was active in films and was the director
of the Éditions de la Sirène. Immediately after the war he may have done

some work for Pathé – scenarios, synopses, dialogue, and editing for a series called 'La Nature Chez Elle.' In 1917-18 he worked for Abel Gance on *J'accuse:*

> ... dans *J'accuse,* je faisais tout: l'homme de peine, l'accessoiriste, l'éléctricien, l'artificier, le costumier, de la figuration et de la régie, l'aide opérateur, le vice-metteur en scène, le chauffeur du patron, le comptable, le caissier et dans *Les Morts qui reviennent,* je faisais un macchabée, tout empoissé dans de l'hémoglobine de cheval car on m'avait fait perdre mon bras une deuxième fois pour les besoins de la prise de vue. Vous savez la chanson:
>
> > Quand Jean Renaud de guerre vint
> > Portant ses tripes dans sa main...
>
> Ca c'était du cinéma!... [20]

For the end of the film Gance had required swarms of wounded soldiers rising from their graves, and the banker Paul Lafitte, owner of La Sirène, had put him in touch with Cendrars, who recruited 'les gueules cassées,' the mutilated survivors of the war, and played his own part alongside them (see page ix). After *J'accuse* Cendrars was the assistant on Gance's famous *La Roue* (originally called *La Rose des rails*), which was some two years in the filming, from Nice to Arcachon to Chamonix, Grenoble, and Saint-Gervais. Cendrars recruited Honegger to write the accompanying music, which became known as *Pacific 231.* Cendrars has often been credited with the concepts of quick cutting for the train sequences which made the film an avant garde classic in editing and even subject matter four years before Eisenstein's *Potemkin.* [21] Gance's previous work, epic in intention but thoroughly sentimental and hardly inventive, lends credence to the influence of the poet of *Le Transsibérien* and *Le Panama,* just published in 1918 in the form and appearance of the Union Pacific Railroad schedule, with the Chicago to San Francisco routes reproduced among the lines of the poem. What was further Cendrarsian at this point in the history of film-making was the use of natural settings, such as Mont Blanc and the railroad yards, and non-actors like the railwaymen themselves. And it seems doubtful Gance would have made the train itself so much the film's central interest.

At the end of 1918 Cendrars was in Paris for a hectic and dramatic two weeks. [22] He was obtaining equipment and raw stock for *J'accuse* (being shot in Nice) and attending the publication of his *J'ai tué* in a special edition designed by François Bernouard. He helped at the typesetter

through the nights and saw friends back from war by day, Léger and
Apollinaire especially. The latter was gravely ill from Spanish influenza
and died on 9 November. He was buried the 11th, Armistice Day, while
the streets overflowed and, as legend has it, reverberated with 'A bas
Guillaume,' the final irony for the 'poète assassiné.' On the 15th the
launching of *J'ai tué* at the Théâtre Impérial was well attended but not a
copy sold. Raymone and Pierre Bertin, among others, read Cendrars'
poetry. The following 'review' by Pierre-Albert Birot for his journal *Sic*
is half-mocking yet also quite moving in the end; it adds to the information
Cendrars gives us by mentioning that he closed his own reception with a
personal farewell to Apollinaire:

> Or nous allâmes au Théâtre Impérial
> Vers la 16me heure
> Le 15 de Novembre
> C'était le temps
> Où Cendrars était en même temps
> Contrôleur et Poète
> Ah qu'un homme au contrôle
> Seigneur voit les choses de haut
> Et comme on est petit au pied de ce bureau
> Et puis après on est entré dans la salle
> On s'est assis dans un fauteuil
> Et l'on a tiré le rideau
> Et les liseurs grâce à l'escabeau
> Sont montés sur la scène
> J'AI TUÉ LE PANAMA LA FIN DU MONDE LA GUERRE AU LUXEMBOURG
> Tout cela nous fut lancé à la tête
> Entre 5 et 6
> Heureusement pour nous et pour l'auteur
> Que Pierre Bertin a lu
> Droitement
> LA FIN DU MONDE
> Tant qu'aux œuvres
> Ce que j'en pense est mon affaire
> Et n'a rien à faire ici
> Chacune est ou sera livre
> Un œil noir les attend
> De pied ferme si j'ose dire
> Le mien est vert
> Et puis on a peut-être un peu pleuré je ne sais
> La salle était sans lumière

Quand Cendrars à la place des siens
Vint dire LE JET D'EAU ET LA COLOMBE POIGNARDÉE
Poème de Guillaume Apollinaire[23]

By the time he died Apollinaire had grown depressed and increasingly difficult for even his good friends, no doubt from his severe wound. His confidence had been failing, and he was particularly hurt when *Les Mamelles de Tirésias* foundered, sabotaged he thought. In the posthumously published *La Femme assise* (1920) he attacked Max Jacob and Picasso, and Cendrars under the guise of Waxheimer, whose pseudonym is Ovide du Pont-Euxin; Apollinaire calls this character 'le faux Ovide.' And yet, at the very moment of the death of 'le mal aimé' Cendrars edited and published a collection of his journalism, *Le Flâneur des deux rives,* for La Sirène. Cendrars appears as the unnamed 'Errant des bibliothèques,' recognizable from the libraries in cities he knew.

In 1919 Cendrars was doing some work for Pathé at Vincennes, and some other unspecified film work in Vienna. He was in Paris for a reception in his and Erik Satic's honour held by Léonce Rosenberg, the art dealer, on 19 February 1919, and his address in Paris about this time was, very intermittently of course, the Hôtel Mirabeau, rue de la Paix. After *La Roue* was finished – its première was in Paris at the huge Gaumont Palace in 1921 and the train sequences caused an uproar – Cendrars travelled first to England and thence to Rome to work on his own film, *La Vénus noire,* with a Hindu star of the Paris Opéra comique, Dourga. Shooting was finished for Rinascimento Films when he returned to Paris in October of 1923:

> Je rentrais bredouille, victime du krack du Banco di Sconto, ce scandale financier soigneusement monté par le baron F... qui devait empocher d'un seul coup, à l'aube du régime de Mussolini, tous les capitaux de l'industrie cinématographique italienne si opportunément amassés durant la Grande Guerre et porter à cette industrie un coup dont le cinéma italien ne s'est jamais relevé. Personnellement, je trinquais pour 8.000 livres Sterling, soit 1.250.000 francs en chiffres ronds, le change étant à 160, mon premier million gagné par mon travail depuis que j'avais dit adieu, non pas à la poésie, mais aux poètes et à Paris, et pour toujours. La septième année de ma vie d'homme commençait. Et j'étais de retour à Paris. Et je repartais de zéro.[24]

The script for this film was already being published as *La Perle fiévreuse* in *Signaux de France et de Belgique* from 1921 to 1922. From what we can tell the film was a spoof on current detective fiction, with Fantômas, Nick

Carter, Arsène Lupin, Gustave Lerouge, Conan Doyle, Maurice Leblanc (author of the Arsène Lupin stories), and Rouletabille (hero of a series by Gaston Leroux) as a kind of Keystone cops trying to solve the disappearance of two women. But that was the end of Cendrars' career as a filmmaker, before it had really begun. Later in Brazil he was to plan a movie, but this time a full-scale revolution intervened.

While he was in Rome, in 1921, Cendrars met Sinclair Lewis through Harold Loeb, who published material by Cendrars in his expensive avantgarde journal *Broom.* Cendrars was interested, at one point, in translating *Main Street,* perhaps for La Sirène.[25] Cendrars directed Paul Lafitte's venture into publishing from about 1918 to 1924, when it folded. I have not been able to trace the 221 volumes he spoke of in 1949[26] (naturally the number may have been purposely impressionistic), but many more than just those he named can be found, so it is quite likely there are many more yet. The following sampling shows his mark (also the mark of Cocteau, who worked at La Sirène[27]): in 1918, Apollinaire's above-mentioned *Flâneur des deux rives;* Cocteau, *Le Coq et l'arlequin;* Cendrars, *Le Panama;* in 1919, Apollinaire, *Le Bestiaire ou le cortège d'Orphée,* illustrated by Dufy; Baudelaire, *Mon Cœur mis à nu;* Cendrars, *La Fin du monde,* illustrated by Léger; in 1920, Jean Epstein, *La Poésie d'aujourd'hui, un nouvel état d'intelligence,*[28] Cocteau, *Carte blanche* (which contains an article on Cendrars), and his *Escales,* illustrated by André Lhote in a deluxe edition of 440 copies; Stravinsky, *Rag-Time,* with a cover by Picasso (a few years ago this volume was for sale in New York, at $500 – or free as a companion-piece to the original drawing by Picasso, which was on sale for $15,000!); Lautréamont, *Les Chants du Maldoror*[29]; de Gourmont, *Pensées inédites,* illustrated by Dufy with an introduction by Apollinaire; in 1921, Cendrars, *L'Anthologie nègre,* with a cover by Csaky; in 1923, Ivan Goll, *Le Nouvel Orphée,* with illustrations by Robert Delaunay, Grosz, and Léger.[30] There were books meant to sell well, in order to support the others, such as five novels by Robert Louis Stevenson, but also extravagances which must have kept the firm very much in the red: an edition of *The Thousand and One Nights* illustrated by Van Dongen and costing 1,200 francs a volume (ordinary volumes cost 6 to 8 francs), and Casanova's *Mémoires* in twelve volumes with 370 period reproductions and the first serious scholarly notes.[31] In 1924 La Sirène published the first translation of Joyce's *Portrait of the Artist as a Young Man,* as *Dédalus, Portrait de l'artiste jeune par lui-même* translated by Ludmila Savitsky.[32] But we cannot say if Cendrars was involved in obtaining or approving the book. The contact might have been made through Budgen.

Cendrars had always been a reader of exploration literature, and primitive themes pervade his work almost from the outset, especially as the avant-garde in painting had discovered their own sources in primitive art just before his arrival in Paris. Captain Cook is mentioned in the *Dix-neuf Poèmes élastiques,* of which the seventeenth, 'Mee too buggi,' is entirely about the island of Tonga. In February of 1916 at the British Museum he had written two poems on African themes and by 1921, when he published *L'Anthologie nègre,* 'folklore des peuplades africaines,' he was well known as the central figure in the enthusiasm for Africana and 'le jazz-band' which was sweeping Paris with the help of Cocteau at the drums (Josephine Baker arrived in Paris a few years later, in 1925). Cendrars' interest was always serious, as the research for *L'Anthologie* shows. Kay Boyle has recently written: 'Blaise Cendrars had been in Africa and South America, and had recently translated a book of primitive Negro songs and poems. He brought with him to Mariette's parties explorers, scientists, and anthropologists. The ambition of the moment seemed to become as African-Negroid as possible.'[33] These interests culminated in *La Création du monde* (1923), with music by Darius Milhaud, sets by Léger, and scenario by Cendrars for Rolf de Maré's Ballets Suédois with Jean Borlin.[34] For the following year de Maré and Borlin planned a ballet after a piece by Cendrars called 'Après-dîner,' with music by Satie and sets by Picabia. But at a certain point the others lost contact with Cendrars and became anxious; in his absence Picabia took over, to make *Relâche* – a more decidedly Dada event, particularly with its film interlude *Entr'acte* (the first movie by René Clair).[35]

Cendrars was gone. He would work on no other ballets, as if only a second one began to be too repetitive for him, or any lengthy collaboration too onerous, even if a resounding reputation was certainly to be made at it. He had stayed long enough to leave behind a small piece of the legend, the foreign ballerinas believing his name was Blaise Sansbras, and then he sailed to South America.

4 The Americas, 1924-39

From 1924 Cendrars' foothold near Paris was at Le Tremblay-sur-Maudre, only a short distance from 'la Nationale 10,' the Paris-Biarritz road which is one of the themes of the four novels of 1945-9. His house was named 'L'Oustaou.' Picabia lived nearby in 'La Maison Rose,' and René Hilsum, Ambroise Vollard, Rouault, Picasso, and the famous silent film comic Marcel Lévesque all lived at Le Tremblay during these years. In 1924 *Kodak (Documentaire)* was published by Stock, with a portrait of Cendrars by Picabia and a striking woodcut by Frans Masereel on the cover. It contained poems about America, Canada, and Japan, but we don't know what visits, if any, supplied the occasions for their composition. As has been recently verified, a number of the poems were found poetry, merely cut out of the text of a popular novel by Cendrars' friend Gustave Lerouge.[1] Also in 1924 he published *Feuilles de route* (a rather Whitmanesque title) at Hilsum's Au Sans Pareil. These are poems of his first trip to South America the same year, which was one result of Cendrars' friendship with Paulo da Silva Prado.

Before collaborating with Cendrars and Léger on *La Création du Monde,* Milhaud had been in Brazil, where he had been cultural attaché while Paul Claudel was head of the French diplomatic mission. Cendrars had probably met Prado in the bookstore of Chadanat, the central character of Cendrars' 'Paris, Port-de-Mer' in *Bourlinguer* (1948); Prado remained one of Cendrars' closest friends until his death in 1943.[2] He belonged to one of the richest and most powerful families in São Paulo, and most of that power was based on coffee interests. It is thus quite believable that, at one time or another, Cendrars was involved in business enterprises in connection with his friend's affairs; however, there is virtually no solid evidence of this at the moment. Prado was also a scholar, much interested in Brazilian historical works and from 1923 he was co-director of the influential *Revista do Brasil.* He favoured and supported the Brazilian modernists, who had first burst upon the scene in February 1922 with the shows of the Semana de Arte Moderna, and he invited Cendrars in 1924 to come to see São Paulo and the young modernists on their own ground; for the Brazilian avant-garde, Oswald de Andrade, Sérgio Milliett, Tarsila do Amaral and others (even the somewhat better established Villa Lobos) spent much of their time in Paris, looking for artistic guidance. There seems little doubt that Cendrars was able to provide them with one thing at least, the conviction that the roots of their modernism had to be autochthonous, to be found in an authentic Brazil. Thus he chose to illustrate the product of his first trip, *Feuilles de route,* with 'primitive' drawings by Tarsila; and Oswald's *Pau Brasil,* published by Au Sans Pareil in Paris in 1925, was dedicated 'A Blaise Cendrars, à l'occasion de la découverte du Brésil,' the discovery working for both the Frenchman and the Brazilian. Indeed, Cendrars had come to discover Brazil for himself, but his eyes revealed to the modernists of the *Pau Brasil* and the subsequent *Antropofagia* movements that their seemingly provincial homeland was nothing to be ashamed of; quite the contrary, it was everything of importance. Cendrars must also have been enchanted to find one source of his own name, *braise,* to be the source of the country's name. He arrived in Rio, where he was met by many of the modernist poets, painters, and journalists (he was first stopped by officials who thought he was a new immigrant; they didn't want any one-armed labourers), and then went on to Santos and São Paulo. He travelled with some of his new friends to the São Paulo State coffee-plantations belonging to the Prado family and much further inland to the sites of early Paulist conquest and the goldmine towns of the late seventeenth century in Minas Gerais. It even seems that Cendrars led the others on, and that some abandoned the group along the way. In Congonhas do Campo he marvelled at the soapstone Stations of the Cross by the eighteenth-century architect and sculptor Aleijadinho, and for many years had plans for a novel on Aleijadinho's life. He wrote *L'Or* instead, about another gold rush, and Aleijadinho was much later transformed into the Manolo Secca of *L'Homme foudroyé* (1945), a twentieth-century sculptor who stands the characters of the Passion in automobiles.[3]

Between 1924 and 1929 Cendrars went to Brazil five times, and there were a few more voyages in later years. He also went to Argentina, Paraguay, and Chile, possibly travelled as far as Patagonia and the sites of *Dan Yack* (1929): the island of Chiloe and parts of Antarctica, probably visited on a modern whaler. One of the poems of *Feuilles de route* tells us what literary baggage he took with him on the first trip to Brazil in January of 1924 aboard the boat *Le Formose:*

Voici ce que ma malle contient

Le manuscrit du Plan de l'Aiguille que je dois terminer le plus tôt possible
    pour l'expédier au Sans Pareil

Le manuscrit d'un ballet pour la prochaine saison des Ballets Suédois et
    que j'ai fait à bord entre Le Havre et La Pallice d'où je l'ai envoyé à
    Satie

Le manuscrit du Cœur du Monde que j'enverrai au fur et à mesure à
    Raymone

Le manuscrit de l'Equatoria

Un gros paquet de contes nègres qui formera le deuxième volume de mon
    Anthologie

Plusieurs dossiers d'affaires

Les deux gros volumes du dictionnaire Darmesteter.

[from 'Bagage']

In fact *Le Plan de l'Aiguille* did not appear until 1929 (by which time a companion volume, *Les Confessions de Dan Yack,* had been added), and many of the other projects mentioned in 'Bagage' were delayed or came to nothing, less because of Cendrars' travels than because of other work not mentioned in the poem, such as his two volumes of poetry, and two novels.

Cendrars' first novel was *L'Or, la merveilleuse histoire du général Johann August Suter* (1925); this was mainly written in six weeks at Le Tremblay, from 22 November to 31 December 1924, although he must have researched the book over any number of years, and the subject is mentioned in *Le Panama* of 1913-14.[4] After the first voyage to Brazil, from April to November of 1925 Cendrars was in Biarritz at 'La Mimoseraie,' home of Mme Errazuriz, one of the Parisian Maecenases who was especially friendly with Cendrars.[5] Here he finished his second novel, *Moravagine,* part of which had been written in Amazonia. He was in South America again in the early part of 1926, and in a letter from São Paulo dated 25 April 1926 sent Oswald some poems for the catalogue of an exhibit by Tarsila; Oswald is invited to add more poems if he wishes, and can sign them 'de mon nom,' Blaise Cendrars.[6] Two months later, in June, he was in Paris again, and he stayed through the winter in Le Tremblay. Then we find him in Spain at the wheel of a *Ballot,* at 'La Redonne,' an empty house he discovered overlooking a *calanque* west of Marseilles, and back in Brazil. At 'La Redonne' he began work on *Les Confessions de Dan Yack* but, he said, it was fatal trying to work in front of a window facing on the sea. And so he would be off again.

It was about this time, in 1929 most likely, that John Dos Passos met Cendrars, probably at a party of Gerald Murphy's. In 1923 Cendrars was to be found among the celebrities at the Murphys' famous *péniche,* or river barge, party for Stravinsky after the première of *Les Noces.* Gerald Murphy's paintings, now considered pre-Pop Art, were made between 1922 and 1929 and in both technique and concern reflect his close friendship with Léger (they also seem to foreshadow the famous posters of Cendrars' friend Cassandre). Through Léger Murphy received a commission for an 'American' companion piece to *La Création du monde* for Les Ballets Suédois, and he in turn enlisted Cole Porter to write the music. The result was *Within the Quota.* Murphy's backdrop was a huge front page with the main headline 'Unknown Banker Buys Atlantic.'[7] But while he imported ironic American myths to France Murphy must also have been the intermediary for at least one current in the other direction. He most certainly acquainted his friend Gilbert Seldes with some of the work of Cendrars; for this critic, among the first to see the value of the popular arts, praised Cendrars in *The Seven Lively Arts* (1924) for proving that the cinema could have a beneficial effect on writing, rather than the much proclaimed opposite.

Dos Passos for his part had written an article on Cendrars, 'Homer of the Trans-Siberian,' published in 1926 in the *Saturday Review of Literature* some time before they met.[8] In 1929 John and Kate Dos Passos saw Cendrars in Paris and visited him in Monpazier, where he was researching his reportage on Jean Galmot, the hero of *Rhum* (1930):

> They cooked wild goose and venison in a huge oldfashioned chimney and we had truffle omelets every noon for lunch.
>
> Cendrars had lost a hand in the war. It was hairraising to spin with him around the mountain roads. He steered with one hand and changed gears on his little French car with his hook. We visited Les Eyzies and every other prehistoric cave within reach. Cendrars took every curve on two wheels.[9]

Then, on his trip back to the United States, 'I translated the *Panama* book on the ancient Spanish line steamer *Antonio Lopez* and used some sketches I did on the same trip as illustrations. The reason? I enjoyed his poetry. His obsessions and manias coincided with many of my own.'[10] Cendrars was in New York in 1931 to sign copies of this now rare volume, *Panama* (a letter to Dos Passos dated 23 March 1930 indicates that he had already been in the States twice in the preceding twelve months); *Panama* contained translations of *Le Transsibérien, Le Panama,* and poems from *Kodak* and *Feuilles de route,* all of which had been quoted, along with *Dix-neuf Poèmes élastiques,* in Dos Passos' article of 1926. A number of letters from Cendrars to Dos Passos covering the years 1929 through 1932 are in the possession of the University of Virginia and reveal that Cendrars was involved with the translation of *The 42nd Parallel.*[11] Gallimard, Dos Passos' publisher, apparently lost interest, and Cendrars arranged a contract with Grasset. There is a good deal of complaining in the letters about the job of writing as a sort of forced labour, and in a hand-written one dated 19 October 1930 he reminisced about a camel they both saw, or heard about, in Monpazier:

> Et j'ai retrouvé le dromadaire chez un paysan, travaillant dur, attelé à une charrue! Quelle tristesse et quelle image du poète! Au sujet de poésie, merci d'avoir traduit les miennes et quelle corvée pour vous! hein? Moi, je suis si loin, si loin de tout ça. Ma jeunesse. On vieillit. C'est moche de devenir un dromadaire attelé.

Two critical books discuss the literary relationship of Dos Passos and Cendrars: Georges-Albert Astre's *Thèmes et structures dans l'œuvre de John Dos Passos* and George Wickes' *Americans in Paris, 1903-1939.*[12] Both scholars consider there is a strong connection. Astre sees in Cendrars' work a direct influence on *Manhattan Transfer,* and Wickes, happily avoiding the influence game altogether, sees the sort of identification Dos Passos himself points to when he speaks of obsessions and manias coinciding with his own. Wickes writes: 'Dos Passos assimilated Cendrars so completely that he did not need to imitate. In spirit, form and style Cendrars' poetry became the very fiber of *USA.*' One may read *L'Or* and *Rhum* as novel-length versions of *USA*'s capsule biographies, narratives in rapid-fire free verse. American critics who do not know Cendrars have naturally assigned the main influence of this sort to Joyce and Eisenstein, but Dos Passos himself put Cendrars closer to the source of what he was getting at in his own work:

> Cendrars and Apollinaire, poets, were on the first cubist barricades with the group that included Picasso, Modigliani, Marinetti, Chagall; that profoundly influenced Maiakovsky, Meyerhold, Eisenstein; whose ideas carom through Joyce, Gertrude Stein, T. S. Eliot (first published in Wyndam Lewis's 'Blast'). The music of Stravinski and Prokofieff and Diageleff's Ballet hail from the same Paris already in the disintegration of victory, as do the windows of Saks Fifth Avenue, skyscraper furniture, the Lenin Memorial in Moscow, the paintings of Diego Rivera in Mexico City and the newritz styles of advertising in American magazines.[13]

Furthermore, both Eisenstein and Joyce were great technical innovators, but neither was especially close to the modernity of life as represented in

that last sentence, or to the life of the city as found in *Manhattan Transfer.*
Congo Jake in that novel bears quite a resemblance to Cendrars, with his
missing limb (a leg, however), his youth in Port Arthur, and his little song:
'J'ai fait trois fois le tour du monde / Dans mes voyages ... '

Also about 1930 Eisenstein met Cendrars in Paris in order to obtain the
rights to *L'Or*, which has been translated into English as *Sutter's Gold* and
Russian as *Zoloto*, both in 1926. Eisenstein's attempt to make films in
Hollywood was short and fruitless. He first prepared Dreiser's *American
Tragedy*, and then *Sutter's Gold;* company politicking at Paramount under-
mined both projects. The script for this first of three versions of *Sutter's
Gold* survives in the collection of the library of the Museum of Modern
Art of New York and is reprinted with sketches for sets and camera angles
in Ivor Montagu's *With Eisenstein in Hollywood.* Although Cendrars was no
longer making films himself he must have maintained many contacts with
people in the industry. In 1934 the producer of Jean Vigo's famous film
L'Atalante, Jacques-Louis Nounez, approached Cendrars for a revision of
Vigo's dialogue (the film starred the very Cendrarsian Swiss actor Michel
Simon), but Cendrars found no fault with it.[14]

When in Paris between 1930 and the next war Cendrars could be found
at the Alma-Hôtel, or at any number of addresses on the avenue Montaigne near the Théâtre des Champs-Élysées, and he would meet with
friends at Chez Francis, a café made famous later by Giraudoux's *La Folle
de Chaillot.* At lunchtime friends and acquaintances knew he could be
found in the kitchen of the Alma-Hôtel, and people from all walks of life
would arrive uninvited to trade favours, stories, and no doubt a bit of
business. He was involved in different business affairs of which he rarely
spoke; one that fell through has recently come to light – a two- or three-
year voyage around the world to record in sound and image all sorts of
supernatural phenomena, voodoo, poltergeists, levitation, and so forth.
The doctor-financier Ferral at first found interested backers, including the
Ford and Rockefeller Foundations, but himself went bankrupt in 1929.[15]

From about 1930 to 1937 Cendrars published no fiction (I include in
the term fiction what he called 'histoires vraies,' in the same way that *L'Or*
may be considered fiction). *Rhum* was a reportage for the weekly *Vu.* He
worked on two similar books, the lives of John Paul Jones and Jim Fisk,
but neither of these was finished. At least three chapters of *John Paul Jones,
ou l'Ambition* appeared in different journals, and a great deal of detailed
research must have been done, as witness, for example, the chapter entitled 'Ivy Close,' although there is a very peculiar enigma about that name
(see my discussion of *Dan Yack* below, page 171).[16] The Fisk material has
been discovered in his papers, and published in the *Inédits.*[17] In 1930
Cendrars edited a series at Au Sans Pareil called 'Les Têtes Brûlées.' Only

two 'firebrands' would see the light: a volume of memoirs, *Feu le Lieutenant Bringolf* (1930), and *Al Capone le balafré* (1931). Both of these books were translated by others and reworked by Cendrars. A few years later he translated two works himself for Grasset: Al Jennings' *Through the Shadows with O'Henry* as *Hors la loi!...* (1936), and, from the Portuguese, Ferreira de Castro's *A Selva* as *Forêt vierge* (1938). Cendrars' own rather restricted output during these six or seven years included one collection of earlier articles and out-of-print prose in *Aujourd'hui* (1931), which is a most important volume for the study of Cendrars as it contains all the earlier prose pamphlets, *Profond aujourd'hui, J'ai tué, Éloge de la vie dangereuse,* etc.; his only avowed piece of autobiography, *Vol à voile* (1932), which deals with his running away from home in Neuchâtel; and two reportages, *Panorama de la pègre* (1935) and *Hollywood, la mecque du cinéma* (1936). For *Panorama* he must have travelled a great deal, and with very good connections, in the Basque country, on the French-Belgian border, in Marseilles (the novelist Henri Bosco said in a television interview that Cendrars was one of the rare people who knew Marseilles without being a native), and among the Paris underworld; *Hollywood, la mecque du cinéma,* serialized in *Paris-Soir* in its year of publication, was written after Cendrars visited California for the opening of *Sutter's Gold,* which after many years had finally been produced.

This trip to the United States, one of many Cendrars made aboard the famous *Normandie,* was the maiden crossing, 29 May to 3 June 1935, and Cendrars was in the company of others who were to cover the voyage for different Paris publications: Colette, Madeleine Jacob, Claude Farrère, and Gérard Bauer, who wrote that Cendrars was rarely to be seen: 'Il ne quitta jamais les soutes et n'en ressortit assoiffé et huileux que lorsque nous fûmes amarrés à la pier 53 – pour se perdre dans New York.'[18] If Cendrars was covering the record-breaking crossing of the luxurious liner for a Paris newspaper the text has yet to be recovered.

Sutter's Gold had been planned as an important and elaborate production. Originally Howard Hawks had begun to direct it, with Charles Laughton playing the lead. William Faulkner had written the script, but there is no telling what, if anything, was retained for the final version. In the end James Cruze directed Edward Arnold, Lee Tracy, and Binnie Barnes with twenty-five hundred extras and seventy-five sets. The opening was a grand occasion; *Time* magazine reported:

> When the picture opened last week, Governor Frank Finley Merriam of California proclaimed Gold Week, and Sacramento held a warm-up for its 1939 Hometown Jubilee. There was a Governor's 'Sutter's Gold Ball.'

Carl Laemmle and entourage arrived in five private cars. Local merchants
displayed themselves in 1849 costumes and sideburns.

However, the film was poorly received and has been totally forgotten.
'Tedious, illogical and fanciful,' the *New York Times* reviewer called it
when it opened at Radio City Music Hall.[19] What angered Cendrars most
was the spurious appearance of a Russian countess, Binnie Barnes' Bartoff-
ski; let us hope Faulkner had nothing to do with that.

Near the end of 1934, on 14 December, Cendrars visited Henry Miller
at the Villa Seurat. He had read *Tropic of Cancer,* and, no doubt pleased
to find himself mentioned there, he came to greet the new American
author. On the first of January he wrote at the head of a short article on
Miller: 'Un écrivain américain nous est né.'[20] This is the first public
recognition of Henry Miller and was soon followed with reviews by
T.S. Eliot, Herbert Read, Aldous Huxley, Dos Passos, Pound, and Or-
well. Cendrars' visit is described to Anaïs Nin in Miller's letters, and his
account is quite a revelation, for the famous truculent Miller was entirely
overwhelmed. He found himself cowed, without words and, it would
seem, outdone at the very games of *Tropic:*

> Perhaps the finest moment in my life, in one sense. But it went flat. I had
> nothing to say. I wondered how long it would continue. I was a perfect
> ass. And trying at intervals to break away. Finally we go out, four of us
> now, and we must have some more alcohol in the bars along the Boulevard
> in Montmartre. Whores hanging on to us, and Cendrars hugging them like
> a sailor, and urging me to take one, take two, take as many as you want.
> After two or three of these bars and more whores hanging on our necks
> I ducked – very unceremoniously too. An au revoir. I don't know what
> he must think of me.[21]

Henry Miller's admiration for Blaise Cendrars is boundless. In *The Books
in My Life* Cendrars is quoted in epigraph (the only living author in a list
of five quoted), is the subject of the first chapter devoted to individual
writers, and in Miller's list of 'the hundred books which influenced me
most' is the only writer for whom Miller includes 'virtually the complete
works'[22] There are even quotations from Cendrars on the walls of Miller's
most recent home in Los Angeles.[23] But Cendrars' immediate effect on
Miller is quite different from that of his very modern poetry on John Dos
Passos. For Miller, Cendrars was a very special sort of man, and his writing
is exactly the mirror of that man,

ce 'Chinese rock-bottom man' de mon imagination, l'homme que D. H.
Lawrence eût aimé être, l'homme universel qui ne sera jamais identifié,
l'homme enfin qui renouvelle la race en replaçant dans le creuset l'humanité tout entière. 'Je méprise tout ce qui est,' dit Cendrars. 'J'agis, je
révolutionne.'[24]

Miller has made a religion – a business, some would object – of becoming
himself such a man, and it is to some degree of success in this that he owes
the best part of his considerable following today. But, as Hesse's Siddhar-
tha discovered, there are many levels of understanding the essence of
things, each one quite immeasurably beyond the one before it, and if
Miller moves on one mystical stage, in his own mind Cendrars acts on
another well beyond that one:

> My dear Cendrars, I will never know you, not as I do other men, of that
> I am certain. No matter how thoroughly you reveal yourself I shall never
> get to the bottom of you. I doubt that anyone ever will, and it is not vanity
> which prompts me to put it this way. You are as inscrutable as a Buddha.
> You inspire, you reveal, but you never give yourself wholly away. Not that
> you withhold yourself! No, encountering you, whether in person or
> through the written word, you leave the impression of having given all
> there is to give. Indeed, you are one of the few men I know who, in their
> books as well as in person, give that 'extra measure' which means every-
> thing to us. You give all that can be given.[25]

Miller recognizes that Cendrars' stance, close to reality as it is, is paradoxically a solitary one:

> In the ocean of humanity Cendrars swims as blithely as a porpoise or a
> dolphin. In his narratives he is always together with men, one with them
> in deed, one with them in thought. If he is a solitary, he is nevertheless
> fully and completely a man. He is also the brother of all men.[26]

In this paradox we can find what links the modernist that Dos Passos
admired and the mystic that Miller needed to discover and emulate. Only
ten days before meeting Cendrars Miller had quoted relevant passages
from C. G. Jung's essay 'The Spiritual Problem of Modern Man' to Anaïs
Nin in his letters.[27] A year later he would quote the same essay again and
at greater length in a letter to Michael Fraenkel in their long correspondence *Hamlet*.[28] I also quote Jung at some length, as his idea of the modern
man is central to my understanding of Cendrars:

... the man we call modern, the man who is aware of the immediate present, is by no means the average man. He is rather the man who stands upon a peak, or at the very edge of the world, the abyss of the future before him, above him the heavens, and below him the whole of mankind with a history that disappears in primeval mists. The modern man – or, let us say again, the man of the immediate present – is rarely met with. There are few who live up to the name, for they must be conscious to a superlative degree ... He alone is modern who is fully conscious of the present.

The man whom we can with justice call 'modern' is solitary. He is so of necessity and at all times, for every step towards a fuller consciousness of the present removes him further from his original 'participation mystique' with the mass of men – from submersion in a common unconsciousness. Every step forward means an act of tearing himself loose from the all-embracing, pristine unconsciousness which claims the bulk of mankind almost entirely ... Only the man who is modern in our meaning of the term really lives in the present; he alone has a present-day consciousness, and he alone finds that the ways of life which correspond to earlier levels pall upon him. The values and strivings of those past worlds no longer interest him save from the historical standpoint. Thus he has become 'unhistorical' in the deepest sense and has estranged himself from the mass of men who live entirely within the bounds of tradition. Indeed, he is completely modern only when he has come to the very edge of the world, leaving behind him all that has been discarded and outgrown, and acknowledging that he stands before a void out of which all things may grow.[29]

The meaning of this for Cendrars is that he was avant-garde in the most quintessential sense. The reality of the present is made by man in a basically unconscious state, the best-trained scientist knows not what he does; at work he tinkers and in himself he lives a hundred years behind the meaning of his own tinkering. By the time literary movements such as Cubism, Dada, and Surrealism had consolidated and approved of a 'new' present, Cendrars was gone; for he consolidated nothing. Although we may consider *Profond aujourd'hui* or *L'Eubage* surrealistic in tendency and implication, we never find that Cendrars was a surrealist, or an any 'thing-ist.' This elusive passing-through – as opposed to a position – is what Miller saw in Cendrars, and sought for himself. Part two of this volume shows that Cendrars was this 'modern' man. For the finest picture in fiction of the modern solitary man read *Dan Yack*.

Cendrars told Miller at that first meeting that he would have liked to translate *Tropic of Cancer* but was returning to Brazil in January (1935). In 1936-7 Cendrars may have covered the Spanish Civil War at Burgos; his reports, if published, have not been reprinted. In 1937 he published the first of three volumes of short stories, *Histoires vraies,* followed by *La Vie dangereuse* (1938) and *D'Outremer à indigo* (1940), all narratives which he always insisted were 'histoires vraies.' He was obliged to insist because they read like tall tales indeed; yet my position is that we must take them for fact (or dismiss the relevance of veracity, which is another possible tack). Appreciation of Cendrars depends largely upon the resolution of this problem. In their involution and personal involvement these narratives prefigure the great autobiographical novels of 1945-9. It is these works, from 1937 to 1949, which put Cendrars himself on stage in an extraordinary world perhaps as mythical as Homer's Greece. They merit the same serious attention.

5 Aix-en-Provence, 1939-48, and Paris, 1948-61

In the summer of 1938 Cendrars had been planning a round-the-world voyage aboard a four-masted sailing ship, the *Moshulu,* but war was threatening and the voyage was cancelled. The next year he was war-correspondent for a number of French newspapers: *Paris-Soir, La Petite Gironde, Le Petit Marseillais, Le Républicain Orléanais, La Dépêche Algérienne, La Vigie Marocaine, Le Mémorial de Saint-Étienne, La Dépêche de Breste* – quite a journalistic 'tour de France.' He and colleagues representing other papers (J.-H. Lefèbvre, *Le Jour* and *l'Écho de Paris;* M. Chenevier and P. Ichac, *L'Illustration;* R. Lacoste representing l'Agence Havas; P. de Lacretelle, *Le Petit Journal;* B. Franklin, *L'Intransigeant;* and André Maurois *Le Figaro*) travelled to Britain to report on the readiness for war, and were then attached to British Headquarters in France. Edmond Buchet of Buchet/Chastel éditions tells of Cendrars coming to see him on 25 November 1939, before he began to write his articles on the war preparations:

> Il nous propose son journal de guerre. Nous acceptons, bien entendu, avec enthousiasme.
>
> J'ai été l'élève de son frère, professeur de droit à l'Université de Genève ... On ne peut imaginer contraste plus absolu entre ces deux frères. Autant Blaise est vivant autant l'autre était ennuyeux, autant il aime l'aventure, autant l'autre était pantouflard. Ils ne s'entendent d'ailleurs pas du tout, me dit Blaise.[1]

The journal Buchet mentions, *Chez l'armée anglaise,* was printed by May 1940 but Buchet, out of prudence, held off publication. Cendrars was covering the war in Belgium. Following defeat upon defeat he was in Lille, Arras, Amiens, and Paris, where he picked up Raymone and her mother and drove them south to safety; then he drove north against the streams of fleeing Frenchmen as far back as Reims. A photograph dated 12 May 1940 shows him in the baggage car of a train out of Amiens, lying on the evacuated gold reserves of the Bank of France, 280 million francs' worth.[2] Wrote Maurois:

> It was a nightmare trip. German airplanes followed us and tried to destroy the tracks; we had nothing to eat. The engine proceeded at a walking pace, and at each grade crossing we found again the sad, rosecolored tide of refugees which spread out over the tracks and kept us motionless for hours.[3]

Although Cendrars only learned of it later, his younger son Rémy was shot down on 19 May and interned at Stalag 17, at Kaisersteinbrück. Cendrars was at Troyes, Blois, Nantes, and finally in Marseilles where he was arrested for his 'English' uniform. Pétain had called for an armistice on 17 June and the English naval base had already been evacuated:

> On pourra lire mes aventures durant 'la drôle de guerre' dans *101.000 killomètres pour rien,* si jamais j'écris ce livre dont le titre m'a été donné par le compteur de ma voiture, chiffre qui indique le kilomètrage que j'ai parcouru seul, au volant, du 3 septembre 1939 au 14 juillet 1940, jour où j'ai remisé la voiture dans un garage d'Aix-en-Provence.[4]

In October the edition of *Chez l'armée anglaise* was confiscated by the Germans, and Cendrars and his works were put on the 'Otto' list. He later found his house in Le Tremblay completely sacked.

From 1940 to 21 August 1943 Cendrars wrote absolutely nothing, nor did he move very much from the town of Aix, where he lived at 12 rue Clemenceau, a narrow lane off the Cours Mirabeau. The quick, fawning submission of France seems to have overwhelmed him, and Edouard Peisson, who saw him almost daily, wrote: 'Peu à peu, Cendrars redevint le pauvre bougre qui avait vécu seul à New York, le soldat qu'il avait été dans les tranchées.'[5] However, it is entirely likely that Cendrars was involved at least in small ways in resistance activities, though his opposition to, even disgust at, the collaboration of local authorities must have been too well known for him to have risked anything overt. The *miliciens* came after him at his house twice, but in each case he had been warned and was away (a week before the end of the war they wrecked his car). I have it from the late Jacques-Henry Lévesque that Cendrars was instrumental in helping the film director Max Ophuls and his wife and child out of France. It is known that Ophuls was hiding in Aix after 1940, that he

worked for a short time in Zurich with Jouvet's company (of which, as I
have said, Raymone was a member), and that he was obliged to flee soon
after to the United States. What makes the story particularly interesting
is that that child was Marcel Ophuls, director of *La Chagrin et la pitié*
(*The Sorrow and the Pity,* 1972), the epic documentary on collaboration and
resistance in Vichy France.[6] Cendrars himself wrote that when Allied
planes circled overhead the German soldiers marching in the streets
would shout 'Licht, Licht!' and, remembering that these were Goethe's
last words, Cendrars would light his candle. They shot out his windows.[7]

Suddenly, on 21 August 1943, after a visit from Peisson, Cendrars
began to write again, more voluminously than ever before. One of the
more practical reasons he gave was that a German officer was billetted
next-door, and the total absence of any papers about his house was indeed
grounds for suspicion, for a writer! But this excuse alone could never
account for the quality of the work he did. The opening of the first volume
describes its genesis in Cendrars' association of the depthless night and
loneliness in Aix with nights in the trenches of 1914, and in these intense
narratives the phoenix, always waiting in his adopted name, rose again:

> Et alors j'ai pris feu dans ma solitude car écrire c'est se consumer ...
>
> L'écriture est un incendie qui embrase un grand remue-ménage d'idées
> et qui fait flamboyer des associations d'images avant de les réduire en
> braises crépitantes et en cendres retombantes. Mais si la flamme déclenche
> l'alerte, la spontanéité du feu reste mystérieuse. Car écrire c'est brûler vif,
> mais c'est aussi renaître de ses cendres.[8]

Cendrars did research in the Méjanes library in Aix, and mixed erudition
and a rich past in four autobiographical novels which were published in
fairly quick succession when the war ended: *L'Homme foudroyé* (1945), *La
Main coupée* (1946), *Bourlinguer* (1948), and *Le Lotissement du ciel* (1949).
La Main coupée is dedicated to his sons Odilon and Rémy, but at the last
moment is prefaced by the discovery of Rémy's death. After spending the
war as a prisoner he had been killed in a training accident in North Africa,
on 26 November 1945.

The first three of these books were written at Aix, and *Le Lotissement du
ciel* was finished in 1949 at 'Saint-Segond,' in close-by Villefranche-sur-
mer. There, Cendrars also wrote about ninety pages of text for Robert
Doisneau's 130 photographs of *La Banlieue de Paris* (1949). It was a return
to the old haunts of 1913-14. The four long novels trace so many elaborate, world-searching concentric circles around an immobile, contemplating man, all four together resembling the Mayan wheel in *L'Homme*

foudroyé, alphabet, calendar, zodiac, ideogram all in one. *La Banlieue de Paris* draws yet other circles, around a new self in an old setting, and they predict, as if at their centre, a final Parisian series to come.

In a letter dated September 16, 1950 Cendrars wrote to Henry Miller:

> Après avoir pris un an de vacances (15 sept. '49 – 15 sept. '50), me marier, un peu voyager en Suisse, Luxembourg, Hollande, Angleterre, Belgique, soigner mes yeux, faire trois mois de radio, déménager, me réinstaller à Paris – je me suis remis au travail, hélas! ... Petit à petit je vais m'enfoncer dans cet univers qui contient tous les autres comme une goutte d'eau des myriades de microbes, la goutte d'encre qui coule de la plume ... C'est extraordinaire ... et je n'arrive pas à m'y habituer ni ... à y croire![9]

Earlier Cendrars has resisted returning to Paris, and when Guy Tosi, then literary director of Denoël, had asked him to come up for the promotion of *Bourlinguer* in 1948 he demurred (Cendrars had attended neither of the two earlier launchings):

> [Villefranche] lundi 15 [mars 1948]
> ... Il m'est impossible de venir actuellement à Paris: j'ai trop de travail; je ne veux pas risquer d'interrompre mon horaire de travail et la rédaction du 'Lotissement du ciel' dans laquelle je suis en plein; un séjour à Paris comprend trop de risques pour moi actuellement après tant d'années d'absence: affaires à liquider, gens à aller voir, 2-3 déménagements, etc. etc ... L'avant-dernière fois que j'étais venu à Paris, pour 3-4 jours, histoire de signer un contrat de cinéma, j'y suis resté 4 ans! – et je ne veux pas m'exposer aujourd'hui au même risque, surtout que les gens de cinéma me relancent une fois de plus et m'ont déjà envoyé ici 3 fois une voiture pour m'enlever! Et je tiens bon, car je dois écrire... [10]

Cendrars and Raymone came to Paris nevertheless, and succeeded in returning to Villefranche after a few days. But perhaps those few days in Paris sufficed for making other commitments. At any rate, in 1950 he moved into a venerable old house on rue Jean-Dolent, across the street from the walls of the Santé prison, a house Napoleon had given to his general Masséna and where, later, Renoir had painted a pretty tenant.

If his purely literary production seems slim for the ten years from 1950 to 1960 it is partly because he was so much occupied with another medium, the radio. Years earlier *Les Confessions de Dan Yack* had been 'written' by dictaphone, and in 1938 he had written the short story 'La Femme aimée' (in *La Vie dangereuse*), where all the action is centered about a radio set. The same year of 1938 had seen the production of *L'Or* on Radio-Luxembourg, adapted by Jacques-Henry Lévesque, and 'La Femme aimée' as well was produced in 1939. *L'Or* was broadcast again, in a new adaptation for La Radio-Diffusion française in 1946 and in 1951. *La Fin du monde* was produced for the same network in 1949, in an adaptation by Madeleine Milhaud to music by Darius Milhaud. The three months of radio Cendrars referred to in his letter to Henry Miller represent the interviews with Michel Manoll, called 'En Bourlinguant avec Blaise Cendrars,' recorded 14 to 25 April 1950 and heard from 15 October to 15 December 1950 in thirteen twenty-minute interviews. These were published as *Blaise Cendrars vous parle...* in 1952, and serve as one of the main sources of information about the author's life and times, though they can often be misunderstood if one fails to recognized Cendrars' impatience with Manoll's manner and general attitude toward 'Art' (the situation is much clearer on the tapes themselves, as one could tell from the samples in the television program on Cendrars produced on 29 January 1972 for Antenne 2).

In 1954, for the opening of Fernand Léger's exhibition 'Le Paysage dans l'œuvre de Léger' at the Gallery Louis Carré, 19 November to 31 December, Léger, Carré, and Cendrars walked through the show discussing the paintings into a tape-recorder. In his introduction to the published transcription Cendrars deplored the fact that the voices could not be heard, and repeated from his 1929 volume *Dan Yack:* 'Quel dommage que l'imprimerie ne puisse pas enregistrer la voix de Dan Yack et quel dommage que les pages d'un livre ne soient pas encore sonores. Mais cela viendra. Pauvres poètes, travaillons... '[11] But by the time the volume appeared, in 1956, Léger had died, in August of 1955, and Cendrars added a post-scriptum in which he emphasized no longer the disparity between voice and printed word, but rather how much closer to life the live tape had brought the words on the page:

> Un enregistrement au magnétophone n'est pas une oraison funèbre, ni un faire-part. C'est un document vivant. Le nôtre ne comporte pas même un message et ne s'adresse pas à la postérité. C'est une simple conversation entre amis, mais combien émouvante par sa simplicité et sa résonance, hélas! déjà posthume. On eût aimé entendre cette note humaine chez Vasari dans son précieux recueil des *Vies des meilleurs peintres du XVIe siècle*, pour nous, si souvent pontificants et dont seule l'érudition semble avoir fait école dans la critique d'art moderne... Mais les machines modernes

s'emparent de l'homme, de tout l'être, et grâce à elles, Léger est tout proche.[12]

Between these two texts we may see Cendrars' essential modernity. He was always interested in innovation for the renewal of human expression which could be found within it. 'Cette note humaine' was in fact one of the few constants in an ever-changing life, from that letter to Suter when he went to his first war, 'Réaction ou Révolution – l'homme doit devenir plus humain,' to this short farewell text to Léger. Cendrars was not much interested in the developments of science and technology for their application to 'progress,' but rather for the renewal of lyricism, as may be seen in the following *avertissement* to *Films sans images,* a collection of three original dramas written for radio, *Sarajevo, Gilles de Rais,* and *Le Divin Arétin:*

> Écrits pour la radio, ces 'films sans images' sont donc faits pour parler à l'oreille, aux millions d'oreilles qui se trouvent à l'autre bout d'un micro.
>
> Il s'ensuit qu'ils sont aux dimensions de la légende et non de l'histoire: on ferait fausse route en y cherchant autre chose que 'des voix.'
>
> N'empêche que la poésie de notre temps (et des autres) se nourrit aussi de légendes et de voix: on peut la découvrir en tournant le bouton d'un appareil de radio.
>
> Mettons qu'il s'agisse de poésie populaire, et tout le monde sera content, y compris les auteurs.[13]

Radio did not diminish legends at all; progress remained transparent, and if you were concerned with the human it would shine through brightly enough.

After 1949, the year of *Le Lotissement du ciel,* Cendrars wrote only two books. One is *Trop c'est trop* (1957), which assembles many short pieces written in the fifties, as well as a few earlier ones. *Trop c'est trop* represents a great deal of multifarious activity, if only one volume; the bibliography covers over two pages and runs from elephant hunting to Greta Garbo. The other book is a novel, a 'roman-roman' this time as he called it, entirely different from any that came before and an astoundingly vital, tumultuous performance for a man of sixty-nine, though he was himself younger than his heroine – his first heroine. *Emmène-moi au bout du monde!...,* published in 1956, is an improvisation on themes embodied in barely disguised Parisian celebrities (and many of the reviews were highly critical of Cendrars' ill treatment of these notables):

> (N.B. Le présent ouvrage est un roman à clef. J'espère bien que per-

sonne n'aura l'inélégance d'y appliquer les clefs, les clefs du Mensonge,
ni n'aura la pauvreté de s'y reconnaître en regardant le voisin par le trou
de la serrure. Par ailleurs, ce livre est écrit selon l'esthétique de quelqu'un
qui croit à ce qu'il raconte, comme Coleman Hawkins, saxo-ténor, et ses
musiciens du ciel, Billy Taylor, piano, Emmett Berry, trompette, Eddie
Bert, trombone, Jo Jones, batterie, et Milt Hinton, contrebasse, le 'Time-
less Jazz,' des as, racontent une belle histoire, *Lullaby of Birdland*, qui se
déroule dans l'espace, hors du temps et de l'époque. B.C.)[14]

Interviewed by Paul Guth in 1954 for *La Revue de Paris*, Cendrars discussed the projects of the moment. Most of *Emmène-moi* was by then
written, and a sequel, which we can see would have been about the
legionnaire of *Emmène-moi*, was planned. This second volume never appeared, and as with *Dan Yack* we may wonder if the import of *Emmène-moi*
would not have been much clearer with the help of its intended second
part. Four other projects were in the works: *L'Amour à l'américaine, La
Femme aimée, La Femme et le soldat,* and *La Carissima,* the life of Mary
Magdalene which Cendrars had already been researching at Aix-en-Provence.[15] None of these works is mentioned in the long listings of works
in progress Cendrars gave on half-title pages in *Emmène-moi, Trop c'est trop,*
or the very last work published during his life-time, *A L'Aventure* (1958),
excerpts from the four post-war novels rearranged in chronological order.
On the other hand, all three of these published books announced three
other forthcoming works: *L'Avocat du diable, La Vie parisienne,* and *Culs
terreux et grands petzouilles,* as well as what always appeared as the last item
in these bibliographies: 'sur le chantier/33 volumes,' which Cendrars
once explained: 'La liste des 33 volumes que j'annonce depuis plus de
quarante ans n'est ni exclusive, ni limitative, ni prohibitive, le nombre 33
étant le chiffre clé de l'activité, de la vie.'[16]

None of these many projects will see the light. In the summer of 1956,
the year of the perfect embodiment of the symbolic number 33, *Emmène-
moi au bout du monde!...,* Cendrars suffered his first attack of hemiplegia,
at the Château d'Ouchy (in the old town of Lausanne). Other attacks
followed. He and Raymone moved from the rue Jean-Dolent to a ground-
floor apartment on the rue José-Maria de Hérédia, from which Cendrars
could more easily reach the street; from there, one has a close view of the
Eiffel Tower, which played such an important part in Cendrars writing. In
1959 Malraux presented him with 'la cravate de commandateur de la
Légion d'Honneur,' and we may see a photograph of the two, Cendrars
terribly diminished, in *Le Magazine Littéraire.*[17] On 17 January 1961, he
was awarded the 'Grand Prix Littéraire de la Ville de Paris,' his very first
literary prize; but he was no longer well enough to attend. It will always

be difficult to imagine Cendrars receiving official recognition and ac-
colades. One of the stories of the legend recounts that he almost won the
'Prix de Monaco,' but that at the last minute a jury member opposed to
him circulated a photograph from Gance's *J'accuse* (apparently the one to
be found in Parrot's *Blaise Cendrars* published by Seghers), and the final
vote went against his uncouth face.

Blaise Cendrars died three days after his 'Grand Prix,' on 20 January
1961, at the age of 73. Nino Frank reports: 'Un de ses derniers mots est,
paraît-il: "construire."'[18] He was buried in the Batignolles cemetery. We
have a short meditation on Cendrars' end in the memoirs of Georges
Simenon. Earlier, in November of 1960, he had been asked for an article
on Cendrars for *Les Nouvelles Littéraires* when Blaise was supposed to get
the 'Prix National des Lettres':

> Comme pour le Grand Prix de la Ville de Paris, on attend, pour ce prix-là,
> que les gens soient mourants et on le leur remet presque toujours dans leur
> lit ... Cendrars, depuis plus de deux ans, est paralysé et, si je ne suis pas
> allé le voir c'est parce que, à ce qu'on m'a affirmé, il se sent humilié devant
> ses amis.

In July, a few days after the death of Hemingway, Simenon compared
the two authors:

> Parmi les stupidités que les journaux écrivent sur le suicide (probable)
> d'Hemingway, il en est une qui me frappe. Presque tous considèrent cette
> fin comme à peu près fatale. Étant donné le tempérament de l'écrivain, il
> devait réagir ainsi devant la menace d'une mort lente, d'un amoindrisse-
> ment progressif.
>
> Or, il y a moins d'un an mourait un autre écrivain, Blaise Cendrars, dont
> le caractère et la légende ressemblaient assez à ceux de Hemingway.
> Cendrars aussi a couru le monde à la recherche d'aventures, a chanté dans
> ses romans les joies brutales et la noblesse du mâle sans peur.
>
> Il a pourtant choisi la solution contraire. Loin de se suicider, il a vécu
> plusieurs années malade, paralysé, luttant contre la maladie avec acharne-
> ment et on dit (?) qu'il refusait tous les médicaments qui auraient apaisé
> ses souffrances, afin de rester lucide malgré tout. Je le crois. Cela lui
> ressemble. Car, lui, je l'ai bien connu.
>
> Aujourd'hui, je pense beaucoup à ces deux hommes aux vies parallèles
> et aux fins différentes.[19]

Hemingway, it is now assumed, failed to live up to the legend he had
fashioned for himself. Cendrars, on the other hand, may seem more of a

paradox, since he insisted upon living on doggedly through his incapacity. Obviously he could distinguish between himself being a legend, and the necessary mythical qualities of poetry and fiction. Whatever adventures were actually his own, he knew where truth and relevance lie in those and in the others. Hemingway wrote in *A Moveable Feast:*

> ... the only poet I ever saw [at the Closerie des Lilas café] was Blaise Cendrars, with his broken boxer's face and his pinned-up empty sleeve, rolling a cigarette with his one good hand. He was a good companion until he drank too much and, at that time, when he was lying, he was more interesting than many men telling a story truly.[20]

For his epitaph Cendrars put himself in a whale. Was it a lie? It's not what you believe, but how you believe it:

> Là-bas gît
> Blaise Cendrars
> Par latitude zéro
Deux ou trois dixièmes sud
Une, deux, trois douzaines de degrés
> Longitude ouest
Dans le ventre d'un cachalot
Dans un grand cuveau d'indigo.[21]

PART TWO
In place of fictions

6   Homer of the Transsiberian

Salut au Monde!   WALT WHITMAN

It is ironic that the first appreciable treatment of *Les Pâques à New York* is given by Professor Durry in her first volume on *Alcools,* for she is mainly concerned with an analysis of 'Zone.'[1] Yet *Les Pâques* is a beautiful and anguished modern religious poem. Malraux wrote in 1920 that it was 'd'une beauté douloureuse et grave (parfois rimbaldienne)'[2]; in 1919 Charles-Henri Hirsch, the important reviewer for the *Mercure* wrote:

> C'est une suite de dix-sept pièces d'une couleur violente et d'un sens plein qui va sans défaillance. Voilà un des efforts les plus sérieux, une des réalisations poétiques les plus voisines du parfait, que l'on doive à un poète depuis longtemps.[3]

And in 1946 Géo-Charles, in a long article reviewing all of Cendrars' work up to that date, could write: '*Les Pâques à New York* sont un pur chef-d'œuvre. Je les tiens pour un des plus grands et des plus émouvants poèmes de notre littérature.'[4] Professor Durry herself does not underestimate the strengths of the poem and clearly states that her preference for 'Zone' is a personal one. The main difference she finds between the two is a very important one – that 'Zone' is basically a poem of *'entremêlement,'* whereas *Les Pâques* is *'centré.'* She speaks of the latter as

> ... cette composition de *Pâques,* à la fois centrée, et quoiqu'on ait dit, d'une très forte continuité. Tout concourt, la régularité du battement litanique; la répétition insistante de certains vers ou débuts de vers; la figuration de la Face sans cesse re-surgissante ...[5]

This analysis of the poem's focus is particularly interesting since *entremêle-ment* could be used to describe almost all of Cendrars' production, from short stories to full-length novels. Actually, Cendrars always deals with a unified core of concerns or themes, and interweaving, as we might translate Mme Durry's word, is a necessary technique for searching out an elusive and complex centre. In the case of this poem something of the reverse seems to obtain, for the diverse images appear to be flung away from the central image of Christ, as if he can no longer control them. One may be reminded of Yeats' 'Second Coming,' in which the falconer has lost dominion in the 'widening gyre'; however, the comparison quickly underlines this main distinction, that Yeats was more concerned with his renovated mythology.

The centre of *Les Pâques* is the difficulty of resurrecting the faith we already had. While it is Easter, the celebration of the resurrection of Christ, the modern world, New York, goes about its crass and deepeningly oppressive business. Christ fails to rise, and in New York gather the poor and the rejected of the world who had hoped for salvation in this New World but find only that,

> Seigneur, la Banque illuminée est comme un coffre-fort,
> Où s'est coagulé le Sang de votre mort.
>
> [ll. 119-20][6]

Twelve years before his novel *L'Or,* Cendrars writes of cupidity undermining faith and sullying man, sun, and God:

> Une foule enfiévrée par les sueurs de l'or
> Se bouscule et s'engouffre dans de longs corridors.
>
> Trouble, dans le fouillis empanaché des toits,
> Le soleil, c'est votre Face souillée par les crachats.
>
> [ll. 191-4]

The difficulty of faith is not the result of modern life exclusively, for although the banks may be bigger and the buildings more numerous and higher, essentially nothing is changed:

> Seigneur, rien n'a changé depuis que vous n'êtes plus Roi.
> Le Mal s'est fait une béquille de votre croix.
>
> [ll. 129-30]

> Ceux que vous aviez chassés du temple avec votre fouet,

Flagellent les passants d'une poignée de méfaits

[ll. 115-16]

There is no especial grudge against the modern world, and the poem is more concerned with the plight of the poor, which has no doubt never been much different; but New York is particularly saddening to the poet because it brings together many different peoples, by implication all people. They have come to the city of money for salvation, and Christ along with the poet may be as lost as any of them. About fifty years later Allen Ginsberg would write about this city in a similar manner in *Howl:* 'Moloch whose skyscrapers stand in the long streets like endless Jehovahs!' and

They broke their backs lifting Moloch to Heaven! Pavements, trees, radios, tons! lifting the city to Heaven which exists and is everywhere about us!

New York for both poets amply illustrated the deprivation and degradation of the suppliants to Mammon. Lines 60 to 110 of *Les Pâques* (of a total of 205) are four pleas to Christ to pity immigrants (Greeks, Spaniards, Russians, Bulgarians, Persians, Mongolians), Jewish refugees, prostitutes, and thieves. Some of these have other gods, some none at all, but Cendrars repeats for each, 'Seigneur, ayez pitié ... ' The lives of these people are tragically impoverished, and in one case the poet asks Christ to give a thief money for a rope with which to hang himself. Part of the anguish the poet feels is that he cannot love and give of himself as Christ did, though he tries. To the thief he gives opium, 'pour qu'il aille plus vite en paradis' (l. 104), but with the prostitutes he fails:

Seigneur, quand une de ces femmes me parle, je défaille.

Je voudrais être Vous pour aimer les prostitutées.
Seigneur, ayez pitié des prostitutées.

[ll. 94-6]

There is not enough of Christ for all the stricken of New York, nor is there strength enough in the poet to love on the scale he aspires to. As the poem advances the Passion of Christ is re-enacted, but also the parallel passion of the poet, who devines a Christ and brother in the next room at the outset and who finds himself in the end forsaken and as if buried in his own room. He and Christ are one, his failure to love is the failure

of Christ. Each time the poet addresses Christ he speaks to himself in a
dialogue with his conscience.

The epigraph to the poem provides the central meaning (this is invariably the case with Cendrars, although often the epigraph seems to bear no
relation to the poem at all). Cendrars quotes the Gallic Latin poet Saint
Fortunatus, from Remy de Gourmont's *Latin mystique,* in a prayer to the
cross exhorting it to bend its 'branches' and relax its pressure on the body
of the Saviour. This inflexible cross in the poem is the city: 'N'écartèle pas
si rudement les membres du Roi supérieur ... ' writes Fortunatus; in *Les
Pâques* the landscape is already bloodied by Christ's martyrdom:

> Je descends à grands pas vers le bas de la ville,
> Le dos voûté, le coeur ridé, l'esprit fébrile,
>
> Votre flanc grand-ouvert est comme un grand soleil
> Et vos mains tout autour palpitent d'étincelles.
>
> Les vitres des maisons sont toutes pleines de sang
>
> [ll. 29-33]

As faith is torn asunder by the vast profusion of misery and suffering, the
wandering poet gives many different images of Christ's Passion – in a
German canticle, in a church in Siena, in intaglio in a precious stone – and
finally he imagines the Chinese might have crucified Him. This is a cruel
and degrading death in which, as the reader attempts to visualize Christ
among Chinamen, faith appears a stranger, alien, incomprehensible, and
punished as only a false prophet is punished. So this saviour is not strong
enough for the world, and the point is emphasized by following the
passage of the Chinese crucifixion with a nostalgic evocation of Catholic
traditions in language reminiscent of Villon's famous *ubi sunt* ballad:

> Je pense aux cloches tues: – où sont les cloches anciennes?
> Où sont les litanies et les douces antiennes?
>
> Où sont les longs offices et où les beaux cantiques?
> Où sont les liturgies et les musiques?
>
> [ll. 159-62]

To have faith in these older, familiar terms is not sufficient for a seemingly
vaster, more diverse and tumultuous world, and the poem is tense with

the dismemberment of Christ, a unifying image, rent among the deluded pleadings of lost souls from the world over.

As I have said, it is such dispersed imagery which will dominate Cendrars' poetic production and for which he is best known; in this poem, however, faith, in the image and the treatment of the image of Christ, manages to control dispersal. This is not always obvious in the statements of the poem; it is true that Christ as saviour seems to have failed, that no one in the poem feels saved, the poet first and last of all. Nevertheless, the poet's despair has the quality of a believer's, the quality of Job's doubt. The poem as a whole is a litany and throughout is medieval in tone, at least to modern ears, from the epigraph to the apparent awkwardness, the repetitions and the simple bluntness of many lines and expressions:

> Je suis triste et malade. Peut-être à cause de Vous,
> Peut-être à cause d'un autre. Peut-être à cause de Vous.
>
> [ll. 67-8]

> Seigneur, faites-leur l'aumône de gros sous ici-bas.
>
> [l. 110]

> Ainsi, Seigneur, vous auriez souffert toute l'infamie,
> Car il n'y a pas de plus cruelle posture.
>
> [ll. 151-2]

It is this bare, unassuming style which, almost alone, holds the cross together. The verse is flatter, more prosaic than the traditional and always sophisticated alexandrine of most French poetry hitherto, but it is different as well from the liberated *verset* of Claudel's *Odes* of a few years before, which is always biblical and exalted in tone. This is where Cendrars and Claudel, after both being influenced by Whitman, part company. *Les Pâques* has little sound of the Church in its prayer, no exaltation, no polish at all it seems. All of its religious tone is contained in the mundane events and objects of daily, despairing life, and much of the beauty of the poem comes from finding precious the demeaned and factitious aspects of the city:

> A la chanteuse au chapeau de paille avec des roses de papier;
> Je sais que ce sont eux qui chantent durant l'éternité.
>
> [ll. 107 – 8]

So often in the poem, it is not Christ who is failing but rather his familiar

images; he is now invisible, perhaps next to one, but at any rate not the
elaborate image handed down by centuries which have adorned and an-
notated him into transubstantiated irrelevance:

> Dans la chambre à côté, un être triste et muet

> Attend derrière la porte, attend que je l'appelle!
> C'est Vous, c'est Dieu, c'est moi, – c'est l'Éternel.

[ll. 18-20]

> Je connais tous les Christs qui pendent dans les musées:
> Mais Vous marchez, Seigneur, ce soir à mes côtés.

[ll. 27-8]

Thus the longest single description of Christ is that as seen, in the poet's
imagination, by the Chinese, who tear out his tongue and eyes and throw
the corpse to the pigs. It is a vision consistent with medieval prints of
people suffering in hell, or on their death beds while angels and devils
fight over their souls. Ugliness is not transcended, and the transubstantia-
tion of Christ's blood is not an abstraction, but a vulgar reality:

> Votre sang recueilli, elles ne l'ont jamais bu.
> Elles ont du rouge aux lèvres et des dentelles au cul.

[ll. 37-9]

   The stripped, innocent style, mixing naïve allegory and common obser-
vations, permits Cendrars to use the simplest aspects of life in the filthy,
teeming streets and yet relate them to some sort of faith. He eludes the
language of propriety, which by transcending or modifying the common-
place also misplaces the holy. It would be a tribal prayer, or ritual, if it
were not for the modern, or New York, fact. The multifarious population
provides images which, each in its own culture, would be ordinary but
which for the reader are exotic, baroque, and grotesque. These images
mix in a depravity more bewildering than any single act or apparition,
examined in depth, could convey. The effect is not of evil, but of confusion, which is itself the depravity. The logic of statements can be halting,
as if shaken:

> Je voudrais être Vous pour aimer les prostituées
> Seigneur, ayez pitié des prostituées.

[ll. 94-6]

Here, Christ is first assumed to love all, he is an absolute measure of love; but in the second line one is no longer sure. The repetition in lieu of a rhyme emphasizes the inability to move on, the obligation of trying again with the same obstacle which, if it cannot be loved – even by God! – will have to settle for pity.

The shadows cast upon the central symbol of the poem could not be better exemplified than by the very last line (l. 205), which stands alone, preceded by 102 couplets: 'Je ne pense plus à Vous. Je ne pense plus à Vous.' This line of course implies its own contradiction; repeated, protesting, it is also cut short as if our sense of the many preceding couplets should provide one more line of utter silence. The end seems to state the necessity for the poet to believe if he is to think about faith at all, especially if he doubts; as Pascal wrote, 'Douter de Dieu, c'est y croire.' In *Les Pâques à New York* the poet is saddened, then anguished at the failure of an older faith within himself, a faith overcome by a confusion of not getting and not spending; and yet he seems condemned to believe, he has no choice. At the end he is as if dead, alone in his tomb-like room, cold, feverish, with a Christ who refuses to die within him. That undying Christ survives in the small gestures of calls to pity witnessed during this long night in the city of horrors. The morning after Easter finds what sort of resurrected man? An almost destroyed one, unrecognizable even to himself, perhaps dying, one who, we may extrapolate from the later work of Cendrars, would only sustain faith within a context of despair, which would have to be its necessary condition. It is as if the only sign that Christ still lives is the mere need of him, the fact that the poet lives. The manner in which the poet is Christ – a familiar idea, to be sure – is that the only loving in the poem, along with the failure to love, is the emotion of the poet's voice. The poet must embrace the world at large, he demands it of himself and so far fails, for the most part. But the voice contains the desire, and the curiosity of a lover, a hungering interest in what people are doing and what they are rather than a narcissistic obsession with his own despair. The two despairs battle silently in 'Je ne pense plus à Vous'; but if to doubt is to believe Narcissus must lose.

Prose du transsibérien et de la petite Jehanne de France is a poem concerned with travelling through the modern, this time physically, devastated world and searching out one's frail identity in terms of that disintegrating world. Since it is Cendrars' most famous and most reprinted poem it has been discussed in many places, from dissertations to school anthologies. Walter Everett Albert, in an unpublished dissertation, examines much of the poem's imagery and formal structure in detail, but along with most of the other commentators he says nothing of the extraordinary appearance of the poem when it was first published.[7]

As Michel Hoog, curator at the Musée d'art moderne in Paris, indicated in an article for *La Revue du Louvre*, Sonia Delaunay and Cendrars went further in *Prose* than any of their contemporaries, the only previous experiment of comparable note being Mallarmé's *Un Coup de dés.*[8] The poem itself is printed in more than ten type faces and sizes, and in different colours as well, on a single sheet two metres long. A few feet of this six-and-a-half foot poem of 445 lines are reproduced on pages 99-101 to give an idea of the variety, the extreme freedom of the verse, and the use of type to reiterate or play variations on themes.[9] This long poem, of which there were to be 150 copies, so that the whole edition if stood on end would equal the height of the Eiffel Tower, takes up the right-hand side of the sheet; on the left is an abstract painting by Sonia Delaunay of the same length and width as the printed poem.[10] At the very bottom of this 'synchrome' painting a small Eiffel Tower is recognizable. Also, much of the text side is coloured. The large sheet was folded once across and then 'en accordéon,' like a pleated map; it then appeared as an ordinary paperback pamphlet with a map of Russia on the cover. Of this production Cendrars wrote:

> Le simultanisme de ce livre est dans sa représentation simultanée et non illustrative. Les contrastes simultanés des couleurs et le texte forment des profondeurs et des mouvements qui sont l'inspiration nouvelle.[11]

Mme Delaunay's painting is definitely meant not to be an illustration. The poem and painting are one, and not a pictorial collage, since the words are of equal importance and must be read. In an article attacking Henri-Martin Barzun's claims to being the first simultaneist Apollinaire wrote:

> Blaise Cendrars et Madame Delaunay-Terk ont fait une première tentative de simultanéité écrite où contrastes de couleurs habituaient l'œil à lire d'un seul regard l'ensemble d'un poème, comme un chef d'orchestre lit d'un seul coup les notes superposées dans la partition, comme on voit d'un seul coup les éléments plastiques et imprimés d'une affiche.[12]

It is clear that the important word here is *contrastes.* The two concepts of contrast and invention, sometimes joined, are probably the most important in Cendrars' work. In a short article written after the war on Robert Delaunay and 'le contraste simultané' in his work Cendrars wrote:

> Le contraste n'est pas un noir et blanc, un contraire, une dissemblance.

Le ciel est comme la tente déchirée d'un cirque pauvre dans un petit village de pêcheurs
En Flandres
Le soleil est un fumeux quinquet
Et tout au haut d'un trapèze une femme fait la lune.
La clarinette le piston une flûte aigre et un mauvais tambour
Et voici mon berceau
Mon berceau
Il était toujours près du piano quand ma mère comme Madame Bovary jouait les sonates de Beethoven
J'ai passé mon enfance dans les jardins suspendus de Babylone
Et l'école buissonnière, dans les gares devant les trains en partance
Maintenant, j'ai fait courir tous les trains derrière moi

Bâle-Toumbouctou
J'ai aussi joué aux courses à Auteuil et à Longchamp
Paris-New-York
Maintenant, j'ai fait courir tous les trains tout le long de ma vie
Madrid-Stockholm
Et j'ai perdu tous mes paris

Il n'y a plus que la **Patagonie**, la Patagonie, qui convienne à mon immense tristesse, la **PATAGONIE** et un voyage dans les mers du Sud
JE SUIS EN ROUTE
J'AI TOUJOURS ÉTÉ EN ROUTE
JE SUIS EN ROUTE AVEC LA PETITE JEHANNE DE FRANCE
LE TRAIN FAIT UN SAUT PÉRILLEUX ET RETOMBE SUR TOUTES SES ROUES
LE TRAIN RETOMBE SUR SES ROUES
LE TRAIN RETOMBE TOUJOURS SUR TOUTES SES ROUES

« Blaise, dis, sommes-nous bien loin de Montmartre? »
Nous sommes loin, Jeanne, tu roules depuis sept jours
Tu es loin de Montmartre de la Butte qui t'a nourrie du Sacré-Cœur contre lequel tu t'es blottie
Paris a disparu et son énorme flambée
Il n'y a plus que les cendres continues
La pluie qui tombe
La tourbe qui se gonfle
La Sibérie qui tourne
Les lourdes nappes de neige qui remontent
Et le grelot de la folie qui grelotte comme un dernier désir dans l'air bleu
Le train palpite au cœur des horizons plombés
Et ton chagrin ricane...

« Dis, Blaise, sommes-nous bien loin de Montmartre? »
Les inquiétudes
Oublie les inquiétudes
Toutes les gares lézardées obliques sur la route
Les fils téléphoniques auxquels elles pendent
Les poteaux grimaçants qui gesticulent et les étranglent
Le monde s'étire s'allonge et se retire comme un harmonica qu'une main sadique tourmente
Dans les déchirures du ciel les locomotives en furie
S'enfuient
Et dans les trous

Les roues vertigineuses les bouches les voix
Et les chiens du malheur qui aboient à nos trousses
Les démons sont déchaînés
Ferrailles
Tout est un faux accord
Le *broun-roun-roun* des roues
Chocs
Rebondissements
Nous sommes un orage sous le crâne d'un sourd...
« Dis, Blaise, sommes-nous bien loin de Montmartre? »

ABOVE AND OVERLEAF An extract (lines 137-304) from the page proofs of the original 1913 edition of *La Prose du transsibérien* corrected by the author
Photo Bibliothèque nationale

Mais oui, tu m'énerves, tu le sais bien, nous sommes bien loin
La folie surchauffée beugle dans la locomotive
La peste le choléra se lèvent comme des braises ardentes sur notre route
Nous disparaissons dans la guerre en plein dans un tunnel
La faim, la putain, se cramponne aux nuages en débandade
Et fiente des batailles en tas puants de morts
Fais comme elle, fais ton métier...

« Dis, Blaise, sommes-nous bien loin de Montmartre ? »

Oui, nous le sommes, nous le sommes
Tous les boues émissaires ont crevé dans ce désert
Entends les mauvaises cloches de ce troupeau galeux
Tomsk Tchéliabinsk Kainsk Obi Taïchet Verkne-Oudinsk Kourgane Samara Penza Touloune
La mort en Mandchourie
Est notre débarcadère est notre dernier repaire
Ce voyage est terrible
Hier matin
Ivan Oulitch avait les cheveux blancs
Et Kolia Nicolaï Ivanovitch se ronge les doigts depuis 15 jours...
Fais comme elles la Mort la Famine fais ton métier
Ça coûte cent sous en transsibérien ça coûte cent roubles
Enfièvre les banquettes et rougeoie sous la table
Le diable est au piano
Ses doigts noueux excitent toutes les femmes
La Nature
Les Gouges
Fais ton métier
Jusqu'à Kharbine...

Vers à mettre j'ai

en gras

ils (sont)

« Dis, Blaise, sommes-nous bien loin de Montmartre ? »
Non mais... fiche-moi la paix... laisse-moi tranquille
Tu as les hanches angulaires
Ton ventre est aigre et tu as la chaude-pisse

C'est tout ce que Paris a mis dans ton giron
C'est aussi un peu d'âme... car tu es malheureuse
J'ai pitié j'ai pitié viens vers moi sur mon cœur
Les roues sont les moulins à vent du pays de Cocagne
Et les moulins à vent sont les béquilles qu'un mendiant fait tournoyer
Nous sommes les culs-de-jatte de l'espace
Nous roulons sur nos quatre plaies
On nous a rogné les ailes
Les ailes de nos sept péchés
Et tous les trains sont les bilboquets du diable
Basse-cour
Le monde moderne
La vitesse n'y peut mais
Le monde moderne
Les lointains sont par trop loin
Et au bout du voyage c'est terrible d'être un homme et une femme *avec*

« BLAISE, DIS, SOMMES-NOUS BIEN LOIN DE MONTMARTRE ? »

J'ai pitié j'ai pitié viens vers moi je vais te conter une histoire
Viens dans mon lit
Viens sur mon cœur
Je vais te conter une histoire...

Oh viens ! viens !

Aux Fidji règne l'éternel printemps
La paresse

L'amour pâme les couples dans l'herbe haute et la chaude syphilis rôde sous les bananiers

Viens dans les îles perdues du Pacifique !
Elles ont nom du Phénix, des Marquises
Bornéo et Java
Et Célèbes à la forme d'un chat
Nous ne pouvons pas aller au Japon
Viens au Mexique !
Sur les hauts plateaux les tulipiers fleurissent
Les lianes tentaculaires sont la chevelure du soleil
On dirait la palette et les pinceaux d'un peintre
Des couleurs étourdissantes comme des gongs,
Rousseau y a été
Il y a ébloui sa vie.
C'est le pays des oiseaux
L'oiseau du paradis l'oiseau-lyre
Le toucan l'oiseau moqueur
Et le colibri niche au cœur des lys noirs

Viens !
Nous nous aimerons dans les ruines majestueuses d'un temple aztèque
Tu seras mon idole
Une idole bariolée enfantine un peu laide et bizarrement étrange
Oh viens !

Si tu veux nous irons en aéroplane et nous survolerons le pays des mille lacs,
Les nuits y sont démesurément longues
L'ancêtre préhistorique aura peur de mon moteur
J'atterrirai
Et je construirai un hangar pour mon avion avec les os fossiles de mammouth
Le feu primitif réchauffera notre pauvre amour
Le Samowar
Et nous nous aimerons bien bourgeoisement près du pôle
Oh viens !

Jeanne JEANNETTE Ninette nini ninon nichon
Mimi mamour ma poupoule mon Pérou
Dada dindan
Carotte ma crotte
Chouchou p'tit-cœur
Cocotte
Chérie p'tite-chèvre
Mon p'tit-péché mignon
Concon
Coucou
Elle dort.

Elle dort
Et de toutes les heures du monde elle n'en a pas gobé une seule
Tous les visages entrevus dans les gares
Toutes les horloges
L'heure de Paris l'heure de Berlin l'heure de Saint-Pétersbourg et l'heure de toutes les gares

Et à Oufa, le visage ensanglanté du canonnier
Et le cadran bêtement lumineux de Grodno
Et l'avance perpétuelle du train
Tous les matins on met les montres à l'heure
Le train avance et le soleil retarde
Rien n'y fait, j'entends les cloches sonores
Le gros bourdon de Notre-Dame
La cloche aigrelette du Louvre qui sonna la Barthélemy
Les carillons rouillés de Bruge-la-Morte
Les sonneries électriques de la bibliothèque de New-York

Le contraste est une ressemblance. On voyage pour connaître, reconnaître les hommes, les choses, les animaux. Pour vivre avec. On s'en approche, on ne s'en éloigne pas. C'est dans ce que les hommes ont de plus commun qu'ils différencient le plus. Les deux sexes font contraste. Le contraste est amour. C'est par contraste que les astres et les cœurs gravitent. C'est le contraste qui fait leur profondeur. Le contraste est profondeur. Forme.[13]

The real form of the poem then is the poem and the painting together, and the depth of their movement arises from the contrasting juxtaposition. We note in this connection the necessity for the painting to be abstract, so that it have no narrative, no story to compete with the epic of the text. It is, in fact, one of the very earliest abstract paintings on record. We cannot 'follow' the painting from top to bottom as we read down the page of text; yet there is a movement imposed upon the eye, a sequence which perhaps we should say the words *try* to dictate. Verbal linearity contrasts with paint strokes, and the contrast increases the appearance of movement on the painted part of the 'poem.' The coloured designs then bathe the lines as they are read, a background which is not in the back at all but all over, a parallel foreground out of which the words emerge as if spoken. Then, of course, the lines of print are themselves visual forms, constantly varied; for example the reader might examine the lines I have reproduced and note the different type faces which answer, as it were, the reiterated question, 'Dis, Blaise, sommes-nous bien loin de Montmartre?' which comes back five times and itself is in a different typeface each time. Each contrast underlines the emotion of the poet as he tries to console 'la petite Jehanne,' then is exasperated by her, later pities her, and finally, after line 280, puts her to sleep. There is then in this poem contrast between painting and words, and between words in their visual forms. Contrast, as Cendrars explains it, is the artist's way to movement and depth, since it obliges different forms to come together, forces gravitation, which is Cendrars' unity, a sort of multiple and synchronic dialectic –'le contraste simultané.'

Lyrical though it is, the work is called a *Prose.*[14] Certainly the word may refer to some extent to the prosaic rhythms of the poem, but Cendrars had something more precise in mind which he explained in a letter dated 23 December 1913 to a friend who was to give a lecture on the poem: 'Pour le mot Prose: je l'ai employé dans le Transsibérien dans le sense bas-latin de "prosa," "dictu." Poème me semblait trop prétentieux, trop fermé. Prose est plus ouvert, populaire.'[15] Frank Budgen reported hearing Cendrars read the poem: 'He intoned it in the manner of a psalm pointed as in the Anglican liturgy.' Rilke's opinion was then sought, and Budgen reports he called it ' "Die höhere Bänkelsängerei," which might be roughly translated "superior street corner balladry." '[16]

The form was certainly open. The poem exhibits the freest of verse; some lines contain only one word, while many run the full length of a wide page which provides room to leave each line intact and which, in this respect, reminds one of Whitman's first edition of *Leaves of Grass* (very few lines are longer than the width of the page; line 154 is the only one in the third of the poem reproduced here.) The right margin is often used to establish the position of lines, so that order comes from both sides of the page. At a distance the typography gives the impression of great inter-weaving and even confusion, but every detail is carefully placed, position playing an important role in meaning (the galley corrections are revealing in this respect). For example, 'viens' within line 241 becomes the call starting lines 242 and 243, successively more intimate, then acquires a new meaning in 'Oh viens! viens' in the right margin, the call to a special dream world (and the story of 'je vais te conter une histoire'); then the terms reversed 'Viens! ... Oh viens!' and again 'Oh viens!' (ll. 265, 269, and 278) at the left margin frame an idyllic love. By lines 289-90 the girl has succumbed to the story: 'Elle dort' appears once in the middle of the page, then again as the beginning of a new section at the left margin. The plea 'viens dans mon lit / ... / Je vais te conter une histoire' has worked, and the poet is rid of the obsessive question 'Blaise, dis, sommes-nous bien loin de Montmartre?'

The major contrast within the poem's language is indicated in the long, explicit title – the train and Jehanne. The train represents the terrible flight of a boy of sixteen who wants so much of the world and life that he is on the verge of breaking everything about him:

> Et je n'avais pas assez des sept gares et des mille et trois tours
> Car mon adolescence était alors si ardente et si folle
>
> [ll. 5-6]

> Et j'aurais voulu broyer tous les os
> Et arracher toutes les langues
>
> [ll. 33-4]

> Je pressentais la venue du grand Christ rouge de la révolution russe
> Et le soleil était une mauvaise plaie
> Qui s'ouvrait comme un brasier.
>
> [ll. 36-8]

The Transsiberian is a modern demon spanning a world of war and revolution and the measure of the demon in the boy. This Christ, obviously, is not the one of *Les Pâques,* but a vengeful and apocalyptic god. The same imagery used to describe the bloody dismemberment of Christ by New York is now used to embody actions the young narrator wishes to perpetrate, or which he embraces in the shape of coming cataclysms. The poem is mostly about a youth much younger than the poet of *Les Pâques,* but it ends when he is older, in a Montmartre café. The story of the youth is told in the past tense, starting in Moscow as he boards the Transsiberian:

> En ce temps-là j'étais en mon adolescence
> J'avais à peine seize ans et je ne me souvenais déjà plus de mon enfance
> [ll. 1-2]

> Or, un vendredi matin, ce fut enfin mon tour
> [l. 65]

The train ride of a few weeks compresses years of ageing. The poem ends in the present, Paris looming abruptly without explanation as if it were the last stop of the train as it travelled eastward:

> JE DÉBARQUAI A KHARBINE COMME ON VENAIT DE METTRE LE FEU
> AUX BUREAUX DE LA CROIX-ROUGE
> Ô PARIS
> Grand foyer chaleureux avec les tisons entrecroisés de tes rues et vieilles
> maisons qui se penchent au-dessus et se réchauffent
> Comme des aïeules
> [ll. 410-13]

So along with a train ride through Russia there is a trip through time from a faraway adolescence in Moscow to manhood in Paris.

The train ride itself is the most extraordinary apocalyptic vision, 'véritable *Train saoul* après le *Bateau ivre,'* wrote Jean Cocteau,[17] a world of social and moral catastrophe as Rimbaud or Lautréamont might have seen it, far more devastating, far more *real* one might say, than the Futurists' theories had envisaged and certainly a direct predecessor of Dada's will to destroy, as Victor Klemperer has described the poem.[18] Lines 172-219 describe the long, oppressive, finally hysterical voyage through the Siberian – and interior – wasteland onward to the Russian front lines in 1904. Lines 354-410 are more brutal, for they describe the Russian debacle. Throughout, the train is the only sufficient vehicle for a man's quest – 'J'ai toujours été en route' (l. 156) – and although it is a terrible demon – 'tous les trains sont les bilboquets du diable' (l. 233) – the machine, a virtuoso we made to surpass ourselves, remains the acrobat who will surmount all obstacles:

> Le train fait un saut périlleux et retombe sur toutes ses roues
> Le train retombe sur ses roues
> Le train retombe toujours sur toutes ses roues
>
> [ll. 158-60]

And it is for this reason that one must discover, understand and even come to love somehow this machine, for it represents ourselves, the contemporary manifestation of our strivings and thus our faith:

> Et je reconnais tous les trains au bruit qu'ils font
> Les trains d'Europe sont à quatre temps tandis que ceux d'Asie sont à cinq
>   ou sept temps
> D'autres vont en sourdine sont des berceuses
>
> [ll. 400-2]

> J'ai déchiffré tous les textes confus des roues et j'ai rassemblé les éléments
>   épars d'une violente beauté
> Que je possède
> Et qui me force
>
> [ll. 404-6]

> La Compagnie Internationale des Wagons-Lits et des Grands Express
>   Européens m'a envoyé son prospectus
> C'est la plus belle église du monde.
>
> [ll. 423-4]

It is Cendrars' successful use of the train as a modern but viable objective correlative for feeling in the poem that makes him the modern poet earlier theorists such as Beauduin, Guilbeaux, Marinetti, and Barzun tried, but failed, to become. They preached the necessity of being sensitive to the modern, changed, and changing world, as Whitman had been, but they were in fact not sensitive. Symbolism had left too strong an influence and the generation before Cendrars remained poets who could not function without proven correspondences. As we shall see, Cendrars was the poet of the train, of the Eiffel Tower, of publicity, cars, phonographs, newspapers, even dime-novels; he is the poet of these objects not because they were new and novel, but because they were really there, with him and part of his condition. In Valery Larbaud the train had been exotic and adventurous, the latest style of *dépaysement.* Yet there is something serious functioning even in fashion. In Cendrars the Transsiberian is also a new adventure, but most importantly it is a new symbol. Quixote's road of life would now be too leisurely, Huck Finn's river too bucolic, despite the violence. Cendrars' 'road of life' was the one the new century had made for itself, quite unselfconsciously, and was thus the natural means of reaching man in this century. Jacques-Henry Lévesque wrote:

> Intégrer le monde moderne dans la poésie, en parler tout naturellement parce qu'il existe, et parce que c'est en plein cœur de ce monde que nous vivons, et qu'on ne peut cesser de le voir et en faire abstraction que par l'acte tout arbitraire d'un esprit timoré qui ne veut ou ne peut pas assumer le réel, c'était évidemment ce qu'il fallait faire pour que les hommes du XXe siècle puissent trouver une poésie à leur mesure, et, à travers cette poésie, se sentent en contact avec le fonds permanent de l'homme.[19]

Or, as Paul Ginestier has written: 'If Whitman boasted of being 'the poet of the locomotive,' it is because during his time that machine was the symbol of the greatest, the most dynamic force possible.'[20] For Whitman and Cendrars the machine was, in itself, poetic. If, for example, a man had little choice but to find himself on a train (or in a car, or surrounded by advertisements), then only the view from the train afforded a true vision of the constraints and freedoms of his condition.

It is the modern world, 'Que je posséde / Et qui me force,' which itself, without preconceived codes, creates the very special 'prose' of Cendrars' poem, the contrasts, the juxtapositions, the interweaving required to convey this new vision. The seven-foot poem and parallel colours, the extravagant typography, the brutal images and descriptions all contrive to express the world as seen from the express, body and soul uprooted and hurled singlemindedly over foreign and fearsome landscapes:

> Entends les sonnailles de ce troupeau galeux Tomsk
> Tchéliabinsk Kainsk Obi Taïchet Verkné Oudinsk Kourgane Samara
>   Pensa-Touloune
> La mort en Mandchourie
> Est notre débarcadère est notre dernier repaire

[ll. 203-5]

In contrast to that vast new world, representing what M. Lévesque called above 'le fonds permanent de l'homme' which the poet is always striving to reach, stands 'la petite Jehanne de France.' Jehanne carries all the human misery of New York in *Les Pâques*, the eternal misery of flesh and soul which in the earlier poem the poet did not have the strength to face and for which he implored 'Seigneur, ayez pitié ... ' Cendrars has put her on the train, and the youth cannot escape her. Christ's imputed pity is now the poet's, as he comforts the fragile girl who knows nothing but the obsessive cry of returning home:

> 'Dis, Blaise, sommes-nous bien loin de Montmartre?'
> J'ai pitié j'ai pitié viens vers moi je vais te conter une histoire
>
> [ll. 240-1]

But his concern for her runs the gamut, from lyric pity to impatience to cruelty. Lines 114-33, in tall frail capital letters, form a twelve-line poem of great delicacy – 'Elle est toute nue, n'a pas de corps – elle est trop pauvre' (l. 129). Lines 130 to 133, with the repetition of *fleur,* the assonant *fleur, seul, cœur,* the internal rhymes *fluette, poète,* are a throwback, for a moment, to an earlier poetry, the grace and musical sadness of Verlaine's 'Il pleure dans mon cœur.' Later he answers her: 'Mais oui, tu m'énerves, tu le sais bien, nous sommes bien loin' (l. 193), 'Non mais ... Fiche-moi la paix ... laisse-moi tranquille' (l. 221) and the simple but cold 'fais ton métier' (l. 199) and 'Fais comme elles la Mort la Famine fais ton métier' (l. 211). By lines 220-6 the youth has realized that what he hates is not the girl but the misery that has made her; then he cares for her again:

> C'est tout ce que Paris a mis dans ton giron
> C'est aussi un peu d'âme ... car tu es malheureuse
> J'ai pitié j'ai pitié viens vers moi sur mon cœur
>
> [ll. 224-6]

Le Transsibérien is written in Jehanne's honour, as the end of the poem tells us. She is perhaps Jeanne d'Arc, virgin become prostitute, a faithful, delicate country violated and betrayed by the times. Certainly she is meant to be the poor, beaten soul of humanity, dismembered in the train as Christ was on Fortunatus' cross:

> Nous sommes les culs-de-jatte de l'espace
> Nous roulons sur nos quatre plaies
> On nous a rogné les ailes
> Les ailes de nos sept péchés
>
> [ll. 229-232]

So the poet charms her with a paradisiacal sanctuary where they will love 'bien bourgeoisement' (l. 277). But that is only a story. Reality is tougher, more brutal, madness on the scale of all Russia tearing past the train windows, the future obliged to vanish swiftly into the past:

Toutes les gares lézardées obliques sur la route
Les fils télégraphiques auxquels elles pendent
Les poteaux grimaçants qui gesticulent et les étranglent
Le monde s'étire s'allonge et se retire comme un accordéon qu'une main
     sadique tourmente
Dans les déchirures du ciel, les locomotives en furie
S'enfuient

[ll. 176-81]

La folie surchauffée beugle dans la locomotive

[l. 194]

Tous les matins on met les montres à l'heure
Le train avance et le soleil retarde

[ll. 298-9]

Et le monde, comme l'horloge du quartier juif de Prague, tourne éperdue-
     ment à rebours.

[l. 311]

Jehanne is protected, shielded from the madness and her own desperation,
and she disappears from the poem of the train after 'Elle dort' at line 290,
reappearing only at the end in memory. The poet carries on in her name,
and in a passage describing the 'failure' of modern artists he indicates their
stance before a world which is 'bien loin de Montmartre,' that picturesque
country of their childhood:

Autant d'images-associations que je ne peux pas développer dans mes vers
Car je suis encore fort mauvais poète
Car l'univers me déborde

[ll. 336-8]

J'ai peur
Je ne sais pas aller jusqu'au bout
Comme mon ami Chagall je pourrais faire une série de tableaux déments
Mais je n'ai pas pris de notes en voyage
'Pardonnez-moi mon ignorance
'Pardonnez-moi de me plus connaître l'ancien jeu des vers'
Comme dit Guillaume Apollinaire

[ll. 342-8]

The poet, like Jehanne, is afraid, but this *Prose* is the only means he can muster, the only way he can sing. John Dos Passos wrote of the poem, 'Here's the hymn of the Transsiberian ... We need sons of Homer going about the world beating into some sort of human rhythm the shrieking hullabaloo, making us less afraid.'[21]

The poem ends in Paris, the train gone with youth. The city is both the new and the old, with colourful posters and buses, but also cows on the Montmartre 'butte' and memories of the past. It is the great crossroads of desires and inhibiting memories:

Ô Paris
Gare centrale débarcadère des volontés carrefour des inquiétudes
[ll. 420-1]

The poem almost ends in the old Paris, in thoughts of youth and of 'la petite Jehanne' remembered over drinks at the Lapin Agile café, the symbol of bohemian youth for the preceding generation.[22] But, as in *Les Pâques à New York,* the very last line combines the new and the eternal in an ambiguous note, half praise and half despair: Paris, city of the Eiffel Tower, 'central station' of suffering and the wheel of life (specifically, *La Grande Roue* was a huge Ferris wheel near the Tower, built for the same exposition and dismantled before the first world war). It is perhaps this wheel which permits us to return to Paris so suddenly upon leaving a train in Manchuria; a return only foreshadowed by line 408, 'Je ne vais pas plus loin,' which obviously refers to the train ride but can also describe the poet who can go no deeper. We are left with a hymn and a question about the escaping sense of the new world as it speeds into the old, a question Cendrars later used as the framework in a long section of *Bourlinguer:* 'Est-ce cela la Roue des Choses à laquelle les Hommes sont liés, semant le Mal, selon ce que le vieux lama enseignait à Kim, cette Roue dont les ornières sont les faubourgs des grandes villes, pleins de mauvaise semence?'[23] In the next poem the narrator would divide into seven or eight 'ornières', all off in different directions, with Paris as the hub and, again the end of the line or lines.

Whereas *Les Pâques* is a plea and *Prose du transsibérien* a search, *Le Panama ou les aventures de mes sept oncles* (1918) is a discovery, the discovery of one's place among the events and places of the world and among the manifestations of oneself in others who went before.

Again the presentation of the volume is important. Soft-covered, the book was folded down the middle so that the back cover constituted both back and front. In this shape the book was only 10 centimetres across by

23 long and seemed to invite a casual pocketing; for it now resembled, with a life-preserver on the front and back, a steamship schedule (see page xii):

> Je connais tous les horaires
> Tous les trains et leurs correspondances
> L'heure d'arrivée l'heure du départ
> Tous les paquebots tous les tarifs et toutes les taxes

[ll. 166-9]

Within the text itself twenty-five 'tracés de chemins de fer américains' provide links between stanzas of unequal lengths. Often these train-routes seem to indicate a pause, a new paragraph. They reproduce, for the most part, lines between San Francisco and Chicago; but lines are not repeated, or if they are the stops vary. There is also a full-page prospectus, authentic and in English, for 'Denver, the Residence City and Commercial Center.' This advertisement becomes relevant and lyrical by the way Cendrars places it in the text as a display of the ambitions of a city calling from miles away; the poet ducks under the Eiffel Tower and springs across the Atlantic to industrious, self-congratulatory American cities or, on the page facing, to lazy and sensual scenes in South America (see pages 111-13 reproduced from Le Panama; the links were not meant to be obscure: the old Gare d'Orsay near the Tower and the town it served, Saint Nazaire, then an important international port for the Americas). The format, train-routes and cover of Panama are those of an old Union Pacific Railroad schedule. The one I found and reproduce on page xiii is dated 15 February 1918, and Cendrars may have used a slightly earlier copy; but most details are identical or very close, down to the lettering of the word Panama which replaces the words Union Pacific System in the same box, on the same red and blue cover with a modified life-preserver. Many of the variations are naturally purposeful, such as the removal of the borders around the routes (along with the dates in the lower right-hand corners) in order to integrate lines and text. Also, a number of routes, along with the Denver ad, come from other companies' schedules. Indeed, Cendrars collected and knew 'tous les horaires.'

As may be guessed at from lines 350 to 359, images succeed each other at a rapid pace, and the trains actually slow this rhythm and make it more measured. Lines are, as a rule, much shorter than in the Prose, and as every line is an idea or image the speed of the poem is dizzying, making it even seem incoherent. Most of these jumbled cries are concentrated in sections of the poem dealing with the poet's confused wanderings, while sections

A la brebis qui broute

Femme-tremplin

Le beau joujou de la réclame

En route !

Siméon, Siméon

Paris-adieux

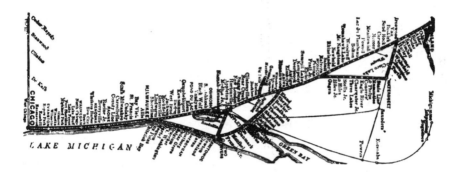

C'est rigolo

Il y a des heures qui sonnent

Quai-d'Orsay Saint-Nazaire

On passe sous la Tour Eiffel — boucler la boucle — pour
retomber de l'autre côté du monde

ABOVE AND OVERLEAF Three pages (lines 350-72) from the
original 1918 edition of *Le Panama*
Photo Bibliothèque nationale

Puis on continue

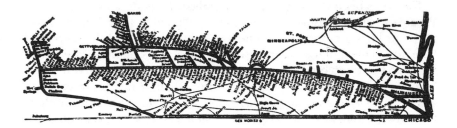

Les catapultes du soleil assiègent les tropiques irascibles
Riche Péruvien propriétaire d'une exploitation de guano
    d'Angamos
On lance l'Acaraguan Bananan
A l'ombre
Les mulâtres hospitaliers
J'ai passé plus d'un hiver dans ces îles fortunées
L'oiseau-secrétaire est un éblouissement
Belles dames plantureuses
On boit des boissons glacées sur la terrasse
Un torpilleur brûle comme un cigare
Une partie de polo dans le champ d'ananas
Et les palétuviers éventent les jeunes filles studieuses

about the seven uncles are much clearer and lyrical in an entirely different manner. The two kinds of lyricism trace the two main themes, to be fused into one discovery, like the same city at the end of two different voyages.

The poem begins by announcing a number of motifs: books in lines 1-3, Panama in line 2, business in lines 4-5, childhood in lines 6-8, the seven uncles in lines 9-10, and their letters in lines 11-13. Little time is wasted here, for all these things are important to the poem. Cendrars' care cannot be emphasized too often, for many critics take exception primarily to the 'disorder' in his writing, whereas the truth is simply that his imaginative and associative reach is longer than what we are accustomed to. In these few lines the interweaving has already begun, firstly of Panama with books and childhood.

There are essentially two kinds of books for the poet. In the first lines all books seem to be in disfavour, but soon one becomes valuable to a young boy for its pictures of far-away places and animals, in the same way that the exotic stamps on his uncles' letters are the call to a new and adventurous life (Rimbaud's verses are said to be inscribed on these stamps). But the boy is young, perhaps six or seven, and even these pictures frighten him. Later, books are again despised – 'Et j'ai jeté tout cela / ... / Les livres' (ll. 107, 110) – along with other aspects of sedentary life. How can he prepare exams, he asks, when one of his uncles' letters is pushed under the door? Throughout the poem are mentioned far more unusual books than those read for school: *'Histoire de la Cuisine à travers tous les âges et chez tous les peuples,/ En 12 vol. in-8°,' 'La Vie des Saints,' 'Navigation de Jean Struys, Amsterdam, 1528.'* And there are other things to read, newspapers, posters, ads, signs, letters, and, in lines 478 to 481, a whole list of things in life 'Pour vous apprendre à épeler l'A B C de la vie sous la férule des sirènes en partance' (l. 482). For there are books which are alive and books which are dead, as defined in similar terms in another poem written about the same time, 'Bombay-Express' – 'Je ne lis plus les livres qui ne se trouvent que dans les bibliothèques / Bel A B C du monde'.[24]

'Le Canal de Panama est intimement lié à mon enfance ...' (l. 6) because the boy's father lost his savings and those of friends in the famous project. This financial failure catapulted the boy out of a repressed, bourgeois life in which he played quietly at home, dissecting flies under the table, into a life of poetry on the scale of the wide world where whaling replaces lurking among furniture:[25]

C'est le crach du Panama qui fit de moi un poète!
C'est épatant

> Tous ceux de ma génération sont ainsi
> Jeunes gens
> Qui ont subi des ricochets étranges

[ll. 57-60]

We have been told communications have made all the world a small, intimate village. Already Cendrars could feel how a man with a shovel in Central America controlled the destiny of a small boy playing under a table in Naples, and how, consequently, the stock exchange had become a new god: ' ... les bulletins de la Bourse [sont] notre prière quotidienne' (1. 5). This does not mean that the boy enters into that business world, quite the contrary. Lines 4 and 5 say that clearly enough, and all of the poem goes against the sense of business as a settling in, a monstrous routine. But the poet is not, should not try to be, free from the effects. The catastrophe wrecks his home, setting him free from it: 'On s'embarque' (1. 64). And the picture-book tells him where to go:

> L'ours le lion le chimpanzé le serpent à sonnette m'avaient appris à
>   lire...
> Oh cette première lettre que je déchiffrai seul et plus grouillante que toute
>   la création

[ll. 69-70]

We are given, dispersed through the poem like the train-routes, six letters, one from each of six uncles. Each letter is a rapid and brilliant sketch in just a few lines of a man making his way in some lost corner of the globe. The means are not glorious, but always special, infused with a determination which, perhaps, is measured by the distance from home – butcher in Galveston:

> C'est moi qui ramène les bêtes saignantes, le soir, tout le long de la mer
> Et quand je passe les pieuvres se dressent en l'air

[ll. 74-5]

golddigger in Alaska:

> Je n'ai jamais trouvé plus de 500 francs d'or dans ma pelle
> La vie non plus ne se paye pas à sa valeur!

[ll. 130-1]

revolutionary in Bombay:

> Tu es convict
> Ta vie circoncise

[ll. 242-3]

valet in South Africa, chef in Chicago, guide in Patagonia. Here is life that
is poetic at its core, the right books to read:

> Tes menus
> Sont la poésie nouvelle

> [ll. 332-3]

Taking his cue from this uncle, whom he may have invented anyhow,
Cendrars later writes up menus as poems in *Kodak.* These men are the
poet's models. At first they are only dreams in the shape of a few misspelled words; then they are landmarks the poet searches for; finally, in
a metaphorical union, the seventh uncle becomes the poet, who is still an
unknown quantity, about to embark:

> Mon septième oncle
> On n'a jamais su ce qu'il est devenu
> On dit que je te ressemble

> [ll. 446-8]

There are two sorts of outbound travelling for the poet: searching for the
others and going on his own voyage. The uncles are as elusive as dreams,
and only one is ever seen – the valet, who returns home, sleeps for two
weeks, goes mad, and dies. The boy sees him only asleep and never sees
any of the others; four are dead, the Buddhist is in jail, the chef, like
Cendrars, never stays in one place, nothing is known of the seventh. In
the case of all but the chef and the seventh, who doesn't write, each letter
is followed by the poet's passage through the uncles' haunted landscapes.
As we read, with the poet, between the lines of four of the letters that

> ... il y avait encore quelque chose
> La tristesse
> Et le mal du pays

> [ll. 77-9, 134-6, 214-6, 256-8]

we see why the poet commemorates an uncle's memory by going after
him, retracing the voyage in an adventure become ritual.

The fourth uncle, the valet, comes to him, and is buried by him. The
fifth, the chef – 'toujours ... partout où il se passait quelque chose'
(l. 330) – whose menus are the new poetry, is the only one who was never
homesick, and his example predicts the last few lines of the poem. The
sixth uncle is the only one to write to the poet personally, not at home but
in South America: 'Attends-moi à la factorerie ...' he writes, but never

arrives. The seventh uncle is the closest, symbolically, to the poet, and an enigma. Each metamorphosis of Uncle comes closer to the poet, who has contrasted his own anguish in the guise of *Wanderlust* to his models' *mal du pays* until all begins to dissolve, poet and uncles into each other, *Wanderlust* and *mal du pays* into the independence of the last lines. But before union the young narrator is a lost, searching soul. Between letters a boy breaks dishes and fails exams, an adolescent crosses the Atlantic, gathering snippets of useless conversation:

> Ce petit train que les Soleurois appellent un fer à repasser
> Je téléphonerai à mon consul
> Délivrez-moi immédiatement un billet de 3ᵉ classe
>
> [ll. 191-3]

a poet assaults Paris, Rastignac-like, and leaves it behind:

> On passe sous la Tour Eiffel – boucler la boucle – pour retomber de l'autre
> côté du monde
>
> [l. 359]

a young man loafs in Argentina. He is never happy; there is impatience, disgust, resignation:

> Je tourne dans la cage des méridiens comme un écureuil dans la sienne
>
> [l. 160]

> Je quitte le bord comme on quitte une sale putain
>
> [l. 199]

> Il n'y a pas d'espérance
> Et il faut travailler
>
> [ll. 295-6]

> J'ai quitté tout cela
> J'attends
>
> [ll. 334-5]

In line 421 he affirms that, indeed, there remain good stories, to read and to tell. One is that of Panama after the French had left, and that will, perhaps, be the story of the poet, who looks like the seventh uncle. If the seven voyagers are only made the poet's uncles to give unity and kinship to their travels, perhaps this seventh is Monsieur Bertrand, a bartender in

Panama to whom the poem is dedicated. It is Bertrand who has told the poet how the jungle world of his youthful reading has taken over de Lesseps' invasion of its domain, how the modern adventure of Panama has rejoined the young boy's adventures in a picture-book of strange animals:

> Le palmier greffé dans la banne d'une grue chargée d'orchidées
> Les canons d'Aspinwall rongés par les toucans
> La drague aux tortues
> Les pumas qui nichent dans le gazomètre défoncé
> Les écluses perforées par les poissons-scie
> La tuyauterie des pompes bouchée par une colonie d'iguanes
> Les trains arrêtés par l'invasion des chenilles
>
> [ll. 461-7]

Thus does reality come to fulfil and even surpass the yearnings of the imagination, and with that recognition of the world as being *enough,* the two searches, for uncles and for self, come together, and to an end which says, Start! Panama itself is only one of the many 'belles histoires' (l. 422) to be told, for as the two searches meet, the whole world presents itself to the poet. The world is always new, and its poetry is just as new, ready; it starts today as the poet walks out his door, grabbing his hat and the first train, as Cendrars said he did when he first ran from home:

> Ce matin est le premier jour du monde
>
> [l. 473]

> Le Los Angeles limited qui part à 10h. 02 pour arriver le troisième
>   jour...
>
> [l. 480]

> J'ai du pain et du fromage
> Un col propre
> La poésie date d'aujourd'hui
>
> [ll. 484-6]

The ending is more frenetic than ever, the spring winding up rather than down. The last train-route appears after the section on the seventh uncle (l. 448), and then lines 487 to 494 speed beyond trains:

> La voie lactée autour du cou
> Les deux hémisphères sur les yeux

>   A toute vitesse
>   Il n'y plus de pannes

[ll. 487-90]

In the next few lines he covers land and sea, with 'le mal du pays' like his
uncles and a fear of mailboxes, of returning home. Then he invokes the
skies agains, and there are no limits to what he can look forward to;
'J'ATTENDS,' he writes in the right-hand margin, poised to take off from
the Rotonde café while the literary men gossip on, though the lack of
punctuation obscures the poet's distinctness from them and their drinking
(also, in a pun, these chatterers take their *train*). Finally the end is swift
and emphatic, as the poet seems to disperse, to disappear among the fifteen
suburban towns where the poem was written :

>   Soleils lunes étoiles
>   Mondes apocalyptiques
>   Vous avez encore tous un beau rôle à jouer
>   Un siphon éternue
>   Les cancans littéraires vont leur train
>   Tout bas
>   A la Rotonde
>   Comme tout au fond d'un verre

J'ATTENDS

>   Je voudrais être la cinquième roue du char
>   Orage
>   Midi à quatorze heures
>   Rien et partout

>   Paris et Sa Banlieúe.
>   Saint-Cloud, Sèvres, Montmorency, Courbevoie, Bougival, Rueil,
>   Montrouge, Saint-Denis, Vincennes, Etampes, Melun, Saint-Martin,
>   Méréville, Barbizon, Forges-en-Bière

Juin 1913-juin 1914

[l. 504 to end]

This finale is a dissolving, yet a positive one despite the often reiterated
'j'attends' and the two expressions in lines 512 and 514 which usually
denote uselessness. Cendrars has embraced this 'nothingness,' which is
obviously not the contrary of 'being.' Henry Miller sheds some light on
this peculiar 'positive absence' in a passage which also emphasizes, in the
metaphor of the wheel of life, the contrast of hub and periphery:

> Out of desperation and humility he had created for himself the most human role of the antagonist ... He refused to spread himself thin over an illusory pattern of grandeur; he muscled deeper and deeper into the hub, into the everlasting no-principle of the universe.[26]

To be 'rien et partout' was the dream of Kipling's lama, who may never have attained it without dying; Kim, on the other hand, launched himself without selfish goal into activity, performing meaningless yet somehow solid acts. As Whitman wrote in 'Song of Myself':

> ... there is no trade or employment but the young man following it may become a hero,
> And there is no object so soft but it makes a hub for the wheel'd universe ...
>
> [section 48]

The 'dating' of the poem with its list of fifteen little villages surrounding Paris serves as the positive answer to 'Je voudrais être ... ' These villages, the author's proclaimed places of composition, illustrate 'partout' as well as the South America or India of the poet's uncles or imagination might (and if the poem was not really written in all those places their mention becomes even more important to the meaning of the poem). In 1925, Fernand Divoire wrote an amusing apology-introduction to his *L'Homme du monde* about how, despite the voice of Cendrars calling to him from a South American jungle (where Cendrars actually was at that time) he, Divoire, still had a world in his small study: 'Cendrars, j'ai aussi un genre de forêt, et un genre de croix du sud, et un genre d'espace. En attendant.' This should not be taken as a view of Cendrars as merely a poet of exoticism, and the reverse should become more and more apparent in this study. Exoticism means escape. When we call Cendrars the poet *Du Monde entier* (the title of the three poems under discussion published together by the NRF in 1919) we are not thinking of him as an escapist, the man running away from himself, but quite the contrary, the man running to everything, curious about life in all its manifestations because these cannot but have a bearing on his own life. This is the opposite of the narrow parochialism we ascribe, with Baudelaire, to the artist in the long quotation that follows, which in its description of 'l'homme du monde' shows the sort of man Cendrars was and what sort of poet he was becoming in these three long poems. The citation is part of Baudelaire's attempt to define modernity with the example of his friend the painter Constantin Guy:

Pendant dix ans, j'ai désiré faire la connaissance de M. G., qui est, par
nature, très voyageur et très cosmopolite ... Lorsqu'enfin je le trouvai, je
vis tout d'abord que je n'avais pas affaire précisément à un *artiste,* mais
plutôt à un *homme du monde.* Entendez ici, je vous prie, le mot *artiste* dans
un sens très restreint, et le mot *homme du monde* dans un sens très étendu.
Homme du monde, c'est-à-dire homme du monde entier, homme qui com-
prend le monde et les raisons mystérieuses et légitimes de tous ses usages;
artiste, c'est-à-dire spécialiste, homme attaché à sa palette comme le serf à
la glèbe. M. G. n'aime pas être appelé artiste. N'a-t-il pas un peu raison?
Il s'intéresse au monde entier; il veut savoir, comprendre, apprécier tout
ce qui se passe à la surface de notre sphéroïde. L'artiste vit très peu, ou
même pas du tout, dans le monde moral et politique. Celui qui habite dans
le quartier Breda ignore ce qui se passe dans le faubourg Saint-Germain.
Sauf deux ou trois exceptions qu'il est inutile de nommer, la plupart des
artistes sont, il faut bien le dire, des brutes très adroites, de purs ma-
nœuvres, des intelligences de village, des cervelles de hameau. Leur conversation, forcément bornée à un cercle très étroit, devient très vite insup-
portable à l'*homme du monde,* au citoyen spirituel de l'univers.

Ainsi, pour entrer dans la compréhension de M. G., prenez note tout
de suite de ceci: c'est que la *curiosité* peut être considérée comme le point
de départ de son génie.

La foule est son domaine, comme l'air est celui de l'oiseau, comme l'eau
celui du poisson. Sa passion et sa profession, c'est d'*épouser la foule.* Pour
le parfait flâneur, pour l'observateur passionné, c'est une immense jouis-
sance que d'élire domicile dans le nombre, dans l'ondoyant, dans le
mouvement, dans le fugitif et l'infini. Être hors de chez soi, et pourtant se
sentir partout chez soi; voir le monde, être au centre du monde et rester
caché au monde, tels sont quelques-uns des moindres plaisirs de ces esprits
indépendants ...

C'est un *moi* insatiable du *non-moi,* qui, à chaque instant, le rend et l'ex-
prime en images plus vivantes que la vie elle-même, toujours instable et
fugitive.[27]

The voyage out into unstable reality is always the voyage back, and in.
Divoire's voyage around his room might bear the same fruit, except that,
as Baudelaire warns, for most artists their room has become a privileged
domain, isolated and arrogant. But the voyage back from *non-moi* makes
the *moi* anew, thus real. As T.S. Eliot has written in 'Little Gidding':

We shall not cease from exploration

And the end of all our exploring
Will be to arrive where we started
And know the place for the first time

[ll. 241-4]

Thus these three progressively longer poems end at 'home,' *Les Pâques* in a small room and both *Prose* and *Panama* quite suddenly in Paris. Paris is a special hub, the place where these *'Prose'* epics are written and to be sung. It is likely that Paris even lurks in the title of *Panama,* since *'Paname'* is well-known slang for Paris. There are further distinctions however; *Prose* ends at the Lapin Agile café in Montmartre whereas *Panama* ends at the Rotonde, a newer meeting place for artists when bohemia shifted to Montparnasse.[28] The voyages move their centres, and reach further in each poem, in geographical distances from their centres, in the amount of travel within each poem and the amount of time the telling takes to return: *Pâques* through downtown New York and back to a room in 205 lines, *Prose* from Moscow through Manchuria and back to Montmartre in 445 lines, *Panama* around the world – and around Paris – and back to Montparnasse in 516 lines. The emotional equilibrium from one poem to the next also shows a clear progression, from the constriction of faith, through rebellion and apocalyptic destruction to an expansive readiness for the unknown new; it is a delicate balance of systole and diastole, and one that will be closely repeated, in entirely new voyages, in Cendrars' three novels of the twenties: *L'Or,* about gold and faith; *Moravagine,* about the arch-anarchist; and *Dan Yack* on emotional renewal. But in this poetic triptych of plea, search, and discovery, much more than in the novels, the one constant subject is the survival of man and poet in modernity; the achievement of constancy in and by very virtue of change – Heraclitus' flow, Spenser's Mutabilitie, Baudelaire's modernity as defined in his articles on Constantin Guy:

> Ainsi il va, il court, il cherche. Que cherche-t-il? A coup sûr, cet homme, tel que je l'ai dépeint, ce solitaire doué d'une imagination active, toujours voyageant à travers *le grand désert d'hommes,* a un but plus élevé que celui d'un pur flâneur, un but plus général, autre que le plaisir fugitif de la circonstance. Il cherche ce quelque chose qu'on nous permettra d'appeler la *modernité* ... Il s'agit, pour lui, de dégager de la mode ce qu'elle peut contenir de poétique dans l'historique, de tirer l'éternel du transitoire.

[p. 466]

The most powerful, effective aspect of these poems is precisely that contrast ('contraste simultané') of lyrical mysticism with the seemingly transitory, contingent nature of all the terribly solid, real objects and terribly passing acts.

7 The elastic Kodak

I accept Reality and dare not question it,
Materialism first and last imbuing
...
I find I incorporate gneiss, coal, long-threaded moss, fruits, grains, esculent roots,
And am stucco'd with quadrupeds and birds all over

WHITMAN, 'Song of Myself'

While Cendrars was writing *La Prose* and *Le Panama* he was also writing much shorter poems and publishing them in such avant-garde magazines as Canudo's *Montjoie!, Les Soirées de Paris, Der Sturm, De Stijl,* and others. These poems were much in demand as emblems of the new poetry, for they appeared in the very first issues of *Montjoie!,* Breton's, Aragon's, and Soupault's soon-to-become-Dada *Littérature,* and Hugo Ball's *Cabaret Voltaire,* the very first Dada publication (work by Cendrars also appeared in the first issues of Florent Fels' *Action,* Roger Vitrac's *Aventure,* Ribemont-Dessaignes' *Bifur,* Jacques-Henry Lévesque's *Orbes,* and others). Yet these earlier short poems were comparatively few in number since they were collected in 1919 as *Dix-neuf Poèmes élastiques.* The only others published before that date are the three 'Sonnets dénaturés' (1916), 'Shrapnells' (October 1914 – the only poem Cendrars wrote while he was in the war), 'Hommage à Guillaume Apollinaire' (November 1918), the longer *La Guerre au Luxembourg* (1916), and the fragments of 'Au Cœur du monde' (1917). It is not a very great amount of poetry.

These last two works, the latter incomplete at that, are the only examples of poetry by Cendrars which is entirely 'linear.' Thought is consecutive and the development simple to follow. 'Hôtel Notre-Dame' in 'Au

Cœur du monde,' for example, is clear and logical, the movement building single-mindedly from a quiet sadness to the declaration of independence at the end, as the poet takes his own road and his own, invented name. The poem is more modest in technique, more discursive – for there is no imagery at all – and more intense, with its single, direct focus, than other work by Cendrars, with which it nevertheless shares common themes:

> C'est pourquoi je ne regrette rien
> Et j'appelle les démolisseurs
> Foutez mon enfance par terre
> Ma famille et mes habitudes
> Mettez une gare à la place
> Ou laissez un terrain vague
> Qui dégage mon origine

La Guerre au Luxembourg, written in October of 1916, describes children playing at war, during the real war, in the Luxembourg Gardens which bridge the Latin Quarter and Montparnasse. We can sense in the voice of the narrator observing these innocent games the long wait for the end to the Great War:

> Croix-Rouge
> Les infirmières ont 6 ans
> …
> On enlève les yeux aux poupées pour réparer les aveugles
> …
> Et ceux qui faisaient les morts ressuscitent pour assister à la merveilleuse
> opération

The last part of the poem predicts the return of the real soldiers, who will be received like children:

> Tout le monde voudra LES voir
> Le soleil ouvrira de bonne heure comme un marchand de nougat un jour
> de fête

There is no ellipsis in this poem, and it resembles in its directness and sharpness, and a certain attitude of patience, Cendrars' poetic prose of *L'Or* (but in a novel such writing no longer seems quite discursive enough!). Certainly these poems would have been the most accessible of Cendrars' work for the readers and critics of the time. However, at the risk of practically ignoring them I shall concern myself with the more avant-garde poetry in the interest of discovering what I feel to have been the general direction of Cendrars' work. This bias makes no adverse value judgement upon works of which, as I quoted in the introduction to this study, Max Jacob could write in a letter to Jacques Doucet, 'Les deux dernières pages de *La Guerre au Luxembourg* sont parmi les plus belles choses que j'ai jamais lues.'

All but the last of *Dix-neuf Poèmes élastiques,* 'Construction' (February 1919), were written in 1913 and 1914, before the war. Perhaps the particular number of poems did not matter to Cendrars, for in the original edition of *La Guerre au Luxembourg* he announced 'sous presse, *Dix-sept Poèmes élastiques.'*[1] Or possibly (and more in keeping with Cendrars' playful fondness for numbers) in order to provide one for each year of the new century, the poems had to be stretched from seventeen for 1917 to nineteen for 1919. The poems are not pretentious and most often they are intimate. Each seems the spontaneous epiphany – in Joyce's sense – of a fleeting moment. In a 'notule d'histoire littéraire' appended to the original volume Cendrars wrote: 'Nés à l'occasion d'une rencontre, d'une amitié, d'un tableau, d'une polémique ou d'une lecture, les quelques poèmes qui précèdent appartiennent au genre si décrié des poèmes de circonstance.'[2] The poems are immediate responses to occasions in which relatively minor occurrences or objects call up personal, often obscure associations in the poet: reading a newspaper, having a drink, Chagall painting; or six colours, a train, his own portrait. Many artists and poets figure in these poems: nos. 5 and 11 are about *littérateurs,* no. 2 is dedicated to Delaunay, no. 4 is on Chagall painting 'with his life,' no. 6 on Sonia Delaunay and her *simultané* clothes, no. 7 on Apollinaire, no. 8 on Canudo, no. 14 on La Fresnaye, no. 18 on Archipenko, and no. 19 on Léger as he paints the author's portrait. No. 10 is the mere transcription of a newspaper article, and no. 15 is about *Fantômas.* In general, the scene of the whole volume is the Left Bank before the war, and there is usually the effect – supported by some amount of fact – that the poems were jotted down in a café, with no formality at all.

The style of the poems is that of the very personal, jagged sections of *Le Panama* where the youth jumbled fragments of his confused life. The poems are 'elastic' in two main ways; by what they permit themselves to include and by what they choose to omit. Almost anything connected with the life of the moment has bearing upon the meaning of that moment as the poet apprehends it. Each poem brings together, as did the Picasso and Braque collages of the time, the everyday materials at hand. Some of the poems were in fact collages themselves, rearranged items from other sources; no. 16, for example, most likely tells us in its title that we are reading phrases cut from newspaper headlines, though line one is from Rimbaud's prose poem 'Barbare':

16 'Titres'

Formes sueurs chevelures
Le bond d'être
Dépouillé
Premier poème sans métaphores
Sans images
Nouvelles ...

Roger Allard, who was not generally impressed by 'cubist' or Dada poetry, could see he was not dealing with just a fad when he reviewed the collection for the NRF in 1919:

> L'élasticité des poèmes de M. Cendrars me paraît hors de conteste. Il est
> même équitable de constater que ces poèmes sont les plus élastiques et les
> plus extensibles de tous les poèmes en forme de vide-poche, où l'auteur
> jette pêle-mêle des lignes de journal, des enseignes de bistro, des vers
> d'almanach, de vieux feuillets de son calepin, et des mégots de la conversa-
> tion. M. Cendrars a coutume de porter dans ces exercices une franchise
> et une liberté d'allures sympathiques, et quelque chose de viril qui manque
> aux jeux de certains esthètes.[3]

The *vide-poche* does not necessarily mean a random inclusion, since there falls out on that plate only what the author has in his pockets, what he has collected for himself, regardless of how poorly he knew his purpose when he started out that day; what Leopold Bloom carried about on his person is practically the story of *Ulysses,* though in such abbreviated form as to be obscure indeed. In Cendrars' nineteen poems we are called upon, through the style, to trust that the grab bag will make sense, that there is a sense, a circumstance behind the pieces. The frankness, virility, *élan,* often plain friendliness of the language suspends our doubting until closer or repeated reading or reflection puts things together.

All the links are, of course, omitted; thus the second elasticity derives from the first. Heterogeneous elements have been jerked together into radical relationships[4] with purpose but no or very little explanation. At every line we are in the situation Wallace Stevens so often presents us with when he gives a poem a seemingly irrelevant title; the whole meaning resides in the connection between poem and title. This abridgment of explanation and transition is the mainstay of modern poetic technique, the manner in which pure picture, or Imagism, becomes meaningful. From acutely perceived but naturally fragmented reality we infer relationships which draw relevant patterns. It is the technique of Apollinaire's 'Zone' and Cendrars' *Panama;* of Eliot's *Waste Land* and Pound's work from 'Mauberley' onward. The two Americans writing in London probably started a bit later with the fragmentation of sense, as they were first preoccupied with the image. Eliot collected 'fragments I have shored against my ruins,' a poetry of unredeemable discontinuity, whereas Pound was closer to what Cendrars did in *Dix-neuf Poèmes élastiques* by being interested in something coming out of the juxtaposition. Jean Epstein enthusiastically described these abridgments, full of pages of unspoken poetry, for the English and American readers of *Broom:*

> The poem of Arthur Rimbaud, one of his simplest, of which I cited a few lines above ['Bottom,' *Les Illuminations*], presents in fifteen lines, nineteen abridgments. You see what a gallop the thought must take in order to understand this poem during a reading aloud. 'Aux cinq coins,' a poem by Blaise Cendrars, contains sixteen abridgments in ten lines, in ten half-lines, without counting the title which is, for all that, a meteor ... *Le Potomac* by Cocteau is not one book for me but four books; perhaps it will be five. And the *Dix-neuf poèmes élastiques* of Blaise Cendrars, I affirm to you, is a volume of eight hundred pages accompanied by thirteen hundred full page plates.[5]

These abridgments, if less numerous and pregnant than Epstein pretends, are further complicated by all the imprecision and resulting ambiguity of life's being seized on the run, as it appears without dress-up. This lack of intellectual precision, the puns, mispronunciations, slips of the tongue, inconsistent associations,[6] are intended to betray the real, if irrational, meaning lurking behind an unpoetic world shackled by well-ordered words and syntax. Still, 'Aux 5 coins' is obscure only until we realize that the title is the name of a Paris café at the corner of Boulevards Saint-Germain and Raspail, nor far from where Apollinaire lived at the time; then we see that poetry stands at this crossroads (in the fifth poem, 'Ma Danse,' Cendrars wrote, 'Tu n'as plus de coutumes et pas encore d'habitudes / Il faut échapper à la tyrannie des revues'), and that the fate of poetry hangs upon the recognition of a new lyricism in the workman's ordinary but emphatic language (though this does not prevent the poet from making *another* language out of that one).

13 'Aux 5 coins'

Oser et faire du bruit

Tout est couleur movement explosion lumière
La vie fleurit aux fenêtres du soleil
Qui se fond dans ma bouche
Je suis mûr
Et je tombe translucide dans la rue

Tu parles, mon vieux

Je ne sais pas ouvrir les yeux?
Bouche d'or
La poésie est en jeu

The last line implies a danger, and I shall speak later of Cendrars' sense of life as dangerous down to its smallest and most ordinary events. Here, the danger is somewhat specialized, for the poet especially; what threatens is that he may miss the beauty around him because the vehicles are not the expected ones. The *Dix-neuf Poèmes élastiques* play in a world of heightened awareness where the most unassuming occurrences can knock the poet off his feet. And, for Cendrars, all the better. He stands under the apple tree waiting, and ready, for the ripe fruit to fall – and he falls with it:

On dirait un aéroplane qui tombe.
C'est moi.
...
On a beau ne pas vouloir parler de soi-même
Il faut parfois crier

Je suis l'autre
Trop sensible

[from 'Journal']

In these poems abridgments, errors, ambiguity, and metamorphosis contribute to short-circuiting the usually discursive and sensible nature of language to throw the reader through language conceived of as a barrier into untranslatable fact and association.[7] This is, of course, quite the reverse of the process some structural critics propose as proper to the making of good poetry, in which, they feel, language is not at all transparent, but is poetic by virtue of holding the attention and becoming its own most important referent. The direction of Cendrars' success with language is the reverse – utter transparency; and more, since he has magnified the referent and recreated it as a thing living in association with himself.

In *Dix-neuf Poèmes élastiques* the objects of the world are bent, pulled,

rewired, and rebuilt until they are thrown into a new motion, a dance with
the poet's senses:

> Je suis un monsieur qui en des express fabuleux traverse les toujours
>   mêmes Europes et regarde découragé par la portière
> Le paysage ne m'intéresse plus
> Mais la danse du paysage
> Danse-paysage
> Paritatitata
> Je tout-tourne
>
> [end of 'Ma Danse']

And yet, it is important to distinguish this effect from that of a dream, or
an early version of Surrealism, in which the objects lose their solidity, and
disappear into the imagination. Cendrars' objects matter and maintain
their independence. This is not, in fact, a poetry of 'possession du monde,'
as it can be so easily taken to be, and it is precisely Cendrars' strength that
he is not acquisitive. His radical transformations leave his subjects real,
and their new lives remain consistent with their more ordinary ones, even
reinforce them, return them to themselves in a stronger light:

> Et le soleil t'apporte le beau corps d'aujourd'hui dans les coupures des
>   journaux
> Ces langes
>
> [end of 'Mardi Gras']

> J'envie ton repos
> Grand paquebot des usines
> A l'ancre
> Dans la banlieue des villes
>
> [from 'F.I.A.T.']

> Il dort
> Il est éveillé
> Tout à coup, il peint
> Il prend une église et peint avec une église
> Il prend une vache et peint avec une vache
> Avec une sardine
>
> [from no. 4, without title]

Thus the subject of the poem takes the poet in hand and paints his own portrait. There is an extreme identification of poet, means, and subject, and perhaps the most essential elasticity of the operation is the workings of the poet's sensitivity become visible as part of the mechanical world, yet without losing in delicacy or humanity:

'Sur un portrait de Modigliani'

Le monde intérieur
Le cœur humain avec
   ses 17 mouvements
    dans l'esprit
Et le vaetvient de la
     passion[8]

If one were to think of *Dix-neuf Poèmes élastiques* as a grab bag of seemingly unrelated film clips, each without context, all hastily edited together, *Kodak,* as the name indicates, and *Feuilles de route*[9] might be two much longer series of static snapshots, what M. Lévesque has called 'instants privilégiés.'[10] A number of the poems in these two works are so short and simple they seem to contain nothing but the blandest of literal meanings:

'Grotte'

Il y a une grotte qui perce l'île de part en part

                [OC 1: 179]

Such poems are no more than the notation of a fact, 'photographies verbales,' as Cendrars called them, with no 'elasticity' at all; I shall return to this sort of poem presently. Many more of the poems, however, though they seem similar to the verbal photography variety, make two statements rather than only one:

'Léger et subtil'

L'air est embaumé
Musc ambre et fleur de citronnier
Le seul fait d'exister est un véritable bonheur

                [OC 1: 120]

A photograph with a note on the back, as it were. The two statements are emotionally related, though again logic is short-circuited. In this case, as in many instances in these poems, the image constitutes the terms of a state of mind. Always, however, the relationship is delicate, 'léger et subtil,' to borrow Cendrars' title, and it can come as a surprise, if usually a small one. The poem is a discovery, an insight, and the essential poetry of the few lines resides not in what is said outright but what is implied in the interplay of the two parts. Again we find how important contrast is in Cendrars; for it is the juxtaposition, the contrast, which contains all the depth of the poem, each of the two terms remaining almost entirely prosaic. Here is another example:

> 'Hic Haec Hoc'
>
> J'ai acheté trois ouistitis que j'ai baptisés Hic Haec Hoc
> Douze colibris
> Mille cigares
> Et une main de bahiana grande comme un pied
> Avec ça j'emporte le souvenir du plus bel éclat de rire
>
> > [OC 1: 176]

All the poems of *Kodak* and *Feuilles de route* may be divided between photo-style poems and what we might think of as Western versions of the Japanese haiku, or hokku principle (and part of *Kodak,* including the section containing 'Léger et subtil,' deals with Japanese subjects). Some of the poems are rather long for haiku (I speak of their relative length; naturally none of them could be seventeen syllables long); for example 'Trestle-work' (OC 1: 102), which builds towards its effect just as the bridge itself is being built. Still, Cendrars manages to bring off the obvious end with a touch of magic, of his own surprise at how clear and necessary the end is; this magic is the essence of the haiku's purpose – revelation, as you turn the corner, of two perspectives crossing and meeting. A few of the poems are very much haiku in the purest sense, the second term not more than a touch of the wind:

> 'Villa Garcia'
>
> Trois croiseurs rapides un navire hôpital
> Le pavillon anglais
> Des signaux optiques lumineux
> Deux carabinieros dorment sur les fauteils du pont
> Enfin nous partons
> Dans les vents sucrés
>
> > [OC 1: 139]

However, the best poems for Western tastes are no doubt those which contain more emotion. 'Îles' is probably one of Cendrars' best known short poems:

'Îles'

Îles
Îles
Îles où l'on ne prendra jamais terre
Îles où l'on ne descendra jamais
Îles couvertes de végétations
Îles tapies comme des jaguars
Îles muettes
Îles immobiles
Îles inoubliables et sans nom
Je lance mes chaussures par-dessus bord car je voudrais bien aller jusqu'à
    vous

[OC 1: 158]

The poetry of these two volumes rests in two distinct areas: in the single abridgments or juxtapositions in each poem, and in the cumulative effect of the poems in their series. In the first respect these poems represent the smallest unit in Cendrars' interplay of inner and outer worlds, one bead on the elastic band. In 'Villa Garcia' the last few words constitute the first and only shift in the poem, slipping from description of an unstable human scene to the embodiment of the senses in nature. Cendrars is making the same use of the haiku that Pound meant to, particularly in his only famous one (which takes place in Paris incidentally), 'In a Station of the Metro':

The apparition of these faces in the crowd,
Petals, on a wet, black bough.

Pound wrote of this: 'I dare say it is meaningless unless one has drifted into a certain vein of thought. In a poem of this sort one is trying to record the precise instant when a thing outward and objective transforms itself, or darts into a thing inward and subjective.'[11] Again, we see the similarity to Cendrars' intentions as I have interpreted them; Donald Davie makes the same important distinction for Pound as regards the integrity of the outer world:

Here once again one sees the traffic being run all the other way from the symbolists. For to Pound it is the outward that transforms itself into the inward, whereas to the devotee of the objective correlative it is always the

inward (the poet's state of mind or state of feeling) that seeks in the
outward world something to correspond to itself.[12]

These two volumes of poetry collect what Pound called 'precise instants' into series which Cendrars hoped would put the reader 'into a
certain vein of thought,' one in which he will open to the slightest glimpses
of countryside, streets, or history as privileged snapshots. Their poetry
resides as much in their contribution to the volume as a whole as in
themselves. The haiku are those especially revealing notes in what is, after
all, the account of a voyage more than a collection with strictly symbolic
or thematic sequence. *Feuilles de route* really constitutes a new form, a
verbal photographic album which, taken in its entirety, has great evocative
power. When Cendrars died John Dos Passos wrote: 'When I go to Brazil
I still see the ascent from Santos to Sao Paulo through Cendrars' eyes.'[13]
Essentially it is *Kodak,* or *Feuilles de route,* which is lyrical as a whole and
by a progression of revealing, or merely well-chosen, glimpses without
comment. The best comparisons might be Butor's *Mobile,* or Virginia
Woolf's *Jacob's Room* in which an attempt is made to approach the meaning
of a man's life through almost insignificant, short scenes viewed from the
outside, an album of photographs. Such an album holds advantages over
a conventional psychological novel or an exhaustive travelogue. It seems
to respect the secrecy of the character, or of the landscape, while the
precise and careful choice of what *is* shown hints at the subject's reserves.
Thus, as in 'Îles,' we touch the islands only from a distance, and they
always await us. Further, the album plays on these reserves by leaving the
reader suspended and obliging him to return to an apparently bland photo
to search out the clues of, for example, two people standing at a certain
peculiar angle to each other, or:

'Keepsake'

Le ciel et la mer
Les vagues viennent caresser les racines des cocotiers et des grands tama-
    rins au feuillage métallique

[OC 1: 121]

The instants call for attentions which a developed and even-flowing text
does not require. But, paradoxically, the effect of the whole volume is not
static precisely because it is not enough of a solid piece. Rather than build
a structure of closely laid elements Cendrars has only outlined the pattern;
the reader is not permitted to hold the voyage firmly, but is obliged to
relinquish the fixed moment and pass from one *instantané,* as rapid photo-

graphs are called, to the next, for each one always calls for the next. Even the last two do not end the succession of these *Feuilles:*

'Podomètre'

Quand on fait les cent pas sur le pont...

'Pourquoi j'écris?'

Parce que...

[OC 1: 182]

In the same way that each poem springs forth and then disappears into the next without transition, the volumes also prefer to dissolve rather than make a final, all-encompassing statement of import and thereby become static. Cendrars' view is elusive, like the place itself which is only willing to give up small vistas. A poem points to more poems of the same sort, 'instants privilégiés,' and asks us to be 'disponible,' as James said of Isabel Archer, to all the possibilities of such instants.

In retrospect it is not difficult to see the relationship of these volumes to earlier poetry by Cendrars. One might imagine that a young poet would most likely work up from the shorter forms to the longest and most ambitious. Here, the reverse has taken place, from epic *Prose* through elastic *Dix-neuf Poèmes* to one-line *Feuilles.* Any number of short-circuits have been successively reduced to the single abridgment and juxtaposition of the haiku, then to a single statement which cannot be abridged but which suddenly takes its place in a simple, fleeting series, a voyage's remembered moments. The relationship to the next work to be published after *Feuilles de route* is also clear. Although Cendrars' next step is to the novel, and thus to the longest work to date, the language and tone of *L'Or* are that of the simple one-line poems I have been discussing. It is the most direct, the starkest of novels imaginable, yet through its sparseness it is poetic, as the novelist Joseph Delteil, reviewing it for the NRF, perceived when he wrote: 'il y a une poésie des faits, la plus belle.'[14] From 1913 to 1925, the span of almost all of Cendrars' published poetry, we come full circle from poetry as *Prose* to prose as poetry. The living fact itself may be poetic and demand only to be chosen and placed. Years later Cendrars wrote that Gustave Lerouge, a popular writer he greatly admired and whose own novels and tracts were to be found montaged into *Kodak,* would force himself to

détruire l'image, ne pas suggérer, châtrer le verbe, ne pas faire style, dire des faits, des faits, rien que des faits, le plus de choses avec le moins de

mots possible et, finalement, faire jaillir une idée originale, dépouillée de
tout système, isolée de toute association, vue comme de l'extérieur, sous
cent angles à la fois et à grand renfort de télescopes et de microscopes, mais
éclairée de l'intérieur. C'était de l'équilibrisme et de la prestidigitation. Ce
jongleur était un très grand poète anti-poétique. [15]

Cendrars must have intuited from the beginning that he was headed in the
direction of this anti-poetic poetry; just as the second uncle in *Le Panama*
provides the story for the later volume *L'Or,* the fifth uncle, a chef in
Chicago, announces 'la poésie des faits': 'Tes menus/sont la poésie nouvelle' writes the poet (ll. 332-3), and so eight menus, without comment
or context and merely in themselves an extraordinary progression, end
Kodak:

III Saumon de Winnipeg
    Jambon de Mouton à l'Écossaise
    Pommes Royal-Canada
    Vieux vins de France

IV Kankal-Oysters
    Salade de homard cœurs de céleris
    Escargots de France vanillés au sucre
    Poulet de Kentucky
    Desserts café whisky canadian-club

V Ailerons de requin confits dans la saumure
    Jeunes chiens mort-nés préparés au miel
    Vin de riz aux violettes
    Crème au cocon de ver à soie
    Vers de terre salés et alcool de Kawa
    Confiture d'algues marines

[OC 1: 131-2]

The facts themselves may constitute, for Cendrars, a rich enough diet
with little need of embellishment, only the well-directed focus of the
poet's eye, whereupon the object's interior light flashes out at him and
cleaves to him – thus Whitman's poet 'stucco'd' over with animals and
rocks. To quote again the end of 'Journal,' the luminary poem of *Dix-neuf
Poèmes élastiques* addressed to the Christ of *Les Pâques:*

On dirait un aéroplane qui tombe.
C'est moi.
...

Je suis l'autre
Trop sensible

[OC 1: 54]

Cendrars pushed the poetry of facts as far as it can go and wrote, as early
as 1913, what may well be the first example of found poetry, no. 10 of
Dix-neuf Poèmes élastiques, 'Dernière heure,' copied out of *Paris-Midi.* Cen-
drars amiably plagiarized others or stole anonymous materials for any
number of his poems – probably more frequently than we yet know. Parts
of *Le Panama* were apparently lifted from travel magazines; in *Dix-neuf
Poèmes* at least three poems are 'found,' or montages of found material
('Dernière heure,' 'Titres,' and 'Mee too buggi,' which is the reorganized
Cubist version of the voyage to the Tonga Islands by a follower of Captain
Cook); and much of *Kodak* was snipped out of a novel by Lerouge, *Le
Mystérieux Cornelius,* to prove, Cendrars said, the statement quoted above
about Lerouge's style.[16] Poetry would indeed be made by all, as Lautréamont had demanded; it was merely a matter of how you looked at
things. 'La poésie est dans la rue,' as Cendrars never tired of repeating.
What is most revealing in this respect about Cendrars is how little his
much-maligned fictions might be fiction; at very worst they were his
personal re-creations of the stories of others. In 'Mee too buggi' he
bypassed the European's point of view to extract the native's song out of
a condescending narrative, and in the first two lines, his only original ones,
he made his reason clear:

Comme chez les Grecs on croit que tout homme bien élevé doit savoir
    pincer la lyre
Donne-moi le fango-fango

[OC 1: 78]

The title *Kodak* was not a fanciful choice – and its replacement, *Documentaires,* confirms that – but we must not underestimate the work done in the
darkroom. Future research will no doubt reveal more 'plagiarisms' by
Cendrars – he often gives the clues himself – but they will always bear the
mark of his sensitivity, his eye on their inner light. Furthermore, as the
next chapter shows, he could never be accused of lacking in imagination.

8 Profond aujourd'hui

All truths wait in all things,

...

Logic and sermons never convince,
The damp of the night drives deeper into my soul.

...

I believe a leaf of grass is no less than the journey-work of the stars.

WHITMAN, 'Song of Myself'

After the war in which he lost his arm Cendrars wrote a number of relatively short pieces in prose – prose poems, in fact, poetic in outlook and style but appropriately prose works because they were largely philosophical, the definition of an attitude toward life. This attempt at definition was made after the epic and 'elastic' poems and before the writing of *Kodak* and *Feuilles de route*. *Profond aujourd'hui* (1917) gives Cendrars' attitude its most concise expression, but it is too concentrated to be enough of an explanation. *L'Eubage* (1923) and *J'ai tué* (1918), along with the later *Éloge de la vie dangereuse* (1926), provide more details and illustrations.

La Fin du monde filmé par l'Ange Notre-Dame (1919) and L'Eubage are works of fiction of an entirely unrealistic kind, surrealistic even, and they might be fruitfully studied in the light of surrealist theory. Both involve voyages to other worlds, metaphors for the strangeness of this world. *La Fin du monde* was apparently meant to be a film script, or perhaps an imitation of one. It certainly would have made an unusual film, with God cast as a ruthless and oblivious businessman out of a Chaplin comedy running a circus show of biblical stories on Mars and destroying the earth as a promotion stunt – something of a cross between Méliès' *Voyage dans la lune* and Lang's *Metropolis*. *La Fin du monde* as it stands, published in a beautiful limited edition with colour illustrations and painted typography by Fernand Léger,[1] views sardonically the ludicrous prostitution of the spiritual powers which could permit and even promote the first world war. Appropriately, at the end of *Moravagine* Cendrars attributes *La Fin du monde* to his demented, dying hero.

L'Eubage is surreal without social or political implications. It is a work of great lyrical beauty, entirely invented since it pretends to be 'la relation pure et simple du voyage que j'ai fait dans les montagnes suprastellaires, région inexplorée qui est comme l'hinterland du Ciel, où prennent sources les Forces et les Formes de la Vie de l'Esprit.'[2] This dedication is then signed 'L'eubage en exil, B.C.' What is an *eubage*? The *Petit Larousse*, where Cendrars says he found the title,[3] tells us he is a 'prêtre gaulois qui étudiait les sciences naturelles, l'astronomie, la divination.' On this voyage science is put to use for the discovery of something so basic, the forces and forms of life and of the spirit, that we approach a religious endeavour. Many of the details reinforce the image of the *eubage*. The book was conceived with numerous illustrations, all of mechanical or scientific apparatuses and descriptions of their functions.[4] This enterprise might be compared to Duchamp's and Picabia's invented machinery as art. Cendrars' production attempts to transform science and machinery into something more human, or to find something essentially human in the machine's movements; this was clear to a well-known critic of the time, Maurice Raynal, who had access to the original version of the book:

> Sous la poussée de son imagination virulente, Cendrars refait la science. Seul un poète comme lui peut entreprendre une tâche devant l'aridité de laquelle échouerait la médiocrité ... Ce qui fait son mérite le plus grand c'est qu'elle [l'œuvre] vit dans une sorte d'harmonie telle qu'en pourrait dégager une machine.[5]

After the first dedication of *L'Eubage* to Doucet there is a second one to another, modern *eubage,* Conrad Moricand, astrologer and companion to Montparnasse artists, later a friend of Henry Miller and Anaïs Nin and her circle.[6] Another *eubage* is referred to at the end of chapter 8 – Robert Fludd, the English mystic philosopher, doctor, and Rosicrucian. All these explorers of the 'sky's hinterland' point in the same direction – to the failure of rationality to chart the real depths of life, which include the life of the spirit, for, as Cendrars wrote in another place, 'Vivre est une action magique.'[7] Appropriately, *L'Eubage* is a magical, fantastic voyage. In chapter 5 the narrator and his crew hunt down a monstrous but beautiful animal in the river of time, but during the chase their ship is threatened with destruction: 'Et c'est à cet instant précis que j'eus la vision de la folie

de notre entreprise. Mon esprit fut accablé par l'erreur de nos recherches
et l'inanité de nos efforts scientifiques.' The problem is not miscalculation
or misuse of a valid science, but the inherent inability of any science, of
any rational formulation, to cope with this magical beast, a butterfly 'aux
ailes isochromes, et dont l'une est le matin, l'autre le soir,' whose body
is peopled by the twelve symbols of the zodiac. Before this celestial
personification of life in its most lavish form illusions of scientific evaluation are dwarfed and shattered:

> Non, il n'y a pas de lois; non, il n'y a pas de mesures. Il n'y a pas de centre.
> Pas d'unité, pas de temps, pas d'espace. Notre raisonnement scientifique
> est un pauvre petit instrument d'analyse; un filet aux mailles de plus en plus
> serrées qui capte et ligote les termes inertes de notre dialectique; un filtre
> qui dépouille les mots de tout esprit, de toute image, de toute force
> créatrice, de toute connaissance, qui les isole, les décortique, les lave, les
> purifie, les dépouille de toute attache, de tout granule, de toute scorie
> qu'ils apportaient avec eux en naissant, pour arriver à circonscrire, à pré-
> ciser une chose unique, donc métaphysique, c'est-à-dire *rien,* puisque tout
> se tient, se lie et rebondit, 'et que l'on ne peut définir un brin de paille
> sans démonter l'univers.'[8]

The subtitle of *L'Eubage, Aux antipodes de l'unité,* describes a world
where rationality holds no power, itself becomes a quaint dream, for all
things are new, different, and changing. The discoveries of science fail to
confirm the reductionist experiment – and by its obsession with unity and
pattern on a human scale almost all science is axiomatically reductionis-
tic – but instead only uncover new differences, and thus confirm what was
always known by the wise man under a tree in this passage from *Éloge de
la vie dangereuse:*

> Une fois de plus la vie change du tout au tout et recommence. 'Donnez-
> moi le septième cil de la paupière gauche, le septième de la rangée supéri-
> eure, à compter de la glande lacrymal,' disait le sage des Indes ...
> Aujourd'hui, je suis aux antipodes ... Savoir. Quoi? L'arbre de la science,
> comme ceux de cette forêt ou le figuier sous lequel radote le vieux sage
> des Indes, n'a pas deux feuilles identiques. Tu peux toujours chercher. Il
> n'y a pas d'unité. Munis-toi de loupes, de verres grossissants, de réactifs
> chimiques, d'un révélateur, d'un atlas, d'un herbier, je te défie de trouver
> deux feuilles pareilles, deux palmes semblables.[9]

The rational attack upon the unknown is futile because it is abstract; 'La
quadrature du cercle n'est pas le Verbe,' Cendrars wrote later,[10] and all

abstractions, including language, lead away from life itself. The inclusion of language can be found in an essay on poetry which makes the link between the view of life being examined here and Cendrars' translation of it into an aesthetics, or should we say a non-aesthetics, of lyricism:

> Le langage va du concret à l'abstrait, du mystique au rationnel. Les langues des sauvages abondent en catégories concrètes et particulières, celles des civilisés n'ont plus guère et de plus en plus que des catégories abstraites et générales.
>
> Le lyrisme plonge par ses racines dans les profondeurs de la conscience individuelle, c'est de là que la poésie tire sa force pour s'épanouir sur les lèvres des hommes.
>
> C'est pourquoi nous n'avons pas le droit de considérer une langue rationnelle et abstraite, parce qu'elle est la nôtre, comme supérieure à une langue concrète et mystique.[11]

Poetry for Cendrars must return to the concrete, the only repository of a mystical reality: 'Sans superstition aucune, l'instinctif balbutiement d'un enfant fait accourir l'univers, le range autour de son berceau et lui fait gracieusement don de sa réalité.'[12] The eyelash, the leaf, the child's instinctive first cry partake of the essential reality. They are *profond,* at depths unsounded by reason or principle, rock-bottom 'no-principle,' as Henry Miller has it, a phenomenologically apprehended irrationality. To grasp this concrete world outside of abstract structures of reason means to intuit existence and its meanings. To intuit, without halting to fathom, without stopping to formulate experience in systematized and usable generalizations, is to live in a constantly and forever changing world, Bergson's duration. Time assumes a different meaning, because there is no more acquiring, accounting, debits, losses, and profits to carry. Each instant of life becomes important enough, sufficient to supply superb possibilities, all of which but one – the one which chooses or which is chosen – are immediately lost without regret, new ones opening up with the next moment – *aujourd'hui.* This bears on the technique of *Feuilles de route,* where every instant is privileged and all instants on their way. Paradoxically, to live in such an unorganized fashion, at the mercy, it would seem, of accidents, coincidences, the contingent, is to live freely. Cendrars improvises. His identification with a changing and irrational existence is the demonstration of a powerful freedom, not philosophical theory as it cannot be avoided here in discussion, but practised, in art as well as, I suspect, in life. A frequent contributor to the Dada journal *Orbes* wrote:

> Cendrars ne met pas en question, dans des livres sophistiques, les conven-

tions, l'art, les influences, il les supprime net. Pour lui, se libérer, c'est
rentrer dans son naturel. Il ne discute pas dans des utopies imprimées ce
consentement mutuel, cette alliance étroite des âmes impossible à généra-
liser; il produit avec une violence dont les chaînons sont incessamment
resserrés par le marteau de la nécessité. Les novateurs modernes écrivent
des théories pâteuses, filandreuses et nébuleuses, ou des romans autobio-
graphiques, mais Cendrars pratique! Il est clair comme un fait, il est logique comme un coup de poing. [13]

Here Jean Van Heeckeren is telling us that a free man living an irrational
existence makes of action his only logic. He is an act himself, equal to
circumstance. 'He takes his stand in relation,' as Martin Buber has it in
I and Thou, and having accepted the relation Cendrars takes a stance which
is nothing if not confidently aggressive, for in its irrationality life is dangerous; I extend the quotation above from *Éloge de la vie dangereuse:*

> ... je te défie de trouver deux feuilles pareilles, deux palmes semblables.
> Deux brins d'herbe, deux pensées, deux étoiles. Deux verbes synonymes.
> Dans aucune langue du monde. Il n'y a pas d'absolu. Il n'y a donc pas de
> vérité, sinon la vie absurde qui remue ses oreilles d'âne. Attends-la, guette-
> la, tue-la. [14]

Irrationality and the word 'absurd' of course open up a special vista.
Referring to a comment on the absurdity of life in *Moravagine,* Jean-Claude
Lovey writes: 'Par cette affirmation d'un nihilisme absolu, Cendrars re-
joint tout le courant existentialiste de la littérature française au XXe siècle.' [15] Lovey's book on Cendrars is devoted, to a large extent, to the
demonstration of this opinion. No doubt there are many connections to
be made with Sartre and Camus, but Cendrars is not an existentialist. To
find life absurd is not enough, nor will Lovey's fairly vague and generalized idea of an existentialism which can group almost indiscriminately
Sartre, Camus, Malraux, and Montherlant fit Cendrars much better than
it fits all the others. Existential literature is much more a literature of and
for ideas, which, as I have just said, Cendrars' writing is not. Sartre and
Camus are so often illustrating their point. As Van Heeckeren says, Cendrars acts, with far greater freedom. Camus tells us we must force ourselves, at every moment, to face vigilantly the essential absurdity, to
maintain our awareness of the difficulty of giving meaning, responsibility,
commitment, to our acts. Typically, the Sartrian hero may give definition
to his life by one exhausting, drastic move which, because of its singular
importance, is achieved at the end or climax of the fiction. Cendrars finds
himself in no such battle with absurdity, for he likes it and lives right inside

it, and his heroes move dangerously and drastically at every turn. Again, it is a matter of opposed apprehensions of time: the existentialist is counting, he is a businessman of morality; Cendrars is prodigal, for he is never afraid of running out. Further, as philosophers the existentialists have polarized an absurd existence and a quite separate, rational man, and they have thus posited a dilemma. Cendrars sees no need of polarization, no need to 'capture and bind the inert terms of our dialectics.' Sartre tells us we are all condemned to choose; yet in the light of *J'ai tué,* for example, that condemnation is not a universal, philosophical problem, but a personal, psychological one for a particular protagonist (and this accounts for much of the strictly literary value in Sartre and Camus). For Cendrars' persona can make his choice before being condemned; that is, before he accepts *Angst* as a condition of his choice, without which there is no existentialism.

A more relevant description of Cendrars' outlook is given in Lévesque's introduction to Cendrars' *Poésies complètes,* where he places the emphasis on Zen Buddhism, Krishnamurti, and Bergson.[16] I might summarize Cendrars' attitude toward the absurd by the example of a Zen koan. When the master had his class meditate on how to get a goose out of a bottle without breaking the bottle or killing the goose he had indeed given it an 'existential' problem, compounded by a second, implicit one of how the goose got there in the first place. Existential theory would call for sweating attention to this dilemma, which if it could be solved would provide a victory over one's failure to be. However, koans were conceived without solutions, and the master broke the bottle.

In *J'ai tué* the narrator kills a man. Everything in the text confirms to us that war is disgusting, demeaning, a horror; but the killing of the German is a victory, without guilt. All of *J'ai tué* up to this killing depicts the vileness of war so vividly that one reviewer called Cendrars barbaric and wondered if this could be called art at all.[17] Officers run out; men hide, pick pockets, and play dead; dupes fall crying 'Vive la France,' or 'C'est pour ma femme'; bodies fly about dismembered; the narrator's face is splashed with blood. He describes how women in factories are worked to exhaustion to provide him with the material to go on shooting. Meanwhile, financiers make money, like God the businessman in *La Fin du monde.* But despite the stupidity of this most absurd of wars there comes a point when, to continue to live at all, one must assault another human being, brushing aside moral hesitations and becoming as intransigent as nature herself, unless one prefers to become the victim of the absurdity by refraining from the immoral and basically pointless act. It is far too late to condemn an irrational war in which men have themselves suspended morality. Cendrars' persona takes the initiative and considers himself a poet for having instinctively embraced reality rather than ethics:

> Me voici les nerfs tendus, les muscles bandés, prêt à bondir dans la réalité. J'ai bravé la torpille, le canon, les mines, le feu, les gaz, les mitrailleuses, toute la machinerie anonyme, démoniaque, systématique, aveugle. Je vais braver l'homme. Mon semblable. Un singe. Œil pour œil, dent pour dent. A nous deux maintenant. A coup de poing, à coups de couteau. Sans merci. Je saute sur mon antagoniste. Je lui porte un coup terrible. La tête est presque décollée. J'ai tué le Boche. J'étais plus vif et plus rapide que lui. Plus direct. J'ai frappé le premier. J'ai le sens de la réalité, moi, poète. J'ai agi. J'ai tué. Comme celui qui veut vivre.[18]

Éloge de la vie dangereuse also tells us the stories of two men who have killed. The first stabbed his rival, tore out his heart, and ate it on the spot. The second man has killed forty-seven, all for matters of honour. That is what the first man calls personality:

> 'Il faut avoir de l'initiative. C'est ce que j'ai enfin compris. De l'automa-tisme tant que vous voudrez, mais n'oubliez pas votre personnalité et qu'elle soit à votre disposition à la seconde précise ... dites bien à vos amis, les poètes, que la vie est dangereuse aujourd'hui et que celui qui agit doit aller jusqu'au bout de son acte sans se plaindre.'[19]

These killings are the most dramatic illustrations of Cendrars' lesson of action. Before he says 'j'ai tué' he says 'j'ai agi,' and that verb is used again above, 'celui qui agit.' The first killer acts superbly, going straight to the heart, 'Au Cœur du monde,' to use the title of a group of poems by Cendrars. It is a drastic vision, a frightening metaphor, but the shock is meant to shake us deeply and stands as the most emphatic example of a freedom to be gained many times in innumerable small ways against a backdrop of absurdity:

> L'action seul libère.
> Elle dénoue tout.
> C'est pourquoi je prends toujours part et parti, bien que ne croyant plus à rien.[20]

Henri Perruchot explains the violence and brutality of Cendrars' writing as a necessary technique which leaves the reader no respite, no civil sanctuary, which forces confrontation with sleepy premises and habits:

> Cendrars est de ceux pour qui la vie, loin d'être donnée à l'homme, doit
> être constamment créée par lui. Il est de ceux pour qui le monde doit être
> constamment bouleversé, telle la terre qui n'est féconde que lorsqu'elle est
> périodiquement éventrée. Le monde, la vie doivent être mouvement inin-
> terrompu, création continue. Il faut empêcher les hommes de dormir, leur
> reprocher comme un crime la stabilité, qui cache toujours conformisme et
> stagnation. Non pas le bonheur, la béatitude somnolente, mais l'action, le
> plus-être, le devenir. Non pas l'acceptation, mais le vouloir. Non pas
> l'ennui de vivre, mais l'ivresse de vivre.[21]

If *J'ai tué* and the view of M. Perruchot seem to open the way to a fascist
and egotistical disdain for human values, *Moravagine* and *Dan Yack* will
demonstrate the exact reverse of such egotism, and each in totally opposite
protagonists. It is perhaps only the natural complacency of readers as M.
Perruchot characterizes them which has focused attention on the more
brutal aspects of action in Cendrars. But there is no limit to the kinds of
actions in the world, whether on the battlefield or in the imagination. Only
each move must respond to the instant, match the requirements of a
chance situation for which there cannot be sufficient planning in advance.
That is why it is life that is dangerous, and not so much death; and why
'vivre est une action magique.' To refrain from acting because of danger
or pointlessness makes every moment a personal failure, an ending. 'Do
I dare,' asks Eliot's Prufrock, 'Do I dare / Disturb the universe?' and then
he relegates action to a moment in the future which he will never engage:
'In a minute there is time / For decisions and revisions which a minute
will reverse.' But every moment in which one acts is a beginning, for as
Hesse wrote in *Magister Ludi (The Glass Bead Game)*, 'A magic dwells in
each beginning.' From the danger of contingency and choice the poet culls
the essential marvel of existence and existing; after the battle with the
butterfly in *L'Eubage* the men examine the body:

> En explorant la trompe, je fis couler une goutte de miel.
>   La vie est efficacement, manifestement, formellement de l'espace et du
> temps sublimisés, fondus, aromatisés. Du miel.[22]

To live in the absurd for Cendrars is to improvise at every moment – to
invent, re-create, or discover (it is not so important which of the three)
the drop of honey, the vital essence of that precarious moment: 'En
somme, rien n'est inadmissible, sauf peut-être la vie, à moins qu'on ne
l'admette pour la réinventer tous les jours!'[23]

These are the principle meanings epitomized in the phrase 'profond
aujourd'hui.' The short essay by that name is the acute, vertiginous realiza-

tion of the presence of a real world. Everything dances about in the mind of the speaker and becomes distorted in surrealistic images which remind one of paintings by Chagall at first and develop into full-blown Surrealism (Cendrars is writing in 1917, seven years before the official beginning of Surrealism):

> Tu fonds le monde dans le moule de ton crâne ... Tout fait la roue sur les quais alors que le lion du ciel étrangle les vaches du crépuscule. Il y a des cargaisons de fruits par terre et sur les toits. Des tonneaux de feu. De la cannelle. Les femmes européennes sont comme des fleurs sous-marines devant le travail farouche des débardeurs et l'apothéose rouge-sombre des machines. On reçoit un tramway dans le dos. Une trappe s'ouvre sous votre pied. On a un tunnel dans l'œil. On monte au quinzième étage tiré par les cheveux ... Je suis empalé sur ma sensibilité.[24]

It seems that modern inventions have only accentuated the madness and confusion of the world; the microscope and the typewriter do not simplify or rationalize but rather bring the madness closer, and the poet finds himself as lost in a supposedly organized and practical world as primitive man was lost when he contemplated the stars: 'Je ne sais plus si je regarde un ciel étoilé à l'œil nu ou une goutte d'eau au microscope ... Les cosmogonies revivent dans les marques de fabrique.'[25] Every move is into a strange new world, a café, a store, a train-station, a hotel room. Each place confuses, rearranges the senses. 'L'œil tend à toucher; le dos mange; le doigt voit.' The body reverts to pre-human reflexes: 'Les cuisses se souviennent et font des mouvements de nageoires.' Then the emptied mind slowly reconstitutes the simplest elements, the simplest distinctions, a man, a woman. Still the madness dominates, for we are at the most profound depth of life's nonsense, sheer idiocy. For a moment the poet contemplates flight, that is, suicide, but he as quickly recognizes that the last thing the absurdity demands is abnegation, for he is himself creator of, and thus at least potentially master of, the absurd, 'Cette tentative de suicide est régicide.' Having thus struck bottom, he has the world revealed to him. His own bleeding is turned to light, and out of the silence of nothingness the ever waiting present snaps into place:

> Cette tentative de suicide est régicide. Je suis empalé sur ma sensibilité. Les chiens de la nuit viennent lécher le sang qui me coule le long des jambes. Ils en font de la lumière. Le silence est tel qu'on entend se bander le ressort de l'univers. Un déclic. Soudain tout a grandi d'un cran. C'est aujourd'hui.[26]

The confusion is dissipated, and we enter into harmony with our own minds, our senses, the moment; synaesthesia stabilizes; we accept the all-encompassing, hallucinating chaos as the only natural order of things:

> Crois-moi, tout est clair, ordonné, simple et naturel. Le minéral respire, le végétal mange, l'animal s'émeut, l'homme se cristallise. Prodigieux aujourd'hui. Sonde. Antenne. Porte-visage-tourbillon. Tu vis. Excentrique. Dans la solitude intégrale. Dans la communion anonyme. Avec tout ce qui est racine et cime, et qui palpite, jouit et s'extasie. Phénomènes de cette hallucination congénitale qu'est la vie dans toutes ses manifestations et l'activité continue de la conscience. Le moteur tourne en spirale. Le rythme parle. Chimisme. Tu es.[27]

Life is a congenital hallucination, obsessed with continuation. Like Whitman, Cendrars communes with a mystical yet concrete essence of life. In Cendrars there is more chaos at the heart of things, though not more variety, differentiation. The 'today' aspect of the phrase 'profond aujourd-'hui' indicates that such communion does not arise from the contemplation of spiritual perfection, immobilized values. In his last book of essays Montaigne wrote: 'Je ne peints pas l'estre. Je peints le passage' ('Du Repentir'). Cendrars too entered into a pact with a dangerous, passing time. Then, abandoning his persona, he turned from poetry and prose-poetry in which he spoke of 'I' to the three novels of the twenties in which three men not himself demonstrated the obsession of continuation, building, destroying, rebuilding. He was not to return to 'I,' the personal 'profond aujourd'hui,' until the forties.

9 'Construire ... '

I harbour for good or bad, I permit to speak at every hazard,
Nature without check with original energy.

WHITMAN, 'Song of Myself'

Having been in preparation for as long as twelve years, Cendrars' first three novels appeared in fairly quick succession: *L'Or* in 1925, *Moravagine* in 1926, and *Le Plan de l'Aiguille* and *Les Confessions de Dan Yack* together in 1929. *Le Plan de l'Aiguille* was printed in 1927, but publication was withheld to await the companion volume; the two were not published as one volume until 1946, under the title *Dan Yack*. There is a fourth work, *Rhum,* less of a novel than a reportage, published in 1930.

The subtitle for *L'Or* is 'la merveilleuse histoire du général Johann August Suter' and for *Rhum* 'l'aventure de Jean Galmot.' Both Sutter (in the French, Suter) and Galmot were real men who engaged in the activities Cendrars ascribes to them, and both of these volumes involved considerable research on his part. Cendrars planned a book on another real man, John Paul Jones, but only a few passages were ever published (see details above, page 73n). On the other hand, *Moravagine* and *Dan Yack* are termed 'romans,' and they are bona fide works of fiction, about men who seem no less real than the historical figures of the romanced biographies despite the fact that their lives are even more exceptional. We shall see that the real, historical world supplied some of the most exceptional pieces in the fictions.

Although they tell the stories of real men, both biographies use objects for their titles. At the same time we note that the novels are named after their respective heroes. Whereas in his fiction Cendrars was concerned with a man, or a force personified by a man, in his biography he preferred to avoid the person and emphasize the force or obsession. I shall examine this obsession and its attendant ironies in *L'Or* only; the lesser known *Rhum* is discussed in the next chapter.

L'Or remains Cendrars' most popular work. It has gone through more than fifteen different editions in France and has been serialized in *L'Humanité* (in 1927) and as far away as Saigon. It has been translated four times into German (not counting the complete works in progress of translation into that language) and Spanish, and at least once into Czech, English (thence into braille), Hungarian, Italian, Russian, Swedish, Flemish, Portuguese, and Serbo-Croatian. Much of this popularity is no doubt due to the topic itself – the poor immigrant becoming the Emperor of California who, when Cendrars' book appeared, had been all but forgotten.[1] The biography was in later years criticized for containing errors of fact, but these were actually very few in number. It must also be remembered that Cendrars was one of the first to research the life of this fellow-Swiss, and that he was a novelist with other concerns than the scholars.[2]

The most immediately remarkable aspect of *L'Or* is the sparseness of its style. Although John Charpentier, reviewing for the *Mercure de France,* found the art of the book 'limited,' he could not avoid sensing the basic power which distinguishes simplicity from poverty: 'Il est sec ou schématique à souhait, et l'on sent toujours dans son style le muscle, sinon l'os même, sous la chair.'[3] And Joseph Delteil wrote in his review for *La Nouvelle Revue Française:* 'Cendrars l'écrit avec sécheresse, une froideur incroyables. C'est le style des bilans. Non, plus rien, absolument rien du vieux Cendrars, du Cendrars des *Poèmes élastiques.* Plus une image, plus une belle alliance des mots. Mais des chiffres, des faits. Le journal de bord d'un homme d'action.'[4] No prose Cendrars wrote before or after, including pure newspaper work, was as terse and bare as *L'Or.* In fact it went entirely counter to the general development of his prose style when we consider that of the earlier, short prose, that of *Moravagine,* and then the writing of his last five novels where the language is nothing if not baroque, a style of massive inclusion, with sentences running on occasion over five closely printed pages. The language of *L'Or* in fact only resembles that of Cendrars' immediately preceding poetry, *Kodak* and *Feuilles de route.* Some parts of the menus which end *Kodak* even reappear in *L'Or,* on the table Sutter sets at the height of his success:

> La table était splendide. Hors-d'œuvre; truites et saumons des rivières du pays; jambon rôti à l'écossaise; ramiers, cuissot de chevreuil, pattes d'ours; langue fumée; cochon de lait farci à la rissole et saupoudré de

farine de tapioca; légumes verts, choux palmistes, gombos en salade; tous
les fruits, nature et confits; des montagnes de pâtisserie. Des vins du Rhin
et quelques vieilles bouteilles de France qui avaient fait le tour du monde
sans s'éventer tellement on en avait pris soin.[5]

In the novel Cendrars was using this material to illustrate Sutter's idea of
himself and a world he had created around him; but the descriptions in
L'Or, which so often give the effect of a documentary accumulation, have
nothing of the lavishness one expects from more romantic works such as
Flaubert's *Salammbô*, for example, for the details are not treated evoca-
tively; they are too solid to permit the reader's reverie, just as they so often
undermine or disfigure the hero's nostalgic reconstructions. Thus the
poetry of fact streamlined his prose, in at least the case of this one novel,
abbreviating comment and self-indulgence.

In *L'Or* Cendrars concentrated on a single, linear, wilful line of action,
consciously stripping his prose of images, of simultaneity (thus of 'short-
circuits' for the purpose of juxtaposition), of interweaving, and, for the
most part, of authorial intrusion. Having done so, however, and unlike
Hemingway who was making similar experiments at about this very time,
Cendrars never again reported the activities of men in such simple and
direct terms; Cendrars' world was never again so narrow in terms of the
hero's consciousness, though, as one might expect, the objective world
was as vast, in *L'Or*, as in any book following so many travels. Sutter
encompasses very little, but rather plunges onward on his track. The point
of *L'Or*'s style was to report fact and ever-pressing action as fast as action
itself. To bring the story still closer to the reader's sensitivity Cendrars
wrote the novel in the present tense, though he did it in a manner so
natural that reviews rarely noticed the innovation. Almost twenty-five
years later Cendrars described *L'Or* as

> ... un livre auquel je pensais depuis plus de dix ans, un manuscrit quasi
> abondonné et auquel je ne travaillais que par intermittence, une histoire
> merveilleuse que je me mis tout à coup à élaguer et à dépouiller pour en
> faire une histoire vraie, un récit que je réécrivis entièrement au présent
> de l'indicatif, celui des cinq modes du verbe qui exprime l'état, l'existence
> ou l'action d'une manière certaine, positive, absolue ... écrit linéaire ex-
> actement le contraire du mode d'écriture polymère ou polymorphe mais
> semblablement universel que j'emploie présentement pour tracer le por-
> trait d'un somnambule.[6]

Sutter could easily have played the role of one of Cendrars' uncles, for
he was the Swiss who gave up a sedentary and bourgeois life to search for

his fortune in the New World. Cendrars followed Sutter's 'Odyssey'[7]
from the time of his departure from Switzerland to Paris, New York, and
the West, up and down the Pacific coast, and eventually to Sutter's New
Helvetia (to become Sacramento) with no comments, overt or implied,
upon his robbing – and being robbed – cheating, slave-buying, or other
improper or illegal activities. In Sutter we decipher less a moral being than
the incarnation of a force of nature in the shape of an obsession which is
hypnotic. The effect is definitely cinematographic, particularly if we think
of a silent film, and one without dialogue cards, one, in fact, where the
characters have nothing to say to each other![8] We are presented with a
single consecutive series of actions, broken into short tableaux, which
affords no opportunity for verbal reflection and never any possibility of
standing still and questioning, only the necessity of going forward. Sutter
himself hardly utters more than a few sentences in the whole novel. The
speed and directness of the action lends the narrative a cool objectivity
which is rare in Cendrars; in one instance the somewhat omniscient author
intervenes to announce the destruction of Sutter's short-lived equilibrium–to warn that his 'film' will not stop:

> Rêverie. Calme. Repos.
> C'est la paix.
> Non. Non. Non. Non. Non. Non. Non. Non. Non: c'est l'OR!
> C'est l'or.
> Le rush.
> La fièvre de l'or qui s'abat sur le monde.
> La grande ruée de 1848, 1849, 1850, 1851 et qui durera quinze ans.
> SAN FRANCISCO![9]

Such infrequent transitions in an otherwise straightforward narrative – this
constitutes one whole chapter, out of only seventeen in all – show us a
fatality working behind the scenes against which no amount of dogged
action on Sutter's part will avail. A passage such as the above hints at the
ironic premise of the story: the ruin of a millionaire by the discovery of
gold on his own land. For Sutter, after all, built a solid empire upon
farming and industry, upon real productivity, and it was taken from him
by an abstraction. The title clearly announces this irony, since gold is
Sutter's downfall, the last thing he wants. As Emile Szittya wrote, *L'Or* is
'contre l'or, pour le blé.'[10]

The novel and Sutter are against gold, but gold is the subject, and the
obsession of all men in the novel except Sutter. Although his rise to power
is not in the least moral and legal, we are never brought to consider his
downfall at the hands of the forty-niners and their American government

a moral retribution; rather it is a tragic irony, his defeat at the hands of forces he cannot control yet which he himself set into motion. Sutter's obsession is with the land itself, the age-old obsession of a good peasant, in fact, and he adroitly wrestles valuable and productive life from that land. But as he walks, and soon has to ride for days, over it, surveying his successful industry, beneath his steps his destiny patiently waits and the reader is forewarned.

It must be noted that Sutter makes no attempt to dig gold for himself, and given his previous activities we might have been inclined to distrust Cendrars' portrayal, if this had been fiction. Herein lies one aspect of Cendrars' interest in this and many another historical figure; the reality of the 'histoire vraie' as it violates expectation, one man's irrational but all too poignantly human choice of course of action and his illogical and often self-destructive ascent. A number of times Sutter declares, 'L'or est maudit.' After being ruined, he is afraid of seeking compensation for his Californian empire because he has seen the corruption, madness, suicide even, that overtake the gold seekers, and he maintains a self-preserving moral sense: 'L'or porte malheur; si j'y touche, si je le poursuis, si je revendique ce qui m'en revient de plein droit, est-ce que je ne vais pas être maudit à mon tour ... ?' (p. 193). Sutter nevertheless decides to sue for compensation, for justice. Very quickly he is no longer concerned with property values, for he comes to see himself engaged in a holy war. Gold becomes an obsession for him, but as an enemy. Near the end of his fight, and his life, the events in California after the rush become in his mind a fulfilment of the *Apocalypse:*

> La Grande Prostituée, qui a accouché sur la Mer, c'est Christophe Colomb découvrant l'Amérique.
> Les Anges et les Étoiles de saint Jean sont dans le drapeau américain, et avec la Californie, une nouvelle étoile, l'Étoile d'Absinthe, est venue s'inscrire dans la bannière étoilée.
> L'Anti-Christ, c'est l'Or. [p. 222]

The two forces in conflict, well beyond Sutter's control, are his basically peasant instinct to build and society's cupidity. Sutter's instinct is constructive, despite the harm it may bring to whatever and whomever may happen to be in its path. It sweeps aside moral considerations, but then again it builds civilizations. Sutter is the personification of such an instinct outside of good and evil, a representative man in the deep sense which Carlyle and Emerson may have intuited when they wrote of the hero in society; but he is also singly human, and just as he always carries the book of the *Apocalypse* with him on his odyssey, he also carries within himself a defeat as sure as his instinct. Gold is the oracle's prediction. The failure of the gold seekers to prefer Sutter's way, husbandry, to the quicker but spiritually as well as socially destructive way of gold draws a dark picture of society as a whole which in part vindicates Sutter, who had made, when we put them in the balance, infinitely less serious moral errors. He too had left the land of his birth, unsatisfied. He demanded, exacted satisfaction from the fates, and this is the arrogance of the others; but unlike them, he retained, quite blindly, the inner need to make, to build with the land, whereas the gold diggers only dreamed of taking, of making a desperate killing without returning anything of substance (the more modern sense of 'gold digger' shows that the popular imagination understood this failure to exchange).

Sutter had substance, because the land was more than dust. A few years later Cendrars made the judgment in his own voice, praising the modern innovation of monoculture in 'La Métaphysique du café,' where he concluded that Brazilian coffee represented 'une lente conquête de l'esprit humain qui s'entoure d'ordre et d'harmonie dans sa lutte contre la nature' and thus was 'une entité métaphysique, au même titre que les autres produits de la terre et tout le labeur de l'homme.'[11] As for the 'handful of dust,' gold, a number of pages in Le Lotissement du ciel lash out at the effects of man's cupidity (with good biblical authority, of course, against cupidity though not money in itself) in what may well be the most angry and abusive language to be found in Cendrars, who never minced words in any case. Gold is

> Hostie métallique de l'économie politique!
>
> L'or est un leurre.
> Et dire que depuis la nuit des temps l'homme social n'a jamais su faire mieux que de s'hypnotiser sur cet artifice! [pp. 485, 486]

L'Or represents the battle between the actions of a man who pursues a metaphysical or spiritual endeavour in the ever solid and renewing earth and those of a society grasping for an insubstantial artifice, what I called earlier an abstraction. Spirituality is different from abstraction because the endeavour which fulfils the spiritual need is by that very activity constructive; it is a quality of the endeavour, and not the goal of it. Spiritual worth is discovered by practice and in practising; hence the familiar, time-honoured value of producing from the land and the age-old warning against cupidity; hence also the present tense of the narrative. 'Johann August Suter est un homme d'action,' writes Cendrars (p. 129), action signifying to be building. His Eldorado was the soil upon which he must erect a substantial, conservative reality. But he became in turn literally 'El Dorado,' the man of gold, and was stripped by his idolators. Cendrars concludes in *Le Lotissement du ciel* that death must be the lot of the avaricious, and that death on the grand scale, a war to end all wars, is the lot of a social world divided between Communism and Capitalism but united in its dedication to gain rather than freedom.[12] We might call this grim position, in its political aspect, Anarchism, and it might be compared to John Dos Passos' often misunderstood position. Sutter is not after gain, for he does not hoard. He is a sort of benign anarchist, ignorant of politics because politics have no understanding of his age-old economics.

It may seem paradoxical that this peasant should travel so far and venture so much. In Sutter, Cendrars united what seem two opposite poles of human nature, the need to hold to the land and the need to hold more land, to fructify beyond what was given at birth. It is one of the American dreams, which is to say, a European's dream about an America where he might repeat for himself his own gentry's original land-grab. Thus Faulkner pictured Thomas Sutpen in *Absalom, Absalom!* wresting his hundred acres from Indians and swamps, the main difference between Sutter and Sutpen being the latter's ancient need for a son. Interestingly, both Cendrars and Faulkner decided to maintain a certain distance from their American archetypes; this is clearly discernable in *Absalom, Absalom!* where four different narrators attempt to reconstruct Sutpen's story years after his death. In this novel as in *L'Or* the reader is kept at a distance from the hero's achievements, which resembles that separating the hero from his dream of a vast and perfect home.

In going so far to be reborn on his Swiss farm, Sutter incarnated the peasant's revolt. He was a perfect persona for Cendrars, who no doubt could feel something of the *mal du pays* of his 'uncles,' and there is much which is typically Swiss in the contradiction, as Robert Kanters suggested in his *Neuf siècles de littérature française:* 'En un sens, la Suisse, pays d'extrême milieu, reste fidèle à sa vocation ... en donnant à la littérature française de l'époque, comme deux grands pôles extrêmes, Ramuz, le paysan, et Cendrars, le voyageur.[13] These extremes are the two sides of one and the same coin, represented in this case by Sutter; to build well, at any cost, somewhere.

At the same time Cendrars was writing of the defeat of the builder at the hands of greed he was also working on a force opposite to Sutter's, the destructive force of Moravagine, an 'idiot,' who like an avenging angel casts the world into apocalyptic chaos. *Moravagine*[14] is the work for which Cendrars is most famous as a writer of fiction. The book's fame, in fact,

preceded its publication, for it was praised and quoted at length by Pierre
de Massot in his *De Mallarmé à 391,* a now rare monograph of great
importance for the development of Dada. Massot wrote, in 1922, that
Cendrars was 'un des esprits les plus brillants et les plus féconds de cette
époque, esprit largement en avant du mouvement contemporain.' Quoting some three pages from portions of *Moravagine* which had appeared in
Les Écrits Nouveaux in 1921 Massot commented: 'Là, Blaise Cendrars ne
ressemble à personne, n'imite personne, montre ce dont il est capable.
Une ironie cruelle, voilée avec tact; une imagination de féerie; un lyrisme
éclatant et sobre; un style ramassé, farci d'images.'[15] By the time *Moravagine* was published in 1926 it could no longer be relevant to Dada as a
movement, nor very much even to an infant Surrealism, which will be
discussed later. Yet, as Jacques-Henry Lévesque pointed out, this novel,
which was conceived before the war, contained all the elements of these
two movements: 'vie intérieur, folie, vie active, esprit de révolte, crime
gratuit, révolution, évasion dans le rêve, conflit entre la liberté et la
nécessité, sexualisme, absurdité du monde.'[16]

Moravagine personifies more powerfully than almost any character in
fiction all of these demented forces. It was perhaps necessary, then, that
he be a created fiction, though in recent years many novelists and critics
have opined that the reverse is true and that the real world is supplying
horrors and fantasies no fiction could hope to match. Cendrars incorporated many details from real events or circumstances into the novel and
its characters; these were not the least fantastic ones and virtually never
served to make an extraordinary tale less so. For example, it is possible
to navigate up the Orinoco River in Venezuela and emerge, without
portage, in the Amazon, as Raymond and Moravagine do. Thus one of the
book's sections least likely to sustain a willing suspension of disbelief is not
the product of the author's negligence or indifference but his consciously
sought out geographical freak, a natural violation of nature's laws. The
Casiquiare Canal, a natural waterway linking two theoretically separate
river basins, also separates veracity from logic and common sense. The
sense of a fantasy voyage reminds one of *L'Eubage,* but reality has supplied
the fantasy. Another case, Moravagine's capricious flight, during the war,
to bomb Vienna, finds its precedent in one Lieutenant Marchal who flew
1,300 km to raid Berlin in 1916. Marchal was later decorated, and we shall
see that Raymond's opinion of Moravagine's exploit is quite different. But
the mad stories are there, to be used.

There is no one source for the numerous activities of Moravagine. My
own first candidate for the essential anarchistic aspect is Otto Gross, the
German psychoanalyst who preached the destruction of the prevailing
social order and practised his preaching more than most (see the biograph-

ical section above, page 41, for Cendrars' knowledge of Gross); he had many mistresses, and his relationships with them were as open as his relationship with his wife. A number of them bore his children, all of whom were dealt with equally. One of these mistresses was Frieda Week-ley, née Von Richthofen, soon to be Lawrence, and Martin Green makes a good case for D.H. Lawrence's ideas to be those of Gross as transmitted by Frieda.[17] Gross gave at least two of his female patients the means to commit suicide, and they did. In 1913 he was committed to an asylum by his father, a world-renowned criminologist. In *The Life and Work of Sigmund Freud* Ernest Jones reports that Jung treated Gross's schizophrenia in a clinic in Switzerland and that Gross escaped from the clinic by going over the wall; the resemblance with *Moravagine,* with Raymond then cast as Jung, the young and ambitious doctor about to break with Freudian orthodoxy (schizophrenia is usually considered to be incurable), is striking; however, Jones's story may be at least a partial fabrication and finds no confirmation in Green's book.

Raymond, the opening chapter of the novel tells us, may not really be named Raymond; and Cendrars knew he could not pretend that he was, in historical reality, Raymond-la-Science, the cool intellectual member of the Bonnot gang who was executed in 1913. Cendrars is using the name as an emblem, as one might say in a novel where we are pretending to protect the hero's identity, 'Let's call him Gavrilo Princip.' However, Raymond is not, in the novel proper, a killer but rather the professional observer, and in this respect he takes on part of Gross's projection into the novel, the mad scientist, a Dr Frankenstein who does not have to create his monster from pieces of others – as Cendrars does – but only lets him out of his cage.

Specific actions of Moravagine also have precedent. His activities in Berlin are announced as those of Jack the Ripper, but we do not have to travel back thirty-five years for the real source, which was the subject, if not the obsession, of German Expressionist films in the twenties: *The Cabinet of Dr Caligari,* directed by Robert Wiene in 1920, treats themes similar to those of *Moravagine,* and the main plot evolves around the use by Caligari, the director of an insane asylum, of a patient to murder his enemies. Cendrars may have known the painters who designed the famous sets, Herman Warm, Walter Rohrig, and Walter Reinmann, Expressionists from the *Sturm* group; he certainly knew the film, as he wrote a critical review of it in 1922 (see chapter 3, footnote 26). One of the most famous sequels to *Caligari* was Paul Leni's *Waxworks* of 1924, where two of the historical characters who come back to life are Ivan the Terrible and Jack the Ripper.

Moravagine's activities in pre-revolutionary Russia must owe something to the life of Azev, the extraordinary double agent who was a rank-
ing agent of the police at the very same time he assassinated Plehve, and
many others, as a member of the Terrorist Brigade. Much information
could have come from Boris Savinkov, a former terrorist who could often
be found at La Rotonde café and who later published his memoirs, including a chapter on the exposure of Azev, in 1931.[18] Azev's position in the
terrorist movement was so secure that no one would believe he could be
a traitor when he was first accused, and when the case was proven the
movement's morale never recovered from the blow. It was impossible to
accept that he had no allegiance at all; yet this is precisely why Moravagine
resembles him so closely, and why the novel *Moravagine* is in many respects
a true story, one made easier to believe in the shape of a fiction, or a myth.
In *Moravagine* Cendrars has generalized many separate realities.

At the age of four Moravagine sets fire to all the carpets in the château
where he is reared as the last descendant of a royal family deprived of the
Hungarian throne (Cendrars wrote in the 'Pro Domo' appended to the
novel that this also was a real man, one Sadory who was one of Rodin's
workmen [p. 431]). At six he is married, thereafter to see his 'wife,' the
Princess Rita, once a year. Obsessed with her and with her image, the day
after her second visit he cuts the eyes out of all the paintings in the château.
At ten he attempts to run away by strapping himself to the belly of his mare
and setting fire to the stables; but the fleeing horse is shot and he is crushed
under the weight. He survives with permanent damage to his leg. Much
later, in Russia, Raymond will have to amputate a toe from this leg before
they board a train to escape the police. At fifteen he puts out his dog's eyes
and breaks its back. He begins to find satisfaction and even sensual plea-
sure in inanimate objects, and eventually he comes to compare Rita's
features to the perfections of metal, egg, stone, and grass. At eighteen,
when one day Rita announces that she will not return again, he kills her
savagely. He is imprisoned for ten years, and then sent to the asylum for
another six, where Raymond finds him. The year is 1900. The old order
has managed to keep him at bay for thirty-four years, during the last six
well hidden as a madman, which no doubt he is, thanks to what that order
thinks of human nature. With the new century he is set loose by Raymond.
It is at this point that the novel opens, with Raymond, ambitious and fresh
out of medical school, on his way to his first job. Raymond wants to live
with and observe clinically – or so he says – this 'grand fauve humain' who
no sooner jumps the wall of the hospital than he kills a little girl who is
collecting wood there: 'Ceci fut le commencement d'une randonnée qui
devait durer plus de six ans à travers tous les pays du globe. Moravagine

laissait partout un ou plusieurs cadavres féminins derrière lui. Souvent par pure facétie' (p. 270). As Yeats writes in 'The Second Coming':

> And what rough beast, its hour come round at last,
> Slouches towards Bethlehem to be born?

There is not room to detail Moravagine's and Raymond's activities. In Berlin, Moravagine becomes a second Jack the Ripper (he shares with his prototype the need to destroy the belly, as his name, 'death to the vagina,' implies). They are obliged to flee to Russia, where they join a revolutionary cell. This is the longest episode, entitled 'Mascha' after the woman revolutionary who has a tempestuous affair with Moravagine. When their coup fails they flee again, to the United States, whence they are obliged to escape to South America. They travel up the Orinoco, stay with the Jivaro, or 'Blue' Indians, whom they practically destroy; then they flee again, up the Orinoco to join the Rio Negro and come out into the Amazon. They now return to France, where Raymond had started out, and, separating, fight in the first world war, the inevitable culmination of Moravagine's prophetic activities. Shortly before Moravagine's death Raymond, who has lost a leg, discovers him in another asylum, taking morphine (there are almost no places left on his body soft enough to take the needle), completely crazy, and writing thousands of manuscript pages about his travels to Mars. Moravagine does not recognize his faithful companion, but when Raymond first comes upon his 'grand fauve humain' in this last prison (for this war-time neurological centre is the old fort on L'Ile Sainte-Marguerite, off Cannes, where the man in the iron mask was held) in answer to the nurse's surprised question, 'Comment, vous le connaissez?' as if it were inconceivable that any human knew him, Raymond replies, 'Je pense bien, Mademoiselle, c'est mon frère' (p. 404).

The whole novel is the devastating, progressive revelation of the kinship between Moravagine and the dark side of Raymond and, through him, of ourselves – 'Hypocrite lecteur, – mon semblable, – mon frère!' However, this accusation, as it were, of brotherhood does not allude to *l'ennui,* as it does in Baudelaire's 'Au Lecteur,' nor to the discovery of man's living death, as it does in Eliot's use of Baudelaire's line in *The Waste Land.* Far from being oppressed by life, Moravagine lives with great energy and momentum, and the rich style of the writing underscores this at every moment; for in him resides the yet deeper force of hate and revenge which has already been repressed in Baudelaire's and Eliot's poems to produce self-inflicted guilt and pain. Moravagine is never afraid to kill, for he has no morality. Christine Morrow in *Le Roman irréaliste*[19] shows how Moravagine is the perfect fulfilment, in advance, of André

Breton's demands in his second Surrealist Manifesto, published in 1930. Interestingly, both Cendrars and Breton after him begin with the medical analysis of a madman in an asylum. In many places Moravagine illustrates Breton's theory, for as he jumps the asylum wall he takes upon himself the primitive revenge of twentieth-century man entangled in a plethora of superficial and demeaning conventions and institutions, all sublimations which have been robbed of purpose. Breton wrote:

> ... on conçoit que le surréalisme n'ait pas craint de se faire un dogme de la révolte absolue, de l'insoumission totale, du sabotage en règle, et qu'il n'attende encore rien que de la violence. L'acte surréaliste le plus simple consiste, révolvers aux poings, à descendre dans la rue et à tirer au hasard, tant qu'on peut, dans la foule.[20]

Of course this resembles the program of Dada, as my quotation above from M. Lévesque indicates. The essential difference lies in Surrealism's emphasis on the unconscious and its meaningfulness, and in this respect *Moravagine* is surrealistic. But often Moravagine's actions seem to go beyond the scope of motivation as we understand the word, a cause at least somewhat proportionate to the actions we observe. Breton, after all, goes on to make serious reservations about his 'acte le plus simple.' But personal motivation in Moravagine quickly dissolves into purely archetypal activity through both the extent of his destructiveness and Cendrars' treatment of it. We might say that the nightmare of *Moravagine* plunges below the field of the Surrealists' Freudian, personal dream to a Jungian, collective dream of universal and objective rather than individual and subjective meaning; and as it does so it probably becomes more Dada. We are warned of this complex oneiric aspect of the novel in the epigraph from Remy de Gourmont, which announces a dream and also sets the stage for the confusion between dream and fact (fictional fact, that is) which is so important to the book's effect: 'Je montrerai comment ce peu de bruit intérieur, qui n'est rien, contient tout, comment, avec l'appui bacillaire d'une seule sensation, toujours la même et déformée dès son origine, un cerveau isolé du monde peut se créer un monde ... '[21]

So at the very outset we may wonder just what is meant to be the dream: the adventures? Moravagine himself? *Moravagine?* Also, and possibly a more immediate question, who is the dreamer? It is natural to assume Raymond is, since he is the narrator. But Cendrars offers another possibility when Raymond recognizes the resemblance of his and his comrade's revolutionary activities to Moravagine's childhood fantasies:

> N'étions-nous donc que les pâles entités jaillies de son cerveau, les medi-

ums hystériques que sa volonté mettait en branle ou des êtres consternés
que son cœur généreux nourrissait du meilleur de son sang? Parturition
d'un être humain, trop humain, surhumain, tropisme ou extrême déprava-
tion, en nous regardant agir, en nous observant de près, Moravagine
étudiait, contemplait son propre double, mystérieux, profond, en communion avec la cime et la racine, avec la vie, avec la mort, et c'est ce qui
lui permettait d'agir sans scrupules, sans remords, sans hésitation, sans
trouble et de répandre du sang en toute confiance, comme un créateur,
indifférent comme Dieu, indifférent comme un idiot. [p. 310]

A case of the dreamer dreamed, as it were. The dreamer then might not
be a person at all, but a force, creator, god, or idiot, an *élan* of death
projecting its power into the minds of blind men. I shall return to the
dream aspect of the novel at the end of this section.

   Moravagine is precisely that force, feeding Raymond's quest for
anarchy (we learn in the beginning of the novel that Raymond will
become a regicide) while destroying in him the search for some sort of
rationality which is, after all, his excuse for the whole enterprise. Moravagine tells him:

> 'Tu n'as donc pas encore compris que le monde de la pensée est fichu et
> que la philosophie c'est pis que le bertillonnage. Vous me faites rire avec
> votre angoisse métaphysique, c'est la frousse qui vous étreint, la peur de
> la vie, la peur des hommes d'action, de l'action, du désordre. Mais tout
> n'est que désordre, mon bon ... Pourquoi voulez-vous y mettre de l'ordre?
> Quel ordre? Que cherchez-vous? Il n'y a pas de vérité ... La vie c'est le
> crime, le vol, la jalousie, la faim, le mensonge, le foutre, la bêtise, les
> maladies, les éruptions volcaniques, les tremblements de terre, des mon-
> ceaux de cadavres. Tu n'y peux rien, mon pauvre vieux, tu ne vas pas te
> mettre à pondre des livres, hein?... '
>   Moravagine avait tellement raison que trois jours plus tard, un di-
> manche, jour fixé pour leur envolée merveilleuse, c'était la guerre, la
> Grande Guerre, le 2 août 1914. [p. 393]

We find here the theme of action in a world of disorder which runs
through much of Cendrars' work, particularly in these three novels of the
twenties, and one which has been examined at length in chapter 8. But
in *Moravagine* action, though an identification of the human with the
natural, can be the reverse of constructive, as it is in *L'Or.* In my epigraph
from Whitman we may see that he too, despite his reputation for indis-
criminate optimism, could feel that the essential energy of nature bore no
relation to good and evil, only to necessity. Destructive though Morava-

gine is, he embodies a return to instinct, thus to nature, which is the reflex of an oppressed, over-socialized civilization heading straight for the catastophe of world war. When Raymond and Moravagine spend the first three years of their adventure together in Berlin, Moravagine studies music in a search for the essential rhythm of life. But he abandons this theoretical study to embody the rhythm in his own demented living. His life is a curse, but he abandons himself to it because it is life, which the study of life manifestly was not. Raymond explains:

> C'est ainsi que l'étude serrée d'une partition musicale ne nous fera jamais découvrir cette palpitation initiale qui est le noyau autogénérateur de l'œuvre et qui dépend, en sa climatérique, de l'état général de l'auteur, de son hérédité, de sa physiologie, de la structure de son cerveau, de la rapidité plus ou moins grande de ses réflexes, de son érotisme, etc. Il n'y a pas de science de l'homme, l'homme étant essentiellement porteur d'un rythme. Le rythme ne peut être figuré. Seuls quelques très rares individus, les 'grands détraqués,' peuvent en avoir une révélation véhémente que leur désorientation sexuelle préfigure. Aussi était-ce bien en vain que Moravagine s'ingéniait à trouver une cause extérieure à son malaise de vivre et cherchait-il une démonstration objective qui l'autorisât d'être ce qu'il était.[22]

From the study of music Moravagine goes straight to murder, the rhythm his world has prepared him for.

Raymond often remains unaffected by his friend's actions because his presumably professional observation of them gives him no real understanding, no penetration of his complicity, just as the music professor has no real understanding of rhythm. At moments, under the great pressure produced by living with Moravagine, he comes to feverish and desperate insights such as the following:

> Tout ce que l'on peut admettre, affirmer, la seule synthèse, c'est l'absurdité de l'être, de l'univers, de la vie. Qui veut vivre doit se tenir plus près de l'imbécillité que de l'intelligence et ne peut vivre que dans l'absurde. Manger des étoiles et rendre du caca, voila toute l'intelligence. Et l'univers n'est, dans le cas optime, que la digestion de Dieu.[23]

Moravagine's actions have no goal, as Sutter's always did. Or we may say he has an anti-goal. He destroys with equanimity whatever happens to cross his path, which most often is a path of escape. But, and this is his genius, he always dominates his opportunistic actions, and never gives the impression of fleeing because he has no pride; he is never hurt by defeat

or loss and thus always takes away in his flight a perfect sense of victory
for whatever has been achieved. In turn, every new situation falls under
his guidance; he is successful because he is a man of action who has no
prejudices, carries no imperative and compelling past, and thus instinctively discovers and submits himself to the revealing rhythm of all he
encounters. That undecipherable rhythm of life, as Raymond explains it
at length, is what appears to ordinary men as luck or chance, or, if one
can put it all together, destiny:

> Il y a aussi dans l'action le contentement de faire quelque chose, n'importe
> quoi, et le bonheur de se dépenser. C'est un optimisme inhérent, propre,
> conditionnel à l'action et sans lequel elle ne pourrait se déclencher ... cet
> optimisme aiguise l'esprit, il vous donne un certain recul et, à la dernière
> heure, il fait tomber dans votre champ visuel un rayon perpendiculaire qui
> éclaire tous vos calculs précédents, les coupe, les trie et vous tire la carte
> du succès, le numéro gagnant. C'est ce qu'on appelle après coup la chance,
> comme si le hasard n'avait pas figuré dans les données du problème sous
> forme d'équation à la n-ième puissance et n'avait déclenché l'action. Un
> joueur qui perd est un amateur, mais un professionnel gagne à chaque
> coup, car il tient toujours compte de cette puissance et s'il ne la résout
> mathématiquement, il la chiffre sous forme de tics, de superstitions, d'au-
> gures, de grigris, tout comme un général à la veille de livrer bataille, qui
> suspend son action, parce que le lendemain est un 13 ou un vendredi, ou
> parce qu'il a ceint son épée à droite et que son cheval a répandu de l'avoine
> à gauche. En tenant compte de ces avertissements, on contemple comme
> le visage de son destin et c'est cela qui rend grave, sérieux, et qui plus tard
> fait croire au spectateur ou au témoin que le gagnant, que le vainqueur
> était un être élu des dieux. Celui qui triche au grand jeu du destin est
> comme un homme qui, se regardant dans un miroir, se ferait des grimaces,
> puis se mettrait en colère et, perdant tout contrôle de lui-même, briserait
> le miroir et finirait par se claquer. C'est un enfantillage, et la plupart des
> joueurs sont des enfants, c'est pourquoi ils enrichissent la banque et que
> le destin semble invincible.[24]

Thus Moravagine is capable of joining and dominating any kind of activity
wherever he finds it. He is a picaro-demon, with no illusions or misconcep-
tions, never the Quixote-like victim of his ideals about the voyage. The
unity of the novel does not come, as it usually does in the picaresque
genre, from an attempt to define oneself in relation to diversified experiences, and in this sense the plot rambles more than usual for the genre.
Cendrars often quoted in his later novels the biblical line from John, 'Le
vent souffle où il veut.' That is chance as destiny, or, to use the words of

my epigraph from Whitman, 'the original energy' of 'nature without check' charging 'every hazard.'[25] Moravagine's energy is negative, and unity, 'aux antipodes de l'unité' as the subtitle of *L'Eubage* runs, is found in the successive collapses of all the scenes he enters.

Moravagine's destiny is the insatiable yearning for anarchy, and beyond if possible, for his freedom is at infinity. But in much of his work Cendrars considered the practice of action more constructive, and we find in *Moravagine* two notable instances of his optimism which remind us of Whitman's overall attitude. Both of these passages are eulogies of work and workers.

The first is all of chapter 'm' – each chapter is designated by a letter and the book runs from 'a' to 'z,' enclosing completely Moravagine's life and death – 'Nos randonnées en Amérique,' published separately in 1926 and again later in the collection *Aujourd'hui* as 'Le principe de l'utilité.' These pages of *Moravagine* constitute a praise of pragmatism and of work, and of the United States, a new world which practises the principle of utility, basic to the activity of living from primitive societies on down to our time, but atrophied in Europe:

> Les machines sont là et leur bel optimisme.
>
> Elles sont comme le prolongement de la personnalité populaire, comme la réalisation de ses pensées les plus intimes, de ses tendances les plus obscures, de ses appétits les plus forts; elles sont son sens d'orientation, son perfectionnement, son équilibre et non pas des réalités extérieures douées d'animisme, des fétiches ou des animaux supérieurs.
>
> C'est le grand honneur du jeune peuple américain d'avoir retrouvé le principe de l'utilité et ses innombrables applications dont les plus élémentaires bouleversent déjà la vie, la pensée et le cœur humains. [pp. 350-1]

Most important, Cendrars considers this pragmatism to generate directly the finest art, the poetry of constructive, useful action:

> Voyez ce premier avion dont le volume, la surface portante, la forme, dont les lignes, les couleurs, la matière, le poids, dont les angles, dont les incidences, dont tout est méticuleusement calculé, dont tout est le produit des mathématiques pures. C'est la plus belle projection du cerveau. Et ce n'est pas une œuvre de musée, on peut se mettre dedans et s'envoler! [p. 350]

This functionalism is the first key to Cendrars' enthusiasm for machinery and modern inventions, as well as for folk and popular art. Functionalism is in itself a moral force, opposed to usury. And exactly as for Henry

Adams in 'The Dynamo and the Virgin,' its power, mystical and 'occult,' as Adams has it, displaces that of the cross, and restores Eros.[26] A machine's 'optimism' is the degree to which it fulfils the dream that built it, the degree to which the body can actually, now, fly with the imagination. In the United States Moravagine kills no one.

The second striking instance of optimism in the worker occurs when Raymond and Moravagine return from South America to a grey and bourgeois Paris: 'Mais où était donc l'or de la France, la nouveauté, les Hommes nouveaux?' exclaims Raymond. They are finally found working on an airplane, 'La plus belle projection du cerveau.' This is perhaps the passage in Cendrars which most resembles the pure Whitmanesque style:

> Peuple magnifique de Levallois-Perret et de Courbevoie, peuple en cotte bleue, peuple de la voiture-aviation, nous suivions vos bandes quand vous rentriez chez vous et nous étions encore là, le matin, quand vous vous rendiez au travail. Usines, usines, usines. Usines de Boulogne à Suresnes. Seules communes de Paris où il y ait des enfants dans les rues. Nous ne fréquentions maintenant plus que les bouillons de cette zone et les brillants apéritifs-concerts du soir. Tous les samedis poule au gibier. Il y a de grands billards, des gramophones géants et des appareils à sous tout neufs. On dépense. On ne compte pas. Appétit, gaieté, luxe, chants, danses, musiques nouvelles. Familles nombreuses ... il n'y a que toi de vrai, que toi de Français, peuple en cotte bleue, peuple de voiture-aviation. Vous êtes tous des Poilus et des As.[27]

These people are valued for their work with modern machinery, but especially for not being subservient to it. Their freedom comes from their prodigality, their desire to spend their lives – unlike the rest of Paris, all guarded savings and guarding bureaucracy.

Moravagine too is, as a person, a man of involvement who has great optimism in his acts. But as a force of destruction he represents the opposite of this 'peuple magnifique,' and he is magnificent only in the purity and disinterestedness of his terrible acts. Gide's Lafcadio is squeamish in comparison, his 'acte gratuit' a dilettante's experiment with his own personal doubts. Through Moravagine acts the revenge of a violated principle of utility, or again of the violated rhythm. Like much of Zürich Dada, Moravagine personifies the revulsion at the forces which were clearly urging war for years before 1914. They did so in the name of civilization, and it is thus appropriate that such a society be physically and morally assaulted by Dada, and by Moravagine. Late in the novel we find Raymond critical of Moravagine for having failed in this sacred assault. In chapter 'p' Moravagine becomes an aviator. Raymond does not join this enterprise, the goal of which is to fly around the world. Since their return from the Americas Raymond seems less dependent. When they had escaped the Blue Indians, he had almost died of tropical fever, and his slow recovery, as they work their way out of the jungle, seems to have served as a sort of purgatory. Now the two seem to part, going to war separately. Later we discover that Moravagine in his airplane attempted to bomb the Emperor's palace in Vienna. Raymond is disappointed in this show of personal vengeance:

> Moravagine avait raté la plus belle occasion de sa vie. S'occuper de François-Joseph alors que le monde entier marchait sur ses traces et que moi, je m'attendais à le voir surgir pour détruire toutes les nations!
> Quel lâche!
> J'en restai profondément déçu... [p. 396]

Now Moravagine is reduced to personal, if grandiose, acts, but has transmitted greater ones to his aspirant. The man Moravagine has imposed himself as dream.

We see that Raymond had never really abandoned Moravagine, or at least the image he formed of him. As we approach the end we are brought to wonder even more how much of the anarchy is due to someone called Moravagine and how much to Raymond's view of his so-called 'fauve.' Raymond is of course the narrator. He speaks in the first person, and some have hastily identified an apparently ingenuous or careless author with the first person singular of the novel, and thus with the dreaming anarchist. But Cendrars suddenly appears near the end of the novel in his own person, working on the wing of the Borel airplane (p. 390). This produces something of a jolt in the reader, a little bit as if he had come across himself in the book. The effect is furthered when Raymond requests of Cendrars to publish one of Moravagine's manuscripts (p. 417). He is speaking of a book called *La Fin du monde,* which Cendrars indeed published a few years earlier under his own name; if Cendrars relinquishes paternity, perhaps indeed it was written by someone named Moravagine. As Raymond and Moravagine alternately go in and out of focus, the dreamer shifts to the dreamed and back. And the dream is so vivid, its irrationality so closely integrated with the quotidian, that the story as a whole stays real, if hallucinatory: 'hallucination congénitale qu'est la vie.'

If we now focus on Raymond as a participant rather than an observer outside the dream, we quickly recognize that he is quite demented in his own right. Though it be in the name of science, he unleashes upon the world a power which we know he understands will only destroy. In the very first chapter he presents his theories about mental illness. The argument is adroit and logical enough, but the conclusion, that sickness might be the real nature of man and so-called health a retrograde artificiality, leads us directly to his involvement with Moravagine. For the most part, Moravagine confidently acts and Raymond follows, analysing, making scientific excuses for his actions. Moravagine's funeral oration, as Raymond calls it, is a medical report of his progressive nervous disorder:

> 'Quelques jours s'étaient à peine écoulés que le malade présentait une série de troubles intéressants: le pouls, d'irrégulier qu'il était, devient franchement arythmique et filant; les battements du cœur sont moins nets, un peu étouffés. La pression artérielle au Pachon est de 15 Mx et de 9 Mn. De temps en temps on note des extrasystoles.
>
> 'L'examen du sang ne nous montre rien de particulier: une légère lymphocytose seulement.
>
> 'Le 10 octobre, c'est-à-dire huit jours après l'institution du traitement spécifique, le malade présente des troubles de la parole; celle-ci devient lente, scandée, traînante, monotone à la manière de la dysarthrie des pseudo-bulbaires. Pas de dysphagie.
>
> 'On suspend le traitement spécifique.' [p. 409]

This strange report, running a full chapter, obviously fails to describe the life of a man who personified such incredible forces; he haunts, ghostlike, an objective and lifeless account of his nervous system which reveals to the doctors nothing especially unusual. To a large extent it is the doctors' very language, their key to insight, which precludes any perception of Moravagine. In this respect Raymond the doctor is condemned while at the same time Raymond the friend is vindicated, for he can see, or wants to, and his language give us quite a different picture of Moravagine.

We are given another important clue to Raymond's personality and its relationship to Moravagine's. Raymond has never slept with a woman, nor even lain next to one. In the scene where he does so for the first time he is nauseated by the presence of Mascha's body. When she reveals that she is pregnant he almost shoots her, but refrains and runs to tell Moravagine, who is the father. It is typical of Raymond that he cannot act and that Moravagine must do so for him. As far as we know, it is *not* Moravagine who kills Mascha, for he does not seem to care about her eventual betrayal. However, all of his murder-victims are women. The sexual basis of Moravagine's madness is obvious, even to Raymond, and the work of Freud is discussed – and Freud mentioned – as early as page 2 of the novel. Also, there is a long tirade by Moravagine against women in which he declares love masochistic and all women masochists. Woman contrives towards the reabsorption of the male and thrives on his resistance. The theory in fact closely resembles Shaw's views in *Man and Superman,* as proposed by a hero who succumbs anyway in the end, with a sort of resigned relish. There, the woman represents the life force of home and hearth, continuation, thus civilization; but man is important in his search for freedom, and he creates beyond the always-conservative home. So Shaw resolves his eternal sexual conflict by approving of the never-ending antagonism. But Moravagine withdraws all constructive value from the woman, and his freedom is not in leaving her – in order to return later with new furniture – but in destroying her, with her home. This is also a variation on Otto Gross's call for anarchy, all-out war against the perverted super-ego of civilization; but Gross's obsession, perhaps the only one possible in the German context of his time, was the father, whether his own, the *Vaterland* or, eventually, Freud himself. For him civilization was not epitomized by the home but by authority. Both Cendrars, in this novel, and D.H. Lawrence, influenced by Gross's ideas through Frieda, preferred to see Western civilization as they had inherited it from the nineteenth century as feminine. The premise bears further variations between the three artists: Shaw's hero fled a mate, Lawrence's persona in *Sons and Lovers* fled a mother, and Moravagine has neither mother nor mate, nor father for that matter – in fact, as they function in the fictions, the heroes of *Moravagine, L'Or,* and *Dan Yack* are all without parents, somewhat like Cendrars himself when he wrote of adopting his pseudonym:

> Je ne suis pas le fils de mon père
> Et je n'aime que mon bisaïeul
> Je me suis fait un nom nouveau

> Pourtant je suis le premier de mon nom puisque c'est moi qui l'ai inventé de toutes pièces.[28]

The female principle, as Moravagine calls it, is considered to be the principle of destruction: 'La femme est masochiste. Le seul principe de vie est le masochisme et le masochisme est un principe de mort' (p. 293). This morbid hate of sexuality, quite Freudian in many respects, including its pessimism,[29] is not only Moravagine's, but clearly Raymond's as well. In Raymond it is merely repressed. In Moravagine it reaches its full symbolic value, a principle of anti-generation. But Moravagine would never have begun without Raymond, who, suppressed, had access to authority. Together they are capable of dreaming against the flow of time and generation, though it is only Moravagine who might be considered the archetypal dreamer who, like Joyce's Finnegan, can project out of his imagination and dominate all of the apparently real world. The two men are an indissoluble pair, the seemingly coincidental, but actually destined, or 'synchronistically' (see Jung, my note 24 above) determined meeting of an ambitious but weak, overcivilized doctor with a 'fauve humain' who has no ambition but is extraordinarily powerful and entirely uncivilized. In this meeting of pure force and its repressed aspirant Cendrars split the schizoid personality of the times into its two natural parts, each hidden from the other. Thus separated, the beast became mythical, and the socialized recognized his own cruel depths. The letter 'reproduced' for us in the preface, written the night before Raymond is to be executed for regicide some ten years after Moravagine's death, seems to show a coolness we found only in Moravagine himself, as if Raymond had eventually become his real and active brother after the madman's death, perhaps in order to continue the 'Grande Guerre, 1914-2013,' the ninety-nine-year war of Moravagine's manuscripts.

It is the note of terrible brotherhood which ends the novel: chapter 'y' contains a few sample signatures of Moravagine, his portrait by Conrad Moricand as he sat at the Rotonde café, and the following short text which warns against the scientist's blindness to human necessity, a text Moravagine writes in his last cell:

> Jeune homme, considère la sécheresse de ces tragiques facétieux. N'oublie pas qu'il n'y a jamais progrès quand le cœur se pétrifie. Il faut que toute science soit ordonnée comme un fruit, qu'elle pende au bout d'un arbre de chair et qu'elle mûrisse au soleil de la passion, hystiologie, photographie, sonnette électrique, téléscopes, ciseaux, ampères, fer à repasser, etc. – tout ça c'est pour épater le cul de l'humanité.
>
> Ton visage est autrement émouvant mouillé de larmes et prêt à crever de rire.[30]

Chapter 'z' then might seem to go against the sense of brotherhood, for under the title 'Épitaphe' it reads:

> On peut lire sur une tombe dans le cimetière militaire de l'île Sainte-Marguerite l'inscription suivante tracée au crayon-encre:
> CI-GÎT UN ÉTRANGER

Moravagine had spent the first thirty-four years of his life separated from the rest of humanity, for very good reason, but Raymond knew the kinship could not be broken; here lies a stranger, my brother.

Moravagine resembles the ithyphallic and destructive god Siva in his cosmic dance of death, and perhaps as well Siva's consort, the black Kali, covered with skulls and blood (I am reminded that in 1921 Cendrars was making a film in Rome with the Hindu actress and dancer Dourga, which was one of Kali's other names). But Siva is also the god of regeneration – resurrection being impossible, and undesirable, before the soul is cleansed of depravity and error. It is thus that Sutter and Moravagine, builder and destroyer, are joined and function as a Siva in both his manifestations to engender a far more human figure, Dan Yack, a failing man rebuilding his life and the lives around him. Our proximity to his failings, his difficulty to love in particular, gives him much of his humanity, and *Dan Yack* is certainly Cendrars' most poignant and beautiful work of fiction precisely because its hero is more human than Sutter or Moravagine, and his few victories contain the suffering of a very real man at grips with both objective reality and himself. In neither *L'Or* nor *Moravagine* were we told much about the inner workings of the main protagonist, for myths demand to stand at a distance and tell everything in their performances. In *Dan Yack*, however, the whole second half is, as the title tells us, *Les Confessions de Dan Yack.*

The specific sources of *Dan Yack* remain veiled in unknown voyages, by Cendrars or by others whose accounts he read, and in Cendrars' personal life. The trip to Antarctica resembles Sir Douglas Mawson's of 1911-14 more closely than any other, but not enough. Both left from Hobart in Tasmania, Mawson on 2 December 1911, Dan Yack on 4 March 1905 (to spend the winter night, which explorers or scientists obviously avoided); but from the outset Cendrars describes at length landscapes which Mawson doesn't bother with.[31] Mawson lost his two companions and survived tremendous hardship alone, and Cendrars might have hoped his heroic struggle to stay alive and reach camp would be in the minds of some of his readers. Dan Yack does not perform heroic feats to stay alive, but his will to live is one of the main points of the voyage. Dan Yack and his crew winter on one of the Balleny Islands, which, as far as I can tell, have not concerned explorers much, except inasmuch as their existence was noted at longitude 164° 3' east (Greenwich), and latitude 67° 5' south, which Cendrars correctly uses as a chapter heading. They live on 'Struge' Island, which should properly be Sturge; it is an odd combination, this consistent spelling or typographical error with the exact and correct location. On the other hand, Cendrars was not likely to make a mistake with Balleny since that name, which came from the whaling captain John Balleny who discovered the group of islands in 1839, bore such a close resemblance to one of the subjects of the book, whales, or *baleines.*

   In the artists who accompany Dan Yack to Struge Island are bits and
pieces drawn from Parisian artistic life. Arkadie Goischman is a poet, but
his surreal dreams of a Jewish boyhood in Russia remind one of Chagall
(Goischman even dreams of a woman named Bella, like Chagall's wife).
Other dreams and reminiscences recall scenes from Cendrars' own past,
notably his impoverished stay in New York. The musician André Lamont
does not present any readily identifiable Parisian traits, but the sculptor
Ivan Sabakoff personifies certain cubist tendencies, illustrated below, and
one comment points to Alexander Archipenko (who was praised in 'La
Tête,' no. 18 of the *Dix-neuf Poèmes élastiques*): 'Ne plus sculpter la main,
mais l'espace infini qui circule entre les doigts écartés.'[32] Further, artistic
personalities are slightly disguised, and rudely handled, behind the men-
tors and friends of the three artists of the novel, and I presume we are to
associate them: thus Lamont with Stravinsky and Sabakoff again with
Archipenko:

   'Mon Dieu, avoue cyniquement André Lamont, notre plus grand musicien
   russe vit bien avec une grande couturière parisienne, pourquoi est-ce que
   je n'en ferais pas autant ici?'

   ' ... ton ami, ton Dieu, Alexandre, oui, Alexandre Korolenko, dont tu nous
   as tant rabattu les oreilles, l'inventeur de la ligne, du cube, de la sphère,
   le rénovateur de la sculpture moderne, l'apôtre de la sculpture pure, de
   la sur-sculpture, il a toujours eu des belles femmes. Quelle tare! Je me
   demande, entre parenthèses, comment un artiste, un grand artiste, peut
   vivre avec une belle femme et produire. L'art ne lui suffit donc plus? Hé
   bien, ton Korolenko, qui vivait à Paris avec la plus belle femme de France,
   je l'ai rencontré dernièrement à New York, il avait épousé une Allemande
   (il paraît que c'est la plus belle femme d'Europe) et ne travaille plus que
   pour le dollar. En plus de ses deux maîtresses, sa femme et sa sculpture,
   il a encore trouvé un maître: le dollar. Quel génie!' [p. 15]

   More personal experiences are behind the second volume, *Les Confessions de Dan Yack.* These are related to the film work Cendrars was doing
with Abel Gance on *La Roue* around Mont Blanc between 1919 and 1921.
The scene of this second volume is set at 'Le Plan de l'Aiguille,' which is
the title of volume one (also, volume one is dedicated to Gance). 'Le Plan'
is the first stop on the *téléphérique,* or lift, from Chamonix to L'Aiguille du
Midi. A photograph in t'Serstevens' *L'Homme que fut Blaise Cendrars* (after
page 144) is dated 1923 and shows Cendrars in a cabin at Le Plan, and
this cabin appears to be identical to the one used in the film; a photograph
of the two leads, Séverin Mars and Ivy Close, together inside appeared in

L'Illustration in 1921.[33] One of the apparently more fanciful details of *Les Confessions* is Dan Yack's formation of a film company for his wife, Mireille, La Société des Films Mireille. This gesture emulates the creation of Ivy Close Films, a company formed by Ivy Close's husband and director, Elwin Neame (their son is the well-known director Ronald Neame). Some of Ivy Close's films before *La Roue* remind one of the ethereal roles Mireille plays: *Dream Paintings, The Lady of Shalott, Sleeping Beauty* (all of 1912) for example.[34] One other, rather mystifying, item suggests that Ivy was important to Cendrars beyond being a source for Mireille. This is the chapter entitled 'Ivy Close' from the unfinished novel on John Paul Jones published in 1928, just between the two volumes of *Dan Yack*. The available documents indicate that Jones returned to England from Jamaica with no woman at all, let alone one named Ivy Close. Cendrars' otherwise scrupulously documented account is sprinkled with references to film, and one wonders if this admittedly invented description of a voluptuous woman bears any relation to Ivy Close herself, and whether the whole thing is not part of a hoax, history fleshed out to please a lady just as Neame and Dan Yack after him made economics fit the heart:

> Mais ce qu'aucun biographe ne raconte, c'est que John Paul Jones ne voyage pas seul. Il est à bord en compagnie d'Ivy Close.
>
> Ici, si j'étais faiseur de scénarios, je présenterais Ivy Close sous la figure d'une touchante jeune fille comme l'exigent la vieille tradition du roman anglais et la routine toute récente du cinéma américain; je penserais à la petite Annie de Thomas de Quincey ou à la malheureuse Sibyl Vane d'Oscar Wilde pour attendrir mes lecteurs et leur faire verser des larmes. Mais je ne pense pas à mes lecteurs, je pense à John Paul Jones, à son type de femme, à ses amours avec la Duchesse de Chartres, au coup de foudre qu'il ressent à la vue de Catherine II et c'est pour serrer la réalité de plus près encore que je ferai d'Ivy Close une femme mûre, haute en chair et gourmande, pleine d'expérience et de coquetterie, avec un lourd passé et d'une élégance à la dernière mode, en un mot une belle frégate, une femme dans le genre de la Moll Flanders de Daniel de Foe.[35]

Essentially Dan Yack is rewriting all of his life previous to the beginning of the novel until, after many rejections and revisions, he finds a place to start anew, with better understanding. Dan Yack (he insists upon being called that, neither more nor less) loves three women at different times in the novel, and it is love which prompts all of his activities. His love for Hedwiga in Saint Petersburg sends him to Antarctica when she decides to marry someone else. His love for his partner's wife makes him leave the community he establishes in the Antarctic. *Les Confessions* are his reading of and comments upon a notebook kept by his wife, Mireille, now dead, whom he realizes he did not love as he should have. In each case Dan Yack is in flight, attempting to fill the void left by a terrible loss with either frenzied action or quiet and solitary contemplation. Hedwiga and Mireille are the most important women in his life, and each dominates her volume of the novel. In *Le Plan de l'Aiguille* we are shown a man who cannot live without the woman he loves reaching a certain balance through the most arduous physical activity, only to discover another woman who reminds him too much of the first (her name is Donna Heloisa). In *Les Confessions de Dan Yack* the same man reveals to us his failure to love the woman he does marry, despite every effort to make her happy. Thus the novel illustrates the Latin epigraph which may be found at the head of each of the volumes as they appeared in 1929: 'Nec sine te nec tecum vivere possum.'[36]

Le Plan de l'Aiguille is the end of a *Bildungsroman* in which Dan Yack, though already a grown man, comes to full and relatively meaningful manhood, precisely 'sine te.' Sutter and Moravagine are virtually infinite forces and never change very much in themselves, only in their actions. But Dan Yack changes from a frivolous man in love to a very powerful actor in the affairs of men, while never losing his youthfulness.

Dan Yack's transformation is dramatically highlighted by the presence of three men who fail to survive what we might call the initiation. He meets these three men, Arkadie Goischman, Ivan Sabakoff, and André Lamont, in a bar in Saint Petersburg where he is drowning in liquor his grief over the loss of Hedwiga. These three men are cursing their fate as men and artists, and Dan Yack, also desperate, offers to take them with him to an island in the Antarctic, anywhere really, where there will be no one and nothing but themselves. Behind him Dan Yack leaves not only Hedwiga but the life of a very rich, very elegant, and superfluous gentleman of Saint Petersburg high society before the Revolution (actually Dan Yack and Moravagine are in Russia about the same time). He is a man who is quite lost without his cane and monocle, accessories despised by his poorer companions who have accepted his offer only because they have nothing else and because they think seclusion from a noisy, superficial, and Philistine city will provide the perfect conditions for work. Dan Yack is anything but an artist; he has, in fact, never been able to read a book. He has no plans at all for his stay on Struge Island. He takes with him a dog, Bari, and a great number of gramophones and recordings of popular operatic songs, national anthems, marches, and animal calls. His dog abandons him for Lamont, the three artists hate his 'music,' and it seems his Saint Petersburg valet neglected to pack a supply of monocles. All the appurtenances of life seem to be falling away from him, and he keeps himself busy by counting and recounting the provisions, that is to say, the essentials.

The three artists, on the other hand, have many plans. Cendrars has, of course, purposely isolated three representatives of the arts and one eccentric dandy-adventurer to test them under the most adverse conditions, a kind of one-year *No Exit* in which each man faces himself even more than he is forced to face the others. Outside is the Antarctic night. Each of the artists plans to compose a great work in the perfect quiet of this island, but each fails to realize the effect such seclusion will have on him. None of these men is capable of working.

Goischman, the writer, daydreams. Immobile at a table, pulling at his nose, he becomes the victim of his memories of a Jewish childhood. These memories become more and more alive to him, but he himself becomes more and more paralyzed, unable to put a single word to paper. He wants to write the novel of his life, but the void around him has destroyed his ability to act in the present, his very character in fact. Cendrars calls Goischman's condition a *dédoublement* and describes it in some detail.[37] This psychiatric term refers to the so-called split personality, or, more precisely, to the sense of cutting away from and observing from the outside one's own existence and actions. This sensation is symptomatic of the overwhelming alienation Goischman experiences in the utter void of the Antarctic. He comes to question his very Jewishness, *goy* meaning gentile (he is, possibly, uncircumcized as well, like Joyce's Bloom: see p. 43). In the end he even loses the feeling of his body; he cuts off his nose, contracts scurvy, and dies by fire. Cendrars describes how he sits in a chair and gazes out of the window in the single wall left standing as the cabin goes up in flames in the middle of a blizzard:

> Jamais Arkadie n'a été aussi lucide.
> Il se porte les mains au nez.
> Il pense avec orgueil.
> 'La mort d'un homme de lettres:
> – Je meurs dans un plagiat et ce plagiat est raté.
> 'En effet, Van Gogh ne s'était coupé que l'oreille droite, et encore, c'était pour une femme. Mais moi!...'
> Il se méprise avec orgueil.
> Inutilité.
> Lucidité spirituelle.
> Il brûle.
> Il gèle.
> Il flambe. [p. 76]

Lamont's difficulties are more obvious to him, for he quickly realizes how much he valued his public, even if it was made up of only a few infatuated women:

> Alors, il pensait à Lulu, la couturière.
> Son auditoire habituel lui manquait.
> Pas une femme! Et petit à petit, il se mit à avoir peur. [p. 41]

Lamont suffers from another social disease, for he has syphilis, now in its last stage. He knows that at this point there is no cure. As soon as he had arrived at Struge Island he had destroyed all the watches, therefore all time in this world of night, and when the sun rises he discovers that he was not able to forestall the inevitable:

> – Mais ... Mais ... le soleil, ânonnait Dan Yack. Le grand soleil du dehors. C'est aujourd'hui le 31 août.
> – Moi qui croyais l'avoir supprimé, dit André Lamont accablé. Et il se mit à geindre:
> – Tout est à recommencer. Ma symphonie est ratée... [p. 62]

Lamont takes to drink, but the new Antarctic sun reveals a final strength to him, and rather than die in the cabin he prefers to walk directly into the emptiness; he disappears resolutely climbing into the ice-field without survival gear.

Ivan Sabakoff, a solid Russian Peasant, is the one Dan Yack finds most sympathetic. During the long winter night Sabakoff eats, polishes lamps, generally hibernates as he awaits the daylight in which he may emerge from aesthetic considerations to sculpt the image of Dan Yack in pure ice: 'Je vais sculpter l'éclair!' he thinks (p. 46). When the summer begins he works every day, but the image is only part of his concern, for he has become obsessed with a theoretical perfection and reduction of that image, and of life altogether. The Antarctic landscape has freed him of the human element, and he pushes past the image, then past even some essence of life towards a final, perfectly cold abstraction:

> 'L'œil!' se disait-il.
> – Non, le monocle! rectifiait-il aussitôt à haute voix.

> 'Il me faut serrer la réalité de plus près encore et la réalité c'est Dieu.
> 'Un cercle, un carré, un cube, une sphère, un disque, une ellipse sont les manifestations de sa perfection.'

> Ivan Sabakoff songeait à une sculpture immatérielle tant son désir de simplification, de purification était grand.
>
> Ah! Se consumer en émettant des formes, comme le soleil, par rayonnement!
>
> Ne plus sculpter la main, mais l'espace infini qui circule entre les doigts écartés.
>
> Et il ne taillait plus dans la paroi des icebergs que d'immenses rondelles de glace qu'il polissait et faisait miroiter au soleil.
>
> – Comme Dan Yack avait raison de porter un monocle, disait-il encore. Le monocle c'est tout. [pp. 66-7]

Sabakoff is led astray by the beauty of the perfect, Cubist void. He falls victim to his own obsession, crushed by his monstrous ice statue of Dan Yack during the great blizzard that also takes Goischman and Lamont.

Symbolically these three men die for Dan Yack. They are also symbolic of the failure of three extreme approaches to art: the narcissistic approach, in which the artist is seduced by himself; the search for fame, in which he is seduced by others, or at least by the esteem he would like them to have for him; and the search for perfection, in which the artist is seduced by an idea. All three men succumb to the pressure of isolation because none can live, even experimentally, without social props. Ivan is more successful than the others because he does find something to do; but he fails finally because his activity was only a means to him, and the end not attainable.

For Dan Yack the most insignificant activity is its own goal, and he never holds any other attitude. But he shares with the others the basic insecurity of us all which requires the plethora of aids society offers, so through the winter night he worries about breaking his only monocle. Counting his stores, he is somewhat like Robinson Crusoe who, in the existential view, constructs a cogent, numbered, and dated world about him out of the nothingness precisely to ward off the sense of nothingness within. Dan Yack's instincts are sounder than this, however, and he dares to play the game of life with fate, throwing bourgeois caution to the winds. Unlike Crusoe, whom we could call the existential bourgeois, Dan Yack stores a certain amount of supplies and throws the surplus away, even though the rescue boat could be weeks late: 'Ce n'est pas une cache secrète qu'il constitue. Non. Il joue son va-tout. Il risque. Avec une fureur et une joie insubordonnées' (p. 52). Dan Yack's approach is always poetic, and that is the essence of his eccentricity. Among the stores is hidden a sixty-pound plum pudding which he has brought for the crew of the *Green-Star* when they come to fetch the four men at Christmas. The day the sun appears Dan Yack plays all his gramophones at once. The appearance of the sun marks a transformation in the foursome. Dan Yack has a mad celebration. Ivan emerges to begin his self-destructive purification. Goischman and Lamont are faced with a light into the void within themselves. The night had been a time of inaction; the day brings destruction. That day, discovering the illnesses of his companions, Dan Yack accidentally breaks his monocle but begins to see.

When he comes upon the statue of himself with the body of Sabakoff beneath it, the scene is reminiscent of Michael Henchard in *The Mayor of Casterbridge* coming upon his own figure floating down the river. Having just left Lamont as he disappeared into the ice-field, and fleeing Goischman who has offered him his nose, Dan Yack is searching for his only friend: '– Ivan, Ivan, murmurait-il, regarde ce qu'ils veulent faire de moi!' (p. 73). All three artists gravitate about Dan Yack as if he were their subject, precisely that aspect of life each artist is grappling with and failing to circumscribe. Goischman attempts to imitate Van Gogh's distorted and irrational sacrifice. Lamont attracts Dan Yack's hitherto faithful dog by his infected body: 'Dan Yack pensait avec amertume: "Jusqu'à Bari qui a opté entre nous et qui s'est attaché à la maladie, pouah!" ' (p. 63). Finally, Sabakoff falls in love, at first with Dan Yack's image, but then with his monocle alone, the epitome of his image. These three demands upon Dan Yack die, and he sees their reflection, at last, when he comes upon his fallen image in ice.[38] Stripped of egotism and conceptualizing, he rises from the ruins of his pathetic images. Discovering his tuxedo, he wears it about the island, eating the festive pudding which is the only food not destroyed. In a pocket he finds a supply of monocles which he counts and then throws away. From a social gentleman he has become what a person of noble birth was supposed to be, a man of superior moral fibre:

> Il n'avait pas de feu, pas de tabac, et rien ne lui manquait! Il ne désirait rien. Il mangeait son plum-pudding consciencieusement, en l'émiettant dans le creux de sa main et, sérieusement, il se lavait au whiskey, à fond. Il ne voulait pas penser à Hedwiga et il s'en prenait à sa barbe pour se distraire. Il était très fier de son smoking. L'uniforme d'un civilisé. Il ne se sentait pas perdu. Il se faisait les ongles avec un silex. Il n'attendait rien.

> Jamais Dan Yack n'examinait l'horizon nord, jamais il ne cherchait au large l'arrivée du bateau.
> Il n'épiait rien.
> C'eût été indigne.
> Il était sûr de lui et saurait attendre.
> Tout.
> Quel enjeu! [pp. 81, 82]

When the *Green-Star* takes him off Struge Island he sees himself in a mirror and discovers the resurgence of a long-lost original strength: 'Il est vrai que c'était la première fois qu'il se voyait sans monocle. Depuis tant d'années. "Quelle victoire, pensait-il. Attention!" ' (p. 88).

With this strength he re-enters the world of human beings, and the remainder of *Le Plan de l'Aiguille* contrasts singularly with the rarified episode of Struge Island. First Dan Yack indulges in a celebration of blaring music-machines, drinking, and exotic sexuality on the Island of Chiloe (off the coast of Chile). Soon, when his family's whaling interests are threatened by Norwegian firms, he throws himself into that business with the same abandon he has shown in all his activities:

> 'Les affaires ne sont pas les affaires, elles sont ce que nous voulons qu'elles soient, nos aventures, nos amours, nos désirs, nos pensées et nos besoins les plus obscurs, nos rêves les plus fous. Est-ce que vous tenez beaucoup à l'argent, vous? Et à vous embêter? Et ne voulez-vous pas vous amuser, c'est-à-dire, détruire, créer, réussir, perdre? bref, faire quelque chose de nouveau et de gai, sans arrière pensée que de jouir, jouir de la minute présente, flottante, incertaine, fugitive, et pourtant violente comme un explosif?' [p. 98]

He establishes a colony in the Antarctic, Community-City, modern, functional, and exclusively devoted to whaling and the processing of whale products. Dan Yack designs this 'city' as both agreeable to live in and practical to work in, a city planner's dream, a sort of 'unité d'habitation.'[39] There is no doubt that Dan Yack has succeeded in rejoining mankind, in building a material world of worth for many more people than just himself. But Donna Heloisa's magical presence destroys for Dan Yack the value of everything he has built. Again he finds that he is not the sort of man for whom conquest of the outside world, of nature or of men, can provide inner peace. He must love and hope to be loved. At the end of this chapter entitled 'Port Déception' (Deception Island is in the South Shetland Islands, between Cape Horn and the Palmer Peninsula), which is also the end of *Le Plan de l'Aiguille,* he watches an iceberg turn over in the water and is once again faced with the reflection of his own life:

> Il y avait déjà un bon moment que Dan Yack le suivait hypnotiquement des yeux quand il le vit tout à coup osciller sur sa base et se retourner. La masse entière s'effondra dans des geysers d'écume, plongea, s'immergea complètement avant de réapparaître la quille en l'air, sale, immonde, rongée par l'eau de mer, boursouflée, fendue, pleine de dents cariées et

de chicots noirs, d'un vilain aspect de maladie honteuse et d'une coloration
vénéneuse, sanglante, due aux diatomées qui la souillaient par en dessous.
Quelle révélation!

Dan Yack eut immédiatement l'impression d'avoir vu chavirer sa
propre vie, et tout ce qui jusqu'à présent l'avait porté, ses sentiments, sa
fierté, son insouciance, sa joie, tout s'en allait à vau-l'eau, tournoyait sous
ses yeux, flétri, terni, pourri, emporté dans un magma de boues et de
débris putrescents. [p. 121]

Les Confessions de Dan Yack indicates in the very first line that the scene
is 'Le Plan de l'Aiguille,' and it thus becomes clear that the first volume
of the novel has always been awaiting this second one in which, secluded
in another icy wasteland, in a cabin above Chamonix, Dan Yack speaks
into a dictaphone, and does little else.[40] Here Dan Yack is again alone,
but from the beginning and for the full length of the volume. The main
action, before the very end, takes place in his mind as he reflects upon his
dead wife's short diary and his life just before and after he met her.

The first of Mireille's *cahiers,* or notebooks, which Dan Yack reads into
his confessions shows how she lived with and loved her father until his
death when she was fifteen. Her account of her childhood, from pages 139
to 149, is one of the most touching narratives in Cendrars and reminds
one of Giono in its evocation of a simple but sensitive child among the
peasantry of Southern France. Mireille's mother is never present, and it
becomes clear to us and to Mireille that she did not care for the child; so
when the father died she sent her to a convent on the rue Notre-Dame
des Champs, and saw her on Thursday afternoons. On the next *rouleau* (the
cylinder upon which Dan Yack records) he rambles on about the February
nights at the Plan de l'Aiguille, Chamonix, and then Armistice Day in
Paris, during which he had driven a bevy of prostitutes and their madam,
Théréson, through the delirious crowds in the street to pick up her daughter, for although Théréson had always assiduously hidden her profession
from the girl, today it made no difference, 'C'était l'Armistice!'

In this manner we come upon Mireille and her relationship with Dan
Yack from two directions, like entering the same scene from both sides
of the stage. We have a double narrator, two points of view each pursuing
the other as his or her subject (Graham Greene did very much the same
thing in the *End of the Affair,* where the hero reads his lover's journal,
which is about him). Behind Dan Yack's seemingly random associations
is the driving force of his concern for Mireille, Théréson's daughter.
Questioned by the young girl, he told of his experiences whaling and in
the war (he did not speak of Struge Island, nor do *Les Confessions* touch
at all upon experiences actually described in *Le Plan,* as if the second

volume was reading between the lines of the first), and he won her heart, as well as his own, in the telling, in much the way Othello wins Desdemona: 'She lov'd me for the dangers I had past, / And I lov'd her, that she did pity them.'

> – Et vous êtes venu vous battre pour la France?
> – Oui, Mademoiselle, je suis venu me battre.
> – Mon pauvre ami! Et vous en avez tué beaucoup?
> – Oui, Mademoiselle, beaucoup.
> – Mon pauvre ami! répétait Mireille tendrement.
> Je lui racontai comment j'avais tué 28 Boches, un jour, avant déjeuner, pour m'amuser, comme on tire les pigeons à Monte-Carlo.
> – Mon pauvre ami, comme j'ai peur pour vous ... [p. 156]

Dan Yack comes to realize, confesses to himself in fact, that he married this girl out of pity, and that he was never able to give her any love other than that of an older brother, who replaced a dead father; 'mon grand,' as she called him. Yet pity had gone both ways, for Mireille had understood that the hardness learned from war was not only a strength but a failure as well. The war occupies much of Dan Yack's thoughts in his cabin, and he too knows how the war has ruined men: 'On dit que la guerre a tout bouleversé, je crois qu'elle a surtout bouleversé l'amour' (p. 170). Dan Yack had fallen in love with Mireille on Armistice Day like a man who, returning from the war, vows to protect a remaining child from the ugliness and brutality of such a world.[41] But such protection was not Mireille's only need, and Dan Yack's brotherly love and indulgence only further weakened her as she became less and less able to cope even with that world of joy and luxuriance Dan Yack provided for her. Continually he tells us he made her laugh, that he devoted his life to doing so, and Mireille's *cahier* confirms his success. But her laughing only tided her over, time and time again, covering an unsatisfied need for love. Dan Yack is not alone at fault, for Mireille had been attracted to him by how well he seemed to fill her father's role, how well he made her forget:

> ... si la gaieté, l'insouciance, l'enfantillage partagent naïvement mon cœur, je crois que le fond de ma véritable nature est très sincèrement la tristesse. J'ai toujours été triste, mortellement triste quand j'étais petite fille, avec des accès d'angoisse qui me serraient soudainement le cœur, et quand je sentais que j'allais me pâmer, vite, vite j'éclatais de rire. C'est pourquoi je sais rire à volonté, mais mon rire me fait toujours mal, chose que j'ai toujours caché à mon grand. [p. 188]

Thus the two confess to each other, and as Dan Yack reads Mireille's notebook into the dictaphone without comment the reader reconstructs two voices finally meeting honestly, pathetically too late for one of them at least.

Dan Yack does more than make Mireille laugh. He had set her up in films:

> Je lui ai constitué une société, la *Société des Films Mireille.* C'est une jolie surprise pour un premier avril, n'est-ce pas? Dire qu'aujourd'hui on peut constituer une société pour faire plaisir à une femme. Cela n'a d'ailleurs aucune importance, pourvu qu'elle soit contente. [p. 173]

But her director insisted upon casting her in languid, ethereal roles, those in fact of Poe's women: '... une femme qui s'appelait tantôt Eléonora, tantôt Ligéia et Ulalume. C'était encore un artiste. Il m'intimidait. Sa conversation était brillante' (p. 173). The artist had again come into Dan Yack's life to steal a part of him. This director exploited aspects of Mireille which Dan Yack could not see because they were too painful. Cast as Poe's muses, Ophelia, or in *Tales of Hoffmann* Mireille was herself, the dying maiden; after all Dan Yack had organized the 'Société Mireille' to distract a little girl from the fatal illness the doctors had diagnosed. Dan Yack had then persuaded her to play Gribouille, a poor fellow not unlike the 'Charlot' (Chaplin) often mentioned in the novel, or Michel Simon's Boudu in Renoir's *Boudu sauvé des eaux* (1932). At last, he had felt, she would portray her real self, but he had been more perceptive than he knew, and too late. Mireille died during the shooting of *Gribouille,* and her diary tells him that, having cast her too well, he was himself partly responsible, for he put her weakness before her on the screen at a time when, all hope gone, dissimulation would have been more kind:

> C'était tellement moi que j'avais l'impression de tourner nue, toute nue, moralement nue.
>
>   Comme j'avais l'air gauche, comme j'étais honteuse, traquée à l'écran! J'avais pitié de moi-même: et plus l'étourderie, la gaucherie, l'imbécillité de Gribouille étaient manifestes, plus mon grand jubilait, et toute la troupe, qui assistait également à la projection de ces premiers bouts d'essai, applaudissait; j'étais seule à m'attendrir sur ce pauvre hère et à comprendre qu'il était irrémédiablement perdu. La vie le blessait, tout tournait mal, rien n'avait de sens pour lui ... Je pleurais à chaudes larmes. Ce n'était pourtant pas la première fois que je me voyais à l'écran. Mais cette fois-ci je n'interprétais plus un rôle, je me voyais révélée à moi-même, c'était moi-même que je voyais évoluer, moi, moi, telle que je suis et telle que

je ne m'avoue pas être, loufoque, éperdue, maladroite, craintive, butée, avec un besoin fou de grandeur et de pureté, et si désarmée, incapable, impuissante, bête. Pauvre Gribouille![42]

Mireille's laugh had been turned against her. But we may also see in this description of Gribouille-Mireille the portrait of Dan Yack, somewhat *loufoque*. Douglas Fairbanks and 'Charlot' both, lonely and sad, carefree and happy, ridiculous and yet heroic, are Dan Yack as we have seen him throughout *Le Plan*. As he did on Struge Island, he has attached himself to another reflection of himself. *Les Confessions* are his meditation upon that dependency and the gestation period of a freedom of sorts from it.

The earlier time of isolation on Struge Island remains an adventure compared to Dan Yack's life at the Plan de l'Aiguille, for he hardly ever leaves the cabin, nor is he in any danger except when he occasionally climbs by choice, to exercise the muscles of *Le Plan*. The two parts of the novel appear in juxtaposition, 'aux antipodes,' as Cendrars would say (the Antipodes Islands are, incidentally, not so very far from 'Struge,' or Sturge Island); the first volume all action, the second contemplation.[43] Cendrars himself has described the dichotomy in the most meaningful terms:

> Le monde est ma représentation. J'ai voulu dans *Dan Yack* intérioriser cette vue de l'esprit, ce qui est une conception pessimiste; puis l'extério-riser, ce qui est une action optimiste.
>
> D'où la division en deux parties de mon roman: la première, du dehors au dedans, sujet du *Plan de l'Aiguille;* du dedans au dehors, objet des *Confessions de Dan Yack,* la deuxième. Systole, diastole: les deux pôles de l'existence. Outside-in, inside-out: les deux temps du mouvement méca-nique. Contraction, dilatation: la respiration de l'univers, le principe de la vie, l'Homme, Dan Yack, avec ses figures.[44]

This is one of the most revealing passages in Cendrars. It defines perfectly his understanding of the relationship between man and his world, and the nature of man's action in it. There are two possible forms of action: one, the *absorption* of experience which permeates the mind, an action of con-traction because the mind, which is all of one's world, is gathering in and shaping; two, the *expression* of experience which has become the mind's own, an action of dilation because the mind is projecting its informed image upon the world, or at least into it. In this view it is the relationship which is all-important, because neither world nor mind can subsist without the other, nor can one be said to be more important than the other. From the point of view of the artist, this defines the making of the work as *re-creation,* a combination of art as mimesis and art as expression. Neither suffices, though *Dan Yack* breaks the concept down. *Le Plan* breathes in, *Les Confessions* out, but only together do they breathe, become Dan Yack.

In this illustration of the two-part cycle which Cendrars calls the principle of life, Dan Yack is as actively alive in part two as he is in part one; a well-known critic René Lalou praised the contemplative volume as a kind of epic: '*Les Confessions de Dan Yack,* lyrique témoignage sur les élans et les misères de notre époque, sont surtout, parmi les tragiques rumeurs de l'action éperdue, l'épopée de la solitude.' [45] In *Les Confessions* Dan Yack rests from the exertions of action, and in *Le Plan* he rests from the burdens of reflection, no less onerous. Or in *Le Plan* he takes on the world, and in *Les Confessions* he takes on himself. The alternation of opposite but complementary activities defines the pulse of life: Sutter the builder opposite of Moravagine the destroyer, Moravagine as man hating opposite of Dan Yack as man loving, and, most true and poignant because contained in the same figure, Dan Yack in the world and Dan Yack in himself. Cendrars considered the first, the man in the world, the more optimistic activity. I have already quoted him on the inherent optimism of action (see page 162 above), but such action cannot stand alone, for the very title of the active volume, *Le Plan de l'Aiguille,* names the isolated place of reflection. Action and contemplation are the same action, or cycle. As Cendrars wrote in a 'premier fragment d'une autobiographie,' 'Je suis une espèce de brahmane à rebours, qui se contemple dans l'agitation ...' [46]

However, there is no reason to assume that the cyclical nature of a man's activity precludes his ability to change; every year's cycle returns while he grows, at least older. [47] The cycle does not stop time, as Dan Yack sadly realizes: 'Aujourd'hui, c'est le 11 juin. C'est l'anniversaire de la mort de Mireille. C'est... Ah! pourquoi est-ce que tout se répète, puisque rien ne revient?' (p. 211). He unburdens himself into his dictaphone, talking more and more about the war until the cycle can be induced to begin again, to emerge from the associations in his story. He remembers that, as they charged up the Crête de Vimy, he had stopped to listen to a bird: 'Je souriais, ébloui. C'était des trilles d'amour. Le printemps' (p. 196). Wherever his mind probes the past he sees birds, and spring. Thinking of Mireille dying, he remembers: 'Oui, le printemps était déjà avancé, car on mourait beaucoup au sanatorium où Mireille se mourait; tous les malades qui avaient duré l'hiver étaient emportés, ils ne résistaient pas au printemps' (p. 201). The goal of taking chances in the war was to go on leave, which meant only one thing, Paris: ' – Allons chercher notre perme pour Panam; aujourd'hui, c'est le Boche qui la tient ... ' (p. 207). Paris is the focal point of wartime dreams: 'Ô Paris, une fois Gallipoli abandonnée, c'est sur toi que devaient se cristalliser tous les désirs des survivants! PARIS ... PARIS ... PARIS ... PARIS' (p. 210). Paris again becomes the goal of all this dreaming of springtime, the sign of the new cycle revving up its motor, for the story of Le Plan is running down:

> Je rentre à Paris. C'est décidé! Je commence à en avoir assez. De quoi, je n'en sais rien. De tout. De rien. Je m'ennuie. [p. 211]

> J'empoigne le volant, j'appuie sur le démarreur, j'embraye et je démarre dans un tonnerre.
> Je vais encore une fois courir ma chance.
> Si seulement je pouvais entrer dans le décor et me casser la figure! [p. 226]

Once again Paris is the ground for new starts, or recuperative endings in the work of Cendrars: thus the sudden finales to *Le Transsibérien* and *Le Panama*, the return to Paris in *Moravagine* to discover working people, the 'perme pour Panam' at the end of *La Main coupée*, the last chapter of *Bourlinguer*, 'Paris, Port-de-Mer.' When Dan Yack says 'je rentre à Paris' he means he is going home, though Paris is never his home in any of the actual scenes of the novel. Cendrars also began there, and then gave it as his place of birth.

A new cycle begins, this time 'tecum,' for he adopts a child. The ending contains two kinds of hope: that of beginning again, inspired in his 'son et lumière' apartment, a whole floor with the partitions knocked out; and the hope that perhaps a son is the one person for whom the love Dan Yack has shown before will now be appropriate. The novel ends:

> Aujourd'hui, c'est mon anniversaire.
> J'ai 52 ans.
> J'ai été me chercher mon fils.
> Ce matin, en rentrant des Halles, je lui ai rapporté un petit lapin rose.
> Il y a déjà longtemps que je rôdais autour des baraquements du boulevard Jourdan et que j'avais fait toutes les démarches pour l'adopter. Au refuge, les petits orphelins russes étaient nombreux. J'ai choisi un petit garçon de onze ans, pâlot, triste, avec des yeux comme ceux d'Hedwiga. Il s'appelle Nicolas.
> Je l'appellerai Dan Yack, comme moi.
> Je lui apprendrai à rire.
> Je le ferai rire.
> Et pour commencer, nous courons déjà tous les trois à quatre pattes sur les parquets, moi, mon fils et le petit lapin rose, dans mon grand appartement vide... [pp. 227-8][48]

Of the nature of things, of his own life in the novel, there are no guarantees. Still, 'vivere possum.'

Sutter, Moravagine, Dan Yack build, destroy, start again. Each time the protagonist both contains and battles his nemisis: gold, war, ice. Of the three, only Dan Yack survives, leaves the fiction open-ended, as if Cendrars had resolved in him the first two forces, entered their centre by combining them in a continually changing balance; we might say that Dan Yack, by working in 'Les Halles,' 'rentre dans le ventre de Paris.' 'Et pour commencer,' he ends, starting out once again closer to the centre of things and himself.

10 From history to story

I carry them, men and women, I carry them with me wherever I go,
I swear it is impossible for me to get rid of them,
I am fill'd with them, and I will fill them in return.

WHITMAN, 'Song of the Open Road'

In *Kodak* Cendrars had been able to make poetic that instant or detail in reality which illuminated the essential, despite the risks he ran at every turn by ignoring all strictures about how to make good poetry. But his obsession with the world at large *per se,* and not as a source from which to appropriate for his own poetry, prompted him to write throughout his career many entirely non-fictional books. These works, translations, essays, newspaper articles, anthropological collections, show his many different interests at the stage of original and fresh curiosity, before they were entirely refashioned into his own manner. We may see, here, first Dan Yack's voyage outward, a soaking up, the meeting of other minds more or less brother to his own, and then his voyage inward, into the world of his own mind as it has been tested by others. The first voyage is illustrated by his research and newspaper work, the second by a few autobiographical fragments. The two antipodes are then unified, in stories termed 'vraies,' where the word means they are true both to history and to a personal view of it. Thus are prepared the vast panoramic novels of the forties in which the vista of the wide world is easily matched by the incredible landscapes of self.

Chronologically, the first of Cendrars' research projects to be published was in African folk literature and mythology, not yet called literature, and which he translated and anthologized in his *Anthologie nègre* of 1921.[1] This was to be the first of a series: a 1926 copy of *Moravagine* announced a second volume, as well as the first of *Anthologie aztèque, inca, maya.* But these compilations, as he called them, never appeared. A few years later he published two other volumes of African stories which he intended for young people: *Petits Contes nègres pour les enfants des blancs* (1928) and *Comment les blancs sont d'anciens noirs* (1930).[2] Both titles show their author's irony about the presumed superiority of white civilization. Cendrars was always interested in the so-called primitive societies because he felt they lived closer to reality in all its particulars. In his 'Notice' to *Anthologie nègre* Cendrars quoted one scholar on the richness of the African languages:

> 'Chaque monticule, colline, montagne ou pic a un nom, ainsi que chaque cours d'eau, chaque vallon, chaque plaine; discuter le sens de ces noms prendrait une vie d'homme. Ce n'est pas la disette, mais la surabondance de noms qui induit les voyageurs en erreur. La plénitude du langage est telle qu'il y a des vingtaines de mots pour marquer les variétés de la démarche, de la flânerie, de la fanfaronnade; chaque mode de marche est exprimé par un mot spécial.' [pp. 211-12]

Cendrars felt that the specificity of the language bespoke the culture's sense of a rich and poetical concreteness. At the same time the material had the appearance of great simplicity and innocence because it was so elemental, as opposed to sophisticated. The very first story in the *Anthologie,* on the creation of man, while resembling the biblical version, differs from it primarily in the friendly closeness of God and man:

> 1 'La Légende de la création'
>
> Quand les choses n'étaient pas encore, Mébère, le Créateur, il a fait l'homme avec les terres d'argile. Il a pris l'argile et il a façonné cela en homme. Cet homme a eu ainsi son commencement, et il a commencé comme lézard. Ce lézard, Mébère l'a placé dans un bassin d'eau de mer. Cinq jours, et voici: il a passé cinq jours avec lui dans ce bassin des eaux; et il l'avait mis dedans. Sept jours; il fut dedans sept jours. Le huitième jour, Mébère a été le regarder. Et voici, le lézard sort; et voici qu'il est dehors. Mais c'est un homme. Et il dit au Créateur: Merci. [p. 215]

The English translation of 1927, *The African Saga,* was reprinted by Negro Universities Press in 1969, and the 1927 introduction by Arthur B. Spingarn has not required revision; on the contrary, his emphasis on Cendrars' discovery of the poetic value of the myths and folklore is what makes the reprinting so interesting and relevant today:

To be sure, Frobenius and some of the others caught a gleam of its poetic
value and its cultural significance. But it was not until the publication of
the *Anthologie nègre* in 1921 that this value and this significance became
evident to the common reader. Blaise Cendrars ... saw its high imaginative
qualities and importance as pure literature. He must have sensed the fact
that most Africans are not 'savages,' that Africa possesses a civilization and
a culture that is rich and varied, primitive, no doubt, but genuine and
beautiful and that in its oral literature much of this has been preserved and
adequately expressed.

Cendrars was constantly attracted by the extraordinary in life and in
men, for in the extraordinarily real he saw the mythical dreams of all men.
What might appear unusual, foreign, exotic to us was only necessity for
those who acted, and his accounting of their case would reflect upon our
own situation. After Sutter, Cendrars tried his hand at another obsessed
builder, the French adventurer and businessman Jean Galmot. *Rhum*
(1930) is not a novel but a long reportage, muckraking in fact, since in
it Cendrars attacks many government agencies, groups, and personalities
which he saw as conspiring to overthrow and eventually assassinate Galmot, the popular *député* from French Guiana re-elected after an uprising
rejected a government stooge. Here Cendrars could write about a man
similar to Sutter, but who had died only in 1928; he could defend the
iconoclast builder's name against vast economic interests which, if they
had already succeeded in ridding themselves of Galmot, could still be
exposed to public opinion.

Cendrars had few illusions about the power Galmot or he himself could
actually wield, and he continually calls Galmot a Don Quixote. The book
Rhum as the 'act' which Cendrars' epigraph announces cannot call for any
victories over evil, but rather the recognition of a tragic sense, of the
inevitable and forced fall of the admirable. Thus Galmot in prison, de-
fiantly refusing to be transferred if it is to be out of pity or indulgence for
his illness, is described by Cendrars as far more free than his oppressors:
'Paroles d'homme libre: bien plus libre au fond de son cachot que tous
ces politiciens, financiers, anciens ministres, procureurs, journalistes,
fondés de pouvoirs, poètes sans talent et gros négociants qui gouvernent
le pays.'[3] With this 'roman' which 'peut aussi être un acte,' as he writes
in the epigraph, Cendrars joins, for a moment, the ranks of the political
anarchists, a specialization within his perennial role as social and cultural
anarchist. Galmot's dream is legality, which is supposed to give justice. At
the end of the book he shies from leading a Guianese revolution for
independence from France, hoping to the end for justice from the judges:

> Pauvre Jean Galmot, Don Quichotte jusqu'au bout! Sa vie ne lui avait-
> elle donc rien appris, qu'il croyait encore à la légalité?... Jamais il ne se
> débarrassera de son fond paysan et de sa mentalité honnête de petit bour-
> geois du Périgord. Il repoussait l'aventure... Pourtant l'occasion était
> belle. [p. 333]

Galmot had been unable, or unwilling, to take on that fine if drastic
occasion, to render justice himself; but his heart had been in the right
place, and this saved him from being a mere capitalist and colonial entre-
preneur. Instead of milking his workers he established unions and co-
operatives. In 1921, about to be imprisoned, he wrote Marcus Garvey in
New York: 'Il faut que la voix terrible du peuple noir, debout dans le
même élan, secoue tous les peuples et leur annonce la libération prochaine
des 400 millions de noirs, la plus prodigieuse puissance humaine. Je suis
avec vous' (p. 322).

Cendrars very clearly saw Galmot gaining his freedom, which the business state would never let him regain for himself, through the freedom
of others, and this is one way to look at Cendrars' own documentary
pursuit of these adventurers. They provided him with 'uncles,' whose
memoirs he wrote. Also, in this decade of newspaper and editing work
running from 1930 to 1940 roughly, they gave him the reasons and means
to travel himself. After *Rhum* he wrote a *Panorama de la pègre* in 1935,
which demonstrates an intimate knowledge of the French underworld,
from Marseilles to the northern border with Belgium and to the Basque
region. In 1936, after covering the first crossing of the *Normandie* from
the hold (while the other reporters sent back copy about the elegant upper
decks), he wrote, also for *Paris-Soir,* a long reportage on his stay in Hollywood.[4] At a later date such documentary books would become far more
personal, such as the 1949 *Banlieue de Paris,* a text to accompany Doisneau's photographs, or *Bourlinguer,* which was at first intended to contain
short essays on places Cendrars had known along with appropriate photographs but which eventually outgrew that format to become a long volume
of complex stories.[5] But already in these earlier, more purely reportorial
books Cendrars was far from hidden away behind the reporter. He was
a celebrity; for example, his picture occupies most of the cover of *Rhum.*
Hollywood, la mecque du cinéma clearly has the tone of a man who knows
the reader is reading *him,* not only about a place he is in. This inclination
to put himself more and more before his audience found its full expression
in two autobiographical pieces, our other antipodes.

In *Une Nuit dans la forêt* (1929) and *Vol à voile* (1932) Cendrars wrote
the only avowedly autobiographical works of his career – and we must
quickly qualify that fact with another, that many commentators believe

they are at least partly fiction. *Vol à voile* is the narrative of young Freddy Sauser running away from the paternal home at the age of fifteen. Quoting from Saint Paul and from the journals of the French flyer Roland Garros, Cendrars shows in his turn how one event or sensation early in one's life may prefigure others, and how the words of an old piano teacher when one is fifteen may remain with one a whole life, guiding it at every turn:

> 'En somme, rien n'est inadmissible, sauf peut-être la vie, à moins qu'on ne l'admette pour la réinventer tous les jours!... ' Propos d'après boire, dira-t-on; oui, peut-être, mais aussi dangereuse boutade d'un esprit enthousiaste, insatiable et insatisfait dont je subis la fascination et sentis le souffle m'enfiévrer, car, comme d'un briquet biscornu peut jaillir une étincelle précaire, mais suffisante pour déclencher un incendie dans un milieu approprié, cette simple boutade d'ivrogne suffit pour ravager mon adolescence et me brûler toute la vie.[6]

Une Nuit dans la forêt is the account of a few hours in Paris between his return from Brazil and a trip to Spain, a few hours during which action is suspended and Cendrars (or at least his persona) gains knowledge of a deep-seated despair. *Une Nuit* is so rich in thought that at times it reads like a string of aphorisms; a single, lonely night translating a myriad of insights about the vast forest one is lost in:

> Mais, en vérité, je n'espère plus en rien. Je le jure. Et j'en donne pour preuve l'amour et cette grande passion que j'habite. (Une dernière pose, mais pour moi seul.) Je n'attends rien de ce que j'aime, mais tout ce que je n'aime pas m'attend.
>
> Et je l'accepte.
>
> C'est pourquoi je ne me prête jamais, mais me donne et me distribue gratuitement.[7]

All of Cendrars' friends have testified to his generosity, and perhaps prodigality has contributed to his being a renegade as much as any other single quality. But it can be seen from the above that a whole complex way of life is epitomized in the simple act of giving. He wrote, 'Life is my only wealth and I spend it, for I am spendthrift.'[8]

If we attempt to generalize quickly about these documentaries of self and of others we find essentially three important elements: firstly, that reality was worth reporting with little embellishment, for its inherent, unsuspected, and possibly unsuspecting lyricism, quite independent from the reporting poet's personal voice; secondly, that the most valuable aspect of reality, for Cendrars, was how men instinctively and daringly

grappled with it in all its incoherence, from the inside, and then indiffer-
ently or compassionately spent the profit; thirdly, that the reporting of this
reality did not exclude his own involvement, whether he was an observer
of others or of himself, because his presence was his only knowledge, his
only medium. In *Hollywood* he wrote:

> Rien n'est aussi émouvant pour un enquêteur qui vient de partir incog-
> nito à l'étranger que de rapporter de cette plongée une actualité vivante,
> palpitante, récalcitrante, mais de signification générale et qui est le seul
> témoignage réel que nous puissions donner de la vie de l'univers, cet
> inconnu ...
>
> Il ne s'agit pas d'être objectif. If faut prendre parti. En n'y mettant pas
> du sien, un journaliste n'arrivera jamais à rendre cette vie actuelle, qui elle
> aussi est une vue de l'esprit.
>
> Aussi, plus un 'papier' est vrai, plus il doit paraître imaginaire. A force
> de coller aux choses, il doit déteindre sur elles et non pas les décalquer.
> Et c'est encore pourquoi l'écriture n'est ni un mensonge, ni un songe, mais
> de la réalité, et peut-être tout ce que nous pourrons jamais connaître de
> réel.[9]

It is through this process of fading into the subject (*déteindre*) rather than
tracing its calcified outline (*décalquer*) that the documentary and the autobiographical merge, the kodak becomes elastic. The writer's presence is
what makes for re-creation. Out of this merger are born his three volumes
of *histoires vraies,* history made real through improbable types.

The stories in *Histoires vraies* (1937), *La Vie dangereuse* (1939), and *D'Outremer à indigo* (1940)[10] are mainly about characters presented to us as real
people Cendrars has known, so we have no evidence that we are dealing
with fiction. Perhaps we are being encouraged to think that we are not.
However, each volume is called a collection of *nouvelles.* One may assume
then that these stories are 'fiction' just as *L'Or* was, facts refashioned and
reorganized for a purpose, and this seems to me the most fruitful premise.
An examination of it as it applies to these stories will discover a few salient
aspects, and these in turn may constitute an outline for the next section,
where the four long autobiographical novels are discussed as one whole.

First, difficulties arise from the assumption that the characters and events
are factual because for the most part we are inclined not to believe in them.
Here, if Cendrars is writing fiction, he has violated consistently one of its
most important tenets (as long as art was still imitation in a narrow sense);
the people and events must be likely or the reader will fail to believe. Most

of Cendrars' fiction and non-fiction seems totally implausible. Just above I quoted him as saying, 'Aussi, plus un "papier" est vrai, plus il doit paraître imaginaire.' This must describe a very special kind of truth. Starting with *Histoires vraies* Cendrars writes of people who he says are real and whom he knows personally; these acquaintances include, for example, Griffith in 'L'Égoutier de Londres,' who knew how to get into the vault of the Bank of England from the sewers,[11] and Fébronio, a religious fanatic who pulled out the teeth of his victims and then murdered them to 'save' them.[12] But, as we have already seen, the most ordinary often seems extraordinary in Cendrars' treatment; for example food, from the simple *menus* in *Kodak* to the two meals in 'La Femme aimée'[13] to the week of dinners arranged for John Dos Passos and his wife as described in *Bourlinguer.*[14] Basic to Cendrars' world is that likelihood or probability is no criterion for the choice of fictional material; the criterion is that it exists, and if it is improbable, all the better. But the extraordinary things which Cendrars depicts are not meant to be interesting for their sensational aspects, for they always serve a meaning. Griffith's cleverness and Fébronio's religious criminality do not in themselves constitute the main significance of their respective stories, as becomes apparent from the emphasis of the narration; they are powerfully embodied symbols – in the first story a foil image for men escaping war, in the second the symbol of conflicting moralities in a culture of diverse and confused origins. So whether Cendrars is reporting fact or inventing fictions, at all times the extraordinary symbolizes our own obsessions uncovered by him, acted out by characters without scruples. In other words, Cendrars has either created or discovered and re-created the archetype in his myth. The veracity of his material is less important than the form it takes, a sort of modern and somewhat personalized mythology. Describing his grotesque heroine in *Emmène-moi au bout du monde!*... Cendrars showed his readers their own reaction to his unbelievable 'reality':

> On hésitait, tant la face paraissait stupide. Et tout à coup, on était emballé et l'on admirait sans aucune restriction mentale l'audace de cette femme qui avait eu recours, probablement sans l'avoir fait exprès, à la terreur religieuse, à la mythologie crétoise, au culte de Minos pour se diviniser ...[15]

The second novelty of these 'histoires vraies' is that Cendrars himself is now the narrator under his own name, reporting reality or merely lying magnificently. He remains on stage throughout these stories and the four autobiographical novels, so called precisely because he seems to be the main character or concern (I shall take issue with this view, however).

Cendrars has purposely relinquished all the advantages of the omniscient author, or of different personae for each story or novel, and no doubt a man who had led a less expansive life – or one who could not lie on such a grand scale – could not permit himself such a luxury, especially in the pursuit of myth. But the purpose of his ubiquitous presence is not to boast of his experiences but to unify experience through the discovery of personal meaning. In 'Le Cercle du diamant' he writes of the chance meeting of two world travellers

> ... qui causent à bâtons rompus, qui trinquent, qui vont se séparer sur une poignée de main sans même avoir eu l'idée d'échanger leurs noms, tellement ils auront eu l'impression de se connaître car, en bavardant du monde entier, ils n'auront fait, au fond, que de parler d'eux-mêmes.[16]

'Je suis l'autre,' or again, 'le monde est ma représentation.' The story always discovers a meaning in Cendrars which is the personal and human value of the mythical experience. The actual story or plot of such a reality, interesting as it may be, does not constitute its primary value, which is the appearance of Cendrars' voice within the event. Only the intention behind that voice renders the unique and unrelated event significant.

This brings us to the third remarkable quality of these stories, the reordering of facts from reality (or the special ordering of facts of fiction). In Cendrars' short stories, in the four later novels, and in much of his other work, the order is always dictated by the voice, the meaning elicited from the outside world. This may be the case with most literature, but rarely have meaning and plot – that is to say, sequential action and related characters – been so much at odds. Cendrars has often been criticized for the disorder of his work, the lack of structure, the rambling of his voice between and to the detriment of the events of his plot; such criticism is undoubtedly the most frequent serious one levelled against him.[17] But it is the expectation of a plot, an *histoire,* which distorts the perspective of such criticism. Indeed Cendrars offers us plots at times, but mostly he only has parts of plots, or the sort of events which look like the material for well-rounded stories without loose ends. Yet rarely is the apparent direction of some striking event the main drift of Cendrars' meaning, and one may often reach the last page before discovering the manner in which everything does in fact tie in. One is reminded, in this respect, of O. Henry, a writer Cendrars had been interested in only two years before publishing *Histoires vraies.*[18] However O. Henry's adroitness with endings was at the service of the surprising plot; in Cendrars the surprise is how apparently disparate actions come to bear an unexpected relationship at a deeper level of sense. Thus a critic who searches for Cendrars the storyteller finds the wrong man, a popular writer having trouble with his dénouements. But such surface action has in fact been entirely undermined. Plot is dispersed or multiple, people come and go – 'I carry them with me wherever I go,' as Whitman says – and they tell us who and where Cendrars is.

'La Femme aimée' illustrates this reorganization of the reader's expectations. It begins with an introduction about being unable to write which runs two pages and seems to be but another of the digressions for which Cendrars is well known. Then we get to the 'subject,' an Englishman named Boyd who wants a story for an opera from Cendrars. During lunch Blaise outlines the story, one of the most improbable for an opera the reader is likely to come across – a polar expedition. 'La Femme aimée' is the beloved of the expedition's leader, and she is never to be on stage; her voice is heard only on a radio transmitter which is the focal point of the play and the main source of its modernity.[19] Boyd suggests that the star singer, Béatrix, would refuse a role in which she would never appear on stage, but Cendrars insists the reverse is the case because the artistic challenge would appeal to her. Béatrix is the link between Cendrars and Boyd; she is the latter's 'femme aimée,' a phrase Cendrars takes from Boyd's conversation for the title of his opera. Behind the outline of the opera lurks another, more important story, that of the two lovers, Boyd and Béatrix. Appropriately the woman never appears on the stage of this narrative except in the form of a telegram. After lunch with Cendrars, Boyd takes a plane for Lisbon where Béatrix is singing that night; he carries two newspaper clippings Cendrars gives him, and which we read in full, about the dramatic possibilities of the radio. These describe Mrs Wallis Warfield Simpson in a villa near Cannes listening to King Edward's voice, 'la voix aimée,' announce on the radio in the evening of 11 December 1936 his abdication from the throne to marry her. This situation is of course another source of the opera's premise. Cendrars returns to his country house where he has a fight with his housekeeper over staying put and working on his book, which she insists he is attempting to avoid. Later that night, unable to work, as he so often is, he finds in the paper that Béatrix' Lisbon concert is on the radio. He searches through the storm static (also an element of the opera) for her voice. Still, although the theme of his opera and his own intention come together here, this is not yet the main import. He cannot get through to Lisbon, but hears an announcement of the crash of a Lisbon-bound plane in this storm. Later Boyd's death is confirmed. Béatrix writes in need, and Cendrars immediately flies to Biarritz to meet her there. After the Cendrars-Boyd episode, then the apparently less important Cendrars-housekeeper episode, now ends the Cendrars-Béatrix story. However, the real 'end' is Cendrars' last words, an ending which tells us that the first two pages contained the essential meaning he was getting at through each of the pieces; how one succumbs to one beloved voice and, the wind having blown one way, another abandoned voice is left to beckon from afar. 'La Femme aimée' ends:

> Pour moi, Biarritz est un monde. J'y ai mes grandes et mes petites habitudes. J'y ai aussi une meute de chiens, une deuxième voiture, une deuxième maison. Aussi, depuis un an, je ne suis pas encore retourné dans mon village, et quand je pense à ce manuscrit qui m'attend étalé sur ma table, dans la petite maison fermée de l'Ile de France, je me demande quelle aventure m'arrivera le jour où je rentrerai chez moi, travailler?[20]

'La Femme aimée' illustrates, I think, some of the density of Cendrars' later writing. There is nothing subtle about the materials themselves, the subtlety is in the way they almost secretly relate. One should not be fooled by the appearance of free association in his narrative, for he remains the man 'qui n'écrit jamais pour rien dire,' as Jean Van Heeckeren has said of him.[21] It is only out of great authorial confidence that he has arranged his work around his own person. The archetypal aspect of his later work is somewhat less apparent in this story, perhaps because it is mainly embodied in a short outline for an opera and two newspaper clippings, and the extraordinary would need more development. But mythopoeia is certainly a major aspect of these stories as a whole, of 'J'ai saigné' and 'Fébronio' for example.[22] The prominence of Cendrars' own voice, the drastic restructuring of plot, and the mythologizing of self and reality together are the three major aspects of Cendrars' art which can be examined in greater depth in the next section dealing with what I consider to be Cendrars' most important contributions to prose literature: *L'Homme foudroyé* (1945), *La Main coupée* (1946), *Bourlinguer* (1948), and *Le Lotissement du ciel* (1949).

His thoughts are the hymns of the praise of things.

Here is action untied from strings necessarily blind to particulars and details magnificently moving in vast masses.

WHITMAN, 1855 preface to *Leaves of Grass*

It is extremely difficult, I think, to *demonstrate* that Cendrars' 'je' is not a purely egotistical entity. In Whitman studies, where the same problem arises, critics are not in the least agreed that the poet was free of a distasteful narcissism,[1] and there also, it seems, nothing can be proven; the reader must determine for himself. However, at least a distinction between what I shall abbreviate as 'self' and 'ego' has been made in Whitman's case, and it may be of use here in the understanding of another writer who is in the Whitman tradition. In his introduction to the 1919 NRF translation of Whitman's poetry (by Gide, Larbaud, Laforgue, Vielé-Griffin, Schlumberger, and Louis Fabulet) Valery Larbaud wrote of what he happily called a 'moi délivré de l'égoïsme':

> ... une poésie du moi délivré de l'égoïsme au sens étroit du mot, du moi agrandi de tout ce qu'il abjure; du moi qui cesse de bouder, à l'écart, ou de se soigner, ou de cultiver ses manies, ou de s'adorer, mais vit en contact avec les autres 'moi,' vit 'en masse.'[2]

Whitman's is a poetry of the self free of egotism. This self should appear to rejoin what we call the mystic self, or again selflessness, abandoning behind the selfishness, the egotism of ordinary, insecure, and materialistic acquisitive living. Malcolm Cowley, the American critic and chronicler of the Lost Generation, writes:

Whitman believed ... that there is a distinction between one's mere personality and the deeper Self (or between ego and soul). He believed that the Self (or atman, to use a Sanskrit word) is of the same essence as the universal spirit ... He believed that true knowledge is to be acquired not through the senses or the intellect, but through union with the self. At such moments of union (or 'merge,' as Whitman called it) the gum is washed from one's eyes (that is his own phrase), and one can read an infinite lesson in common things ... [3]

Cowley's introduction to *Leaves of Grass* leads one to suspect he is a bit suspicious of this 'self,' and it is useful to cite an authority on this concept. The opposition between self and ego, as well as something of an explanation of the mysticism contained in being one's 'self,' is explored in the elusive work of Martin Buber, for whom the distinction defines the difference between the saved world of I-Thou and the lost world of I-It. (In this translation into English the German *Person,* what I call 'self,' is rendered 'person,' and *Eigenwesen,* what I call 'ego,' is translated as 'individuality.')

Individuality makes its appearance by being differentiated from other individualities.
A person makes his appearance by entering into relation with other persons.
The one is the spiritual form of natural detachment, the other the spiritual form of natural solidarity of connexion.

He who takes his stand in relation shares in a reality, that is, in a being that neither merely belongs to him nor merely lies outside him. All reality is an activity in which I share without being able to appropriate for myself.

The person looks on his Self, individuality is concerned with its My – my kind, my race, my creation, my genius. [4]

Buber goes on to distinguish the 'I' spoken by the individual from that spoken by the person who has entered into relation: the I, he says, of Socrates, of Goethe, and the 'unconditional relation' in 'the saying of I by Jesus.' Of Goethe's 'I' in 'pure intercourse with nature' he writes: 'So the spirit of the real remains with it when it turns back to itself, the gaze of the sum abides with the blessed eye that considers its own radiance, and the friendship of the elements accompanies the man into the stillness of dying and becoming.' [5]

As I would judge, with Larbaud, that Whitman's voice is that of self free

of egotism, so I would say that Cendrars' voice is that same 'I' of relation
to 'the spirit of the real.' Nothing could be more relevant to the Whitman
Weltansicht. Whitman's 'Cosmic Consciousness' is precisely his sense of
relation to all of reality, Buber's I-Thou relationship, and Bergson's instinctual identification with the *élan vital.* Through the relinquishing of
egotism (which, of the nature of the act, cannot be willed), of the possession of things, beauty, genius, creation, or whatever, he very simply enters
into contact with others, as Larbaud says; enters things, beauty, genius,
creation, everything that can be the case. And, as Buber says of Goethe,
when such an 'I' in relation turns to look upon itself the same effect
obtains, and such autobiography still draws a picture free of narcissism,
which refers to an attitude and not to a subject.

Larbaud says as much for Whitman, and I apply it to Cendrars. The
enthusiastic integration of the materials of the modern world into poetry
and prose, without the prompting of a theory (or will), is one aspect of
the 'stand in relation.' Another is the constant emphasis on the identity of
world and self, in *Dan Yack* or *Moravagine* for example, or in such frequently repeated phrases as 'Je suis l'autre' and 'Le monde est ma représentation'; or again in the title for the collected poetry re-edited in 1957
as *Du monde entier au cœur du monde.* This Cosmic Consciousness demands
the inclusion of 'I,' the personal voice which must initiate relation and
meaning. But that word *je* is never the centre of a unique attraction, as
must be the case with the egotistical; as Georges Piroué writes of Cendrars: 'Se centrer revient pour lui à jouer les excentriques et décliner son
identité le transforme en Protée. Ce sont là aventures qui lui plaisent:
devenir l'Autre à force d'être soi.'[6]

Cendrars' four autobiographical novels of 1945-9 are uniformly written
in the first person, a first person moreover who calls himself Blaise Cendrars and who fits the knowledge we have of him as a real man. Cendrars
does not talk about himself 'to establish an authoritative apparent self,' as
Buber describes the 'individual.'[7] In fact, although these works are to date
the main source for the details of Cendrars' biography, autobiography is
not their purpose. They are an incidental source, if almost the only one,
for he was consistently reticent about his life and his work, as many of his
friends have testified. In 1929 Nino Frank wrote in an appropriately
entitled article, 'Blaise Cendrars: l'homme le plus seul au monde':

> Quant à savoir quelles sont les affaires qu'il traite, on n'y parviendra
> jamais: 'Ma vie ne vous regarde pas,' est-il toujours prêt à vous répondre
> ... On m'avait demandé d'écrire un livre sur son œuvre et surtout sur son
> existence: 'Le jour même de la publication, quelque soit le ton du livre,
> je publie un démenti dans tous les journaux et je vous fais un procès.'

And a year after the author's death t'Serstevens wrote of his privacy as a
writer:

> Dans tous ces logis de hasard, où je le retrouve, pas un livre, jamais de
> livres, pas un bibelot, rien aux murs, et sur la table pas un papier, jamais
> une seul page écrite. La machine quelquefois, rarement, mais jamais sans
> nulle trace de ce qui est sorti du rouleau d'ébonite. Et il en a été ainsi toute
> sa vie. Je n'ai jamais connu pareille pudeur chez un artisan de lettres. Ceux
> qui l'ont visité n'ont jamais vu que cette table nue, comme si l'écriture –
> et c'était peut-être vrai – lui répugnait.[8]

An intriguing example of Cendrars' 'pudeur' in his writing is that nowhere
in all his stories around 'je,' including the many pages about the war and
the 'récits de guerre' entitled *La Main coupée,* do we find a description of
that terrible moment in a field in Champagne when he lost his arm. We
have accounts of what happened just before that instant and the mysterious
appearance of a severed hand falling out of a clear, quiet sky in 'Le Lys
rouge' in *La Main coupée.* And in 'J'ai saigné,' from *La Vie dangereuse,* we
have the story of Cendrars' hospitalization after the amputation; but this
'histoire vraie' is more about a shepherd, whose horrible death pre-empts
the reader's attention and wrath, and it is even more about Sœur
Adrienne, whose compassion saves the hospital's inmates from both their
wounds and the officer-doctors. It is through these stories about others that
oneself is represented, and that is the method of Buber's self standing in
relation. In connection with *Moravagine* Cendrars wrote:

> Je ne crois pas qu'il y ait des sujets littéraires ou plutôt il n'y en a qu'un:
> l'homme.
>   Mais quel homme? L'homme qui écrit, pardine, il n'y a pas d'autre sujet
> possible.
>   Qui est-ce? En tout cas, ce n'est pas moi, c'est l'Autre.
>   Je suis l'Autre, écrit Gérard de Nerval au bas de l'une de ses très rares
> photographies.
>   Mais qui est cet Autre?
>   ... tous les beaux livres se ressemblent. Ils sont tous autobiographiques.
> C'est pourquoi il n'y a qu'un seul sujet littéraire: l'homme. C'est pourquoi
> il n'y a qu'une littérature: celle de cet homme, de cet Autre, l'homme qui
> écrit.[9]

The wrath and the compassion, which is to say the meaning, of 'J'ai saigné'
belong to Cendrars; but 'je' is always acting, or finding its actions in others.

The array of characters in Cendrars whose numerous attributes and activities are detailed in vast sentences similar in their cumulative technique to Whitman's catalogues is one measure of his vast Other. The reader is not asked to admire Cendrars, as he was not asked to admire Montaigne in his *Essays;* whereas the demand for pity, indulgence, praise, and ultimately admiration are quite imperious in writers like Rousseau or Gide.[10] Cendrars' 'thoughts are the hymns of the praise of things,' as Whitman saw in his own song, and not the hymns of the praise of himself. These things and people are legion but, with the proper insights, the 'I' of I-Thou threads them together to make sense of them. It is what Henry Miller wanted when he printed the following from Emerson as epigraph to *Tropic of Cancer,* another book of 'I' in chaos:

> These novels will give way, by and by, to diaries or autobiographies – captivating books, if only a man knew how to choose among what he calls his experiences that which is really his experience, and how to record truth truly.[11]

In similar terms in *Dan Yack* Cendrars has Goischman discover what must be written in his novel (though Goischman is immobilized and will never write a word of it):

> – Il faut que je trouve un lien de parenté entre toutes les personnes que j'ai rencontrées dans ma vie de vagabond. Les asiles de nuit, les fermes, les châteaux, les émigrants à fond de cale, les cocottes des grands cafés, les anarchistes, les riches. Des bougres de tous les pays et qui ne seront qu'une seul et grand famille, dont je raconterai l'histoire.
>
> Onze mille visages le hantent. C'est sa famille.
>
> Il va écrire le roman de sa vie. Il va raconter sa vie. C'est ça. Ses poèmes ne sont que mensonges. Il va enfin raconter sa vie. La vérité. Tout ce qu'il imagine au sujet des autres, comment il les a rencontrés et pourquoi ils font partie de son cœur, de sa mémoire, de son être le plus intime. Tout est communion.[12]

Goischman's catalogue in the first paragraph above is Cendrars' world. From his voyages, around the world and around his room, Cendrars culls the images of a panorama as vast, diverse, and vigorous as Balzac's.[13] In Balzac the co-ordinates and framework were French society, a complex hierarchy about to disintegrate; in Cendrars it is his self, 'je' in a hundred different places with people scattered throughout or on the fringes of a society that cannot claim them. Examples of this Cendrarsian world, to

look only at those who dominate *L'Homme foudroyé,* are: 'la femme à Mick';
'le père' François, who walks at the bottom of the Meaux canals in a
diving-suit; the many gypsies (Sawo, probably the main hero of the novel,
Marco, the villain, a trainer of bears, 'La Mère,' matriarch of the clan, who
predicts Cendrars' future, 'Le Grêlé,' whose theatre Cendrars calls the
only authentic surreal art); Gustave Lerouge, forgotten author of over
three hundred popular books; his woman, Marthe, whose face was split
by a whip; Paquita, the rich South American who is the heroine of the
novel though she bears no relation to Sawo, only to Cendrars; Fernand
Léger; Manola Secca, the illiterate Brazilian who sculpts the stations of the
cross life-size mounted in automobiles; and, in a haunting image of yearning after sophistication, the group of Peruvian Indians carrying a grand
piano across the Andes.[14] Places also abound, and are not in the least
restricted to being backgrounds for characters, but rather belong to themselves, that is, to Cendrars: La Croix, a trench during the first world war;
La Redonne, Cendrars' momentary retreat where he plans to write *Dan
Yack;* the restaurant Chez Félix in Marseilles; 'La Zone' outside Paris
where gypsies and other impoverished people camped; La Pierre, another
retreat; the Criterion café; 'La Nationale 10,' a road which we might well
consider represents Cendrars himself, a passage to the whole world. What
holds all these disparate people and places together under the same cover
is that Cendrars takes them as his family, as Goischman says; to use Buber's
terminology, the I enters I-Thou.

This self in a world interpreted by it is the organizing medium which tears
up plots to let the pieces fall into its own new order with a new, unified
meaning. I may use *L'Homme foudroyé* as my example. As in the three other
books, no action of one person or of persons in conjunction (some exception would have to be made here for *La Main coupée*) dominates *L'Homme
foudroyé.* An outline shows how dispersed places and people remain:

Part 1 'Dans le silence de la nuit' (pp. 48-73)
         1943: letter to Edouard Peisson
         1915: the French trenches
Part 2 'Le Vieux-Port' (pp. 77-172)
         c. 1927: Marseilles, La Redonne, 'la femme à Mick'
Part 3 'Rhapsodies gitanes'
         1   'Le Fouet' (pp. 175-205): mostly Lerouge
         2   'Les Ours' (pp. 209-249): La Mère, Le Grêlé
         3   'La Grand'route' (pp. 253-290): Paquita
         4   'Les Couteaux' (pp. 293-336): The killing of Marco

We have a first part set in 1943, then 1915; a second about 1927; and a long third part mainly about a few months in 1923, but where we also read a great deal about his experiences in 'La Zone' and with gypsies (1907-17), his attempts to decifer Mayan manuscripts (c. 1923), and various trips on 'La Nationale 10' (perhaps 1924, or 1920 to 1930). Except for Sawo, who is mentioned in parts 1 and 3, these three divisions of the novel apparently share nothing. Even Sawo seems hardly significant as a link, for he is not important at La Croix and barely appears at all in the rhapsodies until the very end, where the novel is abruptly terminated by a ten-page monologue by him at the Criterion café, with only a footnote from Cendrars.

What is Sawo's story? He had run away from his gypsy family and during the war joined the Foreign Legion. He maintains a certain connection with 'La Zone,' however, and with his family; for since his mother is 'La Mère,' and his uncle 'Le Balafré,' elected 'King of Sicily,' that is, leader of Sawo's clan, Sawo is 'Le Fils,' a sort of prince who consequently has definite and inescapable obligations. The most important of these, much as he would like to leave these people to their feuds and continue his life in Paris, is to kill Marco, who has murdered 'Le Balafré.' Thus, although we see hardly anything of him, Sawo is in fact always working behind the scenes throughout the rhapsodies, almost half of *L'Homme foudroyé*, and his monologue at the end explains numerous loose ends in the story of the gypsies' feud. But this feud itself only occupies a small portion of the rhapsodies, in fact it merely provides a scant framework for long sections on other subjects: in the first rhapsody Gustave Lerouge; in the second 'Le Grêlé' and his surrealistic play about bears; in the third Paquita and the deciphering of Mayan manuscripts; and in the fourth, about thirty-three pages on 'La Nationale 10' before the ten pages from Sawo. Here Sawo tells Cendrars of how he defended his family, and how he killed Marco in the end before leaving 'La Zone' and his clan for good. Killing Marco is Sawo's liberation, and this theme of liberation is the leitmotiv of the novel. There is an irony here because, although Sawo wants his liberty from the clan, the gypsies themselves are an image of freedom in the novel. Cendrars lends great romance and mystery to them, if only through all the unsolved questions the reader has about their behaviour up until Sawo's monologue; and, of course, the gypsy is a well-known symbol of independence without Cendrars' help. But Cendrars also shows us how strict the gypsy's mores are, and how oppressive his existence must always remain. In 'Les Couteaux' Sawo kills, but also cuts the umbilical cord.

However, as I have just pointed out, three-fourths of this last section, 'Les Couteaux,' is about 'La Nationale 10,' the road which runs from Paris to Biarritz via Chartres, Tours, Poitier, Angoulême, and Bordeaux. Yet it is the preceding chapter which has for its title 'La Grand'route.' At the end of that chapter Cendrars finds himself tied down, no longer able to work at his manuscripts and oppressed by the *romanis* at the gate of his retreat, La Cornue (Marco, Sawo's enemy is a member of the *romani* clan):

> Partir. Prendre la route. Rouler à tombeau ouvert sur la grand'route, de Paris au cœur de la solitude, de l'autre côté du monde, au volant de mon engin, le pied sur l'accélérateur, rouler sur mes quatre roues à 160 à l'heure, foncer droit devant moi, de borne kilométrique en borne kilométrique, déchirer le monde en deux comme on déchire un prospectus 'en suivant le pointillé.' [p. 288]

It is probably at this point only, near the end of 'La Grand'route,' that we begin to see parts of the book come together: 'Partir. Prendre la route.' It is then time for 'Les Couteaux' to cut the cord for Cendrars as well as for Sawo. After the above quotation we read 'J'avais le cafard'; then a mere listing, over a full page long, of the characteristics of gypsies. A short excerpt from *Genesis* ends the chapter, and 'Les Couteaux' opens, under the heading 'Le Chemin Brûlé': 'Au Tremblay-sur-Mauldre (Seine-et-Oise) la N 10 passe devant ma porte. Un jour, je n'y tins plus, je mis en marche et me voici parti dans le ronflement de mon moteur' (p. 293). This departure is not from La Cornue, not from the physical place of the previous chapter, and thus the theme of leaving must be inferred as a mental state lurking within unrelated scenes and stories. Invariably in at least this volume and *Le Lotissement du ciel* we cannot even guess at a plan until, at one late point, it is revealed to us, and a prose which was full of movement but apparently no order suddenly proves its direction and meaning. So often in Cendrars we are impatient to know where we are being led, and eventually doubtful that we are indeed going anywhere at all; then we discover that the direction had always been there, and this is the climax of the plotless novel; turning back to the epigraph (p. 45) we read:

> ' ... le grand livre du monde... : Voyager, voir des cours et des armées, fréquenter des gens de diverses humeurs et conditions, receuillir diverses expériences, s'éprouver soi-même dans la fortune... '
>   Descartes: *Discours de la Méthode*

L'Homme foudroyé is about becoming a gypsy of the world.

The opening letter to Edouard Peisson celebrates the rebirth of Cendrars the writer after three years of utter silence during the second world war. 'L'homme foudroyé' rises from his ashes (the imagery is Cendrars': see p. 49), and, in fact, *partir* applies as much to the very writing of this volume as it does to disparate narratives and experiences within it. The simplicity and blunt confidence of the first words of narrative are exemplary, and end Cendrars' second war by telling the beginning of his first as if nothing especially interesting had happened between them: 'Donc, la légion était devant Roye' (p. 51). Cendrars follows associations, such as war, without worrying about chronology. 'Dans le silence de la nuit' is about men's fear in war, or, as at the end of 'La Grand'route,' an oppressive melancholy, *le cafard,* that holds the forever waiting soldiers. Two soldiers shoot themselves in the leg to get home, and Sawo simply goes AWOL; 'J'avais le cafard,' he tells Blaise when they meet by chance at the Criterion long after the end of the war (p. 61). Of course this must be the same scene as the one that ends the novel, and from this perspective the whole book is no more than the elaboration – a three-hundred-page parenthesis! – of everything we must know, in Cendrars' view, to understand the larger meaning of Sawo's vendetta. As he elaborates he tells a larger story, and such elaboration is itself more to the point than its supposed origin. Cendrars' attempts at finding a peaceful and isolated retreat, perhaps suggested by Peisson's identical search in 1943 (pp. 48-9), represent at least three cases (at La Redonne in 1927, La Pierre in 1916, and La Cornue about 1923, in that order) of a search for freedom, but each story is a separate, different, and real situation, and the theme gains depth and strength through the great distinctness of its variations. All of them are Cendrars' many versions of Sawo's melancholy. Then the road frees Cendrars, and Sawo tells of his own liberation which now only further illuminates Cendrars' road. It is thus that the result or outcome of the book matters less than what has been happening all along, and the ending is not the culmination of the unconnected involvements but serves to make the reader reflect back upon them, and, in fact, rediscover them. It makes for the most rewarding sort of second and third readings.

My outline above only suggests the complex interweaving of this novel. Cendrars deals in more extended structures than we are accustomed to for the most part, and we must come to him as we do to Faulkner's novels of demolished chronologies. We await Sawo's story from page 61 to page 327, so long that we had written off any continuation of that scene long before it returned, as we had dismissed many other scenes which seemed to be accumulating without point. But the point is always there, as Paul Andréota discovered when he visited Cendrars just after the war:

Qui dira le fin mot de l'écrivain Cendrars? Un autre jour, il me démon-
tra, preuves en main, que sous son débraillé apparent, un ouvrage comme
L'Homme foudroyé avait en réalité été conçu en fonction d'un plan si précis,
si détaillé qu'il eût pu en commencer la rédaction par n'importe quel
paragraphe de n'importe quelle page, le résultat eût été le même.
Prodigieux artisan![15]

Using *Bourlinguer,* a novel I will refer to only a few times, Henri Perruchot
described Cendrars' technique as a sort of discontinuous circling:

Il emploie une technique syncopée, relativiste, qui lui fait découper dans
ses souvenirs, au hasard, dirait-on, sans se soucier d'un ordre chronolo-
gique ni d'un ordre spatial, désarticuler le temps et l'espace. L'on saute dix
ans sans transition, passe d'un atelier de diamantaire de Rotterdam à un
bouge de Valparaiso ou à la cour des shahs de Perse. Le récit se brise
d'innombrables parenthèses, jamais fermées, pleines d'incidences, de rap-
pels, de piétinements, de retours en arrière, de départs inattendus vers
autre chose, où vivent côté à côté, durant quelque lignes ou quelques
pages, des hommes célèbres et des inconnus appartenant à tous les pays
et à toutes les époques, des aventuriers vénitiens ou russes, Picasso, que
Cendrars nomme 'le Philippe II de la peinture moderne,' des maharadjahs,
le marin Papadakis de Samos, un préposé aux douanes de Bordeaux res-
semblant à Joseph Delteil, Tchang-Kaï-Chek ou ce lointain ancêtre du
XVIe siècle, Thomas Platten ... Cette technique est préméditée: par ce
discontinu, par tous ces heurts, Cendrars veut étreindre le maximum de
vie possible, faire éclater les limites de l'homme ... 'Chiffrée à l'échelle,
écrit Cendrars de son héros Moravagine, sa vie aurait figuré une courbe
ascendante qui, retombant, revenant plusieurs fois sur elle-même, aurait
décrit une spirale de plus en plus large autour de mondes de plus en plus
nombreux. Quel admirable spectacle, toujours identique et toujours
varié!'[16]

Thus Cendrars links his technique to the theme of change and cycles
which I examined in connection with *Dan Yack,* and one wonders if he
knew of Yeats' theories of the spiral, or, since he does not mention Yeats
anywhere, if he had not also read Vico.

Cendrars describes his technique in two instances in these autobiographical novels. The first remains somewhat obscure, for it consists at first
of an understanding of the Mayan alphabet. Paquita apparently provides
the key, but as the alphabet itself remains unclear to us we may see only
vaguely:

... c'est Paquita qui me fit remarquer que chaque lettre de l'alphabet maya est mobile et que chaque 'ville sainte' est un horoscope. Elle me disait: 'Si idéographiquement vous placez sous la caverne demi-circulaire par exemple le signe de l'eau, vous verrez que le buste premier, et les personnages secondaires, et l'extérieur de la caverne avec ses signes, ses accents, ses symboles éternels s'y mireront fatalement (ce qui est l'aspect nocturne de la nature des choses, et non pas le monde à l'envers!); mais si vous inscrivez tout cela plastiquement, c'est-à-dire en pictographie, vous fermez le cercle de la caverne et obtenez une roue, la roue de l'Univers, qui est la signature des choses. Voyons, c'est évident, Blaise!' [pp. 287-8, footnote 2]

And at the end of the section on Paquita Cendrars writes:

Ainsi, voici Paquita 'cadrée,' à son tour et selon la méthode, la pure méthode de l'alphabet aztèque.

Je me défends de l'avoir mise sur la sellette mais je l'ai placée au milieu de la Roue pour l'interroger, de la Roue des choses, de la Roue de l'Univers, comme elle m'avait enseigné de le faire pour m'aider à déchiffrer les papyrus du Vatican. Et si je replie la Roue, elle est dans une caverne jusqu'à la fin des temps.

Mais peut-on déchiffrer une femme? [p. 321][17]

Whatever this may mean about the alphabet (or calendar, as it is usually known), it seems a fine image for Cendrars' treatment of his numerous subjects. On the one hand he inscribes them in positions which are juxtaposed but seemingly unrelated until he comes full circle around 'je,' the centre, at which point they are all discovered to be connected by their presence on this particular 'Roue des Choses,' which in this novel is a cycle of moral prisons and escapes. In one instance Paquita sees her life described in one of the many dolls she collects: 'Emma Bovary, c'est mon portrait, je ne pouvais pas la rater. Mais, aujourd'hui, j'ai horreur de cette femme! D'ailleurs la vie des femmes n'est pas drôle. Nous sommes condamnées à attendre. Toujours. Et attendre quoi?... que ça vienne!... ' (p. 317). Only death frees her, as it did Emma. Then there are rows and rows of other dolls. When Cendrars says Paquita is 'cadrée' he is indicating that in order to present a character he must provide a whole world as well, a vast continuum in itself which is the only description, by circumscription. A person must be more than physical and psychological characteristics, and more than the accumulation of his past (which would be a plot), and to attempt to give him to the reader by telling only of these is to immobilize him, whereas Cendrars, to re-create him, wants to keep him moving. So while a character is circumscribed, all the characters making up the circumscription of each, and every one is moving and continually being redefined by his relations. Circumscription is never finished, wrapped up, and Cendrars' 'I' is also best perceived less in itself than in its relation to all its encounters. Sawo is surrounded by his friends of the Legion and the members of the clans, actually inscribed in them, forced to move as they move; Lerouge is inscribed in Marthe, 'La Zone,' publishing, and all the peculiar subjects he writes about; Paquita in lovers, dolls, and Monsieur Jean's 'Enfer'; and Cendrars himself, surrounding all these, is bound by them and by numerous others at La Redonne, Chez Félix, at Meaux, in Paris, etc. In the image of the Mayan alphabet wheel Cendrars combines theme or leitmotiv, juxtaposition as contrast and juxtaposition as relation. The last two were already present in 'le contraste simultané.' The three together, theme, contrast, and relation, are fused in the image of the wheel, and thus in the practice of Cendrars' re-creation.

The second striking instance of Cendrars' explaining his technique bears mostly upon relation, and is found in 'Gênes,' the very long eighth story in *Bourlinguer:*

> Aujourd'hui j'ai 60 ans, et cette gymnastique et cette jonglerie aux-quelles je me livrais pour séduire le mousse, je les exécute maintenant devant ma machine à écrire pour me maintenir en forme, et l'esprit allègre, depuis les années que je ne sors plus, que je ne bouge plus, que je ne voyage plus, que je ne vois plus personne, glissant ma vie comme une feuille de papier carbone entre deux feuilles de papier blanc sous le chariot de ma machine à écrire et que je tape, je tape, au recto et au verso, et que je me relis comme un somnambule, intercalant dans la vision directe celle, réfléchie, qui ne peut se déchiffrer qu'à l'envers comme dans un miroir, maître de ma vie, dominant le temps, ayant réussi par le désarticuler, le disloquer et à glisser la relativité comme un substratum dans mes phrases pour en faire le ressort même de mon écriture, ce que l'on a pris pour désordre, confusion, facilité, manque de composition, laisser-aller alors que c'est peut-être la plus grande nouveauté littéraire du XXe siècle que d'avoir su appliquer les procédés d'analyse et les déductions math-ématiques d'un Einstein sur l'essence, la constitution, la propagation de la lumière à la technique du roman! (*Je fais l'âne pour avoir du son!*)
>
> En d'autres termes donc, j'écris ma vie sur ma machine à écrire avec beaucoup d'application comme Jean-Sébastien Bach composait son *Clavecin bien tempéré*, fugues et contrepoint ... [18]

In *Blaise Cendrars vous parle...* the author stated the idea in less imaginative and more concise terms: ' ... au point de vue composition et exécution, j'ai voulu supprimer le temps, ce qui m'a fait dire que dans la composition

je tenais compte de la relativité d'Einstein et dans l'exécution, de la technique de Jean-Sébastien Bach ...'[19] Einstein did not eliminate time. On the
contrary, he integrated it into systems of energy and space. In this sense
the first of these two quotations, if more obscure, is closer to the truth.
Pre-Einsteinian, absolute time has been dismissed, and time is now flexi-
ble, *élastique*, and disrupted by feeling. Here we are very close to Bergson's intuited duration, for it would seem that measurable time has been
jumbled and the inner voice of 'je' proceeds in a simple but ineffable
duration. Now the moments fall here and there in a continuum of the
mind which is the length of the book. We might say that duration is the
lengths to which Cendrars goes to elucidate his theme. Objective time is
relevant to each variation, because that piece of a story *happens*, but irrelevant to the whole which, for example, might be an emotion which Cendrars felt when Peisson left him in the evening of 21 August 1943. We
must conceive of an obscure and fleeting yet enduring and important
moment which is outside of time as we may more concretely apprehend
it with a clock, but which is obvious and ultimately simple to the mystic.
Jacques-Henry Lévesque gives serious attention to this concept of what he
calls 'l'instant' in his preface to Cendrars' poetry,[20] and I have discussed
it in connection with the snapshot effect of the later poems. It clearly
duplicates the Satori of Zen philosophy. But however mystical that moment may be, our main interest in it is that it has demanded illustration
in Cendrars, a recounting in the form of many events removed from time
so that they may expand into the meaning of the theme. To maintain in
the narrative either chronological time or a single focus on one or more
related characters would be to tell their story rather than circumscribe this
'symbolic action,' as Kenneth Burke terms it. The main import is the
action not of plot but of symbol rooted in experience.

As Paquita is portrayed by circumscription, so the meaning of the book
is not described but illustrated, not so much fashioned and moulded
directly as cut out and away from contingency and chaos. Since Cendrars'
materials are precisely this chaos, the novel often appears to be sheer
improvisation. I would venture to guess that much of the writing *is* im-
provision, but on a chord progression which has been assiduously prepared for all the important variations, and from a hand that has worked
hard and long for its freedom. One may be reminded of the Zen-trained
painter's two- or three-stroke paintings, permitting no corrections and
prepared for by years of study, practice, and meditation. Basic, in fact, to
Zen practice and the more transcendant idea of Cosmic Consciousness is
that such improvisation is the only path to reality because it is the action
of things themselves through the artist, who is more medium than actor,
and whose years of work at his craft represent his learning to listen, to

open himself to the world as Thou; or, in other terms, to relinquish reason
and give himself up to the instinctive interpretation of a pervasive duration. We may find the hallmarks of this attitude towards creation, and all
perception, in Bergson and Buber, in Whitman who wrote in 'Song of
Myself,' 'Dazzling and tremendous how quick the sun-rise would kill
me, / If I could not now and always send sun-rises out of me,' and in
Cendrars, who wrote: 'On n'agit pas. On est agi.'[21] It also motivates my
choice of the word 're-creation' to describe Cendrars' writing. We might
say that the length of duration, in each of these four novels, is each one's
intricate theme, hardly decipherable before all the concrete facts have
fallen out of chaotic clock-time into their new order. Suddenly chaotic
interweaving is turned inside out like a glove, revealing R.P. Blackmur's
'gesture,' that symbolic action which had always directed the book. Revealing pattern only late in the account, Cendrars closely parallels the
manner in which any man comes to self-understanding after years spent
in puzzlement over the relationship of all that has happened to him. He
suddenly gains distance, and, paradoxically, Cendrars' 'je' is just this perspective.

Cendrars' 'relativity' provides perspective in both time and space, neither of which is fixed, but always inscribed in his persona. Conversely, his
persona, a veritable 'family' of themes as Wittgenstein used the word to
avoid a restricting definition, provides the co-ordinates for discovering
time, place, and personalities. The relationship is perfectly fluid, which is
as it should be. Time, plot, 'je' have meshed inextricably into the 'becoming' of a symbolic action. It is important to see that 'becoming' cannot be
pinned down, only continually inferred from the life of the writing, just
as Yeats' line, 'How can we know the dancer from the dance?' (from
'Among School Children') tells us that the meaning cannot be divorced
from the object which carries it. In this sense these four books represent
the final sophistication of the deceptively simple prescription for poetry
which Cendrars gave in his 1926 essay 'Poètes,' in *Aujourd'hui;* the artist
must concern himself with the concrete. I quote again from *L'Eubage:*

> ... tout se tient, se lie et rebondit, 'et que l'on ne peut définir un brin de
> paille sans démonter l'univers.'
>
> Sans superstition aucune, l'instinctif balbutiement d'un enfant fait ac-
> courir l'univers, le range autour de son berceau et lui fait gracieusement
> don de sa réalité. [p. 74]

'No ideas but in things,' as William Carlos Williams often repeated; nothing but 'the the' wrote Wallace Stevens at the end of 'The Man on the

Dump' in answer to the question, 'Where was it one first heard of the truth?' Abstractions or abstract statements are useful for making order but useless for seeing reality. Thus *L'Homme foudroyé* must remain largely at the level of an 'instinctif balbutiement' if it is intended to re-create its world, never quite reaching intellectual definition which would of its nature dismiss the quality of becoming. Appropriately, the books of this series seem to end abruptly, too soon, because in a sense they have not ended, but arrived at becoming. The book breaks off when its meaning comes alive, and the revelation of its gesture, its only point, initiates its first movement in the reader. So not only does the text appear confused, but the eventual elucidation is truncated; yet we are meant to understand, and, I think, even be elated at, this climax in the form of discovery. In 'Crossing Brooklyn Ferry' Whitman wrote:

> We understand then do we not?
> What I promis'd without mentioning it, have you not accepted?
> What the study could not teach – what the preaching could not accomplish
> is accomplish'd, is it not?

The necessity for explication to resort to the materials I have used from Buber, Bergson, and even Zen points clearly to a fact which must have been apparent already in the second section of this chapter. Cendrars is a mystical poet, like Blake or Whitman, a mystical novelist like Hesse. Unlike these, Cendrars is a mystic within a Catholic framework, as we shall see in a moment in *Le Lotissement du ciel;* however, this background does not prevent him from resembling other mystics far more than he does other Catholics. These poets and novelists, along with the Zen master, share a personal relationship with the godhead, the pantheistic essence of life, which transcends religious dogma and idiosyncrasies. For them there is never a church, only God and themselves, I-Thou; religion is a buttress for others, at most a popular iconography for someone like Cendrars. Each of these men understands time differently from other men; eternity is seen only in the relinquishing of it for the instantaneous Present. Or, similarly, understanding does not come from holding life securely in hand, acquisitively, but rather as I have attempted to show it in Cendrars' use of plot, or as Blake describes it in his short poem 'Eternity':

> He who binds to himself a joy
> Does the winged life destroy
> But he who kisses the joy as it flies
> Lives in eternity's sun rise.

Reality is not timed, with eternity arriving thereafter; reality is change, becoming in duration, and only that, which is an eternal continuum. Furthermore, to enter into this I-Thou requires acceptance of it; the relinquishing cannot be willed. Also, such acceptance is not resignation, which is negative and could never suffice for any sort of faith. All these attitudes contribute to the *Anschauung* at the core of this view of Cendrars, which exhibits one more salient characteristic; the materials of such mystical poetry, what we might call the 'Thou' part of I-Thou, are found every day, at every present instant, 'profond aujourd'hui.' Both Whitman and Cendrars tried to fashion their mystical poetry out of the modern world about them (Blake and Hesse were more inclined to search far away, or in the imagination, which of course Cendrars does as well). As to the differences between even Cendrars' and Whitman's mysticism, we may find at least two important ones; Cendrars' much more sure and knowledgeable sense of the past, of traditions and literatures; and his far greater activity, since action was always the first requirement of his brand of mysticism. Thus perhaps his most famous description of himself: 'De plus en plus, je me rends compte que j'ai toujours pratiqué la vie contemplative. Je suis une espèce de brahmane à rebours, qui se contemple dans l'agitation ... '[22] Contemplation is one kind of action, or part of it, but from the perspective of the mystic not necessarily its opposite.

However, more important for my purposes here is the similarity between Walt Whitman and Blaise Cendrars, not the difference between them. Bergson, Buber, Blake, Hesse, Whitman, and Cendrars belong together as mystics. The last four are writers and, I should say, poets essentially; and, as they are mystics, what they write takes the form of vision, or myth. A further distinction is that the last two, Whitman and Cendrars, make myth out of the world of the present.

Mystical poets are not alone in *using* myth, but only they can *make* it. Eliot, Joyce, and Mann are cases in point. Not one was a mystic, but all employed myth to establish archetypal frameworks, extended metaphors, in fact, which were meant to parallel the failures of the present. Thus, if life appeared chaotic, or without sense or grandeur, a previous myth was appealed to for order, or at least a context for order, an unheeded lesson. In this endeavour Eliot, Joyce, and Mann show that they fell entirely within a rational, intellectual artistic tradition, despite their appeal to a previous irrationality. Whitman and Cendrars, however, created myth, a brand new, unprepared-for order, which is quite different from illustrating anew an older construct. Cendrars from the very beginning made magical, religious objects out of the Eiffel Tower and radios, Fantômas and newspapers; and these replaced those magical objects which belonged to another culture:

On m'a souvent demandé quelles étaient les sept merveilles du monde moderne?

Les sept merveilles du monde moderne sont:

1 Le moteur à explosion;

2 Le roulement à billes SKF;

3 La coupe d'un grand tailleur;

4 La musique de Satie qu'on peut enfin écouter sans se prendre la tête dans les mains;

5 L'argent;

6 La nuque d'une femme qui vient de se faire couper les cheveux;

7 La publicité.

J'en connais encore 700 ou 800 autres qui meurent et qui naissent tous les jours.[23]

Perhaps such a new, popular, seemingly prosaic religion does not seem the equal of the ancient myths. But that must remain a subjective judgment, which can change. The myth is not at its inception a fine, delicate, utterly beautiful entity, as Yeats' 'The Second Coming' warns us, but rather an emphatic and uncompromising force which transcends taste (besides, much of the tone of old myths resides in overly refined translations). Cendrars considered that the poetic in reality had to be instinctive and unpremeditated, and could never derive from the purposeful attempt to be art. It was the intrinsic, functional intention which made for poetry, whereas the desire for artistry in itself would fatally disfigure popular truth. Thus:

Combien une humble servante qui lave la vaisselle *en ne pensant à rien* est plus photogénique, à la condition qu'elle se laisse surprendre à son insu par l'objectif, que toutes les métamorphoses pénibles d'une Mary Pickford qui *n'arrive pas à s'oublier* malgré les cent cinquante mille volts qui l'aveuglent.

Je donne toutes les vedettes du monde pour un animal à l'écran, car ce n'est pas l'individu qui vit sous nos yeux, mais la race dans toute son ingénuité et l'espèce.[24]

Through this selfhood free of egotism the mystic comes upon 'la race,' the folk and its myth. His freedom from aesthetic pretentions permits him to see through acting to the so-called anti-poetic. Paradoxically, to be poetic requires not attempting to be so. This is but another case of the necessity of relinquishing will and becoming a medium. The archetypal content of life is available only to the artist as medium, a self free of egotism who can thus see, be visionary.

As a consequence of such an attitude the author has little importance, except to the extent that he is part of the myth too. Cendrars delighted in the works of anonymous authors and in tales told by strangers in planes, on boats, or in some bar at the end of the world. In *Blaise Cendrars vous parle...* he tells of the ten volumes of his novel *Notre Pain quotidien,* 'qui sont écrits mais que j'ai consignés au fur et à mesure de mes pérégrinations dans les coffres-forts de banques en Amérique du Sud et que, si Dieu le veut on découvrira un jour par hasard. Cela n'est pas signé et le dépot est fait sous un faux nom.'[25] *Notre Pain quotidien* illustrates a central aspect of Cendrars' mythmaking; for even if it exists, his claim for it is that it should appear to be an anonymous production. Whether it exists or not, it stands for a man who by it becomes a disinterested legend. And, of course, Cendrars is a legend. He created one out of himself and life about him, and he is thus a part of it, though since he was apparently not concerned with personal glory he was not duped by the tall tale of himself: 'Le plus gros danger pour un écrivain c'est d'être victime de sa légende, de se prendre à son propre piège.'[26] Legends are for the people who come after, not for their creators. Even if most of his extraordinary career and creations are not 'real' to start with, or did not happen exactly as he tells them, Cendrars is not for that a 'liar' in any pejorative sense because the invention is not self-serving, self-aggrandizement, but rather the mystic's 'hymns of the praise of things,' the re-creation of things infused with the writer's faith that they are of inestimable value. Cendrars wrote in *Le Lotissement du ciel,* 'La vertu de la prière c'est d'énumérer les choses de la création et de les appeler par leur nom dans une effusion. C'est une action de grâces' (p. 456). The mystic's praise cannot but render mythical the apparent ordinariness of life.

It is useful to examine for a moment Cendrars' 'lying.' Several articles in the *Mercure de France* special issue *Blaise Cendrars,* those by Piroué, Lanoux, Beucler, Szittya, and t'Serstevens notably, attempt to correct, here and there, errors in Cendrars' story (and t'Serstevens discusses the problem at greater lengths in his book *L'Homme que fut Blaise Cendrars*). Consistently these writers dismiss one claim only to confirm another one just as extraordinary, if not more so, or else only fall into contradictions with each other – no doubt magnificent contradictions are the most fertile soil for legends anyway. Beucler confirms Cendrars' trips at least to Mongolia and Manchuria, but Szittya insists he never went to China.[27] Szittya writes that Cendrars 'se passionnait dans la fabrication des souvenirs,' thus dismissing much of the veracity, I suppose, of the four autobiographical books under discussion here; but if Szittya seems to be reducing Cendrars' activities to those of common men, he also tells us that Cendrars memorized the *Encyclopaedia Britannica.*[28] In her obituary for Cendrars in the

NRF Elizabeth Porquerol writes that there could only have been one or two uncles for *Le Panama,* and suggests that many of 'their' adventures were only Cendrars' own.[29] Only! If we are trying to cut Cendrars down to size we might as well leave him all his seven uncles. On the other hand t'Serstevens writes: 'Je crois bien que *Le Panama* de Blaise est sorti tout entier d'un numéro du *Tour du Monde* où figurent en photo les "bannes d'orchidées," je veux dire les bannes rouillées, pleines de vase et de vegétation exotique.' He adds: 'Mais quelle distance de ce pauvre article de magazine aux poignants paysages du canal abandonné par le krach, tels que Blaise les a recréés!' And above this discussion of *Le Panama* he writes:

> Il m'a donné, d'année en année, six versions différentes de son équipée dans le Transsibérien, toutes plus belles les unes que les autres, et différentes de la version du poème. On ne peut vraiment reprocher à un homme d'avoir l'imagination si féconde qu'elle lui permette de créer sept poèmes avec les éléments d'une seule réalité.[30]

Can we even conclude that Cendrars took the Transsiberian railroad at all? The accounts crisscross, and they slowly come to confirm a core of ascertainable fact; but it becomes obvious that the core cannot represent all of the facts, and, also, that even the bare core is uncommon. Piroué writes 'Cendrars ment beaucoup moins qu'on ne croit.'[31] In fact, in many cases, Cendrars was unusually discreet about his life, and some of the most interesting information is collected from the lives of other people. He was the first to insist that Moravagine and Dan Yack were not himself.[32] He never boasted of furnishing titles for many of Chagall's early paintings,[33] never discussed what business enterprises he was involved in (we have a few teasing details, such as his Paris telegram address in 1929 CENDRARAYM – Cendrars aime – and one for Rio a few years earlier, HOBALGOB.[34]) Cendrars never mentioned anywhere in his published writing, and notably not in the autobiographical novels, the existence of his first wife Féla, the mother of his three children and a woman to whom he was married for some thirty years; as we have seen, a close friend, t'Serstevens, did not even know about her for over a year of their friendship. T'Serstevens now reveals to us that Raymone, Blaise's mistress from 1917 and his wife after 1949, never slept with him.[35] I have been unable to decide, I must admit, whether that is good or bad for the legend!

Cendrars' fictions do no more than match the truth. They stand beside it, and within it, not substituting for weakness, but translating the same power from different angles. The quality of myth is enhanced by the extraordinary truth cleaving to the extraordinary invention because, for the mystic, reality is the fine representation of transcending truth, and not in the least a vulgar failure which he must transcend. Armand Lanoux wrote:

> En fait, Cendrars était l'anti-Rousseau, l'anti-Gide, l'anti-Amiel, hommes aux sincérités interminables, et quelque peu masochistes. Lui, il était le poète en action, l'affabulateur, le conquérant, l'aventurier. Il n'a jamais distingué précisément le réel de l'imaginaire. Le fond même de la poésie de Cendrars est une prodigieuse ornementation du réel, un baroquisme végétal, luxuriant. Il crée son odyssée en même temps qu'il la vit et il ne sait plus demêler ensuite le vrai du faux ...
>   Cendrars était un menteur. Oui. Comme le poète. Comme Cocteau lorsqu'il avoue: 'je suis un mensonge qui dit toujours la vérité.' Comme le plus grand des menteurs, le Grec Ulysse.[36]

When fiction reaches such exaggerated proportions, while remaining true to sense, it has refashioned reality into myth. It is naturally Cendrars' lyrical voice which effects just such a transformation, one which to many appears so fabulous that it may certainly seem pure invention. In a review of Jean Rousselot's *Blaise Cendrars* of 1955 Robert Kemp wrote of Cendrars:

> Quel pouvoir de récréation et d'invention personnelle!
>   Car il y a le 'mensonge Cendrars' qui est une forme du génie. Vivant sur une plaque géométrique, abstraite, sans épaisseur ni couleur, Cendrars eût, les yeux fermés, inventé les Andes et les steppes, élevé des cités, emplis de ténèbres des mines imaginaires et créé les animaux et les plantes, le diplodocus et la mouche tsé-tsé ...[37]

And yet, despite Cendrars' ability to do so, it is not likely that he taxed his imagination this much. It is after all impossible to maintain at one and the same time the two serious accusations against Cendrars' mythmaking: that he stole everything he wrote from other, documentary sources, and that he fabricated everything out of his own incredible imagination. With evidence for both, we must see him as combining them, matching and alternating. To discover the archetypal meanings or to fabulate, these were, for Cendrars, part of the same mythopoeic activity.

A good illustration of Cendrars at work in this mystical and mythopoeic vein, and one of his finest books, is *Le Lotissement du ciel. Le Lotissement* runs 268 pages in the *Œuvres complètes* and is divided into three parts on different subjects: 'Le Jugement dernier' (14 pages), 'Le Nouveau Patron de l'aviation' (124 pages), and 'La Tour Eiffel sidérale' (125 pages). This last is also subtitled 'Rhapsodie de la nuit,' which reminds us of its similarities in manner and mode to the four long rhapsodies of *L'Homme foudroyé,* and, I would add, to 'Gênes' and 'Paris, Port-de Mer' in *Bourlinguer.* The two longer parts are further divided into section and followed by notes 'pour le lecteur inconnu,' a practice of Cendrars' in three of these four post-war books (not in the case of *La Main coupée*).

Part 1, 'Le Jugement dernier,' is a short piece describing how Cendrars brings a certain tropical bird, a *sept-couleurs* (a sort of tanager) from Brazil to a little girl in a poor neighbourhood, 'les Batignolles.' Cendrars has tried upon numerous occasions to bring one back to Europe but none has ever weathered the Atlantic, and this time, deciding against an ant-eater which a native is trying to sell him, he brings 250 birds! Of the ant-eater he writes:

> Je le regretterai toute ma vie car avoir une bête aussi extravagante comme copain vous ouvre les yeux sur les mystères de la création et vous fait toucher du doigt l'absurde de toute cette longue histoire de l'évolution des êtres. Avoir un copain qui vous tient chaud au cœur, et un compagnon de route emmanché comme celui-là vous fait rire du matin au soir. C'est peut-être Dieu. [p. 341]

The birds are equally marvellous to Cendrars, and we quickly realize that the story serves a symbolic function. Only one bird survives, to die the day the little girl sees it (she has it alive for an evening). The title refers directly only to a 'post-scriptum pour les âmes sensibles' in which Cendrars imagines his little friend clapping her hands for a second and final time at the sight of the wonderful bird. The epigraph to 'Le Jugement dernier' is from O.W. Milosz, and reads: 'Il n'y a que les oiseaux, les enfants et les Saints qui soient intéressants' (p. 338).

Part 2, 'Le Nouveau Patron de l'aviation,' is entirely devoted to levitation. It is divided into three sections. Section 1, 'Le Vol arrière,' contains two principal motifs: the life of Saint Joseph of Cupertino, patron saint of flyers because of his frequent levitations – including one backward flight! – and the account of Cendrars' project to write the saint's life in the Méjanes library in Aix-en-Provence during the occupation. The epigraph to 'Le Nouveau Patron' is from a prayer of Saint Joseph of Cupertino: ' ... donnez à mon intelligence la vivacité et la promptitude et éloignez de moi la timidité et de mon esprit les ténèbres ...' (p. 352); Cendrars has undertaken this project for his son, Rémy, who is a flyer during a time of great moral darkness:

A partir du 10 mai 1940 le surréalisme était descendu sur terre, pas l'œuvre des poètes absurdes qui se prétendent tels et qui sont tout au plus des sous-réalistes puisqu'ils prônent le subconscient, mais l'œuvre consciente du Christ, le seul poète du surréal. Il n'a jamais écrit une ligne. Il agit. Et chacun en prenait pour son grade. Logiquement.

Feu, flammes, fumées. Bombes qui attisaient les incendies. Ponts, chemins de fer, écluses sautaient, et sur les routes, les grandes armées alliées qui s'avançaient dans le chant des moteurs et le casque fleuri et qui devaient le soir même être couchées parmi les morts, les survivants en débandade, avaient dès le matin déjà été disloquées par les flots des populations qui fuyaient terrorisées et vu leurs colonnes géantes coupées par les files des longues automobiles américaines de Bruxelles et d'Amsterdam qui se sauvaient en quatrième dans un gloussement de poules de luxe et un crissement des pneus passés au blanc d'Espagne, une féerie de fin du monde, sous un soleil implacable et par un beau temps fixe. Vision biblique, sans parler des pleurs muets des petits enfants perdus dans la tourmente ou de ce corbillard abandonné à un croisement de routes dont le mort, une très vieille femme, embouteillait à lui seul tout un carrefour. Comme dit Goya: '*Yo lo vi,*' je l'ai vu, de mes yeux vu...[38]

Section 2, 'Le Miracle de l'an 1000,' is a forty-four-page account, or rather list, of saints who have levitated, from about the year 1000 to the present, with a short description of the event in each case. This section makes for alternately fascinating and dreary, repetitive reading. The fascination stems from the fact that the descriptions are, after all, those of first-hand witnesses. The great number of levitations under the often incredulous eyes of reasonably serious observers (as we may determine ourselves from the texts) begins to convince the reader, or at least largely suspend his disbelief.[39] The repetitiveness builds an obsessive, incantatory effect which also undermines scepticism, although, of course, the resisting reader is not likely to enjoy this section of the book. Cendrars wrote of it: 'C'est le purgatoire du lecteur.'[40] Section 3 of 'Le Nouveau Patron de l'aviation,' entitled 'Le Ravissement de l'amour,' attempts to intuit the *ravissement* in the heart of Saint Joseph. This section is passionate, lyrical, as concentrated and difficult as Rimbaud's *Illuminations,* as far beyond the ken of intellect as must be the saint's spirit when it accepts the miraculous ravishment. To find other such passages in Cendrars we must return to *Profond aujourd'hui.* Here the religious ecstasy completely submerges realistic narrative. A fifteen-hundred-word sentence apparently about birds is our only sign of Saint Joseph's ravishment, followed by this description of the unsayable, otherworldly silence:

La vertu de la prière c'est d'énumérer les choses de la création et de les appeler par leur nom dans une effusion. C'est une action de grâces.

Il ne s'agit pas de bouger les lèvres ni de faire claquer la langue, de la faire battre. On ne prononce pas les paroles.

Seul Dieu parle.

C'est pourquoi le saint qui tombe en extase tombe aux abîmes, flotte en-Haut, est lévité, gravite dans un transport, fuse et ne se possède plus. Tout au plus pousse-t-il un cri ou un dernier soupir. Il se laisse aller et coule comme une sonde au plus profond de la parole de Dieu. Il plane...

Mort au monde.

L'oraison mentale est la volière de Dieu.

– Dis-moi, bel Oiseleur, mon Fauconnier: y a-t-il plus grande diversité d'âmes que d'oiseaux, de nombres vivant dans l'Unité ou, dans les profondeurs de la mer, de poissons, ces oiseaux des abysses qui bougent perpétuellement des lèvres mais sont muets parce que leur bouche est tactile et que leur corps en double fuseau qui monte et qui descend, qui gravite, est le symbole scellé du CHRIST, dis-le-moi, beau Pêcheur d'âme dans les borborygmes, toi qui sondes les reins, ou y a-t-il plus d'astres au ciel et des étoiles doubles dans l'univers pour chanter ta Gloire? [pp. 456-7]

Part 3, 'La Tour Eiffel sidérale,' is made up of fifteen sub-sections which I shall not attempt to describe independently. This part represents perhaps the most complex reshuffling of plot in all of Cendrars' work. It describes sorting out diamonds in Saint Petersburg (about 1907), travelling to the Morro Azul plantation in Brazil, living in this refuge with its owner, Dr Oswaldo Padroso (about 1924), and, at the bottom of all the ramifications in this part of the book, a night in the trenches in 1915. In the Brazilian jungle Cendrars' voice mainly condemns the attempt of modern political bodies to substitute their materialistic rationales for humane religion. The USA and the USSR are attacked with equal vehemence, for they both embody this subversion. We meet with a theme I have explored in my treatment of any number of works by Cendrars: *L'Eubage, La Fin du monde, L'Or* and *Rhum*:

On connaît les résultats mirobolants et catastrophiques de ce premier triomphe de l'application de la raison à la direction de la vie des hommes réglementées; ce premier essai d'ordre économique créa tous les désordres et fit exploser la Révolution; et les nôtres, que nous escomptons d'avance, seront un véritable cataclysme planétaire parce qu'appliquée à l'échelle de l'univers notre misérable raison ne tiendra pas le coup, ainsi que le prouvent notre dernière guerre, nos idéologies, notre monde actuel scindé en deux par les fanatiques également matérialistes mais divisés sur l'application d'une formule scientifique propre à assurer non pas le bonheur, comme l'affirment les deux partis antagonistes, mais la prompte décadence du genre humain. [pp. 482-3]

For Cendrars economics must not replace ethics, or the self disappears. The difficult trip to the Morro Azul represents Cendrars' own voyage through the darkness of the second world war in previous pages of the book. He rediscovers the 'hole' in the sky over the trenches in 1915 in the 'sac à charbon,' or coalsack in the Brazilian sky near the Southern Cross.[41] This coalsack is the main symbol of 'La Tour Eiffel sidérale.' It reflects the incomprehensible blankness a man may face in his life, in his own constellation, or the blankness all men faced in the war (and this prompts a discussion of Arthur Cravan and the nihilism of Dada). From his look-out point at the front Cendrars stares at himself in the sky:

> Mon créneau, c'était mon esprit qui l'obturait. Mon cœur vissé en objectif. Focalisation. Gros plan. *Longshot.* Une question de degrés, d'engrenages, d'angle, de mise au point, de limbe chiffré.
> La nuit, tout est déformé au front. L'univers venait s'inscrire dans mon créneau équipé d'un obturateur: moi!... [p. 520]

In the trenches Cendrars becomes, for the first time to his knowledge, a contemplative, and a poet (though there can be no writing in that place; Cendrars has often enough insisted upon that). Section 8, 'Les Bêtes animiques,' describes how he searches for the Word, 'Le Verbe,' which will decipher his own coalsack. It must be named, 'pour s'en rendre maître' (p. 529). The otherwise inscrutable sky is filled with man's names. Only through a 'ravissement de l'amour' is the poet given the name of his world; it is a naming and renaming which crashes in upon him like the shells all around him during this night in 1915, and it burns him 'd'incendie d'amour divin,' as he describes the only instance of two saints levitating together, Saint Teresa d'Avila and Saint John of the Cross (p. 467). The coalsack is the unnamed, each man's mystery awaiting the faith necessary to give it a name, which will permit him to occupy his place in concert and communion with all other men, or saints, or stars. Each saint who levitates in the earlier part of the book gains a place in the sky, his *lotissement* as the real estate developer would have it. For Cendrars the poet-traveller – whether the travels were real or imaginary – place, that is geography, was always the principal epistemological arena; thus, in *Le*

Lotissement du ciel the author's famous and obscure saints are allotted their ecstatic spaces, and with new competencies they people all the skyward dreams of the novel's characters. As a boy in Saint Petersburg Cendrars had covered a map of the constellations with the diamonds he guarded in a locked room:

> ... mais il m'arrivait aussi, toujours pour me distraire, de dérouler une carte du ciel sur la grande table et de recouvrir chaque constellation avec des pierres précieuses que j'allais quérir dans le réserve des coffres, marquant les étoiles de première grandeur avec les plus beaux diamants, complétant les figures avec les plus vivantes pierres de couleur, remplissant les inter-valles entre les dessins avec une coulée des plus belles perles de la collec-tion de Léouba, allumant toutes les lampes dont je pouvais disposer, la rampe, le plafonnier, les baladeuses, ma lampe de poche, le projecteur mobile que je braquais et faisais pivoter comme une lance d'incendie ou, plutôt, d'arrosage car, selon celle que je visais, l'inondant de flots de lumière crue, chaque pierre dominait à tour de rôle comme fleurit chaque plante dans le cycle des saisons, comme chaque fille apparaît tour à tour dans une ronde, s'avance, se présente, s'isole un instant, se met en vedette, chante et rentre dans la danse et se cache à son rang et se mêle à ses compagnes:
>
> ... embrassez la plus belle!...
>
> Elles étaient toutes belles! Et je me récitais la page immortelle et pour moi inoubliable de Marbode sur la symbolique des pierres précieuses que je venais de découvrir dans *Le Latin Mystique* de Remy de Gourmont, ce livre gemmé, une compilation, une traduction, une anthologie, qui a bouleversé ma conscience et m'a, en somme, baptisé ou, tout au moins, converti à la Poésie, initié au Verbe, catéchisé. [pp. 546-7]

Portioning into the sky his vicarious riches, the young Cendrars discovers a meaning for each stone. And for his part Dr Oswaldo, as he is called, in his own 'action de grâces' attributes the name of his idol to a place in the sky, his special *lotissement.*

Dr Oswaldo is a man who has loved, from a distance except for one precious moment, 'la divine Sarah' Bernhardt, and in 1924 he wants Cendrars to help him register a new constellation he has discovered,

> ... la *Tour Eiffel Sidérale,* que je voudrais vous entretenir en vous priant, tellement j'ai confiance en vous, monsieur Cendrars, de bien vouloir faire une démarche à Paris pour que l'on enregistre officiellement ma décou-verte (j'en aurais une telle joie avant de mourir!) car, dans ma pensée, c'est

un suprême hommage que je rends à la divine et à la France, en localisant
la Tour Eiffel au ciel et dans notre hémisphère austral... C'est un symbole
... J'ai tant tremblé pour elles deux durant la guerre. Sarah et la Tour sont
les deux projections spirituelles de la France d'aujourd'hui et sont intimement unies dans mon esprit, comme vous le verrez et ainsi que je l'ai
expliqué dans ma communication à l'Académie des Sciences, car ce n'est
point simple toquade... Et l'Institut ne me répond pas, malgré les documents joints, une photographie qui ne laisse aucun doute ... [p. 575]

Charting his coalsack in the only manner possible, out of his personal, if
eccentric, experience and conviction, Dr Oswaldo has in fact appropriated
stars from other, known constellations, and the tower is actually visible
only from a certain angle at the Morro Azul which blots out the major
parts of those other configurations. But the destruction of earlier *lotissements* does not bother him, for they have lost their meanings, and thus any
claim on the imagination:

> Pourtant le ciel n'appartient à personne, ils n'en ont pas l'exclusivité et
> tous les noms vulgaires et vides de sens que les astronomes y ont inscrits
> pour meubler leurs cartes encore si incomplètes et défectueuses, ne signi-
> fient rien, alors que la Tour montée au ciel du Brésil, ma patrie, signifie
> quelque chose digne d'être mémorabilisé ... (p. 582)

The good doctor made his discovery in September of 1914, when France
seemed crushed by the German advances (Dr Oswaldo's account parallels
Cendrars' narrative earlier of the 10 May 1940 debacle), and it symbol-
ized to him then the eventual victory of *la divine*'s homeland. This discovery is his act of faith, name and value assigned to his 'nuit dans la forêt,'
or 'sac à charbon.'

Le Lotissement du ciel is precisely about its title from at least the three
angles I have traced in outline: those of Dr Oswaldo, Saint Joseph (and
innumerable other saints), and Blaise Cendrars, boy and man. Cendrars
peoples the dark shadows of Saint Joseph's prayer in the epigraph to 'Le
Nouveau Patron de l'aviation' with the children, saints, and birds of the
quotation from Milosz which serves as the epigraph to 'Le Jugement
dernier.' Birds abound and fill even the pages of 'La Tour Eiffel sidérale,'
for Oswaldo,

> ... étant une espèce d'ermite vivant dans la solitude, un saint laïque, un
> libre-penseur à l'âme tendre et, comme son maître Auguste Comte, un
> positiviste touché par l'amour ... avait interdit la chasse dans toute l'éten-

> due de sa propriété, le vallon du *Morro Azul,* de la Montagne Bleue était
> le refuge des oiseaux. [p. 477]

And birds are the ostensible subject of the epigraph to the whole book:

'Injustice'

> Devant sa fenêtre du Palais-Royal, Colette contemplait les pigeons et
> les moineaux s'ébattant au soleil.
>   – La plus grande injustice qui existe peut-être dans la création, fit-elle,
> c'est que certains possèdent des ailes... [pp. 335]

In the light of this book (and perhaps in the mind of Colette as well),
'certains possèdent des ailes' refers to people; those who, symbolically, but
really as well, reach the sky. Levitation is the core subject of the book,
rising out of the ashes of an 'incendie d'amour divin' to join the Logos (in
French Bibles, *le Verbe*). We are to believe the levitations of the saints, as
we are not to mock Oswaldo's discovery, and as we are to believe Cendrars' wild stories. In the mystic, imagination and reality are one and the
same because reality is not real without the madness of its lovers: 'Il est
vrai que nous aimons le monde; mais ce n'est pas parce que nous sommes
habitués à la vie, mais à l'amour,' reads the epigraph to 'La Tour Eiffel
sidérale' (p. 476) from Nietzsche, and Cendrars writes:

> Ah! les saints, ces enfants terribles de l'Église! Il n'y a que ça de vrai pour
> ne pas condamner la vie et la maudire les Saints, les Enfants, les Fleurs et
> les Oiseaux, des fous, des dons gratuits qui vous viennent on ne sait d'où,
> des saisonnières et des innocents. Sans tout cela la vie serait impossible.
> [p. 397]

Le Lotissement du ciel is of course Cendrars' levitation, containing within
it the natural, the traditional, and the modern levitations of birds, saints,
and, along with airplanes, the Eiffel Tower! He does not transcend these
things; he takes them with him (like many of the saints who, attempting
to stay down, dragged furniture off the ground with them). The book is
the most overtly religious demonstration of Cendrars' ability, as early as
1912, to see man's nature within the objects of common and popular life,
to see the lyricism of everyday but contemporary existence. Saint Joseph
and Oswaldo each function in a faith that is free of traditional binds, for
Joseph is pathetically ignorant of his own religion, and Oswaldo is ready
to dismiss any established *lotissements* for his own. Each man's instinctual
independence frees him for the only important revelation, 'le ravissement

de l'amour,' and this no matter what its peculiar manifestation may be. Cendrars commits the same basic heresy and raises man's gods out of his pragmatic and essentially unconscious creations:

> Le totem auquel on s'identifie est l'origine de la chose qui engendre l'être, tout comme aujourd'hui les machines en qui se concrétisent non seulement le génie de l'homme contemporain mais encore tous les rêves de bonheur du genre humain et ses aspirations spirituelles de salvation future, et c'est pourquoi le long des autostrades macadamisées les pompes à essence, par exemple, ressemblent tant aux fétiches des sauvages, mêmes formes stylisées, mêmes couleurs criardes, mêmes ornementations, verre, miroirs, cuivre, nickel, ampoules ou perles, mêmes éclaboussures, sang ou cambouis, même astiquage, les slogans électriques des modernes remplaçant les tatouages sacrés des primitifs, les sigles des compagnies d'essence, les marques des trusts concurrents, les grigris de secte des initiés, le même besoin spirituel engendrant la même esthétique pour exprimer la même terreur, DIEU, Dieu le Père, DIEU, et c'est pourquoi les pompes à essence au bord des routes et à la sortie des villes, sans rien dire des hauts fourneaux, des cheminées d'usine et de tout le bataclan industriel, les complexes de tuyauteries, de poutrelles, d'engrenages, de câbles, d'étincelles, de fumées lourdes, de jets de vapeur, de lueurs fulgurantes, de décharges électriques qui font de l'activité de l'homme d'aujourd'hui un spectacle tragique, vont par groupes, font cercle et portent chacune un panonceau comme un masque nègre qui s'anime la nuit et stupéfie. [pp. 540-1]

As man's productions are capable of generating a more essential and human meaning, of levitating in fact, in Cendrars' lyricism, so they gain mythical value. Myth is the folk telling its version. Cendrars plays the teller here, but his 'I' is not personal. We note that only the first fourteen pages are Cendrars' own story; most of the rest is composed of documents and Oswaldo's tale. Cendrars' unlikely story of 250 seven-coloured birds merely takes its place next to the others, stories which are at root anonymous. A truth is wrenched from a likely reality and reported in all its splendid unlikelihood. In a modern, sceptical age credulity is to be recultivated, or the world remains without wonder, crushed under the weight of meaningless objects. Cendrars assaults verisimilitude, yet remains faithful to reality. His lyricism is that wonderment which makes things spiritually and sensually real rather than only objectively and verifiably so; a lyricism which metamorphoses newspapers, cars, streets, buildings, boats, radios, anything we make use of into myth, a version of reality projecting man's longing into the heart of merely real things, 'au cœur du monde.' Whitman predicted: 'They [the poets] shall find their inspiration in real objects today, symptoms of the past and future ...' and 'The direct trial of him who would be the greatest poet is today.'[42] As much as to say, 'profond aujourd'hui'; Cendrars' voice mythologizing modern 'action untied from strings necessarily blind to particulars and details magnificently moving in vast masses.' The chaotic excess of modern life, reflected in the baroque plot, is melted down in an 'incendie d'amour divin,' and then resuscitated, out of 'braises crépitantes et ... cendres retombantes.'[43] The phoenix, a mythical bird and the personification of the 'ravissement d'amour,' rises towards its place among the other extravagant configurations in the sky.

12 'Réinventer la vie'

Salut au Monde!   WALT WHITMAN

In *Blaise Cendrars vous parle...,* which was broadcast in 1950, Cendrars said he was contemplating a real novel, 'un roman-roman' as he called it, and in a footnote dated 1952, the year of the publication of these interviews, he added: 'J'ai commencé ce roman le 1er janvier et j'espère bien l'avoir terminé avant la fin de l'année. Son titre: *Emmène-moi au bout du monde!...*'[1] In this third interview there is much discussion of writing, and of the identification of an author with his characters. Cendrars insists that his own characters are not himself, and he speaks at length of this problem in the case of Flaubert and *Madame Bovary.* Then of travelling in the near future he says: 'Cela ne m'empêchera pas d'écrire que d'être au bout du monde. J'espère même que j'y écrirai tout autrement. Un écrivain vivant doit se renouveler. Et le dépaysement y est favorable.'[2] In 1950 Cendrars had recently returned to Paris, and he remained there until his death eleven years later, thus renewing an old acquaintanceship, or even love. It is thus that we might consider his new *dépaysement* to be Paris; *Emmène-moi au bout du monde!...* (1956) is his first novel about Paris, and his first about a woman.

Only in the eighth interview does Cendrars mention the famous personality from real life who serves as the starting point for his own Thérèse Églantine: the actress Marguerite Moreno.[3] Cendrars warns us, in a prefatory note to the novel already quoted at the end of my biography: 'Le présent ouvrage est un roman à clef. J'espère bien que personne n'aura l'inélégance d'y appliquer les clefs, les clefs du Mensonge ...'[4] I do not think it improves the novel to indulge in such inelegance, for its meaning, as much of it as may be discovered, does not depend on its springboard in reality. Yet we must assume a good deal of irony on Cendrars' part, if not maliciousness, in this little note; it is the novel in which the characters are the most readily identifiable, but the only one in which he warns us not to make the connections. Briefly, the keys are given, or dismissed, in this eighth interview (recorded two years before the novel is begun): Thérèse, the lead in the play *Madame l'Arsouille,* written by Guy de Montauriol and directed by Félix Juin, correspond respectively to Moreno in Giraudoux' *La Folle de Chaillot* directed by Louis Jouvet. Two other keys are that Coco in the novel springs quite obviously from Christian 'Bébé' Bérard, who did the sets for *La Folle,* and, on a more personal note, the dedication to 'La Folle de St. Sulpice' is for Raymone, who played that role in Giraudoux' play.

Emmène-moi au bout du monde!... reverses Cendrars' technique of the four preceding books by having a plot with no flashbacks or disruptions in chronological time. Rather than spanning a great many years, jumping back and forth at the call of associations, *Emmène-moi* covers about twenty-four hours in the first ten chapters. The last three chapters disperse the characters, purposely leaving an open ending; the main point must remain those twenty-four hours. But if Cendrars has written a story with a plot, he has done so only to emphasize the plot's failure. If we concern ourselves with what *happens,* that a man is murdered, we finish only in frustration because there is no solution, and the case remains a mystery, as the chief of police, Jean de Haulte-Chambre, predicts: 'J'y flaire un mystère. Or, j'ai horreur du mystère' (p. 283). Chapters 5 to 9, almost half of the novel, deal with the murder and, like the chief of police, the reader demands some sort of answer. Yet chapter 11 is entitled 'Le Crime parfait,' and is only an account of what the characters do during the next six to eight months, with barely mention of the crime except directly in connection with the police chief's story. Thérèse, who during virtually all of chapter 9 lectures de Haulte-Chambre on the crime (an extraordinary twelve-page monologue), does not mention it at all in the next chapter, and, in fact, we must conclude that once the characters of the novel emerge from the police station the subject almost totally disappears from their minds. The novel is too well handled, with many details and actions dovetailing and a murder held in very clear focus, for us to think that Cendrars has lost control. Rather he has purposely created an elaborate red herring which turns out to be precisely the point, an unsolvable mystery. In this respect the novel strikingly resembles the work of the film director Michelangelo Antonioni, especially in *L'Avventura* (1960) and *Blow-up* (1966). In *L'Avventura* a girl is lost on a small island and the other participants in the trip search for her for about half an hour of film time. It is made quite clear that the girl has entirely disappeared, without possible explanation. The same kind of mystery attends the search for a murderer, as well as the disappearance of the body of the victim, in *Blow-up,* and in both films the mystery serves to make living more difficult; more irrational, unsolvable, contingent. The mystery epitomizes the deep anxiety in the vacuous lives of boredom which most of Antonioni heroes and heroines lead.

As in *Blow-up,* the crime in *Emmène-moi* is unfathomable, and both director and author insist upon pursuing the non-existent answer at great lengths. Antonioni forces his audience into the very heart of pointlessness, as does Cendrars; but, as we have come to see, for him the irrational is not threatening. Thérèse forges right into the unknown with no apprehensions, and she has aspects of the crime incorporated into the play, which is in rehearsal. The plot, a sort of Rorschach test pointing to nothing and anything, becomes the measure of the characters' various relations to mystery; in particular, this self-erasing plot takes the measure of an extravagant 'monstre sacré,' Thérèse Églantine.

So, in a circuitous way, the novel is very much a conventional one. We are presented with a striking array of Parisians, and Cendrars has detailed their characters more fully and with greater interest than we have found in his earlier novels, where only one or two characters counted, or in the autobiographical works, where the main interest was the meanings and variations in the author's voice. We have almost a novel of manners, a Balzacian view of Paris: the theatrical world, the underground, the bars and cafés, the police, and any number of neighbourhoods or *quartiers.* Now if we distinguish – roughly to be sure – those characters who are willing to take risks, who throw themselves into work or play with abandon and enthusiasm – Thérèse; Jean-Jean (or Jean de France), who is her legionnaire lover; Émile, who is shot; Coco, the stage designer – from those other characters who are less inspired but more methodical, determined, selfish, and self-serving – such as Juin, Montauriol, and de Haulte-Chambre – then we have aligned the main figures in two camps: that of the free and spontaneous inside mystery, that of the serious and self-important who take care to stay out:

> Selon la formule d'Henry Miller: *Dieu créa le monde et y entra...,* fidèle au propre de son génie, Coco attendait l'inspiration de la dernière heure pour tout improviser quand les autres perdaient la tête et c'est en frisant chaque fois la catastrophe qu'il atteignait à la maîtrise, d'où ses prodiges au théâtre où le peintre n'avait connu que des succès, une longue suite de triomphes. Il n'en était pas plus vaniteux pour cela, au contraire, il restait humain, pas humble, non, mais caché, toujours comme Dieu dans sa machine.

> Contrairement à Coco, par exemple, qui était tout improvisation, ou à Teresa, qui était toute spontanéité, Félix Juin n'avait pas de génie. C'était

un bûcheur. Il n'avait pas de don et aucune espèce de générosité. Pas de
flamme, peu de goût, pas de passion ... Et l'on peut dire que s'il avait réussi
à tromper le public sur sa véritable personnalité c'était à force de travail,
d'application, de volonté, d'entêtement, de détermination et d'une inaltér-
able patience qui n'était pas dans sa nature mais qu'il s'évertuait à exercer,
ce qui parfois lui donnait la fièvre et l'énervait ou le portait hors de lui.
Quand cela lui arrivait en scène, alors il était sublime. Mais c'était rare, car
il était trop jaloux de lui-même et ne se donnait pas. [pp. 229, 294]

Here Cendrars allows that even calculating Félix Juin is magnificent when
he forgets himself, his ego. It is the first quality of Thérèse, as well as of
her lover Jean-Jean, that she behaves as generously in life as on the stage;
she is inspired, and improvises throughout (she is also shrewd enough to
judge her effect):

De mémoire humaine on n'avait jamais vu ça et de l'avis des rares privilégiés qui eurent la chance d'assister à cette scène improvisée, burlesque,
sanglante, désopilante, de froid calcul et de haute poésie, de don total,
d'abandon de soi-même, d'emportement mais sans aucune frénésie, d'inspiration, d'humilité et de maîtrise ... [p. 239]

In the scene in question, having just arrived terribly late for rehearsal
because of her bout with Jean-Jean, Thérèse makes her grand entrance by
letting fall all her clothes and reciting Villon's ballad, 'Ha! vieillesse
félonne et fière,/ Pourquoi m'as si tôt abattue,' which perfectly describes
her own appearance on the bare stage at the age of 79. A machinist
remarks, 'On voit bien qu'elle est de Montmartre, la môme' (p. 240), and
it is because she instinctively knows herself and reads her audience so well
that she is capable of improvising so brilliantly, as she does in this entrance
and later in her speech to the chief of police. 'Je suis peuple,' says Thérèse,
born near Square d'Anvers in Montmartre; her first husband taught her

... que la tragédie, le drame, la comédie, la farce sont les manifestations
de la vie populaire, que les règles ne sont rien, que chez tous les peuples
à tous les temps, toutes les formes d'art sont permises, que le théâtre est
une acceptation, une soumission commune des hommes et des étoiles aux
lois obscures de la création, une participation à la joie de vivre, un jeu du
sort bon ou mauvais, que la destinée de l'individu isolé n'a aucun sens,
sinon comique, caricatural, et que tous emsemble, acteurs et public, nous
sommes liés dans le délire universel ou féerie qui nous emporte.[5]

This passage describes Cendrars' own view of art and life as I have been examining it throughout. 'Le théâtre est une communion,' Thérèse says, and in the same chapter Cendrars has her elaborate on a statement we have already seen from himself: 'Seule l'action libère et les idées que l'on peut se faire sont de l'action avortée' (pp. 306, 315).

It is this attitude which permits the book to absorb the mystery without becoming obsessed by it. On the one hand life at its most striking, yet gratuitous and absurd, is incorporated into the play – Thérèse's disrobing, which ensures the success of the play, and the mysterious murder, which is the perfect symbol of the incomprehensible. On the other hand the theatre, 'soumission ... aux lois obscures de la création,' invades life, having thus 'sa prolongation dehors, une résonance dans la rue' (p. 369). For example, Juin and de Haulte-Chambre play alternately cat and mouse in the chapter entitled 'Tartufe... Tartuffes'; and later Thérèse out-Tartufes them both in her long monologue, improvising a hypothetical case of her own guilt and at the same time eliminating such a possibility. If 'vivre est une action magique,' as Cendrars has said before and repeats here in the title of chapter 2,[6] then indeed the world is much like an illusion, a theatre in which we must nevertheless not fail to choose actions. It is only those who act forcefully, extraordinarily, often in this novel brutally, who precipitate reality out of illusory existence: Thérèse, Jean-Jean, Émile. Each of these crashes through life, as Thérèse breaks glass panes in doors when she passes through (it is something of a visiting card for her). The crash makes things come alive at that instant, and makes for a super-reality:

> ... je vais m'engueuler une fois de plus avec Félix Juin et le petit Guy qui n'aiment pas l'irruption de mon réalisme dans leur surréalisme un peu bébette, esthétique et conventionnel. Ils vont encore m'accuser d'être trop vraie et de faire ultra. Bien sûr que je fais ultra-vraie, et pourquoi pas... et pourquoi n'essaient-ils pas d'en faire autant, au lieu de canner?... Il n'y a pas plus coco que ces directeurs et auteurs d'avant-garde qui veulent toujours faire du nouveau, rien que du nouveau, à n'importe quel prix et n'importe comment du nouveau-nouveau, c'est leur formule ... [p. 200]

The only sources for 'le nouveau' are the mysterious depths of life, and never its mere forms; not, as described in this case, tricks with aesthetic, theatrical conventions. This is why 'le spectacle est dans la rue,' as one chapter is entitled, chapter 3, which takes place inside the theatre.[7] The play, always ready to fly off in the forms the artists can conjure up, must continually be returned to the home of the anonymous yet modern and new folk. While Jean-Jean makes love to her in the first pages of the novel, Thérèse keeps thinking of the lines:

> Plonger au fond du gouffre...
> Au fond de l'Inconnu pour trouver du nouveau...[8]

This crude lover revitalizes the aging actress; in fact he must maintain the black eye he gives her at the beginning (she has it when she recites Villon in the nude and decides she wants it for the play). It is a number of eccentric and extraordinary people – Jean-Jean, the legionnaire; 'la Présidente,' whose fabulous jewels Thérèse embroiders onto her gown for the play; Émile, brawler, bar proprietor, and murder victim, as well as Thérèse herself – who all epitomize the strengths of the street, and supply the play on the stage and the play of life with a fuller reality, Whitman's 'passion, pulse and power.' Below the stage of this novel, like the river Seine which Félix hears 'par un mystérieux canal du Moyen Age' (p. 295) under the offices of the police station, runs an undercurrent of powerful vitality, a story in itself entirely phantasmagorical, but which seems to supply that 'Inconnu' which is the first source and basis of reality. This is the story of 'la Présidente,' Bahanie-Paceaura Netotsi (Marie-Antoinette), told mostly in chapters 2 and 10. Born legless in 1900, she is sold at the age of fifteen into the famous harem of Moha-Ou-Hammon (in Kenifra, Morocco), who apparently prefers her to all others. The night of the Pasha's nuptials to an eight-year-old she is thrown out of a castle window, by Thérèse! (The colonel Oscar de Pontmartin is also present; he marries 'la Présidente' in 1929. Had it all been arranged?) Beneath the window she is caught by a legionnaire, who was *not* expecting her! She is carried away, and later turns up exhibited in fairs. She becomes an obsession, a talisman for legionnaires, 'Notre-Dame de la Légion,' and, between 1915 and 1929, many die trying to gain possession of her. Mixed up somehow with this story is that of Jean-Jean, for Thérèse learns only now, some thirty years later, of what happened after the defenestration of her friend, 'la Présidente,' from Jean-Jean's legionnaire friend, Owen. All of this incredible story Cendrars affirmed in an interview to be factual.[9] In the same interview he said the novel had originally been conceived to be about the legionnaire, and this is confirmed to us by the following, dated 1951, from *Trop c'est trop,* a collection of stories and essays published in 1957:

> En dernière analyse, *le roman que je n'écrirai jamais* est, je le crains fort et comme chaque fois que je suis en transes, justement celui que je suis en train d'écrire, en l'espèce un livre sur la Légion, dont le sujet est une femme à la Légion et que je n'intitulerai pas *Notre-Dame de la Légion,* mais *Emmène-moi au bout du monde!...* car c'est un roman d'amour. De la bagarre? Bien sûr, mais entre moi et ma machine à écrire.[10]

Thus in *Emmène-moi* a myth-like truth – or so the author tells us person to person, outside of his fiction – underlies an illusory or theatrical world in turn rendered more real by the violent invasion of the myth. The invasion is mysterious, insidious to such a man as the chief of police. No doubt it is a mystery, 'l'Inconnu,' for even such as Thérèse, but she is intimate with it, and personifies it. Its baffling action is the very medium of her freedom, the chord progression for her improvisation: 'Je pourrais donc vous parler durant des heures et des heures de tout ce que vous voudrez et improviser à jet continu sans jamais m'écarter de la réalité ni des faits précis ...' (p. 325). It is this emphasis on improvisation which makes the novel 'un petit roman gai,' as Cendrars called it (see footnote 9 above), despite the terrible seriousness of its premises and its mystery; a novel of *insouciance* as Jacques-Henry Lévesque described it to me. The epigraph, always important as we have seen, insists upon the improvisational nature of the book by comparing the author's aesthetics to those of a jazz band:

> Par ailleurs, ce livre est écrit selon l'esthétique de quelqu'un qui croit à ce qu'il raconte, comme Coleman Hawkins, saxo-ténor, et ses musiciens du ciel, Billy Taylor, piano, Emmett Berry, trompette, Eddie Bert, trombone, Jo Jones, batterie, et Milt Hinton, contrebasse, le 'Timeless Jazz,' des as, racontent une belle histoire, *Lullaby of Birdland,* qui se déroule dans l'espace, hors du temps et de l'époque. [p. 188]

M. Lévesque, himself an early admirer of jazz in his Dada 'little' magazine of the late twenties *Orbes,* quotes from a letter of Cendrars to the French jazz scholar Hughes Panassié: 'Le jazz hot n'est pas de l'art mais une nouvelle façon de vivre.'[11] In *Vol à voile* Cendrars told us how, at the age of fifteen, he had learned to *inventer,* or *préluder* on a musical theme, and I have already quoted this very important passage in which we are told life must be improvised:

> 'Dans la vie, comme en musique, il ne faut pas s'attarder à l'idée reçue, mais se tourner vers l'idée à recevoir, c'est pourquoi, nous deux, nous "inventions" hein?'
>
> En somme, rien n'est inadmissible, sauf peut-être la vie, à moins qu'on ne l'admette pour la réinventer tous les jours!...[12]

Thérèse shatters the suffocating patina of accepted, rationalized ideas to continually rediscover original ideas, with 'original' taken in its two senses; the new identifies the pristine. Improvisation is the only creative 'soumission ... aux lois obscures de la création,' and it is what makes

Thérèse's contributions to the play its main, primal reality, its super-reality. When Thérèse dies she is as young as ever, for her death is no finale, only another variation, a last chorus without arrogance and practically without sadness. She falls out of a cherry tree, like a ten-year-old, and only the grotesque body dies of age.

Thus it was with Cendrars the author, improvising a new life to the very end. *Emmène-moi* is by far his most Rabelaisian work, alternately obscene, bombastic, funny, and tender, a novel not entirely unlike Henry Miller's first success *Tropic of Cancer,* of which Cendrars, apparently Miller's very first reviewer, wrote: 'Livre royal, livre atroce, exactement le genre de livres que j'aime le plus.'[13] *Emmène-moi* is a 'livre royal,' and a 'livre atroce,' and 'un roman "bœuf," ' as André Billy called it in his disgruntled review.[14] It runs quite counter to the direction of the four autobiographical volumes, which culminate, in the last one, with the levitation of saints and author. It would almost seem that Cendrars was debunking himself. As the three epic poems and the three early novels embodied a sort of dialectic of the imagination, the grand finale in the sky of Aix-en-Provence is shockingly returned to earth, to the streets of Paris. Saint Theresa and Saint John of the Cross levitate, Thérèse and Jean-de-France screw. If this is the work of a writer grown old, to the philosophical maturity of a 'brahmane à rebours,' it has been without the loss of any of his youthful toughness, or of his perfect sense of abandon. With *Emmène-moi au bout du monde!...* it is as if that cry of the title were indeed taken up again, an original call to adventure; so that we might end our discussion of Blaise Cendrars as if we were only beginning.

Conclusion: Making discovery

For Cendrars everything was a beginning because every single thing in the world was a marvel. Hesse has written that 'A magic dwells in each beginning.'[1] In that light Cendrars' phrase 'Vivre est une action magique' means that to live is to begin, at every moment, whatever that moment may offer. Of the two lines from Baudelaire quoted at the outset of *Emmène-moi au bout du monde!...* Cendrars wrote:

> De l'inconnu, du nouveau, tout l'est pour qui découvre la vie spirituelle. On peut naître pour la première fois, on peut naître pour la dixième fois dans la même maison, dans une maison qui est toujours la même et où l'on découvre à chaque détour du nouveau. L'écrivain qui fait de nombreux retours sur lui-même, comme moi, ne monte jamais par le même escalier, ne descend jamais dans la même cave, n'est jamais au sommet de la même tour, il découvre sans cesse et toujours du nouveau, tout dépend du climat, de l'heure, du moment, de l'humeur, de l'inspiration, de la sanctification, de l'épuisement, de la fatigue.[2]

The mystical poet is always transforming, reinventing the quotidian. For such continual rebirth one must be continually available, as well as always ready to leave, to take a new departure. In context the above quotation from Hesse reads:

> At life's each call the heart must be prepared
> to take its leave and to commence afresh,
> courageously and with no hint of grief
> submit itself to other, newer ties.
> A magic dwells in each beginning and
> protecting us it tells us how to live.

And Cendrars wrote in *Feuilles de route* 'Quand tu aimes il faut partir.'[3] Thérèse of *Emmène-moi* stays young because she can leave, and begin, as if the heart and mind only age and die from a life-long accumulation of failures at leaving. She, Sutter, Moravagine, Dan Yack, and, it is time to infer, Blaise Cendrars had 'the ability to live spontaneously on primitive levels,' as Matthiessen says of Walt Whitman.[4] Cendrars' spontaneity guarantees the vitality of his work; creation is improvised, if with great care and attention, and in most of his production after years of gestation; it is improvised with the seriousness one must bring to matters of importance, matters beyond self-importance. It is thus that the movement of his work is organic and unified, at the deepest levels, beneath forms.

Beneath Cendrars' many forms and innovations, his seemingly excessive improvisation, we ought to be able to find some inner archetypal patterning since, if mythopoesis can be new, it is unlikely that the impetus itself can be entirely so. Just what is the dominant symbolic action of Cendrars' mythologizing as I have described it? I have established that Cendrars generally eschewed earlier myth narratives as structural devices for his own. Nor does it seem that the most familiar themes are present. As a rule, his work does not seem to embody the usual forms of initiation, or *Bildung,* or – to mention the most common version of these, particularly in American literature – the myth of the fall from innocence. The three epic poems are perhaps the most interested in this theme, but innocence, if it can precisely be called that, has already been lost, at the very outset of *Les Pâques* for example. These poems end in a reconciliation with experience and, I think, a rather surprising return to innocence, instead of the usual accommodation to existence after the fall. There is a return to faith and wonder, so that the direction and meaning of the myth would seem to be reversed. The fallen state in Cendrars actually corresponds more closely to what is considered chaos in cosmological myths, a time and place before existence in faith. If this is not sufficiently clear in the three poems alone it becomes more so in the progression I have followed in my analysis. I have already discussed Cendrars' passage from epic to short – indeed, at times, shortest – poetic forms. A vast panoramic yet discontinuous picture of humanity and Christ is followed by the clear presentation of prosaic objects and events. The particular myth which underlies Cendrars' work involves a regaining of innocence.

The novels of the twenties do not at all follow any scheme of bourgeois initiation into or recovery of money, power, fame; nor do they aspire for the Romantic obverse, the principled rebellion against these values. For Sutter, Moravagine, and Dan Yack such rebellion needs no statement because it predates the beginnings of their fictional lives. Sutter is innocent of fate in Cendrars' portrayal, and he remains so throughout his outer transformations. It would seem that Moravagine is almost what he is before he is even born; he transforms the world around him, overpowers it, and is beyond initiation into anything. From the outset he has all the knowledge of himself he ever needs or desires. In both of these cases fate determines character and action more than initiative can, and the bourgeois hope of making changes for the better never comes into play. Dan Yack does divest himself of worldly values, but at the very beginning of the novel and apparently without much difficulty, certainly with little bearing on his important actions in the two volumes. These do not develop towards a crisis of initiation, but are mostly post-initiation; and, furthermore, as I have said of the poetry, such early initiation is not into experience, but into another innocence. His is not a Romantic rebellion; he is in fact quite a Romantic character, bemoaning his losses, only in the first few pages. Thereafter something more positive is happening, succeeding a Romantic life which pre-dates the novel itself. This is, as I say above, a new beginning, and it underscores the great relevance of *Emmène-moi,* despite the fact that the novel may not be Cendrars' best, nor perhaps even finished.

Cendrars' heroes, including himself, are of mythical proportions without being quite powerful enough, somewhat without the aura of achievement. They do not succeed or overcome; at best they instinctively or compulsively start again, as betrayed by the insistently spontaneous and episodic nature of their lives. Also, they do not fall, again because no matter what the circumstances they seem always ready to start up again, the past failing to weigh heavily. Yet these are not anti-heroes, and they are quite different in quality from the major sort of novelistic hero from Flaubert to Joyce. It is difficult to find a niche for Cendrars' personae somewhere along the imaginary continuum between these two extremes of protagonist, hero and anti-hero. Cendrars' hero is an anarchist actor, a marginal, eccentric, outside man or woman. And the new life he or she is always starting is outside the bounds of social expectancy and conformism, outside expediency. He is extravagant and prodigal. Sutter is not yet a capitalist; he is an aspirant for something not yet specified at the end of an uncharted voyage, which is to say he is an explorer. And Sutter the explorer may dream of his reign and dominion but he never attains it, never gets the chance to become a settled capitalist (further, the examples of Moravagine and Dan Yack demonstrate that if he had, Cendrars would not have found him interesting). Cendrars and his personae are explorers, adventurers, people who go towards something happening; they are always moving towards, and never arriving, consolidating, keeping for themselves and from others. It is a continual, anarchistic youth, a perfect Dada gesture.

The four autobiographical novels constitute the most magnificent, luxuriant stage for Cendrars and his theatre of anarchists, who, there with him, inhabit a *Zone* outside civil, chartered Paris. In these books we are no longer dealing with the single, singular fates of the earlier novels. The outsiders have become a population. We are now offered a picture of someone who chooses to call himself the author looking at, moving towards, joining a whole culture of pariahs, all proudly beating their drums loudly. The call is to youth, to beginning, to announcement and discovery of things rather than accumulation and appropriation of them. There is no end to the drumming, and thus implicitly no real quest, desire, or demand for completion. Each performer is one of Zeno's paradoxical arrows; but, unlike Zeno himself, not one of them worries about the theoretical impossibility of their voyage. After all, as we all know, the arrow *is* getting on, adventuring into the unknown but definitely existing space and time in the nose of the arrow.

Discovery is a version of creation, and the dominant myth in Cendrars is a creation myth in a very significant variant. Cendrars' own initiation was to discovery as a way of life, a rather less exalted or arrogant form of creation. His persona is himself created via discovery, which is to say *re-created,* to use the term which I think best describes Cendrars' artmaking. It is revealing to look again at the particular cosmological myth alluded to in *Le Panama:* 'le dieu Tangaloa qui en pêchant à la ligne tira le monde hors des eaux.'[5] Tangaloa did not make the world, he found it. Yet it did not exist, for mortals, until he found it. Most creation myths are of a different sort, God or Gods making the world out of chaos, that is to say out of no order at all. Cendrars preferred to find one, and to re-create it for his reader. It is thus that much of what he wrote was not fiction, or at least not fiction of his own. Nor did he require that the language of his fictions be his own. He did not feel he had to do better, or differently, or transcend the orders and especially disorders of reality – that would have been to create – he merely had to see them, to pull them out of the obscuring, suffocating waters. It was not, for that matter, a small or insignificant re-creation to find Found Poetry, with the tenth and seventeenth poems of *Dix-neuf Poèmes élastiques,* 'Dernière heure,' dated September 1913 and 'Mee too buggi,' dated July 1914.

Of course the discovery of the world at large, to which I shall return in a moment, cannot be all of creation, or re-creation. Beginning is a continual re-creation of oneself, as object reflects back upon subject and the artist as adventurous discoverer inevitably finds himself, the trained eye finding the seer 'I.' We might term Cendrars' discovery a 'co-naissance,' as the word has been defined, or invented, by Claudel in his *Art poëtique.*[6] The discovery of things in their essences is a rebirth for the soul;

or, inversely, the soul's rebirth is a discovery of the world. Claudel summarizes his argument in a prelude to the first part of his *Art poëtique* as follows: 'Interprétation de l'Univers et de la figure que forment autour de nous les choses simultanées.' We remember the importance of 'contrastes simultanés.' For Claudel world and self are simultaneously born to each other. In the mystical poets – Claudel, Cendrars, Whitman – spiritual and material worlds interpenetrate with equal value, one not at all transcending the other. Whitman sang:

> I hear and behold God in every object, yet understand God not in the
>   least,
> Nor do I understand who there can be more wonderful than myself.
>
> ['Song of Myself']

Each realm offers an accurate and full insight into the other. Hence self-knowledge is knowledge of the world, or to come to know the world is at the same time to come at oneself.

This simultaneous birth finds traditional illustration in the phoenix symbol, which Cendrars used in a number of places, including his pseudonym. It represents a myth of re-creation of self, to which Cendrars has joined aspects of a creation myth of the world. As with the creation, Cendrars puts particular emphasis on one phase of the phoenix story. He has less interest in the long life before and after than in the marvel of birth itself, burning up and starting up at the same time. In this fire Cendrars is being reborn with his objects. It is a *co-naissance* in which the 'I' of Buber's I-Thou is always chancing, adventuring out after the 'Thou' of things and people. These eccentrics are also taking their chances, and the unique, extraordinary, and even ridiculous qualities of people and objects in Cendrars are the symptoms of their open-mindedness, a refusal to conform and settle down, to be done with it all. It is Cendrars' particularly acute sense of time as instants in flow which provides the key to how the conventional myth of rebirth must be seen. Whereas the past inventories time and the future holds the promise that time will be inventoried, the present tense remains the most unresolved; it cannot stop starting, and this with facts at their solidest. Hence the present tense of *L'Or*. For Cendrars the phoenix does not stand for one life and death in the past which gains the right to another cycle in the future, but for a birth which unsettles cycles before and after, which will not let them resolve.

Just as the phoenix in Cendrars will not burn out, the continual refiring of Cendrars does not really let a creation myth form. Cendrars would not let a pattern form, and his works are noticeably unrepetitive, or uncyclical. In what I am calling the re-creation myth the only pattern is the repetition of discovery; there is always emphasis on what is discovered, not on the act of creating, and as what is discovered is always new and unexpected the pattern does not call for resolution. The phoenix always flies into a new fire, and what burns is always unique.

This position of author vis-à-vis the world is the one Jung ascribes to what he would call modern man.[7] And in an article entitled 'Evolution, Myth and the Poetic Vision,'[8] Walter J. Ong examines the responses of modern poets to a modern, scientific view of time and change and finds them wanting, for the same reasons that Jung considered such a 'modern' man to be a rare bird indeed since he would have to liberate himself from the reflexes of the racial unconscious. Yet precisely those qualities Ong is searching for in the make-up of the poet are to be found in the picture of Cendrars I have drawn: a sense of time as change; a distaste for the cyclical and for its related version of the 'epiphany,' a moment in time frozen into an eternity for contemplation; an acceptance, if not espousal, of open-endedness and contingency in which people are unique. It is interesting that Ong finds Americans more particularly inclined to these attitudes, and, among poets, Whitman and William Carlos Williams more so than any others. Yet I wonder if either went as far as Cendrars, if either could begin again so constantly, with such an array of re-creations. How eccentric he was himself it is, and may remain, difficult to say. But the persona of his stories was always extraordinary, for in this manner youth and adventure would be sustained. And the youth and adventure in turn guaranteed, in fact forced, the uniqueness of the objects he collected. If he did not make his world, he made it new; he created discovery. To re-create meant to discover 'God in every object,' as Whitman wrote, with the greatest emphasis not on God, or on ascribing pattern to disparate things, but rather on objects, on the radical diversification and independence of God's manifestations.

Notes

Full bibliographical information on works given in brief in these notes may be found in the bibliography.

INTRODUCTION

1 Marcel Raymond *De Baudelaire au Surréalisme*, 239, 246-7
2 Ilya Ehrenburg *People and Life;* Marie Seton *Sergei M. Eisenstein* (London 1952); Jean-Paul Clébert *The Gypsies* trans. Charles Duff (London 1967); Roger Stéphane ''l'ant que Malraux vivra, on ne pourra pas écrire' *Magazine Littéraire* no. 11 (October 1967) 23-6; Pascal Pia 'Montparnasse, patrie des "louftingues"' 44-7; Jean-Patrick Maury 'Henry Miller ou la littérature scandaleuse' 48-50
3 Raymond Warnier 'Blaise Cendrars, aventurier humaniste du XXe siècle' *Mese Sanitario* (Milan) (April 1961) 3-4
4 William Carlos Williams 'America, Whitman, and the Art of Poetry' *The Poetry Journal* (November 1917) 31
5 In a short survey of Whitman in France the Whitman scholar Roger Asselineau writes: 'Some of our major contemporary poets were, or still are, attracted by Whitman's technique and his cosmic imagination: Blaise Cendrars, Paul Claudel, St-John Perse, for example' (in 'Whitman in France in 1960' *Walt Whitman Review* 6, no. 1 [March 1960]; 4). A few others who have made the rapprochement are: Conrad Moricand *Portraits astrologiques* 35; Alain Borne, untitled article in the *Mercure de France* special number, *Blaise Cendrars* 192; Nino Frank in a letter reprinted in the *Letteratura* special number on Cendrars, 50; Christian Murciaux in a letter reprinted in ibid. 55; Paul Morand in his fine preface to Blaise Cendrars *Du Monde entier*, a *Nouvelle Revue Française* (hereafter NRF) reprinting of the 1919 *Du Monde entier* with other poems (Paris 1967) 11; Louis Parrot *Blaise Cendrars* 25; Maurice Fombeure in 'Douze écrivains et artistes l'évoquent' *Le Figaro Littéraire* 28 January 1961, 12.

6 Unpublished letter (January 1915) in Marcel Adéma *Guillaume Apollinaire* 302; Max Jacob *Correspondance* ed. François Garnier, vol. 1 (Paris 1953) (letter to Jacques Doucet, 17 January 1917); André Malraux 'Des Origines de la Poésie cubiste' 42; Abel Gance 'Blaise Cendrars et le cinéma' *Mercure, Cendrars* 170-1; Philippe Soupault *Le Figaro Littéraire* 28 January 1961, 6; John Dos Passos 'Homer of the Trans-Siberian' 155-67; Henry Miller *Blaise Cendrars* (for the English version of this passage the reader must go to 'Tribute to Blaise Cendrars'; neither of the Cendrars essays in *The Henry Miller Reader* or *The Books in My Life* includes it. Also in Miller's introductory essay to Cendrars *Œuvres complètes* [Denoël] vol. 5 [1960]). For an actual photograph of Miller's rock-bottom Chinese man see *Synthèses* 22 nos. 249/250 (February-March 1967) 29; Georges Simenon 'Simenon écrit à Cendrars.'

7 Philippe Soupault 'Enfin Cendrars vint... ' *Mercure, Cendrars* 87. Also see his *témoignage* in *Œuvres complètes* (Club français du livre) 4: xi.

8 René Hilsum, *témoignage* in *Œuvres complètes* (Club français du livre) 1: xxvii

9 Blaise Cendrars *Blaise Cendrars vous parle...* OC 8: 563. (Hereafter all of Cendrars' work which can be found in the Denoël *Œuvres complètes* will be quoted from that source and indicated by OC, volume number, and page. See the contents of each volume in section A2 of the bibliography.)

10 Frank Budgen *Myselves When Young* 135

11 Jean-Paul Sartre *What is Literature?* trans. Bernard Frechtman (New York 1966) 70

12 Raymond *Baudelaire* 247

13 Cendrars *L'Homme foudroyé* OC 5: 221

14 Guillaume Apollinaire *Textes inédits* introduction, 116

15 Unsigned *glossaire* at the end of Ribemont-Dessaigne's review *Bifur* no. 1 (25 May 1929). These notes on contributors are generally considered his on the evidence of Nino Frank, secretary of the review at the time.

16 Nino Frank 'Blaise Cendrars, l'homme le plus seul au monde' 5

17 *Mercure, Cendrars,* introduction, 7

18 Maurice Nadeau *Littérature présente* 170

19 Blaise Cendrars 'Pro Domo' appended to *Moravagine* OC 2: 429-45

CHAPTER ONE

1 Jean Buhler *Blaise Cendrars, homme libre, poète au cœur du monde.* See details here, and birth certificate facing p. 16.

2 Blaise Cendrars OC 1: 204-6. One could argue that the poem does not in fact say he was born here.

3 André Bourin 'Rendez-vous avec Blaise Cendrars' 15

4 Nino Frank 'Naples et la "Scuola Internazionale" ' in *Mercure de France: Blaise Cendrars* 161. I should add here that the main subject of this article is the school

both Cendrars and Frank attended at a slight interval (see photograph facing p. 28 of this special number).

5 Conrad Moricand *Portraits astrologiques* 35. This book, published by Au Sans Pareil, is dedicated to Cendrars. Among the other horoscopes are those of Van Dongen, Picasso, Cocteau, Jouvet, and André Tardieu.

6 OC 1: 40

7 Buhler *Blaise Cendrars* 15

8 *Vol à voile* OC 4: 266

9 Ibid. 255

10 *Blaise Cendrars vous parle...* OC 8: 537-8

11 *Vol à voile* OC 4: 256

12 Ibid. 257

13 *La Banlieue de Paris* OC 7: 151

14 *Bourlinguer* OC 6: 202-4 (note 2)

15 *Mercure, Cendrars* facing 28

16 *Vol à voile* OC 4: 252-3

17 *Inédits secrets* (Club français du livre, Paris 1969) 132-3

18 *Vol à voile* OC 4: 252

19 *Mercure, Cendrars,* facing p. 28. The caption places this photograph in Moscow.

20 *Inédits* 136, letter to the Azoff and Don Bank. I thank J.-P. Goldenstein for tracing the Russian street name.

21 *Vol à voile* OC 4: 251

22 A. t'Serstevens *L'Homme que fut Blaise Cendrars* 30. He and Cendrars met only in 1913. One wonders how t'Serstevens can feel so sure of his facts when we read that it was almost two years before he knew Cendrars was married and had a child (pp. 69, 78). For the view that Cendrars did indeed make these trips, see the conversation about Russia, Mongolia, Manchuria, and other places in André Beucler 'Blaise Cendrars' in *Mercure, Cendrars* 58. Also, see footnote 19 above.

23 The *Inédits* cite, in one of Freddy's reading lists, Hanns Heinz Ewers' *Moganni Nameh, Novellen und Gedichte,* 1910. Professor M.V. Dimić of the University of Alberta has supplied me with the sources. The phrase is a title in Hafiz' *Divan,* and means Book of the Singer. Both Cendrars and Ewers most likely found it in Goethe's *Westöstlicher Divan,* where it provides the organizing principle of the sequence of poems.

24 *Inédits* 6, dated Saint Petersburg, 31 January 1907

25 Ibid. 13

26 Ibid. 29

27 See *Blaise Cendrars vous parle...* OC 8: 658: 'Je m'intéressais aux abeilles parce que cela me rapportait gros, je ne m'y intéressais pas comme Maeterlinck, soi-disant pour étudier les mœurs des abeilles et en tirer des conclusions morales absurdes, applicables à l'homme.'

28 *Inédits* 42

29 Ibid. 47

30 Ibid. 50. This is a letter from Féla to Blaise dated 12 November 1917. It is unlikely that they were still living together at this late date.

31 Ibid. 105

32 Ibid. 132

33 Ibid. 133

34 Ibid. 139

35 Ibid. 141

36 Letter to me, and, particularly on the poets' early meeting, Raymond Warnier 'A propos de Blaise Cendrars'

37 The day before embarking Freddy spoke of the *Lituania*. There is no explanation given for the sudden change from *Lituania* to *Birma*. One possibility is that he did change boats because the doctor on the first gave him a bad medical report, in connection with his eyes which never troubled him (see *Inédits* 163-5).

38 Ibid. 149-50. This passage and the following ones dealing with the trip itself are part of a projected (and never published) volume *Mon Voyage en Amérique*. A long quotation from 'Léonard de Vinci: *Traité de la Peinture* – chap. XII: de la Figure; p. 134 – Ed. Péladan' serves as epigraph; it is a bitter criticism of the human animal as no better than 'faiseurs de fumiers.' The brackets are in the *Inédits* text, and not explained.

39 The Doucet collection in the Sainte Geneviève Library in Paris owns a copy of *Les Paques à New York* inscribed to Isabelle Bender by Cendrars (and crossed out by her when she sold it to Doucet for 50 francs): 'Paris, November 1912/ à Isabelle/ à mon amie/ à ma femme/ à [illegible].'

40 *Inédits* 159-60

41 Ibid. 151

42 Raymond Dumay 'La Naissance de Cendrars' introduction to Blaise Cendrars *Œuvres complètes* (Club français du livre) 2: v-viii

43 Ibid. viii

44 *Inédits* 173

45 Ibid. 178

46 Ibid. 148. There was a short period, perhaps a month or so, during which the author wrote 'Cendrart.'

47 *Une Nuit dans la forêt* OC 7: 17

48 *Bourlinguer* OC 6: 317

49 A. t'Serstevens 'Cendrars au bras droit' in *Mercure, Cendrars* 81. See the same text revised, with examples, in t'Serstevens *L'Homme que fut Blaise Cendrars* 35 ff.

50 Introduction to Balzac's *Ferragus* OC 8: 492, 496

51 *Bourlinguer* OC 6: 299

52 To be found in *Dites-nous, Monsieur Blaise Cendrars* ed. Hughes Richard, 105

53 *Blaise Cendrars vous parle...* OC 8: 566

54 *Dites-nous* 124; originally in *Les Nouvelles Littéraires* 30, no. 1256 (27 September 1951): 1

55 *Dites-nous* 72; originally in *L'Intransigeant* 50, no. 18.327 (24 December 1929): 4. Cendrars had just finished *Dan Yack.*

56 Frank Budgen *Myselves When Young* 133

57 Letter from Blaise Cendrars in Jean Epstein *La Poésie d'aujourd'hui: un nouvel état d'intelligence* 214

58 Pound wrote in 'Remy de Gourmont: a Distinction Followed by Notes' in *Instigations* (New York 1920): 'De Gourmont prepared our era; behind him there stretches a limitless darkness' (p. 169). Eliot's famous phrase 'dissociation of sensibility' is adapted from de Gourmont (see below, Freddy Sauser's article on de Gourmont). Eliot quotes and discusses de Gourmont in 'The Perfect Critic' in *The Sacred Wood* (London 1920), where he writes: 'Of all modern critics, perhaps de Gourmont had most of the general intelligence of Aristotle' (p. 13). The February-March 1919 issue of *The Little Review* (nos. 10-11) was entirely devoted to de Gourmont and included Pound's article. Also, Pound translated de Gourmont's *Physique de l'amour.*

59 *Inédits* 55-7. This is the 1912 text, and may be much revised from the original one.

60 Some of these editions are: Saint Augustine *Confessions* and *Augustinici Opera* (Paris 1689-1700, 11 vols.); Fortunatus *Opera* (Fortunatus is quoted from *Le Latin mystique* in epigraph to *Les Pâques*); Gregory of Tours, his correspondence with Fortunatus; Saint Gregory of Nazianzus *Vie et poésies; Godeschalki Sequentiae* (Gottschalk supplies the epigraph to Cendrars' own *Séquences*); Hilary of Poitiers *S. Hilarii Pictavorum Episcopi Opera* (Paris 1693); *S. Hildegardis Opuscula, Epistolae, Quaestiones* (Cologne 1556); *Innocenti III Opera* (Cologne 1552); Saint Thomas *Aquinas Opera Omnia* (Rome 1570); Prudentius *Aurelii Prudentii Clementis Qua Extant* (Amsterdam 1667). Among the other authors cited in these lists are Saint John of the Cross and Saint Theresa of Avila, who together play an important role in *Le Lotissement du ciel,* Saints Bernard, Bonaventure, Loyola, and John of Damascus, (Apollinaris) Sidonis, and Thomas à Kempis.

61 *Blaise Cendrars vous parle...* OC 8: 551

62 See letter from t'Serstevens and Cendrars' reply among documents reproduced in *Œuvres complètes* (Club français du livre) 1: n.p., and facing p. 33 of t'Serstevens' *L'Homme que fut Blaise Cendrars.* Cendrars never republished *Séquences,* notably omitting it from the volumes of complete poetry published in 1944 and in 1957. However the editors of both *Œuvres complètes,* Denoël and the Club français du livre, have included it.

    As I shall not speak of *Séquences* in part two, I might quote Michel Décaudin here. His text is from his introduction to 'Amours', three prose poems of Cendrars which also fall under the same influences and were not republished by the author; in *Letteratura*, special number on Cendrars, 8: '*Séquences,* qui parut en 1913, porte, avec son mysticisme érotique traversé de fièvres et de peurs sans raison, la marque du baudelairisme décadent et des *Serres chaudes* de Maeterlinck, tandis que par leur forme les quarante poèmes de ce recueil font penser au *Latin mystique* et aux *Divertissements* de Remy de Gourmont. Nous sommes pourtant loin d'une poésie à la mode de 1890: l'exaspération des sentiments, l'allure volontairement prosaïque qui brise le vers, des platitudes qu'on ne saurait prendre pour des maladresses, tant il eût été facile de les éviter, sont les signes, d'une violence parfois un peu fruste, par lesquels s'affirme contre ses modèles la personnalité du jeune Cendrars.'

63 *Blaise Cendrars vous parle...* OC 8: 562. Nevertheless, a few lines of Baudelaire's 'Voyage' are quoted in and extremely important to Cendrars' last novel, *Emmène-moi au bout du monde!...* He also used the phrase 'esprit catholique' for Henry Miller.

64 The two doctors who worked in Nancy had some influence on Freud, who worked with Bernheim and translated two of his books about the same time he translated two by Charcot: Bernheim *De la Suggestion et de ses applications à la thérapeutique* (Paris 1886) translated as *Die Suggestion und ihre Heilwirkung* (Vienna 1888), with a long introduction by Freud; and *Hypnotisme, suggestion, psychothérapie: Études nouvelles* (Paris 1891) translated as *Neue Studien über Hypnotismus, Suggestion und Psychotherapie* (Vienna 1892). Of Liébault, who wrote *Du Sommeil provoqué* (Paris 1889), Freud said that he 'revived hypnotic research in modern times' (*The Basic Writings of S. Freud* [New York 1938] 513n). Also on Cendrars' list is James Braid, an earlier precursor (d. 1860). The relevance of all this is not Cendrars' use of Freud but rather a parallel interest in dreams, hallucinations, and the unconscious in general, so much so that many of his works, such as *Profond aujourd'hui* and *L'Eubage,* are called surrealistic (or pre-surrealistic: see H.S. Gershman *The Surrealist Movement in France* [Ann Arbor, Michigan 1969] 138). Indeed, I would argue that Cendrars provides, throughout his work, a more faithful embodiment of the interpenetration of the conscious and the unconscious than one can find in most properly 'Surrealist' work, which often confused the irrational with the incoherent: 'Le discours spontané [de l'analysé] est loin d'être une salade verbale, et ceci quelle que soit la liberté de parole dont il se targue. Pour n'avoir pas tenu compte d'une telle différence, pourtant essentielle, André Breton avait pu confondre les associations libres et l'écriture automatique. Certes, l'automatisme de l'écriture effaçait, à un certain degré, le parti pris de l'expression consciente; mais ne retrouvait-on pas un autre parti pris, celui d'une absence intentionnelle de tout sens conscient?' (V.N. Smirnoff 'L'Œuvre lue' *Nouvelle Revue de Psychanalyse* 1, no. 1 [April 1970]: 51-2 and note). Although Cendrars professed to have no interest in psychoanalysis – as such, that is to say, as a praxis, separable from

a theory of the unconscious – the main characters of *Moravagine* are analyst and mad patient. The latter is somewhat based on Otto Gross, one of Freud's prize pupils along with Jung. Jung claimed to have treated Gross's schizophrenia. See my discussion of the sources of *Moravagine* (below, pp. 155-6).

Cendrars, not Breton, it has been shown, deserves the credit for introducing Apollinaire to psychoanalysis: see Marc Poupon *Apollinaire et Cendrars* Archives des lettres modernes (Paris 1969) 42-4.

65 *Inédits* 171. And Goethe, in this case, brings us back to Nerval, translator of *Faust* and author of his own *Poésie et vérité*.

66 Ibid. 178

67 Ibid. 183-4

68 Ibid. 194, 193

69 Ibid. 242

70 Ibid. 209. Nor is *Les Pâques à New York* mentioned in the New York sections of the *Inédits*.

We don't know if Cendrars knew de Gourmont, at this or at any other time. In a last letter to Suter from Saint Petersburg dated 1/14 November 1911 he wrote: 'J'ai reçu de Remy de Gourmont une lettre très stimulante' (*Inédits* 143), but this letter is not to be found in the *Inédits*. We do find, however, on p. 53, one from de Gourmont addressed to Bella Bender in Brussels when Freddy was staying with her, 20 August 1910. In 'Paris, Port-de-Mer' Cendrars says he met de Gourmont and even took him to his first movie, about 1907-8 (*Bourlinguer* OC 6: 266-8).

71 *Trop c'est trop* OC 8: 154

72 *Inédits* 203

73 *Moravagine* OC 2: 385

74 *Blaise Cendrars vous parle...* OC 8: 649

75 *Inédits* 209

76 *Blaise Cendrars vous parle...* OC 8: 651

77 See the letter to Féla dated 14 April 1912 *Inédits* 208-9.

78 *Blaise Cendrars vous parle...* OC 8: 652

CHAPTER TWO

1 *Inédits secrets* 250

2 'Bombay-Express' in *Dix-neuf Poèmes élastiques* (1919), written in April 1914. The line was later used by Picabia in a Dada manifesto – see documents at the beginning of Blaise Cendrars *Œuvres complètes* (Club français du livre) 1.

3 *Inédits* 253. The editors do not give the addressee.

4 Ibid.; also p. 252

5 Ibid. 247

6 The *Inédits* give the date as 29 September on p. 271 and as the 25th on p. 246. The invitation says the 23rd. By my count the closest Friday would be the 27th. This article appeared in German in the October 1912 issue of *Les Hommes Nouveaux* as 'Anarchismus und Schönheit,' signed Jack Lee.

7 *Inédits* 273, 274

8 'La Bande à Bonnot' was a group of anarchists, or possibly just gangsters, that terrorized Paris for almost two years (1911-12). The gang was the first to use cars in their attacks on banks and bank couriers, and rarely hesitated to shoot. The survivors of the massive police assaults finally mounted against them – a veritable army laid siege to a barn where Bonnot was trapped alone – were tried in February of 1913. Kibaltchich, later a well-known socialist writer under the name of Victor Serge, served four years as an accessory. Raymond-la-Science is Raymond Callemin, the most cold-blooded member of the group, and was executed at La Santé on 21 April 1913.

9 Roch Carrier 'Blaise Cendrars: Un début dans la vie' 176. Carrier's ultimate source is t'Serstevens in *Mercure de France: Blaise Cendrars* 77.

10 Émile Szittya 'Logique de la vie contradictoire de Blaise Cendrars' in *Mercure, Cendrars* 75

11 New York 1974

12 *Inédits* 282

13 See Marc Poupon *Apollinaire et Cendrars* 43 for the full text from *Revolution* (Munich) 5-20 December 1913. See Green *The Von Richthofen Sisters* 67 for the general context of Gross' arrest and the ensuing protest.

14 Edmond Buchet *Les Auteurs de ma vie, ou ma vie d'éditeur* 188

15 *Inédits* 280

16 In the poem 'Tu es plus belle que le ciel et la mer' *Feuilles de route* OC 1: 136

17 *Blaise Cendrars vous parle...* OC 8: 652. The drawing, of a man whose head is severed, is reproduced in Louis Parrot *Blaise Cendrars* after p. 40.

18 This is the heading for the chapter on Apollinaire in his *The Banquet Years*.

19 *Inédits* 269

20 Poupon, citing Nicolas Beaudin's article 'Les Temps héroïques' *Masques et Visages* 39, June 1956. That Cendrars saw the show is confirmed in the *Inédits*, p. 284, but there is no mention here of the others, and of course he could have gone any time, alone. Duchamp and Picabia were the organizers of the salon which thus represented the most advanced thought in painting at the time; Duchamp exhibited his famous *Nude Descending a Staircase* at this show, before sending it to the New York Armory Show at the beginning of 1913.

21 Marcel Adéma *Guillaume Apollinaire* 205-6, from Gabrielle Buffet 'Rencontre avec Apollinaire' *Le Point* November 1937

22 Décaudin *Le Dossier d'Alcools* 35 and Poupon *Apollinaire et Cendrars* 13. For those interested in pursuing the debate these are the essential elements: Jules Romains *L'Esprit poétique des temps nouveaux* (La Lanterne Sourde, Brussels

1923) (the relevant passage may be found in almost any of the critics; the most complete version is in Luciano Erba, ed. *Cendrars* [Milan 1961, 10-11]); Robert Goffin *Entrer en poésie*, where the battle is begun (see his further comments in *Fil d'Ariane pour la poésie)*; Marie-Jeanne Durry *Guillaume Apollinaire: Alcools*, vol. 1; Décaudin *Dossier*, a study of the drafts of 'Zone'; Francis J. Carmody *The Evolution of Apollinaire's Poetics, 1901-1914*; Raymond Warnier 'A Propos de Blaise Cendrars'; André Billy *Avec Apollinaire*; Poupon *Apollinaire et Cendrars*; the *Inédits*, and the commentaries by Raymond Dumay in other volumes of the *Œuvres complètes* of the Club français du livre (see next note); J.-P. Goldenstein 'Blaise Cendrars, *Inédits secrets.'* There are any number of resemblances between Professor Goldenstein's text and my own, firstly because we are the only writers to deal with the *Inédits*, and secondly because we talked together a great deal and saw each other's material.

23 *Inédits* 286-7. In his introduction to volume 1 of the Club français du livre *Œuvres complètes* Raymond Dumay has misdated and misquoted this letter – wilfully or through carelessness one cannot say for sure – and used it to help show that Cendrars could not have influenced Apollinaire. He dates the letter 15 December, a month late, thus implying a much later meeting of the two poets, after the appearance of 'Zone' (this makes little difference since Apollinaire probably had a copy of *Les Pâques* quite a while before he met Cendrars). Dumay also quotes the sentence I have just cited, but as follows: 'Il m'a dit que *Pâques* était le meilleur poème publié depuis dix ans dans le *Mercure*' (Dumay xii-xiii). As this statement is patently false it provides, in Dumay's estimation, a sort of *ad hominem* argument against Cendrars. As it turned out, Cendrars was not published by the *Mercure de France* until 1 December 1918, the first number to appear after Apollinaire's death.

24 Goldenstein 'Blaise Cendrars, *Inédits secrets'* 152

25 See Mario Roques *'Le Perceval le gallois* de Guillaume Apollinaire.'

26 Poupon *Apollinaire et Cendrars* 59, and letter in *Inédits* 320-1. See these reviews in Guillaume Apollinaire *Chroniques d'art, 1902-1918;* see p. 295 for the review of 25 March 1913, the one Poupon is quite sure of (as for myself, I cannot tell).

27 Warnier 'A Propos de Blaise Cendrars' 638

28 The poem appeared as 'Apollinaire' in Canudo's *Montjoie!* (April-June 1914) and as 'Hamac' in *Dix-neuf Poèmes élastiques*. It was mistakenly reprinted by André Warnier in the special Cendrars number of *Letteratura*, pp. 11-12, as an uncollected poem by Cendrars.

29 Michel Hoog *Robert et Sonia Delaunay* 124

30 *Inédits* 293-4

31 F.O. Matthiessen *American Renaissance* (London, Toronto, New York 1941) 579

32 Henri Ghéon 'Les Poèmes: Le Whitmanisme' NRF 7 (1 June 1912) 1053. One

of the most relevant critical works of this period is Jacques Rivière's 'The Adventure Novel,' which appeared in three parts in the NRF for May, June, and July of 1913 (see Rivière *The Ideal Reader* [New York 1960] 84-124). This essay constitutes a culmination of the Poe-Whitman dichotomy, with a sort of victory for Whitman (though he is not named) over the symbolists, and also a new bifurcation, as it calls for 'adventure' in fiction in terms that would often apply to no one else *but* Cendrars, yet in fact prepares the way for the new classicism of Gide, Proust, and other NRF authors. We don't know what role Rivière played in the 1919 publication of *Du Monde entier* at the NRF.

33 Apollinaire 'La Vie anecdotique' *Mercure de France* 102 (1 April, 1913): 658-9

34 See Cyrile Arnavon 'Walt Whitman' *Les Lettres américaines devant la critique française (1887-1917)* (in *Annales de l'Université de Lyon* series 3, fasciculus 20, Paris 1951) 67, note 84, for a full listing, which includes Bazalgette and Stuart Merrill. Also see Roger Shattuck 'Apollinaire's Great Whitman Happening' *City Lights Journal* no. 3 (1966) 171-83.

35 Apollinaire 'La Vie anecdotique' *Mercure de France* 106 (16 December 1913) 864

36 Poupon *Apollinaire et Cendrars* 47

37 *Inédits* 358

38 Décaudin *Dossier* 35

39 *Inédits* 359. 'Crépitements' was first printed, without authorization, in the very first Dada publication, *Le Cabaret Voltaire* (Zurich, May 1916). Two points of interest are the fact that Dada felt so strongly the need of this poem and the question of how Hugo Ball, Tzara, Arp, Huelsenbeck, or whoever obtained the poem. The last line may supply a clue: 'Et j'envoie ce poème dépouillé à mon ami R... ,' who could be Ludwig Rubiner. Rubiner wrote a review of *Le Transsibérien* for *Die Aktion* 3, no. 4 (October 1913): 940-1. We also know that Cendrars was one of the very few pre-Dada poets Tzara admired; see, for example, Elmer Peterson *Tristan Tzara* (New Brunswick, New Jersey 1971) 138-9.

40 '*19 Poèmes élastiques*' NRF 7, no. 75 (1 December 1919) 1093

41 Pär Bergman '*Modernolatria*'; for the debate in particular, see Roger Shattuck 'Une Polémique d'Apollinaire'; Robert Delaunay *Du Cubisme à l'art abstrait* 107-14; and *Inédits* 362-72, which contains (pp. 367-8) a 'simultané' chronology Cendrars wrote for *Les Soirées,* but which Apollinaire never published. (In *Der Sturm* 4, nos. 194/195 [January 1914] 167 Robert Delaunay writes that Apollinaire asked Cendrars for this chronology a week before the Salon d'Automne. Cendrars' list is dated October 1913, and the accompanying article dated December 1913 ends: 'Elles ont été demandées à l'auteur par Guillaume Apollinaire pour le No. 17 des *Soirées de Paris.* Le No. 18 vient de paraître et G.A., qui les avait acceptées, ne les a toujours pas publiées.') Cendrars' list resembles the material in Delaunay, which is more detailed but

which itself contains things written by Cendrars. An interesting aspect of the chronology is that at least four or five items are given dates one month earlier than is usually known; for example *Pâques* is dated October and 'Zone' November. Nothing is gained by this acceleration for all, in the way of beating Barzun to the 'simultané' punch or in any other way, and I think we are justified in assuming that these are not erroneous dates of publication, but dates of finished copy or early proofs. If so, the most interesting detail of this list is February 1913 as the date for 'le premier livre simultané' by Mme Sonia Delaunay-Terck and Blaise Cendrars (*Inédits* 368). Delaunay gives the same date, p. 111.

42 In Hoog *Robert et Sonia Delaunay* 141-5. Of one of these advertisements Hoog writes: 'Sans rapport avec les papiers collés cubistes dont elle est contemporaine, ni avec les collages surréalistes, elle annonce plutôt les grands papiers découpés de Matisse' (p. 145).

43 See, on this important distinction, Michel Sanouillet *Dada à Paris* 428-32, and Jacques-Henry Lévesque's letter on Cendrars and Dada in *The Dada Painters and Poets*.

44 Philippe Soupault 'Enfin, Cendrars vint...' in *Mercure, Cendrars* 86

45 Szittya, in *Mercure, Cendrars* 76

46 See Léger's articles collected in his *Fonctions de la peinture* (Paris 1965).

47 The articles appeared from 3 May to 24 July 1919 and are reprinted in *Aujourd'hui* OC 4: 183-94.

48 *Blaise Cendrars vous parle...* OC 8: 642-3. I take the liberty of assuming he refers to the *Sacre*, and not to *Petrouchka* as he says.

49 *Blaise Cendrars vous parle...* OC 8: 551-2; Henry Miller *Letters to Anaïs Nin* 293. Also a frequent collaborator of Stravinsky, the 'Vaudois' (from Vaud, Switzerland) novelist and poet C.F. Ramuz was a friend of both Cingria and Cendrars. Henry Poulaille, in *Nouvelle Age littéraire*, continually puts Cendrars and Ramuz together as a sort of joint fountainhead of the best, most radical writing of the twentieth century (pp. 52, 184, 186, 383).

50 Frank Budgen *Myselves When Young* 133, 136-7. On Fantômas, see the poem by the same name, the fifteenth in *Dix-neuf Poèmes élastiques*. 'St. Sèvres' must be a confusion of Sèvres and Saint-Cloud; Cendrars lived at both. Cravan's very injurious article for his own journal *Maintenant* may be found reprinted in *Maintenant* ed. Bernard Delvaille (Paris 1957).

CHAPTER THREE

1 Roch Carrier 'Blaise Cendrars: Un début dans la vie' 185-6, where the text of the *Appel* appears. Carrier's information comes mainly from *La Main coupée* OC 5: 404-5, where Cendrars writes '*Appel* que j'ai rédigé avec Canudo.' For more details on Cendrars' enlistment and experiences as a soldier see Hughes Richard 'Blaise Cendrars s'en va-t-en guerre' 3.

2 *Inédits secrets* 397-8

3 Jean Breton 'Une Confession inédite de Blaise Cendrars'

4 *Blaise Cendrars vous parle...* OC 8: 646. However, he did write one short poem while at war, 'Shrapnells' (Cendrars' spelling).

5 Le Maréchal Fayolle *Cahiers secrets de la grande guerre* ed. Henry Cantamine (Paris 1964) 104

6 René Jeanne and Charles Ford *Histoire du cinéma* 1 (Paris 1947): 177-8. See the full (and also slightly different) version in *Trop c'est trop* OC 8: 285-90.

7 Document in *Œuvres complètes* (Club français du livre) 10

8 *Le Lotissement du ciel* OC 6: 386

9 Féla in *Inédits* 382, in a text written about 1915, and Sonia Delaunay in *Œuvres complètes* (Club français du livre) 1: xxii. The Delaunays were in Portugal at the time, which she mistakenly gives as 1916.

10 Undated and unaddressed letter reprinted in Richard 'Blaise Cendrars s'en va-t-en guerre' 3

11 Text communicated to me by Raymond Warnier

12 A. t'Serstevens in *Œuvres complètes* (Club français du livre) 1: xxiv-xxv

13 Gabriel Fournier *Cors de chasse, 1912-1914* 101-5; also referred to in Jean-Paul Crespelle *Montparnasse vivant* 134 and in Marcel Adéma *Guillaume Apollinaire* 296

14 Frederick Brown *An Impersonation of Angels* (New York 1968) 158

15 For the letter and more details see Adéma *Apollinaire* 297-8. For Cendrars, and a more critical evaluation of Apollinaire's powers after his wound, see Roger Shattuck *The Banquet Years* 226-7.

16 *L'Homme foudroyé* OC 5: 221

17 The list of projects is given in the *Inédits* 409, with dates of termination added as projects were finished. The *mot* of Picasso may be found, among other places, in André Warnod *Fils de Montmartre* (Paris 1955) 248.

18 *Dites-nous, Monsieur Blaise Cendrars* 176

19 *L'Homme foudroyé* OC 5: 178. For more on this sort of solitude, see the material quoted from C.G. Jung in connection with Henry Miller, pp. 76-7 below.

20 *Blaise Cendrars vous parle...* OC 8: 172

21 See Jacques-Henry Lévesque *Blaise Cendrars* 55; André Lagarde and Laurent Michard *XXᵉ Siècle* (Paris 1965) 360; and especially Georges Charensol *Le Cinéma* (Paris 1966) 110: 'Car en dépit d'un scénario puéril, ce que Gance est parvenu à exprimer ce sont essentiellement les rapports de l'homme et de la machine, et il n'est pas douteux que Blaise Cendrars lui ait apporté une collaboration décisive.' Standish D. Lawder, in *The Cubist Cinema* (Anthology Film Archives Series 1, New York University Press 1975), assumes Cendrars was the film editor (see '*La Roue,* Cendrars and Gance' pp. 79-98), as did many of the early viewers who saw his name in the credits (it was later withdrawn). Ezra

Pound assumed that whatever was good at all in *La Roue* was due to Cendrars (*The Dial* March 1923, 273).

22 See a fairly breathless and more detailed account at the end of *Blaise Cendrars vous parle...* OC 8: 668-73.

23 P.-A. Birot 'Chronique d'automne' *Sic* 3, no. 35 (December 1918) n.p. The next month, in a special Apollinaire number (nos. 37, 38, 39, January and 15 February 1919), *Sic* published a new poem by Cendrars, 'Hommage à Guillaume Apollinaire.' 'La Colombe poignardée et le jet d'eau' is the proper title of this poem of Apollinaire (from *Calligrammes*).

24 *L'Homme foudroyé* OC 5: 177

25 Harold Loeb *The Way It Was*, quoted in Mark Schorer *Sinclair Lewis* (New York 1961) 323. Among the contributions to *Broom* (see bibliography of Cendrars in English) is a critique of the famous German Expressionist film, *The Cabinet of Doctor Caligari*. This item has not been reprinted by either of the two *Œuvres complètes*, and can only be found in *Broom* 2, no. 4 (July 1922): 351 and in *Les Feuilles Libres* 4, no. 26 (June-July 1922); 150.

26 Preface to *La Fin du monde* OC 2: 13

27 Many sources, using some of Cocteau's own declarations, give the two writers as co-directors (see, for example, F. Brown *An Impersonation of Angels* 163 and note, or Jean Cocteau *Entre Picasso et Radiguet* ed. André Fermingier [Paris 1967] 36). However, Cocteau says Cendrars was the director in *Entretiens avec André Fraigneau* (Paris 1951), and in his *Journals*, ed. and trans. Wallace Fowlie (Bloomington, Ind. 1956) 46, speaks of 'la Sirène publishing house, where M. Lafitte obeyed the directives of Cendrars and published our books.'

28 Epstein was a great admirer of Cendrars, and brought him this manuscript in Nice as a totally unknown writer. He soon gave up writing on aesthetics to become one of the most important film-makers in France. In 1927 he directed *Six et Demi Onze*, originally called *Un Kodak*, the title had to be changed for the same reason Cendrars had to change his *Kodak* of 1924 (see chapter 4, footnote 1 below). In 1928 he directed *La Chute de la Maison Usher*, which may be referred to in *Les Confessions de Dan Yack* (1929).

29 Before this edition it was almost impossible to find a copy of *Les Chants* (see bibliography in Philippe Soupault *Lautréamont* [Paris 1946]); it is thus of some importance in the development of Paris Dada and Surrealism (however, excerpts appeared earlier in *Vers et Prose*, and articles in *La Phalange*). André Breton reviewed the La Sirène edition for the NRF (June 1920), reprinted in *Les Pas perdus* (Paris 1969, Collection 'Idées') 68-72.

30 Ivan Goll, whose reputation is only now growing, translated Cendrars' *L'Or* into German as *Gold* (Basel, Zurich, Leipzig, Paris, Strasburg 1925 – the same year as the original).

31 Cendrars was well aware that the 1826-36 edition, which his followed, was

expurgated, as he went to Leipzig in 1919 to see Brockhaus who had the original. Brockhaus would not let him use the manuscripts, and only in 1960 did Plon finally publish the original. Cendrars engaged a number of researchers to document the events reported in the memoirs, and those notes, mainly the work of Raoul Vèze, were instrumental in dispelling the accepted opinion that the work was fiction; the editors of the new edition express their indebtedness to this scholarly work in their introduction (which see; also, Blaise Cendrars, 1949 introduction to the reissue of *La Fin du monde* OC 2: 11-13).

32 Savitsky first approached Rivière for publication by the NRF, but surprisingly he turned it down. One Félix Fénéon accepted it at La Sirène (Centre Culturel Américain, *Les Années vingt, les écrivains américains à Paris et leurs amis, 1920-1930*, catalogue for an exposition held 11 March to 25 April 1959, 55). Other authors published by La Sirène include Villon, Mallarmé, André Salmon, Conrad Moricand, Erik Satie, Paul Lafitte, André Billy, J.-E. Blanche, Max Jacob, Joseph Caillaux, and Jean Roc. La Sirène also published other works by those already cited and a translation of Dreiser's *Sister Carrie*.

33 Kay Boyle and Robert McAlmon *Being Geniuses Together* (New York 1968) 122. Also see Jean Cocteau *Carte blanche* 104 (chapter entitled 'Jazz-Band').

34 For a photograph of all five together, mistakenly dated 1932, see Douglas Cooper *Fernand Léger et le nouvel espace* 23; for costumes, decor, program cover, curtain, etc., for the ballet see pp. 149, 151, 156, 157. Cendrars' scenario may be found in synopsis in *L'Esprit Nouveau* 2, no. 18 (1923): 2113.

35 Michel Sanouillet *Picabia et 391* 2 (Paris 1966) 168-9. The text of Cendrars' 'Après-dîner' is reprinted by Sanouillet (pp. 255-6).

CHAPTER FOUR

1 Cendrars himself said he did this (in *L'Homme foudroyé* OC 5: 187-8), but he did not say which book of Lerouge he had used (although he conveniently named the book in question a few pages on, on p. 205). Cendrars' statement was taken to be merely another in a long series of tall tales until the recent republication of Lerouge's *Le Mystérieux Dr Cornélius* (Paris 1967) with an introduction by Francis Lacassin detailing the 'plagiarism.' Also see J.-P. Goldenstein 'De l'élasticité poétique: Genèse d'un poème de Blaise Cendrars' devoted to a much earlier poem, 'Dernière heure,' the tenth in *Dix-neuf Poèmes élastiques*, which Cendrars called 'télégramme-poème copié dans *Paris-Midi*.' This may well be the very first found poem, but in any case this idea was certainly not new to Cendrars in 1924. Another poem from *Dix-neuf Poèmes élastiques*, 'Mee too buggi,' was a modified found poem: see J.P. Goldenstein 'Blaise Cendrars sur les traces du Capitaine Cook' and my own 'The Voyage Out and the Voyage Back in a Poem by Blaise Cendrars.' Another novelty of *Kodak (Documentaire)* was its title, which used the name of a firm. Cendrars was ready to make a generic term of it even before the company was; the Kodak

Company complained to Stock and the title had to be changed for the next edition to *Documentaires*; however this was not until 1944.

2 Most of my information about Brazil comes from Alexandre Eulálio 'L'Aventure brésilienne de Blaise Cendrars,' which in turn makes use of the numerous articles and documents in Aracy Amaral *Blaise Cendrars no Brasil e os modernistas* (São Paulo 1971). We can expect more information from Professor Erdmute Wenzel White's forthcoming book on the Andrade brothers. Amaral gives a full bibliography for Cendrars in Brazil.

3 'Manolo Secca' was excerpted from *L'Homme foudroyé* and translated by William Brandon, along with other work by Cendrars, for *The Paris Review* 10, no. 37 (Spring 1966): 105-43.

4 See 'Pro domo,' appended to *Moravagine* OC 2: 440. The other dates at the end of *L'Or* indicate Cendrars' great and extended interest in this relative of his friend from Basel, August Suter.

5 Mme Errazuriz was a wealthy Bolivian frequently seen in fashionable artistic circles in Paris. Her story is told by Cendrars in *L'Homme foudroyé*.

6 Amaral *Blaise Cendrars* 133, 138

7 See Calvin Tomkins *Living Well Is the Best Revenge* (London 1971).

8 *The Saturday Review of Literature* 16 October 1926, 202, 222; reprinted in *Orient Express* (New York 1927) 155-67. It was Mr Dos Passos who wrote me that he met Cendrars only after writing the article, and that he probably met him at a party of the Murphys.

9 John Dos Passos *The Best Times* (New York 1966) 203-4

10 Letter to me, 6 March 1967

11 My thanks to Professor Melvin Landsberg for arranging copies of these letters for me, and to Robert Corum for his careful transcriptions from the originals at the University of Virginia.

12 Astre 1 195 and Wickes 99. I have discussed the question more fully in 'John Dos Passos and Henry Miller on Blaise Cendrars,' a paper read at the Canadian Comparative Literature meeting, Learned Societies, 30 May 1972 (McGill University, Montreal).

13 Introduction to Dos Passos' translation of *Panama* vii-viii

14 P.E. Salles Gomez *Jean Vigo* (London 1972) 156-7

15 See the notes to Blaise Cendrars *Œuvres complètes* (Club français du livre) 4:297.

16 The chapters from *John Paul Jones* that appeared were: 'John Paul Jones' in *The Living Age* (1927) 428-31, also in *The European Caravan* ed. Samuel Putnam (1931) 199-204; 'L'Enfance' in *Cahiers du Sud* 91 (June 1927): 438-50; 'Les Négriers' in *La Revue Européenne* 1 (new series), no. 4 (April 1927): 275-98; and in *Orbes* no. 4 (unseen); 'Ivy Close' in *Anthologie de la nouvelle prose française* (Paris, Kra 1928), 274-88. On *John Paul Jones* see W.A. Bradley 'Sur *John Paul Jones* et sur *La Vie et la mort du soldat inconnu*' in *Mercure de France: Blaise Cendrars* 174-5. Some 100 pages were apparently written for *La Vie et la mort du soldat*

inconnu. In *The Books in My Life* (p. 43) Henry Miller writes: 'In the course of his travels, searching for rare documents and buying up rare books relating to John Paul Jones' myriad adventures, Cendrars confessed that he had spent more than tenfold the amount given him by the publishers in advance of royalties. Following John Paul Jones' traces, Cendrars had made a veritable Odyssean voyage. He confessed finally that he would one day either write a huge tome on the subject or a very thin book, something which I understood perfectly.'

17 *L'Argent (Histoire mirobolante de Jim Fisk)* 'chez Grasset, 1935'; see the outline and fifteen pages of text written at Le Tremblay, August 1934, *Inédits secrets* 413-28.

18 Gérard Bauer in the Cendrars number of *Letteratura* 47. Also see *Dites-nous, Monsieur Blaise Cendrars* 117-18 and note. Cendrars arrived in Los Angeles by boat, the *Wisconsin.*

19 See Joseph Blotner *Faulkner* (New York 1974) 851-2; *The Motion Picture Herald,* 15 February 1936, 14-15, and 4 April 1936, 83; 'Gold Week' *Time* 6 April 1936, 46; Frank S. Nugent 'Fact and Fiction Come to Grips in "Sutter's Gold" ' *New York Times* 27 March 1936, 25.

20 First appeared in *Orbes* second series, no. 4 (Summer 1935); reprinted in appendix to Henry Miller *Blaise Cendrars* LXXI-LXXII and in English in George Wickes *Henry Miller, the Man and His Works* (Toronto, London 1969) 23-4

21 Henry Miller *Letters to Anaïs Nin* 143

22 Miller *The Books in My Life* 59-84, 346-8; this list of one hundred books was originally made up for *Pour une bibliothèque idéale* (Paris 1951). The next greatest praise ('His works in general') is given to Conrad, de Nerval, Dostoevsky, Dreiser, Henri Fabre, Hamsun, G.A. Henty, W.H. Hudson, Maeterlinck, Nietzsche, and Rimbaud.

23 Sandra Hochman 'Henry Miller, A World of Joy' *New York Times* 3 November 1968, section 2, p. 33

24 Miller *Blaise Cendrars* XVI. The first part of this homage, pp. XI-XXII, does not appear in the English versions in *The Books in My life* and *The Henry Miller Reader.*

25 *Books in My Life* 65-6, *Miller Reader* 334

26 *Books in My Life* 74, *Miller Reader* 343

27 *Letters to Anaïs Nin* 138 (4 December 1934)

28 Henry Miller and Michael Fraenkel *Hamlet* trans. Roger Giroux and Tanette Prigent (Paris 1956) 120-1 (letter of 16 December 1935)

29 C.G. Jung *Modern Man in Search of a Soul* trans. W.S. Dell and Cary F. Baynes (New York 1968) 196-7. I am quoting from the beginning of the essay; Miller uses the same material with slightly different deletions; also, his emphases vary in the *Letters* and in *Hamlet.*

CHAPTER FIVE

1 Edmond Buchet *Les Auteurs de ma vie, ou ma vie d'éditeur* 58, 59
2 Photo in Jean Buhler, facing p. 113
3 André Maurois *I Remember, I Remember* 269
4 *L'Homme foudroyé* OC 5: 306
5 Edouard Peisson 'Blaise Cendrars à Aix-en-Provence' in *Mercure de France: Blaise Cendrars* 132
6 Information gathered from Claude Beylie *Max Ophuls* (Paris 1963)
7 *Bourlinguer* OC 6: 251
8 *L'Homme foudroyé* OC 5: 49
9 Henry Miller *The Books in My Life* quoted in epigraph, p. 7
10 Guy Tosi 'En relisant quelques lettres de Blaise Cendrars' Cendrars number of *Letteratura* 17
11 *Entretien de Fernand Léger avec Blaise Cendrars et Louis Carré sur le paysage dans l'œuvre de Léger* OC 8: 502
12 Not reprinted in OC. See same title as given in footnote above, published in Paris, by Louis Carré, 1956, post-scriptum on first page, in Cendrars' hand (I have not quoted the full text).
13 OC 8: 312. These three radio plays enjoyed some success. *Sarajevo* was produced in January 1955 and again in September 1958, and was staged in Albi (Palais de la Berbie) in 1955 and more recently in Marseilles (see the 1964 publication of the Théâtre universitaire de Marseille, *Sarajevo*). *Gilles de Rais* was produced in December of 1955 and again in May of 1956; in April of 1956 it received the Prix Carlos Larronde for best dramatic program of 1955. *Le Divin Arétin* was produced in June 1957; Jean-Marie Amato received the Prix Pierre Renoir for his interpretation of Aretino.
14 Note at the beginning of *Emmène-moi au bout du monde!...* OC 7: 188
15 Paul Guth 'Blaise Cendrars' 128-9
16 *Blaise Cendrars vous parle...* OC 8: 591
17 In 'Tant que Malraux vivra, on ne pourra pas écrire,' an interview of Roger Stéphane by the *Magazine Littéraire* no. 11 (October 1967): 24
18 Nino Frank *Mémoire brisée* 225
19 Georges Simenon *Quand j'étais vieux* 153, 365-6
20 Ernest Hemingway *A Moveable Feast* (New York 1964) 81
21 *Dites-nous, Monsieur Blaise Cendrars* 120 (from *Opéra* 6 June 1951, 3)

CHAPTER SIX

1 Marie-Jean Durry *Guillaume Apollinaire: Alcools* 1: 237-301
2 André Malraux 'Des Origines de la poésie cubiste' 42

3 Charles-Henri Hirsch, review in *Mercure de France* 135 (1 September 1919) 139

4 Géo-Charles 'Un Univers poétique: L'œuvre de Blaise Cendrars' 21

5 Durry *Alcools* 273

6 All poetry of Cendrars is quoted from OC 1; however hereafter I indicate the precise lines quoted rather than the page reference, as the reader may find the poems in many places.

7 Walter E. Albert 'The Poetic Works of Blaise Cendrars.' Nor does Professor Albert mention the unusual edition in his otherwise valuable introduction to Cendrars' *Selected Writings* 1-44 (see pp. 16-17).

8 Michel Hoog 'Quelques précurseurs de l'art d'aujourd'hui' 165

9 From the proofs corrected by the author, reproduced in *Le Transsibérien* (Paris, 1966), at the end of the volume. My thanks to the Bibliothèque nationale for this facsimile. It will be noted that there are numerous differences from the final version, which I use in my analysis of the poem.

10 See page x above. One may get a more detailed idea of this edition from Michel Hoog *Robert et Sonia Delaunay* 130-4 and in *Sonia Delaunay* (Garden City, New York, The New York Art Guild 1973), which contains a three-foot colour fold-out. However the fatal drawback of any reproduction less than the full two metres long is that the text is barely legible.

11 Blaise Cendrars in a *prière d'insérer,* or news release, in *Paris-Journal* 17 October 1913. The word *non* is crucial, but does not appear in this passage as quoted by Robert Delaunay *Du Cubisme à l'art abstrait* 114. However, that volume contains numerous errors since it collects many of the painter's unedited notes and rough drafts. My text is also that of Hoog 'Quelques précurseurs' 165-6.

12 Guillaume Apollinaire 'Simultanisme-Librettisme' 323-4

13 *Aujourd'hui* OC 4: 193. The date of this text is 24 July 1919.

14 The description of the poem as prose helps to indicate that it might have been what Jean Royère was referring to when he was interviewed by P. Mansell Jones in the fall or winter of 1913 about the influence of Whitman in France: 'I was advised to ask him [Bazalgette] ... for information about certain poets or *prosateurs* who had written in Whitman's fashion. My interlocutor insisted on a poem about a locomotive, a long, remarkable piece. I couldn't discover whether he meant Whitman's or a French imitation' (P. Mansell Jones 'Talks with French Poets in 1913-14' *French Studies* 2, no. 3 [July 1948] 212).

15 *Inédits secrets* 371. We might also note the similar meanings of the titles *Prose* and the earlier *Séquences,* as both terms refer to a Roman Catholic hymn.

16 Frank Budgen *Myselves When Young* 135

17 Jean Cocteau *Carte blanche* 105

18 Victor Klemperer *Geschichte der französischen Literatur im 19. und 20. Jahrhundert* 2, in a chapter entitled 'Cendrars und der Dadaismus' 248-51. On page 248 he writes: 'Entwicklungsgeschichtlich betrachtet ist hier eine Vermischung des

Futurismus, seines rebellischen Kraftverlangens, mit Rimbauds Bemühen um den bildlichen Ausdruck des Unterbewussten und die Niederschrift des Alogischen gegeben. Und neben dem genialen Rimbaud wirkt der irrsinnige Lautréamont.'

19 Jacques-Henry Lévesque *Blaise Cendrars* 26-7. On page 27 M. Lévesque cites Whitman as a predecessor of this attitude.

20 Paul Ginestier *The Poet and the Machine* trans. Martin B. Friedman (Chapel Hill, N. C. 1961) 19. This book provides a fine analysis of concepts important to my thesis – mainly, the wedding in the twentieth century of a new, material, and outside world with the world of the imagination.

21 John Dos Passos 'Homer of the Trans-Siberian' 158, 167. Although the hymn may lack the ability to play the games of former verses Cendrars manages a touch of irony in the above lines by rhyming Apollinaire's name with his unrhymed lines.

22 For an account of the Lapin Agile (at first the Lapin à Gilles) and the shift of artistic activity from Montmartre to the Left Bank, read Francis Carco *De Montmartre au Quartier Latin* (Paris 1927, Brussels 1928).

23 'Gênes' in *Bourlinguer* OC 6: 130.

24 OC 1: 70

25 In 'Une Nuit dans la forêt,' OC 7: 23-4, Cendrars has free access to the Bugatti belonging to Philippe Bunau-Varilla, the engineer for the French project to build a Panama Canal. If this passage is faithful autobiography, Cendrars could have known Bunau-Varilla fairly well. He was like a character right out of one of Cendrars' novels, fomenting a revolution in Panama against the Columbian government in order to finally sell his dream to the Americans, fifteen years after the French project failed. He had the provisional Panamanian government appoint him plenipotentiary envoy to Washington and signed the Hay-Bunau-Varilla Treaty which gave the Canal Zone to the United States.

26 Henry Miller, preface to Blaise Cendrars *Selected Writings* x. This passage is not in *The Henry Miller Reader* version (New York 1959), but appears in French in Henry Miller *Blaise Cendrars* XXI-XXII.

27 Charles Baudelaire 'Le Peintre de la vie moderne' in *Curiosités esthètiques* (and *L'Art romantique*) (Paris, Garnier 1962) 460-1, 463, 464. It is no coincidence that so many ideas in Baudelaire's art criticism ressemble ideas in Cendrars, who considered the earlier poet a precursor of modernity not in his poetry but in his critical writing. We may note in passing from the passages quoted the very phrase 'du monde entier,' the dislike of being called an artist and of literary gossip, the praise of the *flâneur*, the sense of being at home everywhere, and the love of playing the observer hidden in the crowd.

28 For an interesting account of the new spirit in art at the Rotonde one might look at Ilya Ehrenburg *People and Life, 1891-1921* 142-94. On page 174 he writes: 'A chance visitor might have thought that the *Rotonde* was a neutral

country, but actually it had lived in the grip of catastrophe long before August 2, 1914. In 1913 we had all read Blaise Cendrars' poem *La Prose du Trans-sibérien et de la Petite Jehanne de France.*' Ehrenburg then goes on to quote six lines on the Russian wounded.

CHAPTER SEVEN

1   *La Guerre au Luxembourg,* with six drawings by Kisling, was published in Paris by D. Niestlé in 1916 ('Censuré à 16 heures le 11 Décembre 1916, 861e jour de la guerre, au Bureau de la Presse du Ministère de la Guerre').

2   OC 1: 536. In his dissertation Walter Albert considers the word 'circumstantial' self-condemning (p. 138). However, Jacques Henry Lévesque, in his introduction to Cendrars' *Poésies complètes,* p. 21, note 1, quotes Goethe in his *Conversations With Eckermann* to the effect that all good poetry is 'circumstantial,' and I have already quoted Baudelaire to the same effect. Also see Roger Allard in the following note.

3   Roger Allard, review of *Dix-neuf Poèmes élastiques* NRF 7, no. 75 (1 December 1919) 1093. His review goes on to say: 'Il a raison de protester contre le décri systématique des poèmes "de circonstance." Il appartient au poète de porter tout sujet qu'on lui propose à la hauteur de son génie, s'il en a. Un peintre qui refuserait la tâche de faire un portrait, comme indigne de son talent, serait fort ridicule. M. Cendrars est le seul poète qui ait su quelquefois réussir un *Ersatz* du cubisme plastique. Nul, pas même Apollinaire, ne fut davantage démarqué. Dans une "notule d'histoire littéraire" l'auteur de *Poèmes élastiques* rappelle avec une discrète amertume que "les aînés, les écrivains classés et le soi-disant avant-garde refusaient ma collaboration." J'admire surtout qu'elle soit acceptée sans nulle gêne aujourd'hui par ses imitateurs directs. Il est vrai que le voisinage si dangereux d'un vrai poète n'est guère redouté des mauvais, car ceux-ci sont les derniers à s'aviser de leur infirmité.'

4   I am using here the term as coined by Henry W. Wells in *New Poets from Old* (New York 1940), where he uses the phrase 'radical image' to describe the process of what is more commonly called in English the 'metaphysical image.' Wells' term is closer to the sense of contrast as discussed in the previous chapter.

5   Jean Epstein 'A Necessary and Sufficient Literature' 315. I have reversed the order of these two passages.

6   In 'Poètes,' reprinted in *Aujourd'hui* OC 4: 207-25, Cendrars examined these errors to show that they were the main tools of the new poets. He illustrated, from Aragon, Apollinaire, Desnos, himself, Rimbaud and Cocteau, a number of passages taken from M.J. Vendryes *Le Langage, Introduction linguistique à l'histoire.* The poem 'Coquilles,' in *Feuilles de route* 174, is in praise of such 'errors.'

7 I am in agreement here with Robert Goffin in *Fil d'Ariane pour la Poésie* 234, where he discusses the process in great detail.

8 Blaise Cendrars *Du Monde entier au cœur du monde* (Paris 1957) 15. This is one of six hitherto uncollected poems which were not reprinted in OC.

9 The poems in *Feuilles de route* were published in smaller volumes and in reviews from 1924 to 1928 and brought together under the single title in *Poésies complètes* in 1944.

10 Jacques-Henry Lévesque, *Blaise Cendrars* 56

11 Pound in *Gaudier-Brzeska* (London 1916) 103, as quoted by Donald Davie *Ezra Pound, Poet as Sculptor* (New York 1968) 57

12 Ibid.

13 John Dos Passos, among collected 'Testimonianze' in the Cendrars number of *Letteratura* 49

14 Joseph Delteil, review of *L'Or* 944

15 *L'Homme foudroyé* OC 5: 182-3

16 See p. 68 and footnote 1 of chapter 4.

CHAPTER EIGHT

1 The 1919 edition was published by La Sirène. It had previously been published in the *Mercure de France* 130 (1 December 1918) 419-30, in the same issue as Apollinaire's 'L'Esprit nouveau et les poètes' (pp. 385-96), the text of the lecture given a year earlier at the Vieux Colombier theatre with readings of modern poets, including Cendrars; it is thus possible the *Mercure* editors were using *La Fin du monde* as an illustration of Apollinaire's essay, where he wrote 'Les poètes modernes sont donc des créateurs, des inventeurs, et des prophètes' (p. 394). Apollinaire had died three weeks before.

2 *L'Eubage, Aux antipodes de l'unité* OC 2, dedication to Jacques Doucet, 53. I have described in part one (pp. 60-1) how Doucet paid Cendrars each month for a 'letter' or chapter from him; hence the division of the work into twelve sections, one for each month of the year (although this does not account for starting with March, the first month of the old calendar). For more details on the writing of *L'Eubage* and the relationship with Doucet see Blaise Cendrars *Le Lotissement du ciel* OC 6: 501-5. Herbert S. Gershman calls *L'Eubage* 'presur-realistic' in his *The Surrealist Revolution in France* (Ann Arbor, Michigan 1969) 138.

3 *Le Lotissement du ciel* OC 6: 502-3

4 Some idea may be gathered from the publication of chapters 5 and 6, with the illustrations, in *L'Esprit Nouveau* 1, no. 7 (April 1921): 791-7. This edition was never published though it was in proofs and an advertisement for it in the same journal (2: facing p. 1719) announced that only fifteen copies remained for subscription. Seventy numbered copies were to be sold at 50 francs a copy. The

text was finally published with different illustrations in 1926 by Au Sans Pareil.

5 Maurice Raynal, review of *L'Eubage* in *L'Esprit Nouveau* 1, nos. 11-12 (July?
1921) 1285. Raynal is writing of the one copy in proofs. Publication was
announced for November.

6 Moricand is better known to English readers as the hero (or villain) of Henry
Miller's *Big Sur and the Oranges of Hieronymous Bosch* (New York 1957). He
charted Cendrars' horoscope, along with those of Van Dongen, Picasso, Cocteau, Louis Jouvet, André Tardieu, and others in *Portraits astrologiques,* dedicated to Cendrars 'En souvenir de *L'Eubage.*' The end of Cendrars' horoscope,
p. 35, strikingly ressembles my own interpretation of Cendrars and his writing:
'Un tel être réalise la connaissance sur un plan affectif par une sorte d' "os-
mose." La vision utilitaire du monde lui échappe, non pas qu'il l'ignore, mais
sitôt connue, il la dépasse pour pénétrer au cœur des phénomènes et atteindre
leur sens caché. Une "conscience cosmique," celle qui fut l'apanage de Balzac,
de Whitman, de Jacob Boehme. La connaissance du monde provient non plus
de la simple observation, mais d'une identification aux phénomènes que l'on
perçoit d'une sorte de communion.'

7 Cendrars wrote this often. Notably, it is the title of chapter 2 of *Emmène-moi
au bout du monde!...* in OC 7.

8 *L'Eubage* OC 2: 74

9 *Éloge de la vie dangereuse* in *Aujourd'hui* OC 4: 154-5

10 *Le Lotissement du ciel* 498

11 'Poètes' in *Aujourd'hui* OC 4: 207. In this essay Cendrars quotes from Whitman's 'Song of the Exposition' and 'A Song for Occupations' to illustrate the
new poets' search for a modern yet lyrical language.

12 *L'Eubage* OC 2: 74

13 Jean Van Heeckeren 'Vérité-Force' *Orbes* no. 4 (Winter 1932-3), as quoted in
Lévesque's introduction to *Poésies complètes* 33. Lévesque adds that Van Heeckeren is virtually copying word for word from Balzac's *Splendeurs et misères des
courtisanes.*

14 *Éloge de la vie dangereuse* in *Aujourd'hui* OC 4: 155

15 Jean-Claude Lovey *Situation de Blaise Cendrars* 147. The nihilistic statement
Lovey is referring to here is in *Moravagine* OC 2: 323; it is made by a character
(not the author), a member of a revolutionary cell in Russia, as part of an entry
in his diary during a state of depression. M. Lovey's book has been severely
criticized by Paul Pettiaux in 'Cendrars défiguré.'

16 *Poésies complètes:* Zen 33-4, Krishnamurti 38-9, Bergson 34, Sartre and Camus
36-7. Also see the footnote on pp. 41-2. Other writers mentioned here and of
special relevance to my point of view are Nietzsche, De Gourmont, Heisen-
berg, and Charles-Albert Cingria on the medieval poet Notker.

17 Georges Le Cardonnel, review of *J'ai tué.* On p. 115 he writes that *J'ai tué* has
mostly 'la valeur d'un recueil de sensations.' This is a frequent underestimation

of Cendrars as a creative writer, always to see the power of his prose resulting from mere observation of powerful, unexpected sensations. There is good reason to believe, for example, that the major 'sensation,' killing a man, is not factual. In *La Main coupée* OC 5: 394 Cendrars recounts the identical scene and then reveals to us that the German was dead already.

18 End of *J'ai tué* in *Aujourd'hui* OC 4: 152

19 *Éloge de la vie dangereuse* in ibid. 157, 158. The story of the devoured heart seems unlikely, but Cendrars is not afraid to supply many of the circumstances surrounding the event so that it might be verified in Rio newspapers. Also, his reference to one Peter Kolb's *Caput Bonae Spei Hodierum* (Nuremburg 1719) is entirely correct, and the material there on similar native practices lends credibility to his own story.

20 Blaise Cendrars *Une Nuit dans la forêt* OC 7: 15

21 Henri Perruchot 'Blaise Cendrars, ou vivre est une action magique' 187

22 *L'Eubage* OC 2: 76

23 Blaise Cendrars *Vol à voile* OC 4: 277

24 *Profond aujourd'hui* in *Aujourd'hui* OC 4: 143-4

25 Ibid. 142. Near the end of *Moganni Nameh* OC 4: 103, Cendrars quoted Goethe: 'Mikroskope und Fernröhre verwirren eigentlich den reinen Menschensinn.'

26 *Profond aujourd'hui* in *Aujourd'hui* OC 4: 144. One might compare this passage, as well as others on suicide like 'Bombay-Express' in *Dix-neuf Poèmes élastiques* ('La vie que j'ai menée/ M'empêche de me suicider'), to Camus' ideas on suicide. As the end of *Profond aujourd'hui* shows, Cendrars dismisses suicide in order to enter the absurd. Camus resists suicide because it considers it insufficient as a rebellion against absurdity. Essentially then, Camus remains rational.

27 Ibid. 144-5

CHAPTER NINE

1 See James Peter Zollinger *Sutter, the Man and His Empire* (New York 1939) 343 and Erwin G. Gudde, ed. *Sutter's Own Story* (New York 1936) 234. The earliest biography prompted by Cendrars' novel was Julian Dana's *Sutter of California* (New York 1934). Then Sutter's *New Helvetia Diary* was published in 1939. For more details on the American edition of *L'Or* and the American film *Sutter's Gold* see my article 'La Fortune de *L'Or* en Amérique' in the special Cendrars numbers of *La Revue des Lettres Modernes* expected for the spring of 1977. *The Emperor of California* was the title of a second film made from Cendrars' novel, by Luis Trencker in 1936 (Germany). The film had the dubious honour of winning the prize at the Venice festival when the Germans objected to *La Grande Illusion.* Cendrars sued Trencker for not crediting *L'Or* as his source, but the war left the case in abeyance.

2 Both Zollinger and Gudde (see footnote above) are critical of Cendrars' novel
  as unsound biography. However, Faith Maris, reviewing for the *New Republic,*
  13 October 1926, 227, and M.R. Werner, reviewing for *The Saturday Review
  of Literature,* 30 October 1926, 253, both realized Cendrars was manipulating
  fact for dramatic effect. His changes emphasize the irony and the conflict of
  land versus gold which I am about to examine.
     Cendrars himself explained one of the errors in the radio interviews, *Blaise
  Cendrars vous parle...* OC 8: 584-5; he copied a mistake from Martin Birmann's
  letters (Birmann was Sutter's only correspondent in Switzerland). This error
  Cendrars says he corrected in later editions. Another error can be no more than
  an oversight. He gives Sutter's age as 73 when he dies. However, the novel
  gives dates of both birth and death correctly, by which count Sutter died at 77.
  Pages 583-4 of the interviews give an indication of Cendrars' attitude towards
  historicity in connection with *L 'Or.*

3 John Charpentier, review of *L 'Or*, 452

4 Joseph Delteil, review of *L 'Or* 944. In 1925 Delteil himself became famous
  with his novel *Jeanne d'Arc.*

5 *L 'Or* OC 2: 155. About five of these items are dispersed among the eight menus
  in *Kodak* OC 1: 131-2.

6 *Le Lotissement du ciel* OC 6: 559

7 This word is used a few times in H.I. Brock's partly critical review of *Sutter's
  Gold* for the NYTBR, 3 October 1926, 4. For Brock the book suffered too much
  from the influence of the movies and jazz (Brock, it must be added, disliked
  both), and he called Cendrars a 'Jazz Homer.' Dos Passos used the comparison
  only two weeks later, since 'Homer of the Transsiberian' was first published
  in *The Saturday Review of Literature* for 16 October 1926, 202, 222.

8 A. t'Serstevens, in 'Du *Transsibérien* à *Moravagine:* Cendrars, poète et romancier' 1, wrote of *L 'Or:* 'L'histoire est menée droit au but, par un homme qui
  connaît à merveille tous les effets des projections sur l'écran cérébral et sait
  rendre l'anecdote uniquement visuelle. C'est le plus beau des films, à la meil-
  leure manière de William Hart, avec un grand souffle d'épopée sur de grands
  paysages.'
     Gilbert Seldes, as I have already mentioned, referred to Cendrars among
  other European writers in 'The Cinema Novel,' in *The Seven Lively Arts* 384-90,
  to demonstrate that, contrary to the complaints of some American writers, the
  cinema could promote 'brevity, hardness, clarity, brilliance' rather than 'slop-
  piness.'

9 *L 'Or* OC 2: 160

10 Emile Szittya 'Logique de la vie contradictoire de Blaise Cendrars' *Mercure de
  France: Blaise Cendrars* 66

11 'La Métaphysique du café' in *Aujourd'hui* OC 4: 238, 239. This article was
  written in 1927.

12 *Le Lotissement du ciel* OC 6: 484-5
13 As quoted by Alfred Berchtold *La Suisse Romande au cap du XXe siècle: Portrait littéraire et moral* (Lausanne 1963) 848
14 OC 2: 229-425
15 Pierre de Massot *De Mallarmé à 391* (Saint-Raphaël 1922) 33, 34
16 Jacques-Henry Lévesque *Blaise Cendrars* 64
17 Martin Green *The Von Richthofen Sisters* (New York 1974)
18 Boris Savinkov *Souvenirs d'un terroriste* trans. Bernard Taft (Paris 1931) and *Memoirs of a Terrorist* trans. Joseph Shaplen (New York 1931)
19 Christine Morrow *Le Roman irréaliste* 256-8. Cendrars is discussed in a chapter entitled 'Le Roman de l'inconscient' which also deals with Julien Green, Faulkner, Ribemont-Dessaignes, Crevel, Breton, Chirico and Aragon.
20 André Breton *Manifestes du Surréalisme* (Paris, NRF, Collection 'Idées' 1963) 78
21 *Moravagine* OC 2: 233; from de Gourmont's *Sixtine*
22 Ibid. 282. In connection with this idea of essential rhythm and the civilized, scientific attempt to encompass it epistemologically, I reproduce below most of Cendrars' 'Hommage à Jean Borlin' (director of the Ballets Suédois). The text is further interesting in its reference to Whitman. 'Hommage à Jean Borlin' is not included in the OC.

    'J'ai dit un jour à Jean Borlin: "Mon vieux, tu ne sais pas danser." Et je lui expliquais: "Comprends-moi bien. Tu es sur le même plan que les matelots, les mulâtres, les nègres, les sauvages, et c'est ce que j'admire le plus en toi. Avec tes pieds de paysan suédois, tu te places exactement aux antipodes des Ballets Russes, tu bouscules la tradition du ballet français qui nous revient de Saint-Pétersbourg avec l'ancien régime et l'italianisme. Écoute maintenant le grand cœur de Whitman et laisse-toi aller dans les bras des ouvriers de la voiture-aviation." Et je l'entraînai voir comment l'on danse à Paris. Les endroits où l'on danse à Paris, une fois sorti de la rue de Lappe et de la rue de la Roquette, sont les grands boulevards, les gares, l'aéroport du Bourget, le Vel' d'Hiv', la salle Wagram, l'autodrome de Linas-Montlhéry. Affiches et haut-parleurs vous font oublier les enseignements de l'Académie de Danse, la sciatique et le temps, la mesure et le goût, la mièvrerie et la virtuosité. Quand on a tout oublié, ça y est, on a trouvé le rythme, le beau rythme d'aujourd'hui qui porte les cinq continents nouveaux: la discipline, l'équilibre, la santé, la force, la vitesse' (from *Les Ballets Suédois dans l'art contemporain* [Paris, Éditions du Trianon 1931] 176-7).
23 *Moravagine* OC 2: 323. This is the passage referred to by Jean-Claude Lovey in *Situation de Blaise Cendrars* 147. See footnote 15 of chapter 8 above.
24 *Moravagine* OC 2: 304. The integration of chance into one's plan of action, and the accompanying reliance on signs and their interpretation, in other words, prediction, bring us for a second time to C.G. Jung. For the latter's interest

in the Chinese book of oracles, the *I Ching* (or *Book of Changes*), see his *Memories, Dreams, Reflexions,* ed. Aniela Jaffé, trans. Richard and Clara Winston (New York 1965) 373-6, 388-9, and most especially his essay 'Synchronicity: An Acausal Connecting Principle' in the Bollingen Foundation series no. 51, *The Interpretation of Nature and the Psyche* (New York 1955) 5-146. Here Jung discusses the *I Ching* and its Western equivalents; the name of Robert Fludd appears in this connection, as do those of J.P. Migne and Schopenhauer, two favourite authors of Cendrars. Also note Cendrars' interest in Moricand, and the drawing of Moravagine by Moricand, or so we are told, on page 423 of the novel.

25 Élie Richard, in 'Blaise Cendrars, vagabond du bon plaisir, chante la nostalgie du malheur qui pointe les hommes de son temps,' finishes his article: 'Je suppose que l'ouvrage qu'il annonce sous le signe de Villon, dit-il, nous apprendra où il place le bout du monde, nous livrera le mot de sa philosophie. Il ne serait pas étonnant que ce soit le mot Hasard.'

26 Henry Adams *The Education of Henry Adams* (New York 1931) chapter 25 'The Dynamo and the Virgin' 379-90. This entire chapter in Adams is relevant.

27 *Moravagine* OC 2: 385-6. Also see footnote 22 above on Jean Borlin.

28 Blaise Cendrars 'Au Cœur du monde' ('fragment retrouvé') OC 1: 199, 205

29 Freud wrote: 'Hatred is at the bottom of all the relations of affection and love between human beings; hatred in relation to objects is older than love'; quoted in J.A.C. Brown *Freud and the Post-Freudians* (Harmondsworth, Middlesex 1964) 139. The view that women are basically masochistic is propounded by a Freudian, Helen Deutsch, in *The Psychology of Women* (New York 1944).

30 *Moravagine* OC 2: 422. The text is in Moravagine's handwriting (actually recognizable as Cendrars') and followed by a printed transcription. I here take the liberty of substituting for *oiseaux,* in the printed text in all editions, the more logical *ciseaux.* As for *hystiologie,* perhaps it is meant to mean *histologie* which would be consistent with Cendrars' interest in microscopes.

31 Sir Douglas Mawson *Home of the Blizzard* 2 volumes (London 1915)

32 *Dan Yack* OC 3: 67

33 *L'Illustration* 2 (17 December 1921): 600. On page 598 a photograph of night filming in Nice shows a clear picture of Cendrars (not named, however). The whole article, pp. 598-600, signed by one Robert de Beauplan, seems to show the influence of Cendrars in its emphasis on real workers and the use of dangerous, on-location sets around Mont Blanc (perhaps Beauplan is Cendrars' pseudonym made from 'beau Plan' de l'Aiguille).

34 See Rachel Low *The History of the British Film* 2 (1906-14) (London 1949).

35 Blaise Cendrars 'Ivy Close' in *Anthologie de la prose française* (Paris, Simon Kra 1928) 275

36 'Life is impossible without you, impossible with you.' This epigraph, which so

precisely epitomizes the tragic bind of Dan Yack's life, is not be to found in the OC edition.

37 *Dan Yack* OC 3: 41-2. T.S. Eliot used a similar arctic experience in *The Waste Land* (l. 366, ' – But who is that on the other side of you ?'); alienation is one of the major themes there too, but Eliot's interest is more obviously religious, and he refers as well to the journey to Emmaus.

38 Louis Parrot, in his *Blaise Cendrars* 51-5, compares Dan Yack to Poe's *Arthur Gordon Pym,* and with good reason. At this point in *Le Plan,* pp. 74-5, Dan Yack resembles Pym at the putative end of his narrative when he comes upon a white spectre rising out of the polar waters. Also see J.M. Santraud 'Dans le sillage de la baleinière d'Arthur Gordon Pym: *Le Sphinx des glaces, Dan Yack.*'

39 One may only conjecture, for the moment, to what extent Le Corbusier and Cendrars ever discussed urbanism. They knew each other well, and Cendrars contributed to *L'Esprit Nouveau,* which Le Corbusier and Ozenfant directed. Le Corbusier was born in the same town as Cendrars, La Chaux-de-Fonds, one month later, and he also preferred to pursue his creative career under a pseudonym. See Jean Buhler *Blaise Cendrars, homme libre, poète au cœur du monde* facing p. 81 for a photograph of Le Corbusier, Léger, Raymone, and Cendrars at Le Tremblay-sur-Maudre in 1924. In his *Le Modulor* Le Corbusier reprints a card from Cendrars on which, in response to the architect's request for his opinion of the book, Cendrars writes 'Who gives a goddam.'

40 Reading the two reviews of the two parts of *Dan Yack* by René de Weck, 'Valeur dynamique de Blaise Cendrars; *Le Plan de l'Aiguille*' and '*Les Confessions de Dan Yack,*' one may see how perplexing *Le Plan* seemed alone (despite which de Weck had only praise for the volume!), and how brilliantly clear it became in light of *Les Confessions. Dan Yack* is in this respect a harbinger of the later novels which often appear to be nothing but random associations for as much as three-quarters of their length.

In a prefatory note Cendrars writes that he, like Dan Yack, did not write *Les Confessions,* but *read* them into a dictaphone, so we are to presume something of a 'voice within a voice' method. Yves Gandon attempted to parody the dictaphone method in a 'critique romancée,' 'Blaise Cendrars vue par Dan Yack.'

41 It is interesting to compare the impulse behind Dan Yack's Armistice Day proposal to Cendrars' poem 'Hommage à Guillaume Apollinaire' (OC 1: 191-2) in which he proclaims Apollinaire's symbolic resurrection in the streets that same day (when Apollinaire was buried), in his own person and in the bodies and souls of the next generation. Also, there is a striking similarity between two details. In the poem Apollinaire appears 'à cheval sur le moteur d'un camion américain et brandissait un énorme drapeau international déployé comme un avion.' In the present account of Dan Yack's Armistice Day, as he

drives his Studebaker through the Place de la Concorde, 'un matelot américain s'installa à califourchon sur le capot et déploya une immense bannière étoilée' (p. 155).

42 *Dan Yack* OC 3: 190, 191. The *Petit Robert* dictionary defines Gribouille as a stock character who always falls prey to the very ills he goes to such lengths to avoid.

43 Richard Montegue Payne, in his doctoral thesis 'Blaise Cendrars: From Action to Contemplation,' examines action and contemplation as basically different and opposed, but I am trying to see them as one and the same.

44 As quoted in Lévesque *Blaise Cendrars* 68-9. Originally published in *Diogène* 19 April 1946. This passage is also reproduced in Buhler *Blaise Cendrars* 114 and by Parrot *Blaise Cendrars* 50 (abridged).

45 In his review of *Les Confessions de Dan Yack*

46 *Une Nuit dans la forêt* OC 7: 16

47 In this distinction between change and cycle lies my main difference of opinion with Richard Montegue Payne, who considers that *Dan Yack* represents a change, in Cendrars, from a man of action to a man of contemplation, and thus a moral development in the author. On pages 80-1 of his thesis (see footnote 43 above) he says that the novel ends on a note of hope which is the product of 'reflection, an entirely new approach to life for one of Cendrars' protagonists.' As my quotation from Cendrars should make clear, the 'new' idea is the cycle in a world of constant change, not meditation alone. The new hope of the end is not the product of any new way of life, but rather the natural quality of another new cycle's beginning, as I show below.

48 Nicolas is the name of Dan Yack's son by Hedwiga; see page 206, where he inquires after her child, ignorant of its sex or name, but knowing she had been pregnant.

CHAPTER TEN

1 OC 1: 209-488

2 OC 2: 451-510 and OC 4: 109-39

3 *Rhum* OC 3: 306 ('paroles' does not refer directly to Galmot's defiant letter to his jailer, p. 309).

4 *Panorama de la pègre* OC 4: 279-384 and *Hollywood, La Mecque du cinéma* OC 4: 385-468

5 *La Banlieue de Paris* OC 7: 129-84. The original edition had 130 photographs; Seghers has reissued the volume in paperback with 24 photographs (1966). *Bourlinguer* OC 6: 13-331; the editor, René Kieffer, told me that *Bourlinguer* began as a photograph album he suggested to Cendrars.

6 *Vol à voile* OC 4: 277

7 *Une Nuit dans la forêt* OC 7: 17. Much of the first half of *Une Nuit* deals with *Le Plan de l'Aiguille* and can be seen as a soul-searching pause between the two volumes of *Dan Yack.* On p. 27 Cendrars writes of *Le Plan:* 'En somme, il n'y a qu'un seul personnage et tout se passe dans sa tête.' This suggests an opposite approach to the one I took, though one's conclusions about the novel as a whole would not be so different.

8 S. Kunitz and H. Haycraft *Twentieth Century Authors* (New York 1942) 260. This biographical sketch is written in the first person, and printed in English in quotation marks.

9 *Hollywood* OC 4: 413

10 *Histoires vraies* OC 3: 339-453; *La Vie dangereuse* OC 4: 469-581; *D'Outremer à indigo* OC 8: 7-133; the three volumes contain in all seventeen stories.

11 'L'Égoutier de Londres' *Histoires vraies* OC 3: 362-73. I should note that Cendrars reports this fact as Griffith tells it to him. Critics have not sufficiently distinguished those extraordinary tales Cendrars tells from those he merely repeats from others.

12 'Fébronio' *La Vie dangereuse* OC 4: 523-57

13 'La Femme aimée' ibid. 561-81

14 Dos Passos confirmed the extravagant menus to me (undated letter of November 1967) with a question mark about the last, culminating item, wild swan; he remembered wild goose. The wild swan seems a typical Cendrarsian flourish, but is not impossible; as unheard of as swan for dinner may be to most of us Mr Dos Passos pointed out that both wild goose and swan – if young – are delicious. Incidentally, these feasts took place in Monpazier, where Cendrars was doing research on Jean Galmot.

15 *Emmène-moi au bout du monde!...* OC 7: 207

16 'Le Cercle du diamant' *Histoires vraies* OC 3: 383-4

17 See Maurice Nadeau *Littérature présente* (Paris 1952) 168-74, who finds *La Main coupée* and other work confused. Also see Robert Brasillach *Les Quatre jeudis: Images d'avant-guerre* 347-51 on *Histoires vraies* which, he wrote, nevertheless 'consolent de beaucoup de littérature.'

18 In *Blaise Cendrars vous parle...* OC 8: 605-6 Cendrars praises O. Henry, particularly as a master of form. In 1936 Cendrars translated Al Jennings' *Through the Shadows with O. Henry.* Jennings, formerly an outlaw in the West, had been in jail with the short-story writer.

19 One may be reminded of Minotti's opera *The Telephone,* or of Cocteau's *La Voix humaine,* though this latter strikes me as being less interested in the modernity of the instrument.

20 'La Femme aimée' *La Vie dangereuse* OC 4: 581

21 Quoted in Lévesque's introduction to Cendrars' *Poésies complètes* 35

22 *La Vie dangereuse* OC 4: 487-511, 521-57

CHAPTER ELEVEN

1 See Malcolm Cowley's introduction to the reprint of the original 1855 edition of *Leaves of Grass* (New York 1959) xxvii-xxxiv, where he says Whitman betrayed his 'self.'

2 Valery Larbaud 'Walt Whitman' *Œuvres complètes* 4 (Paris 1950): 287

3 Malcolm Cowley, introduction to *Leaves of Grass* xxi

4 Martin Buber *I and Thou* trans. R.G. Smith (New York 1958) 62-4. Also see, for this mystical distinction between self and ego, J.-H. Lévesque 'Sur Blaise Cendrars: Extraits d'un recueil alphabétique' in *Mercure de France: Blaise Cendrars* 100, under the heading of 'Profond Aujourd'hui.'

5 Buber *I and Thou* 66

6 Georges Piroué 'Cendrars et la Suisse' in *Mercure, Cendrars* 50

7 Buber *I and Thou* 64

8 A. t'Serstevens 'Quand Cendrars bourlinguait à Paris' 13. This text is from one written forty years earlier for *Comœdia* (5 January 1922); the latter is reprinted in t'Serstevens' *L'Homme que fut Blaise Cendrars* 113-17.

9 'Pro domo' appended to *Moravagine* OC 2: 435 (written, apparently, in 1917)

10 Cendrars was harsh on both Gide's puritanism and his self-indulgence; see *Blaise Cendrars vous parle...* OC 8: 559. These qualities represent the alternate repression and defiant indulgence of the same thing, the egotistic self.

11 Henry Miller *Tropic of Cancer* (New York 1961)

12 *Dan Yack* OC 3: 44

13 We note that Blake, Balzac, and Whitman are the only writers of the nineteenth century included by R.M. Bucke in his *Cosmic Consciousness* (New York 1901, 1923). Bucke coined the term of his title. The concept of self discussed here is the subject of a large part of Bucke's work.

14 *L'Homme foudroyé* OC 5: 43-336

15 Paul Andréota, untitled article in *Mercure, Cendrars* 195

16 Henri Perruchot 'Blaise Cendrars, ou vivre est une action magique' 186-7

17 'La Roue des Choses' becomes the obsessive theme of 'Gênes,' in *Bourlinguer.*

18 *Bourlinguer* OC 6: 157

19 *Blaise Cendrars vous parle...* OC 8: 574

20 *Poésies complètes* 33-5

21 André Bourin 'Rendez-vous avec Blaise Cendrars' 16

22 *Une Nuit dans la forêt* OC 7: 16

23 'Publicité = Poésie' *Aujourd'hui* OC 4: 230

24 *Une Nuit dans la forêt* OC 7: 39

25 *Blaise Cendrars vous parle...* OC 8: 591. Details of this novel are given in *Une Nuit dans la forêt* OC 7: 26-7 and cannot but remind one of the material and even part of the technique of John Dos Passos' *U.S.A.* (*Une Nuit* was, however,

written earlier, in March 1927, and published in 1929). Cendrars' friend Henry Poulaille wrote a series of novels entitled *Le Pain quotidien* in the thirties.

26 *Blaise Cendrars vous parle...* OC 8: 576

27 André Beucler 'Blaise Cendrars' in *Mercure, Cendrars* 60; Emile Szittya 'Logique de la vie contradictoire de Blaise Cendrars' in ibid. 66

28 Szittya in ibid. 64, 67

29 'Blaise Cendrars' 518

30 A. t'Serstevens 'Cendrars au bras droit' in *Mercure, Cendrars* 82

31 'Cendrars et la Suisse' in ibid. 47

32 See *Blaise Cendrars vous parle...* OC 8: 576

33 Jean Cassou *Chagall* (New York 1965) 22, 54

34 'Blaise Cendrars, l'homme le plus seul au monde.' I found the Rio cable address in the records of Harpers Bros. in New York.

35 *L'Homme que fut Blaise Cendrars* 95-101

36 'Paradoxe du grand menteur' in *Mercure, Cendrars* 56

37 'La Vie des livres'

38 *Le Lotissement du ciel* OC 6: 387-8. Rémy was killed in a training flight accident just after the war. See the very moving beginning of *La Main coupée,* where Cendrars reprints Rémy's last letter and the messages to Cendrars from his son's comrades in arms and commanding officer. To the extent that *Le Lotissement du ciel* is a biography of Saint Joseph, patron saint of flyers, it is undertaken *in memoriam.*

39 Levitation is not as suspect as one might suppose. The 1967 edition of the *Encyclopaedia Britannica* reports: 'The puzzling thing about levitation is that while it is intuitively rejected as impossible by the mind accustomed to scientific habits of thought, there is nevertheless a great weight of evidence in favour of its occurrence. This evidence would indeed be overwhelming if the phenomenon were intrinsically more likely.'

40 Quoted by Paul Andréota *Mercure, Cendrars* 195

41 Cendrars also uses a symbol of the obverse, Delaunay's pinhole in the window shade to let a ray of light into his darkened room for the analysis of the spectrum; see pp. 510-11 of *Le Lotissement du ciel.*

42 Walt Whitman *Complete Poetry and Selected Prose* ed. James E. Miller, Jr. (Cambridge, Mass. 1959) 425, 424 (the 1855 preface)

43 See pp. 27-8 above and *Une Nuit dans la forêt* OC 7: 17 for the sources of Cendrars' name in Nietzsche. Coincidentally, when Professor Takataro Kigi (Hayashi) inscribed a copy of his *Shibuzura* (collected poems, containing translations of Cendrars' poetry from the English versions by John Dos Passos) (Tokyo, Kongo Shuppan 1967) to Cendrars, he wrote, 'To Mr. Braise Cendrars' (copy in my possession).

CHAPTER TWELVE

1 *Blaise Cendrars vous parle...* OC 8: 575-6
2 Ibid. 576
3 Ibid. 643-4
4 *Emmène-moi au bout du monde!...* OC 7: 188. See pp. 84-5 above for the full text of this note.
5 Ibid. 310. Another point of interest in this little speech is that Cendrars may actually be thinking of Moreno's first husband, Marcel Schwob, who had a strong, if somewhat neglected, influence on Apollinaire's generation. Schwob particularly resembles Cendrars in his taste for odd, even frightening, characters, and in his combination of the erudite and popular.
6 This is the form of the title on the page of contents. As the editors of the *Œuvres complètes* have noted – and preserved it – this sentence appears as running head in the chapter as 'Vivre est un art magique.' In the light of the pervasive theatrical meanings one wonders if the 'error' is not a purposeful, playful variation. One may well wonder which word, *art* or *action,* applies better to this incredible chapter with 'la Présidente.' In the English translation *art* is used in both places.
7 Also see p. 228: '*Le spectacle est dans la rue!* portait une des annotations du générique.' *Le Spectacle est dans la rue* (n.p., Draeger Frères 1936) is a volume of posters by A.M. Cassandre, a famous poster artist and a good friend of Cendrars who wrote the following text for the collection. As it has not been reprinted I give it in full. The first two paragraphs constitute an introduction; each phrase thereafter appears across from, and refers directly to, a poster, but also takes its place in a coherent and poetic sentence:

La Rue, la rue de Paris est assurément un des spectacles les plus prodigieux qui se puissent imaginer. Quand on voit défiler la vie d'aujourd'hui, quand on est pris, emporté dans son tourbillon, quand on se rend compte à chaque pas que les immeubles, que les palaces, que les vitrines, les magasins font tous les jours peau neuve, que les autos, que les avions, que même les mœurs, les coutumes, les habitudes de la société évoluent sur un rythme nouveau qui fait que depuis quelques décades à peine le citadin le plus casanier roule, vole, voyage, il est légitime de se demander quels sont les instigateurs et les artisans d'une pareille métamorphose?

A.M. Cassandre est un de ces hommes-là et je lui suis reconnaissant d'avoir découvert dans la Publicité la fleur de la vie contemporaine, d'avoir compris qu'elle était une affirmation d'optimisme et de santé, la plus chaleureuse manifestation de la vitalité des hommes d'aujourd'hui, de leur puissance, de leur puérilité, de leur don d'invention et d'imagination; je suis reconnaissant à Cassandre de n'avoir pas seulement été un peintre mais surtout un des plus fervents animateurs de la vie moderne: le premier metteur en scène de LA RUE.

de l'évasion ...
... à la conquête
de la nature ...
... à la nature-morte
de la synthèse
... à l'objet
de la violence
à la poésie
du rêve incassable
à la rigueur de l'épure
A.M. Cassandre ...
emploie toutes les données du monde pour ...
CHANTER
... sur les portées de la lumière,
une idée, un nom, une marque D'AUJOURD'HUI.

8 *Emmène-moi* OC 7: 194. The source is Baudelaire's 'Le Voyage' – the last lines of the last poem in the 1861 edition of *Les Fleurs du mal.* Thérèse forgets parts of the lines, and must search for the last word, 'nouveau.' The two lines are meant to read: 'Plonger au fond du gouffre, Enfer ou Ciel, qu'importe? / Au fond de l'Inconnu pour trouver du *nouveau!* '
9 Gabriel d'Aubarède 'Rencontre avec Cendrars' 4
10 'Le Roman que je n'écrirai jamais' in *Trop c'est trop* OC 8: 304-5. From both here and the above-cited interview with d'Aubarède we may gather that a sequel to *Emmène-moi* was intended, perhaps even required, since the novel is not yet about either the legionnaire or 'la Présidente.' I would say the ending of the novel further indicates a sequel. If so, we might have seen a solution to the murder, as well as the tying up of other loose ends. However, my view remains that Cendrars chose to sustain his mystery for at least the length of a publishable book; this novel must be considered sufficient in itself for whatever it does present to a reader.
11 Jacques-Henry Lévesque 'Sur Blaise Cendrars: extraits d'un recueil alphabétique' *Mercure de France: Blaise Cendrars* 101. M. Lévesque reads *Le Transsibérien,* which is, after all, 'dédié au musiciens,' to jazz background on Folkways Records FL9940. 'Le jazz hot' usually refers to jazz played after, and in reaction to, 'Swing.'
12 *Vol à voile* OC 4: 276-7
13 Blaise Cendrars 'Un écrivain américain nous est né' reprinted from *Orbes* second series, no. 4 (Summer 1935) in Henry Miller *Blaise Cendrars* LXXI
14 André Billy 'Un Roman 'bœuf' de Blaise Cendrars'

CONCLUSION

1 Herman Hesse *Magister Ludi* trans. Mervyn Saville (New York 1949) 396
2 *Blaise Cendrars vous parle...* OC 8: 589-90
3 'Tu es plus belle que le ciel et la mer' *Feuilles de route* OC 1: 136-7
4 F.O. Matthiessen *American Renaissance* (London, Toronto, New York 1941) 535
5 *Le Panama* OC 1: 39
6 Paul Claudel *Art poëtique* in *Œuvres complètes* (Paris 1957) 121-217 (the dieresis is Claudel's). The first two parts, Claudel's analysis of a 'connaissance du temps' and a 'co-naissance au monde et de soi-même,' could readily be compared to my analysis of Cendrars.
7 See C.G. Jung 'The Spiritual Problem of Modern Man' in *Modern Man in Search of a Soul* (New York 1968) and as quoted above, p. 77.
8 In *Comparative Literature: Matter and Method* ed. A. Owen Aldridge (Urbana, Illinois 1969) 308-26 (also to be found in Ong's *In the Human Grain*)

Bibliography

This bibliography has been drawn up for students of Cendrars, and it therefore omits material used in this volume which does not refer to him. The bibliography is divided into two main sections: A, works by Cendrars and B, works about him.

Section A is further subdivided:
A1: a chronological listing of the works as they interest this study. (This is not a complete listing; one which is almost complete may be found in OC 8, a descriptive bibliography drawn up by Hughes Richard from the earlier work by Jacques-Henry Lévesque.)
A2: the contents of OC, by volume
A3: a chronological listing of Cendrars' works in English

Section B is further subdivided:
B1: volume-length studies and special issues of periodicals devoted to Cendrars
B2: doctoral dissertations
B3: articles, chapters in books, reviews, etc.

This is not an exhaustive bibliography, but I believe it is a good start, particularly for France and North America. For a bibliography of Cendrars in Brazil see Amaral in B1. For Italy, see the Cendrars number of *Letteratura* in B1. By far the best source for material appearing currently on Cendrars is the *French Bibliography* of the French Institute, New York. Also, we expect soon the first volume of a two or three volume *Calepin* from Hughes Richard (Minard).

A   WORKS BY CENDRARS

AI   CHRONOLOGY

1909 *Novgorode* (Sozonoff, Moscow)
1912 *Les Pâques à New York* (Les Hommes Nouveaux)
1913 *Prose du transsibérien et de la petite Jehanne de France* (Les Hommes Nouveaux)
—   *Séquences* (Les Hommes Nouveaux)
1916 *La Guerre au Luxembourg* (Niestlé)
1917 *Profond aujourd'hui (A La Belle Édition)*
1918 *Le Panama ou les aventures de mes sept oncles* (La Sirène)
—   *J'ai tué* (A La Belle Édition)
1919 *Dix-neuf Poèmes élastiques* (Au Sans Pareil)
—   *Du Monde entier* (NRF)
—   *La Fin du monde filmée par l'Ange Notre-Dame* (La Sirène)
1921 *Anthologie nègre* (La Sirène)
1924 *Kodak (Documentaire)* (Stock)
—   *Feuilles de route* (Au Sans Pareil)
1925 *L'Or* (Grasset)
1926 *Moravagine* (Grasset)
—   *L'Eubage* (Au Sans Pareil)
—   *L'ABC du cinéma* (Les Écrivains Réunis)
—   *Éloge de la vie dangereuse* (Les Écrivains Réunis)
1928 *Petits Contes nègres pour les enfants des blancs* (Éditions du Portique)
1929 *Le Plan de l'Aiguille* (Au Sans Pareil)
—   *Les Confessions de Dan Yack* (Au Sans Pareil)
—   *Une Nuit dans la forêt* (Aux Éditions du Verseau)
1930 *Rhum* (Grasset)
—   *Comment les blancs sont d'anciens noirs* (Au Sans Pareil)
1931 *Aujourd'hui* (Grasset)
1932 *Vol à voile* (Librairie Payot)
1935 *Panorama de la pègre* (B. Arthaud)
1936 *Hollywood, la mecque du cinéma* (Grasset)
1937 *Histoires vraies* (Grasset)
1938 *La Vie dangereuse* (Grasset)
1940 *D'Outremer à indigo* (Grasset)
—   *Chez l'armée anglaise* (Éditions Corrêâ)
1944 *Poésies complètes* (Denoël)
1945 *L'Homme foudroyé* (Denoël)

1946 *Dan Yack* (Éditions de la Tour)
— *La Main coupé* (Denoël)
1948 *Bourlinguer* (Denoël)
1949 *Le Lotissement du ciel* (Denoël)
— *La Banlieue de Paris* (Éditions Pierre Seghers)
1952 *Blaise Cendrars vous parle...* (Denoël)
— *Le Brésil* (Les Documents d'Art)
1956 *Emmène-moi au bout du monde!...* (Denoël)
1957 *Trop c'est trop* (Denoël)
— *Du Monde entier au cœur du monde* (Denoël)
1959 *Films sans images* (Denoël)
1969 *Inédits secrets* (Club français du livre)
— *Dites-nous Monsieur Blaise Cendrars* 'réponses aux enquêtes littéraires de 1919 à 1957,' collected, with preface and notes, by Hughes Richard (Éditions Rencontre)

A2   LES ŒUVRES COMPLÈTES PUBLISHED BY DENOËL (1960-4)

1   (1963) *Du Monde entier au cœur du monde* (complete poetry)
Anthologie nègre
Séquences
Amours
2   (1961) *La Fin du monde*
L'Eubage
L'Or
Moravagine
Petits contes nègres pour les enfants des blancs
3   (1960) *Dan Yack*
Rhum
Histoires vraies
4   (1962) *La Perle fiévreuse*
Moganni Nameh
Comment les blancs sont d'anciens noirs
Aujourd'hui
Vol à voile
Panorama de la pègre
Hollywood
La Vie dangereuse
5   (1960) *Préface* by Henry Miller
L'Homme foudroyé

La Main coupée
6 (1961) *Bourlinguer*
Le Lotissement du ciel
7 (1964) *Une Nuit dans la forêt*
Chez l'armée anglaise
La Banlieue de Paris
Emmène-moi au bout du monde!...
8 (1964) *D'Outremer à indigo*
Trop c'est trop
Films sans images
Textes inédits
Blaise Cendrars vous parle...
general bibliography of the works of Blaise Cendrars

A second complete works was published in sixteen volumes by the club français du livre (1968-71); this edition includes the *Inédits secrets*. A German edition of Cendrars, at first undertaken by Karl Rauch (Dusseldorf), is now in the hands of Arche (Zurich). And Peter Owen has undertaken the translation into English of most of the novels (see below).

A3 CHRONOLOGY OF CENDRARS IN ENGLISH

1919 *I Have Killed (J'ai tué)* Translated by Harold Ward. Five designs by Fernand Léger *The Plowshare* (Woodstock, New York) 8, nos. 6/7 (May-June)
1922 *Profound Today (Profond aujourd'hui)* Translated by Harold Loeb *Broom* 1, no. 3 (January): 265-8
— 'The Cabinet of Doctor Caligari' Review of the film. Translated by (?) from 'Le Cabinet du docteur Caligari (Ciné-Opéra)' (*Les Feuilles Libres* 4, no. 26 [June-July 1922]) *Broom* 2, no. 4 (July): 351
— 'At the Antipodes of Unity' Part of *L'Eubage* Translated by (?) *Broom* 3, no. 3 (October): 182-3
1926 'The Days of '49' Abridged version of *L'Or*. *Hearst's International Combined with Cosmopolitain* (October): 20-5, 211-24
— *Sutter's Gold (L'Or)* Translated by Henry Longan Stuart. Woodcuts by Harry Cimino. New York, Harper; London, Heinemann
1927 *African Saga (Anthologie nègre)* Translated by Margery Bianco.

Introduction by Arthur B. Spingarn. New York, Payson and
Clarke

— 'John Paul Jones' Translated by (?) *The Living Age* (Boston)
133 (July-December) 428-31. French source given as 900
(International French Language Literary Quarterly) Winter
1926-7 [unseen]

1929 *Little Black Stories for Little White Children (Petits Contes nègres pour
les enfants des blancs)* Translated by (?) [unseen]. New York,
Harcourt Brace

1931 'John Paul Jones' See 1927 above. Reprinted in *The European
Caravan* Edited by Samuel Putnam. New York, Putnam,
199-204

— *I Have No Regrets (Feu le lieutenant Bringolf)* Edited by Blaise
Cendrars. Translated by Warre B. Wells. London, Jarrolds

— *Panama (Le Transsibérien, Le Panama,* excerpts from *Kodak* and
Feuilles de route) Translated by John Dos Passos. Watercolours
by John Dos Passos. New York, Harper

1934 *Sutter's Gold* See 1926 above. Reissue by Harpers

— *Sutter's Gold* See 1926 above. Reissue by Blue Ribbon (New
York)

1936 *Sutter's Gold* See 1926 above. Reissue by Grosset and Dunlap
(New York)

1948 *Antartic Fugue (Le Plan de l'Aiguille)* Translated by (?) [unseen]
London, Pushkin Press; New York, Anglobooks

1959 *Panama (Le Panama)* Translated by John Dos Passos. See 1931
above. Introduction by G. Reavey *Chelsea Review* no. 3
(Winter): 3-25

1964 *The Trans-Siberian Express (Le Transsibérien)* Translated by
Anselm Hollo *Evergreen Review*. Reprinted in *Evergreen Review
Reader* edited by Barney Rosset. New York, Grove Press 1968
621-30

1966 'The Art of Fiction' and 'Manolo Secca' Translated by William
Brandon. Eleven poems. Translated by Ron Padgett (from
*Blaise Cendrars vous parle..., L'Homme foudroyé, Du Monde entier au
cœur du monde*). Introduction by William Brandon *The Paris
Review* 10, no. 37 (Spring): 105-43

— *Selected Writings of Blaise Cendrars* Edited, with a critical
introduction, by Walter E. Albert. Preface by Henry Miller.
New York, New Directions

1967 Poetry in *Vice* (England) [unseen]

— Poetry in *The Once Series* (Brightlingsea, England) 1966-7
[unseen]

— *To the End of the World (Emmène-moi au bout du monde!...)*
    Translated by Alan Brown. London, Peter Owen 1967 and
    New York, Grove 1968

1968 'Two Portraits: Gustave Lerouge, Arthur Cravan' (from
    L'Homme foudroyé and *Le Lotissement du ciel)* Translated by
    William Brandon *The Paris Review* 11, no. 42 (Winter-Spring):
    157-70

— Four poems Translated by Tom Clark and Ron Padgett *Works*
    (New York) 1, no. 3 (Spring): 39-42

— *Moravagine* Excerpts. Translated by Alan Brown *Encounter* 31,
    no. 5 (November): 14-27 and no. 6 (December): 3-14

1969 *Moravagine* Translated by Alan Brown. London, Peter Owen
    1969 and New York, Doubleday 1970

— 'A Curious Virgin' Excerpts from *L'Homme foudroyé* Translated
    by Nina Rootes *Queen* (London) 432, no. 5670 (30 April-13
    May): 91, 94, 99, 103

— *African Saga* See 1927 above. Reissue by Negro Universities
    Press, New York; obtainable through Greenwood Press
    (Westport, Conn.)

1970 *The Astonished Man (L'Homme foudroyé)* Translated by Nina
    Rootes. London, Peter Owen

1972 *The Prose of the Trans-siberian and of the Little Jeanne of France (Le
    Transsibérien,* prefaced by an article with the same title by
    Cendrars for *Der Sturm* no. 184-5, November 1913, p. 127)
    Translated by Roger Kaplan. Illustrations by Dejade and others
    Chicago Review 24, no. 3 (December): 3-21

— *Planus (Bourlinguer)* Translated by Nina Rootes. London, Peter
    Owen

1973 *Lice (La Main coupée)* Translated by Nina Rootes. London,
    Peter Owen

B   WORKS ABOUT CENDRARS

B1   VOLUME-LENGTH STUDIES AND SPECIAL ISSUES OF
      PERIODICALS DEVOTED TO CENDRARS

Amaral, Aracy *Blaise Cendrars no Brasil e os modernistas* São Paulo,
    Martins 1970
Buhler, Jean *Blaise Cendrars, homme libre, poète au cœur du monde* Biel,
    Switzerland, Éditions du Panorama, and Paris, Édition Fischbacher
    1960

Chadourne, Jacqueline *Blaise Cendrars, poète du cosmos* Paris, Seghers (l'Archipel) 1973

Europe: Blaise Cendrars. 54, no. 566 (June 1976). Pieces by Philippe Soupault, Claude Leroy, Charles Dobzynski, Michel Décaudin, Pierre Lagrue, Mary Ann Caws, Monique Chefdor, Jean-Paul Clébert, Hughes Richard, Pierre Rivas, Pierre Hourcade, Francis Lacassin, Blaise Cendrars, Gustave Lerouge, Henri Béhar, Jean-Pierre Goldenstein, Michel Delon, Dominique Belot-Perard and Maryvonne Denis, Daniel Leuwers, Bernard Mauralis, Jean-Hughes Malineau, Francis Vanoye, Henri Barbusse, A. t'Serstevens. Chronology and bibliography by Monique Chefdor.

Lepage, Albert *Blaise Cendrars* Paris, Les Écrivains Réunis 1926

Letteratura (Cendrars number) Volume 24 (19 of new series), no. 52 (July-August 1961): 3-70. Pieces by Cendrars, Alessandro Bonsanti, Guy Tosi, Michel Décaudin, R.M. Albérès, Piero Bigongiari, Raymond Warnier, Gérard Bauër, Yves Brayer, A.M. Cassandre, Jean Cocteau, John Dos Passos, Maurice Fombeure, Nino Frank, Paul Gilson, Paul Guth, Jean L'Anselme, Pierre Mac Orlan, Darius Milhaud, Christian Murciaux, Roger Parelon, Édouard Peisson, Gaëtan Picon, Jean Rousselot, Philippe Soupault, A. t'Serstevens, Carlo Bo, Libero De Libero, Corrado Govoni, P.A. Jannini, Arrigo Levasti, Mario Miserocchi, Glauco Natoli, Roberto Papi, Calo Pellegrini, Leonardo Sinisgalli, Ardengo Soffici, Orfeo Tamburi, and Diego Valeri. Bibliography for Italian language material

Lévesque, Jacques-Henry *Blaise Cendrars* Paris, Éditions de la Nouvelle Revue Critique 1947

Lovey, Jean-Claude *Situation de Blaise Cendrars* Neuchâtel, Les Éditions de la Baconnière 1965

Mercure de France: Blaise Cendrars (special number) Paris 1962. Pieces by Cendrars, Raymone, Paul Andréota, Antonio Aniante, Francis Aumaire, Pierre Bertin, André Beucler, Alain Borne, W.A. Bradley, Ferreira de Castro, Sonia Delaunay, Robert Doisneau, Florent Fels, Nino Frank, Bernard Fricker, Abel Gance, Paul Gilson, Robert Goffin, Jean-Claude Ibert, Armand Lanoux, Guy le Clec'h, Raymond Lèques, Jacques-Henry Lévesque, Marcel Lévesque, Pierre de Massot, Darius Milhaud, Henry Miller, Édouard Peisson, Michel Perrin, Georges Piroué, Michel Ragon, Salvador Reyes, G. Ribemont-Dessaignes, Jacques Rouré, Robert Sabatier, Pierre Seghers, A. t'Serstevens, Philippe Soupault, Émile Szittya, F.-J. Temple, and Guy Tosi.

Miller, Henry *Blaise Cendrars* Translated by François Villié. Paris, Denoël 1951

Miller, Henry, and others *Blaise Cendrars Zum Gruss* Zurich, Die
     Arche 1975. Articles and poetry by Henry Miller, Beat Brechbühl,
     Ilya Ehrenburg, Jürg Federspiel, Elisabeth Meylan, Gerold Späth,
     Friedrich Glauser, Werner Helwig, Albert Mermoud, Hughes
     Richard, and short excerpts from essays by artists and writers
     published elsewhere
Orte (Cendrars number) No. 4 (May-June 1975). Pieces by Gaby
     Arrizo, Beat Brechbühl, Werner Bucher, Rolf Hörler, Elisabeth
     Meylan, Henry Miller, and Theo Ruff
Parrot, Louis *Blaise Cendrars* Paris, Seghers (Poètes d'aujourd'hui)
     1948
Risques: Salut Blaise Cendrars Nos. 9-10, 1954. Pieces by Michel
     Décaudin, Jean l'Anselme, Marcel Béalu, Colette Benoite, Jacques
     Boursault, Jean Breton, Louis Calaferte, Henri Calet, Ferreira de
     Castro, Jean Cau, Pierre Chabert, René Char, Jean Cibié, Jean
     Cocteau, Maurice Dekobra, Sonia Delaunay-Terk, Philippe Dereux,
     Jean Digot, Henri-Simon Faure, Jean Fiolle, Bernard Fricker, Pierre
     Garnier, Michel Georges-Michel, Jacinto-Louis Guereña, Guy
     Gérard, Paul Gilson, Robert Guiette, Franz Hellens, Pierre Jerac,
     René Lalou, Fernand Léger, Jean-Jacques Lévêque, Jacques-Henry
     Lévesque, Emmanuel Looten, André Malraux, Adrian Miatlev,
     Darius Milhaud, Henry Miller, Pierre-Jean Oswald, Michel Perrin,
     Pascal Pia, Roger Quesnoy, Michel Ragon, Jules Romains, Jean
     Rousselot, Robert Sabatier, Michel Salès, André Salmon, Pierre
     Seghers, Maurice Serrault, Philippe Soupault, Jean Wagner
Rousselot, Jean *Cendrars* Paris, Éditions Universitaires (Témoins du
     XXe siècle) 1955
Serstevens, A. t' *L'Homme que fut Blaise Cendrars.* Paris, Denoël 1972

A special number of *La Revue des Lettres Modernes* (Paris, Minard),
     edited by Michel Décaudin, is expected for the spring of 1977, with
     articles by Jay Bochner, Yvette Bozon-Scalzitti, Jean-Pierre
     Goldenstein, and Claude Leroy.

B2   DOCTORAL DISSERTATIONS

Albert, Walter E. 'The Poetic Works of Blaise Cendrars' Indiana
     1961
Ames, Sanford Scribner 'The Prose Works of Blaise Cendrars'
     Wisconsin (Germaine Brée) 1970
Bochner, Jay *'Profond aujourd'hui:* Blaise Cendrars and the Whitman
     Tradition in France' Columbia (Daniel Dodson) 1969

Carrier, Roch 'Cendrars et la délivrance de l'homme' Doctorat d'État, Paris 1970

Ekombe, M.L. 'Le Regard poétique de Blaise Cendrars' Liverpool 1962-3

Horrex, S.P. ' "Modernity" in the Poetry of Blaise Cendrars' Reading 1969-70

Jonge, A.H.F. de 'The Imagery of the French Pre-Surrealist Avant-Garde, with Special Reference to Apollinaire, Cendrars and Jacob' Oxford 1969-70

Nitzberg, Howard 'Blaise Cendrars, Epic Poet in the Cubist Years' New York University (Anna Balakian) 1971

Palmer, Judith 'Theory and Practice in Blaise Cendrars' Autobiographical Fiction' Case Western Reserve (J. Alter) 1971

Payne, Richard Montegue 'Blaise Cendrars: From Action to Contemplation' Stanford 1960

Sparks, Jackson Gillen 'The Novelistic Style of Blaise Cendrars: A Study of *Moravagine* and *Dan Yack*' North Carolina (Jacques Hardré) 1967

Stewart, J.A. 'Blaise Cendrars: The Poetry Years (1908-1924)' Missouri (Herbert S. Gershman) 1967

Szautner, Kathleen Anne Marschang 'The Mystery of Women in the Works of Blaise Cendrars' Bryn Mawr (Mario Maurin) 1971

B3   ARTICLES, CHAPTERS IN BOOKS, REVIEWS ETC. ON CENDRARS

Adèma, Marcel *Guillaume Apollinaire* Paris, La Table Ronde 1968

Aeschimann, Paul *'Dix-neuf poèmes élastiques'* Les Marges 17, no. 68 (15 December 1919): 314

Albert, Walter E. 'Blaise Cendrars: A Temporal Perspective' *Texas Studies in Literature and Language* 4, no. 3 (Fall 1962): 321-9

– Introduction to *Selected Writings* See A3, 1966, above.

Aldington, Richard 'Some Recent French Poems' *The Egoist* 15 June 1914: 221-3

Allard, Roger '19 poèmes élastiques' NRF 7 no. 75 (1 December 1919): 1093

Amaral, Aracy 'Cendrars no Brasil: Uma Saudação de Mario de Andrade' *O Estado de São Paulo, Suplemento Literário* 25 January 1969: 6

– 'Cendrars e a descoberta do Brasil – A viagem a Minas' *Minas Gerais, Suplemento Literário* 22 February 1969: 1-7

- 'Paulo Prado e Blaise Cendrars' *O Estado de São Paulo, Suplemento Literário* 17 May 1969: 5
André, Marius 'La Poésie' Review of *Dix-neuf Poèmes. La Minerve Française* 3, no. 14 (15 December 1919): 536-40
Apollinaire, Guillaume 'La Vie anecdotique' *Mercure de France* 102 (1 April 1913): 658-9
- 'La Vie anecdotique' *Mercure de France* 106 (16 December 1913): 864-5
- 'Simultanisme-Librettisme' *Les Soirées de Paris* 15 June 1914: 322-5
- *Le Flâneur des deux rives* Paris, La Sirène 1918
- 'L'Esprit nouveau et les poètes' *Mercure de France* 130 (1 December 1918): 385-96
- *La Femme assise* Paris, Gallimard 1948
- *Textes inédits* Introduction by Jeanine Moulin. Geneva, Droz 1952
- *Chroniques d'art, 1902-1918* Edited by Leroy C. Breunig. Paris, Gallimard 1960
- *Œuvres poétiques* Edited by Marcel Adéma and Michel Décaudin. Paris, Gallimard (La Pléiade) 1965
Arcos, René 'Quelques Poètes modernes' *Mercure de France* 105 (15 October 1913): 677-703
Astre, George-Albert 'Cendrars et la contemplation' *Critique* 5, no. 38 (July 1949): 662-4
- *Thèmes et structures dans l'œuvre de John Dos Passos* 2 vols. Paris, Minard (Les Lettres Modernes) 1956, 1959
Aubarède, Gabriel d' 'Rencontre avec Cendrars' *Les Nouvelles Littéraires* 25 February 1956: 1, 4
Les Ballets Suédois dans l'art contemporain Paris, Éditions du Trianon 1931
Barret, Andrée 'Cendrars et l'esprit nouveau' *Europe* 42, nos. 421-2 (May-June 1964): 137-46
Bauër, Gérard 'Poète et romancier de l'aventure du monde' *Le Figaro* 23 January 1961: 11
Bay, Paul *Le Style coruscant* Brussels, Éditions des Cinquante 1968
Benet, W.R. Review of *Panama* Translated by John Dos Passos *Saturday Review of Literature* 8 (12 December 1931): 378
Berchtold, Alfred *La Suisse romande au cap du XXe siècle: Portrait littéraire et moral* Lausanne, Payot 1963
Berge, André and François 'Interview de Blaise Cendrars sur le cinéma' *Les Cahiers du Mois* nos. 16/17 (1925): 138-42
Bergman, Pär *'Modernolatria' et 'Simultaneità': Recherches sur deux tendances dans l'avant-garde littéraire en Italie et en France à la veille de la*

première guerre mondiale Upsala 1962 (Studia Litterarum Upsaliensia no. 2)

- 'Att resa utan hopp och att vänta förgäves: Tva poem av Blaise Cendrars' *Ord och Bild* 74 (1965): 21-8

Biblio (Cendrars feature) Volume 18, no. 7 (August-September 1950): 3-15. Pieces by Cendrars, t'Serstevens, and Henri Poulaille

- (Cendrars feature) Volume 24, no. 3 (March 1956): 3-10. Pieces by Cendrars, Paul Vialar, and Paul Gilson

Bidou, Henri Review of *Moravagine*. *Revue de Paris* 33, no. 11 (1 June 1926): 694-7

Billy, André *'L'Or' L'Œuvre* 22 July 1925

- 'Un Roman 'bœuf' de Blaise Cendrars' *Le Figaro* 23 February 1956: 17

- *Avec Apollinaire* Paris, Geneva, La Palatine 1966

Bochner, Jay Review of *Moravagine*. *The Globe and Mail* (Toronto) 31 January 1970: 14

- 'The Voyage Out and the Voyage Back in a Poem by Blaise Cendrars' *Exploration* (State University of Illinois) 1 (1973): 22-31

- 'From Walt Whitman to Blaise Cendrars' *Calamus* (Tokyo) 9 (1974): 8-28

Borum, Paul *Poetisk modernisme* Copenhagen, S. Vandelkaer 1966

Bory, Jean-Louis 'Une Aventure d'homme: A propos de Blaise Cendrars' *Mercure de France* 341 (April 1961): 692-6

Bourin, André 'Rendez-vous avec Blaise Cendrars' *Paru* (Monaco) no. 45 (August 1948): 14-18

Brasillach, Robert *Les Quatre jeudis: Images d'avant-guerre* Paris, Éditions Balzac 1944

Breton, Jean 'Une Confession inédite de Blaise Cendrars' *Le Pont de l'Epée* 7, no. 24 (1964): 35-40

Brion-Guerry, Liliane, ed. *L'Année 1913: Les Formes esthétiques de l'œuvre d'art à la veille de la première guerre mondiale* 2 vols. Paris, Klincksieck 1972

Brock, H.I. *'Sutter's Gold'* NYTBR *3 October 1926: 4*

Buchet, Edmond *Les Auteurs de ma vie, ou ma vie d'éditeur* Paris, Buchet/Chastel 1969

Budgen, Frank *Myselves When Young* London, Oxford 1970

Le Cabaret Voltaire One issue (15 May 1916)

Caforio, Guiseppe 'Blaise Cendrars: un poeta da conoscere' *Ausonia* 27, no. 6 (1972): 56-60 [unseen]

Carat, Jacques 'Les Livres: *L'Homme foudroyé*' *Paru* (Monaco) no. 15 (February 1946): 21-3

Carmody, Francis J. *The Evolution of Apollinaire's Poetics, 1901-1914*

Berkeley, Los Angeles 1963 (University of California Publications in Modern Philology vol. 70)

Carrier, Roch 'Blaise Cendrars: Un début dans la vie' *Études Françaises* (Montreal) 2, no. 2 (June 1966): 163-89

– Review of Lovey See B1 above *Études Françaises* (Montreal) 3, no. 1 (February 1967): 115-21

Carrieri, Raffaele, ed. *Blaise Cendrars* An anthology. Milan, All'insegna del Pesce d'oro 1958

Cassandre, A.M. *Le Spectacle est dans la rue* Text by Blaise Cendrars. N.p., Draeger Frères 1936

Castro, Ferreira de *Forêt vierge* Translation, with an introduction by Blaise Cendrars. Paris, Grasset (Livre de Poche) 1966

Caws, Mary-Ann *The Inner Theater of Recent French Poetry: Cendrars, Tzara, Péret, Artaud, Bonnefoy* Princeton, NJ, Princeton University Press 1972

Cederschiold, Gunnar 'A French Poet, Blaise Cendrars' *Plowshare* 8, nos. 10-11 (September-October 1919), n.p. (12 pages)

Chabanieux, Pierre 'Moravagine' *Le Divan* July 1926: 329-30

Chagall, Marc *Ma Vie* Paris, Stock 1931

Charpentier, John 'L'Or' *Mercure de France* 181, no. 650 (15 July 1925): 451-2

– 'Moravagine' *Mercure de France* 189, no. 675 (1 August 1926): 678

Chauveau, Paul 'Le Plan de l'Aiguille' *Les Nouvelles Littéraires* 20 April 1929: 3

Christy, Jim 'Now to Drift in a Mandala' Review of *Lice* (*La Main coupée*). *The Globe and Mail* (Toronto) 1 December 1973: 37

Clébert, Jean-Paul (no title) *L'Arc* 4, no. 14 (Spring 1961): 52

Clouard, Henri *Histoire de la Littérature française du Symbolisme à nos jours.* 2 vols. Paris, Albin Michel 1947

Cloutier, Cécile 'Les Héros de Cendrars' *Liberté* (Toronto) 7, no. 4 (July-August 1965): 337-40

Cluny, Claude-Michel 'Blaise Cendrars: Poésie du premier jour du monde' *NRF* 16 (new series), no. 184 (1 April 1968): 695-700

Cocteau, Jean *Carte blanche* Paris, La Sirène 1920

Connors, Burton 'Henry, Blaise and Ferdinand' *Earth Ship* no. 3 (April 1971): 18-20 [unseen]

Cooper, Douglas *Fernand Léger et le nouvel espace* Translated by François Lachenal. Geneva, Les Trois Collines 1949

Courtines, Pierre Review of *Le Lotissement du ciel. Books Abroad* 25, no. 1 (Winter 1951): 41

Crespelle, Jean-Paul *Montparnasse vivant* Paris, Hachette 1962

– *Chagall: L'Amour, le rêve et la vie* Paris, Presses de la Cité 1969

Décaudin, Michel 'Le Changement de front d'Apollinaire' *Revue des Sciences Humaines* October-December 1950: 255-60
- *La Crise des valeurs symbolistes* Toulouse, Privat 1960
- *Le Dossier d'Alcools* Geneva, Droz; Paris, Minard 1960 (Société de Publications Romanes et Françaises 67)
Decaunes, Luc 'Blaise Cendrars ou le parti-pris de la vie' *Les Cahiers du Sud* no. 294 (1949): 309-13
Delaunay, Robert 'Lettre ouverte au *Sturm*' *Der Sturm* 4, nos. 194-5 (January 1914): 167
- *Du Cubisme à l'art abstrait* Edited by Pierre Francastel. Paris, SEVPEN 1957
Delteil, Joseph *'L'Or'* NRF 12, no. 140 (1 May 1925): 944-5
Denat, Antoine 'De Montaigne à Miller' *Synthèses* 22, nos. 249-50 (February-March 1967): 56-62
Descaves, Pierre 'Blaise Cendrars' *La Revue du Caire* 12, no. 129 (April 1950): 493-8
Divoire, Fernand *Le Grenier de Montjoie!* Paris, Éditions du Carnet Critique 1919
- *L'Homme du monde* Paris, Kra, Éditions du Sagittaire 1925
Dos Passos, John 'Homer of the Transsiberian' *Orient Express* New York, Harpers 1927: 155-67, as reprinted from *Saturday Review of Literature* 16 October 1926: 202, 222
- trans. *Panama* by Blaise Cendrars, with a preface by Dos Passos. New York, Harpers 1931
Droit, Michel 'Il nous emmenait au bout du monde' *Le Figaro Littéraire* 22 January 1962: 13
Dumay, Raymond 'De Sauser à Cendrars' *La Revue des Deux Mondes* (new series) no. 3 (1 March 1969): 523-37. Reprinted in Blaise Cendrars *Œuvres Complètes* 1 (Club français du livre, Paris 1968) iii-xix, under the title 'Des Mythes aux poèmes'
- 'Cendrars à port-enfance' *Revue des Deux Mondes* (new series) no. 6 (June 1970): 633-44
- See his introductions to each of the volumes of the Club français du Livre *Œuvres complètes*
Durry, Marie-Jeanne *Guillaume Apollinaire: Alcools.* 3 vols. Paris, SEDES 1956, 1964
Duvignaud, Jean 'Blaise Cendrars, écrivain picaresque' *Preuves* 17, no. 124 (June 1961): 82-6
Ehrenburg, Ilya *People and Life, 1891-1921* Translated by Anna Bostock and Yvonne Kapp. New York, Knopf 1962
Eisenstein, Sergei *Sutter's Gold* A shooting script. See Ivor Montagu below.

- Synopsis of scenes for *Sutter's Gold*. The Museum of Modern Art
  library collection, New York
Epstein, Jean *La Poésie d'aujourd'hui: un nouvel état d'intelligence,* with a
  letter from Blaise Cendrars. Paris, La Sirène 1920
- 'Le Phénomène littéraire' *L'Esprit Nouveau* 2, no. 13 (1921):
  1431-43
- 'A Necessary and Sufficient Literature' *Broom* 2, no. 4 (July 1922):
  309-16
Erba, Luciano, ed. *Cendrars* Introduction 9-31. Milan, Nuova
  Accademia Editrice 1961
Eulálio, Alexandre 'L'Aventure brésilienne de Blaise Cendrars' *Études
  Portugaises et Brésiliennes* (Rennes, Faculté des lettres et sciences
  humaines) 5, (1969): 19-55
Le Figaro Littéraire 'Les 70 ans de Blaise Cendrars' 31 August 1957: 3
- 'Blaise Cendrars: 12 écrivains et artistes l'évoquent' Pieces by Jules
  Romains, Roland Dorgelès, Georges Braque, Philippe Soupault,
  Marc Chagall, Robert Goffin, Paul Gilson, Marie Dormoy, Maurice
  Fombeure, Alain Bosquet, Charles le Guintrec, and Marc Alyn. 28
  January 1961: 6, 12
Fiorioli, Elena 'Blaise Cendrars, "le vagabond intellectuel"' *Culture
  Française* (Italy) (March-April 1962) [unseen]
Fontainas, André '*Kodak*' *Mercure de France* 175 (1 October 1924):
  178
- '*Feuilles de route*' *Mercure de France* 179, (1 April 1925): 177-8
Fouchet, Max-Pol 'Un Brahmane à rebours' *L'Express* 26 January
  1961: 28
Fournier, Gabriel *Cors de chasse, 1912-1914* Geneva, Pierre Cailler
  1957
Frank, Nino 'Blaise Cendrars, l'homme le plus seul au monde' *Les
  Nouvelles Littéraires* 21 December 1929: 5
- *Mémoire brisée* Paris, Calmann-Lévy 1967 ('Une Mort difficile'
  reprinted from *Mercure de France: Blaise Cendrars*)
- 'Bruit et fureur chez Blaise Cendrars' *Les Nouvelles Littéraires* 27
  February 1969: 6
- 'Blaise Cendrars le mal-aimé' *Les Nouvelles Littéraires* 28 January
  1971: 1
Galimand, Lucien 'Retour à Cendrars' *La Quinzaine Littéraire* 15-31
  May 1967: 18
Gandon, Yves 'Blaise Cendrars vu par Dan Yack' *Les Nouvelles
  Littéraires* 7 December 1929: 5. Reprinted in
- *Mascarades littéraires* Paris, Éditions Trémois 1930
Géo-Charles 'Un Univers poétique: L'œuvre de Blaise Cendrars'
  Maintenant no. 4 (1946): 20-36

Gigon, Fernand *De Tels Hommes* Geneva, Perret-Gentil 1942

Gilson, Paul 'Blaise Cendrars au cœur du monde' *Arts* no. 792 (19-25 October 1960): 1

Ginestier, Paul *The Poet and the Machine* Translated by Martin B. Friedman. Chapel Hill, NC 1961

Goffin, Robert *Entrer en Poésie* Paris, A l'Enseigne du Chat qui Pêche 1948

- 'Châteaubriand et Cendrars' *L'Arc* 4, no. 14 (Spring 1961): 47-9

- *Fil d'Ariane pour la Poésie* Paris, Nizet 1964

Goldenstein, J.-P. 'De l'élasticité poétique: Genèse d'un poème de Blaise Cendrars' *Les Lettres Romanes* 24, no. 1 (1 February 1970): 73-9

- 'Blaise Cendrars, *Inédits secrets*' (article on the Cendrars-Apollinaire debate) *Revue des Lettres Modernes,* nos. 276-9; Archives Guillaume Apollinaire no. 10 (1971): 149-60

- 'Cendrarsiana' *Études Littéraires* (Quebec) 4 no. 2 (August 1971): 244-7

- 'Blaise Cendrars sur les traces du Capitaine Cook' *Revue d'Histoire Littéraire de la France* 73, no. 1 (January-February 1973): 112-17

Gsteiger, Manfred *Westwind. Zur Literatur der französischen Schweiz* Bern, Kandelaber Verlag 1968

Guardian Weekly (Manchester) Review of *Lice* (*La Main coupée*) 9 June 1973: 26 [unseen]

Guth, Paul 'Redevenu parisien après dix ans, Blaise Cendrars raconte sa vie' *Le Figaro Littéraire* 10 December 1949: 6

- *Quarante contre un.* 2 vols. Paris, Denoël 1951

- '4 Portraits: Blaise Cendrars, le cyclope qui redevient parisien' *Les Œuvres Libres* no. 198 (November 1952): 123-31

- 'Blaise Cendrars' *La Revue de Paris* 61 (May 1954): 120-9

Heist, Walter 'Die Luge von der Literatur und vom Leben: Über Blaise Cendrars und fünfzig Jahre französischer Literatur' *Frankfurter Hefte* 19 (1964); 494-502 [unseen]

Hirsch, Charles-Henri Review of *Les Pâques. Mercure de France* 135 (1 September 1919): 139-40

Hoog, Armand 'Cendrars en 1948' *Carrefour* no. 195 (9 June 1948): 7

Hoog, Michel 'Quelques précurseurs de l'art d'aujourd'hui' *La Revue du Louvre et des Musées de France* 16, no. 3 (1966): 165-72

- *Robert et Sonia Delaunay.* Paris 1967 (Musée national d'art moderne, Inventaire des collections publiques françaises no. 15)

Houston, John Porter 'Cendrars' Modernism' Review of *Selected Writings. The Southern Review* (Louisiana) 6 (new series), no. 2 (April 1970): 561-5

Jaloux, Edmond *'Moravagine' Les Nouvelles Littéraires* 11 September
    1926: 3
Jan-Topass 'Essai sur les nouveaux modes d'expression plastique et
    littéraire: Cubisme, Futurisme, Dadaïsme' *La Grande Revue* 103
    (1920): 579-97
Jeanne, René, and Charles Ford, eds. *Abel Gance* Paris, Seghers 1963
Josephson, Matthew 'A Neo-Romantic Poet' Review of *Panama*.
    Nation (2 December 1931): 616-17
Kemp, Robert 'La Vie des livres' Review of Rousselot, *Cendrars. Les
    Nouvelles Littéraires* 8 March 1956: 2
Klemperer, Victor *Geschichte der französischen Literatur im 19. und 20.
    Jahrhundert.* 2 vols. Berlin, Deutscher Verlag der Wissenschaften
    1956
Kwiatkowski, Jerzy 'Anarchista Bardzo Pozyteczny: Opoez ji B.
    Cendrars' *Tworczosc* no. 1 (1962): 81-105
Lagrue, Pierre 'Guillaume et Blaise, poètes contemporains' *Europe* 44,
    nos. 451-2 (November-December 1966): 118-24
Lalou, René Review of *Les Confessions de Dan Yack. La Quinzaine
    Critique des Livres et des Revues* 1, no. 4 (25 December 1929): 184
– 'Le Livre de la semaine' Review of *Le Lotissement du ciel. Les Nouvelles
    Littéraires* 8 September 1949: 3
Lanoux, Armand 'Blaise Cendrars, ou la première fugue du vagabond
    du monde' *Les Œuvres Libres* no. 177 (December 1960): 270-3
– Introduction to Cendrars 'TPMTR' *Les Œuvres Libres* no. 178
    (February 1961): 20
Le Cardonnel, Georges Review of *J'ai tué. La Minerve Française* 3
    (November 1919): 112-15
Leprohon, Pierre *Jean Epstein* Paris, Seghers 1964
Lerouge, Gustave *Le Mystérieux Docteur Cornélius* Preface by Francis
    Lacassin. Paris, Jérôme Martineau 1966
– *La Mandragore magique* Preface and epilogue by Hubert Juin. Paris,
    Pierre Belfond 1967
Leroy, Claude 'Cendrars, le futurisme et la Fin du monde' *Europe* 53,
    no. 551 (March 1975): 113-20
Lévesque, Jacques-Henry Introduction to Cendrars *Poésies complètes* See
    A1, 1944, above.
– Letter on Cendrars and Dada in Robert Motherwell *The Dada
    Painters and Poets* New York, Wittenborn 1951
– 'Cendrars and the Transsiberian' Album notes for *Prose du
    transsibérien et de la petite Jehanne de France,* 'poemontage' by
    Lévesque and Frederick Ramsay, Jr., Folkways Records (FL9940).
    New York 1967

Lévy, Yves '*Bourlinguer* par Blaise Cendrars' *Paru* (Monaco) no. 45
   (August 1948): 19-20
Living Age Review of *Sutter's Gold* 15 November 1926: 375
Loeb, Harold *The Way It Was* New York, Criterion Books 1959
Lutgen, Odette *En Dépit de leur gloire* Paris, Éditions Mondiales 1961
Maggi, Cristiana '*Roman cinéma*: Ungaretti 1914' *Paragone* 24, no. 276
   (February 1973): 70-87
Mallet, Robert 'Blaise Cendrars ou "la belle aventure" ' *Le Figaro
   Littéraire* 16 August 1958: 2
Malraux, André 'Des Origines de la poésie cubiste' *Connaissance* no. 1
   (January 1920): 38-43
Manoll, Michel, interviewer. See *Blaise Cendrars vous parle...*, A1,
   1952, above.
- 'Supplément à mes entretiens avec Blaise Cendrars: Les cent figures
   d'un sans-culotte de la poésie' *Arts* no. 364 (19 June 1952): 7
- 'Cendrars' *Le Figaro Littéraire* 28 January 1961: 6
Maris, Faith 'California Gold' *The New Republic* 48, no. 619 (13
   October 1926): 227
Martins, Wilson 'Cendrars e o Brasil' *Revista do Livro* (Rio de Janeiro)
   5, no. 18 (June 1960): 177-83
Massot, Pierre de *De Mallarmé à 391* Saint-Raphaël, Au Bel
   Exemplaire 1922
Mauriac, Claude 'Avant Apollinaire...' Review of Rousselot *Cendrars.
   Le Figaro* 23 February 1956: 17
- 'Blaise Cendrars et le goût du risque' *Le Figaro* 6 August 1958: 7
Maurois, André *I Remember, I Remember* Translated by Denver and
   Jane Lindley. New York and London, Harpers 1942
Miller, Henry 'Tribute to Blaise Cendrars' *T'ien Hsia Monthly*
   (Shanghai) 7 (1938): 350-6
- *The Books in My Life* London, Icon Books 1952; New York, New
   Directions 1960
- *The Henry Miller Reader* New York, New Directions 1959
- *Letters to Anaïs Nin* Edited by Gunther Stuhlmann. New York,
   Putnam 1965
- 'Reading Blaise Cendrars' *Mademoiselle* October 1973: 58, 62
Montagu, Ivor *With Eisenstein in Hollywood* New York, International
   Publishers (New World Paperbacks) 1967, 1969
Montfort, Eugène Review of *Moravagine. Les Marges* 36, no. 145 (15
   July 1926): 226-7
- *25 Ans de littérature française* 2 vols. Paris, Librairie de France n.d.
Mora, Edith 'Blaise Cendrars' *Les Nouvelles Littéraires* 26 June 1958: 1, 4
Moricand, Conrad *Portraits astrologiques* Paris, Au Sans Pareil 1933

Morrow, Christine *Le Roman irréaliste* Paris, Toulouse, Didier 1941

Muller, Henry 'Adieu au bourlingueur' *Carrefour* no. 854 (25 January 1961): 21

Nadeau, Maurice *Littérature présente* Paris, Corrêa 1952

– 'Blaise Cendrars, poète et baroudeur' *Plaisir de France* 22 (Christmas number 1955): 29-32

Nathan, Jacques *La Littérature du métal, de la vitesse et du chèque de 1880 à 1930* Paris, Didier 1971

Nimier, Roger *Journées de lecture* Paris, Gallimard 1965

Nin, Anaïs *The Diaries of Anaïs Nin* 3 vols. New York, Swallow Press and Harcourt, Brace and World 1966, 1967, 1969

– *The Novel of the Future* New York, Macmillan 1968; New York, Collier Books 1970

Nobili, Paola 'Viaggio, Dolore, Amore in Blaise Cendrars' *Spicilegio Moderno* (University of Bologna, Instituto di Lingue e Letterature Straniere) no. 3 1974: 232-44

Les Nouvelles Littéraires 'Le Poète du monde entier' Paul Gilson, Henry Miller, Blaise Cendrars. Biographical sketch. 26 January 1961: 1, 6

Nunes, Benedito 'Apollinaire, Cendrars e Oswald' *O Estado de São Paulo, Suplemento Literário* 7 February 1971: 1; 14 February 1971: 1

Orbes 2 series, 8 numbers (irregular) 1928-35

Ouellette, Fernand 'Blaise Cendrars ou l'homme aux deux pieds sur les pôles' *Liberté* (Toronto) 1, no. 2 (March-April 1959): 79-84

Parinaud, André 'Blaise Cendrars – Les peintres modernes ont raté leur art et leur vie' *Arts* no. 333 (16 November 1951): 1

– 'Blaise Cendrars – Les foules modernes traversent la vie dans les passages cloutés' *Arts* no. 368 (17 July 1952): 1, 6

– 'Blaise Cendrars – Distinguons les poètes des aventuriers du dimanche des explorateurs scientifiques et des mordus du sport' *Arts* no. 376 (12 September 1952): 10

Parrot, Louis 'La Symphonie du monde' *Les Lettres Françaises* 6, no. 103 (12 April 1946): 5

Pawlowski, G. de Review of *L'Or. Annales Politiques et Littéraires* 86 (January 1926): 7-8

– Review of *Moravagine. Annales Politiques et Littéraires* 86 (June 1926): 664-5

Périer, Gaston-Denys 'Deux Aspects de M. Blaise Cendrars' *Le Thyrse* 19 (1922): 243-6

Périer, Odilon-Jean 'Leçon au professeur sur l'Anthologie nègre' *Signaux de France et de Belgique* 1, no. 9 (January 1922): 451-71

Perruchot, Henri 'Blaise Cendrars, ou vivre est une action magique' *Synthèses* 8, no. 89 (October 1953): 184-91

– 'Blaise Cendrars, quand le destin a-t-il frappé à votre porte?' *Les Nouvelles Littéraires* 15 January 1959: 1, 2

Pettiaux, Paul 'Cendrars défiguré' Review of Lovey *Situation de Blaise Cendrars*. *Les Lettres Nouvelles* October-November 1966: 133-51

Porquerol, Elisabeth 'Blaise Cendrars' NRF 9 (new series), no. 99 (1 March 1961): 517-19

– 'Cendrars-la-Jeunesse' *Bulletin de la Guilde du Livre* (Lausanne) (May 1970) no. 5: 134-7

Portelaine, Henri de 'Hommage à Blaise Cendrars' *La Revue du Caire* 23, no. 247 (March 1961): 175-81

Poulaille, Henry *Nouvelle Age littéraire* Paris, Librairie Valois 1930

Poupon, Marc *Apollinaire et Cendrars* Archives des Lettres Modernes no. 103, Archives Guillaume Apollinaire no. 2 (Paris, Minard 1969)

Putnam, Samuel, et al, eds. *The European Caravan* New York, Putnam 1931

Queneau, Raymond, ed. *Pour une bibliothèque idéale* Paris, Gallimard 1956

Rachilde [Vallette, Marguerite Eymery] Review of *J'ai tué*. *Mercure de France* 131 (16 January 1919): 306

Raymond, Marcel *De Baudelaire au Surréalisme* Paris, José Corti 1969

Raynal, Maurice Review of *L'Eubage*. *L'Esprit Nouveau* 1, nos. 11-12 (1921): 1285

– Review of *Anthologie nègre*. *L'Esprit Nouveau* 2 (n.d.): 1921-2

Rexroth, Kenneth 'Cooey-Booey Cubist' NYTBR 9 October 1966: 4, 20

Reyes, Salvador *Rostros sin Mascara* Santiago de Chile, Empresa Editora Zig-Zag 1957

Richard, Élie 'Blaise Cendrars, vagabond du bon plaisir, chante la nostalgie du malheur qui pointe les hommes de son temps' *Rolet* 19, no. 558 (15 April 1956): 1

Richard, Hughes, compiler. Bibliography of the works of Blaise Cendrars in OC 8, Paris, Denoël 1964

– 'Blaise Cendrars s'en va-t-en guerre' *Le Journal de Genève* no. 229 (2-3 October 1965): iii, v

– ed. See *Dites-nous, Monsieur Blaise Cendrars* A1, 1969, above.

– 'Cendrars ou la volonté du mythe' *Les Lettres Nouvelles* December 1969-January 1970: 105-14

– 'Blaise Cendrars: "Je suis tout autre" ' Review of *Inédits. Marginales* 25, no. 130 (February 1970): 60-2

- 'Mais qui était donc Blaise Cendrars?' Review of t'Serstevens *L'Homme que fut Blaise Cendrars. La Quinzaine littéraire* 1-15 September 1972: 15
- 'Lettres de Blaise Cendrars à Sven Stelling-Michaud' *Écriture 11* (Vevey, Switzerland, Bartil Galland 1975): 160-89

Richter, Mario 'Les Pâques à New York di Blaise Cendrars' *Saggi a Ricerche di Letteratura Francese* 12 (new series) Rome (1973): 409-37

Rim, Carlo [Jean-Marius Richard] *Mémoires d'une vieille vague* Paris, Gallimard 1961

Robinson, Landon Review of *Sutter's Gold. The New York Evening Post Literary Review* 30 October 1926: 4

Roques, Mario 'Le *Perceval le gallois* de Guillaume Apollinaire' *Le Flâneur des Deux Rives* 1, no. 1 (March 1954): 8-10

Rothmund, Alfons 'Blaise Cendrars, humaniste vagabond du XXe siècle' *Die Neueren Sprachen* no. 7 (July 1962): 307-20

Rousseaux, André 'La Poésie brute de Blaise Cendrars' *Le Figaro Littéraire* 7 September 1957: 2. Reprinted in his *Littérature du vingtième siècle* vol. 6 (Paris, Albin Michel 1958): 92-101

Rousselot, Jean *Présences contemporaines* Paris, Nouvelles Éditions Debresse 1958
- 'Une Heure avec Cendrars le précurseur' *Marginales* 19, no. 97 (September 1964): 1-6
- *Mort ou survie du langage?* Brussels, Sodi 1969

Roy, Claude *L'Homme en question* Paris, Gallimard 1960

Rubiner, Ludwig 'Manuskripte: *Die Prosa von der Transsibirischen Eisenbahn*' *Die Aktion* 3, no. 4 (October 1913): 940-1

Sanouillet, Michel *Dada à Paris* Paris, Pauvert 1965
- *Picabia et 391* 2 vols. Paris, Losfeld 1966

Santraud, J.M. 'Dans le sillage de la baleinière d'Arthur Gordon Pym: Le Sphinx des glaces, *Dan Yack*' *Études Anglaises* 25, no. 3 (July-September 1972): 353-66

Sauriat, André 'Littérature 51' *L'Acropole* 3, no. 13 (September-October 1951): 2-7

Scalzitti, Yvette Bozon- *Blaise Cendrars et le Symbolisme* Archives des Lettres Modernes no. 137 (Paris, Minard 1972)

Seldes, Gilbert *The Seven Lively Arts* New York, Harper 1924

Serstevens, A. t' 'Du *Transsibérien* à *Moravagine*: Cendrars, poète et romancier' *Les Nouvelles Littéraires* 26 September 1926: 1
- 'Mon vieux Blaise: L'histoire d'une amitié' *Le Monde* 25 January 1961: 8
- 'Quand Cendrars bourlinguait à Paris' *Le Figaro Littéraire* 22 January 1962: 1, 13

Shattuck, Roger 'Un Polémique d'Apollinaire' *Le Flâneur des Deux Rives* 1, no. 4 (December 1954): 41-5

– *The Banquet Years* London, Faber 1958

– ed. 'Apollinaire's Great Whitman Happening' *City Lights Journal* (San Francisco) no. 3 (1966): 171-83

Sidoti, Antonio '*La Prose du transsibérien* de Blaise Cendrars: Problèmes de composition, d'impression et de publication' *Les Lettres Romanes* 27, no. 1 (February 1973): 71-84

Signaux, Gilbert 'La Place de Cendrars' *La Table Ronde* no. 6 (June 1948): 1017-19

Simenon, Georges 'Simenon écrit à Cendrars' *Les Nouvelles Littéraires* 8 December 1960: 1

– *Quand j'étais vieux* Paris, Presses de la Cité 1970

Simiot, Bernard 'Le Monde d'aujourd'hui... vu par Blaise Cendrars' *La Revue des Deux Mondes* 15 February 1961: 743-5

Somville, Léon *Devanciers du Surréalisme* Geneva, Droz 1971

Soufflet, Edmond 'Blaise Cendrars et Brest' *Les Cahiers de l'Iroise* April-June 1972 [unseen]

Soupault, Philippe 'Mort d'un poète' *Revue de Paris* 68 (March 1961): 158-60

– *Profils*. Paris, Mercure de France 1963. 'Enfin Cendrars vint' as reprinted from *Mercure de France: Blaise Cendrars*

Sourian, Peter 'The Rage of Paris' Review of *To the End of the World*. NYTBR 4 August 1968: 28

Stelling-Michaud, Sven 'Visite à Blaise Cendrars à propos de "Vol à voiles"' *Écriture* 11 (Vevey, Switzerland, Bertil Galland 1975): 190 4

Stenhouse, Charles E. 'Cinema Literature' *Close Up* (London) (7 November 1930): 335-40

Der Sturm: Erster Deutscher Herbstsalon Catalogue. Berlin 1913

Szittya, Émile *Das Kuriositäten Kabinett* Constance, Germany, Seeverlag 1923

– 'Blaise Cendrars, ou l'inquiétude de la fin du siècle' *Lettres Françaises* no. 865 (2-8 March 1961): 4

Temple, F.-J. 'Cendrars le fabuleux' *L'Arc* 4, no. 14 (Spring 1961): 45-7

– *Miller* Paris, Éditions Universitaires 1965

Thiébaut, Marcel 'Blaise Cendrars... et Henry Miller' *La Revue de Paris* 55 (October 1948): 156-9

Time Review of the film of *Sutter's Gold* 6 April 1936: 46

TLS 'Playboy' Review of *To the End of the World* 16 February 1967: 121

– 'No Other God but Life, The Tall Stories of Blaise Cendrars' 26 February 1971: 247-8

- 'Down to the Sea' Review of *Planus* 14 April 1972: 408
Torres, Henry *Souvenir, souvenir, que me veux-tu?* Paris, Del Duca 1964
Van Looy, Grommaire 'Blaise Cendrars' Review of Lepage *Le Thyrse* 23 (1926): 392-3
Vigneras, L.A. 'Blaise Cendrars' *French Review* 14, no. 4 (February 1941): 311-18
Warnier, Raymond 'Blaise Cendrars, aventurier humaniste du XXe siècle' *Mese Sanitario* (Milan) April 1961: 3-4
- 'Blaise Cendrars, voyageur et prophète: Évocation de l'ère cubiste' *Marginales* 16, no. 78 (June-July 1961): 47-50
- 'A propos de Blaise Cendrars' *Studi di Letteratura Storia e Filosophia in Onore di Bruno Revel* Florence 1965 (Biblioteca Dell' 'Archivum Romanicum' vol. 74): 617-59
Wazyk, A. *Od Rimbauda do Eluardo* Warsaw, PIW 1965
Weck, René de *'Kodak'* Mercure de France 177 (1 January 1925): 250-51
- 'Valeur dynamique de Blaise Cendrars: *Le Plan de l'Aiguille'* Mercure de France 212 (15 June 1929): 729-32
- *'Les Confessions de Dan Yack'* Mercure de France 217, (1 February 1930): 706-7
Weelen, Guy 'Robes simultanées' *L'Oeil* no. 60 (December 1959): 78-84
Weightman, John Review of *To the End of the World. Observer Review* 26 February 1967: 26
Werner, M.R. 'The Irony of Life' Review of *Sutter's Gold. Saturday Review of Literature* 30 October 1926: 253
Wickes, George *Americans In Paris* Garden City, New York, Doubleday (Paris Review Editions) 1969
Wurmser, André 'Blaise Cendrars' *Les Lettres Françaises* no. 610 (8-14 March 1956): 2
Zabel, Morton Dauwen Review of *Panama. Poetry* 39 (January 1932): 224-7
Zweig, Paul Review of *Selected Writings. Poetry* 111 (November 1967): 124

Index

This is an index to authors and their works, critics quoted or discussed, avant-garde and important French periodicals, critical terms useful to the study and various other details of interest to literary history. Strictly referential information in the notes is not indexed.

UNIVERSITY OF TORONTO ROMANCE SERIES